Fly Fishing for Pacific Salmon II

Les Johnson and Bruce Ferguson
with Pat Trotter

Fly Fishing for Pacific Salmon II

Les Johnson and Bruce Ferguson
with Pat Trotter
Illustrations by Ron Jenkins

Frank
Amato
PORTLAND

Frank Amato Publications, Inc.
P.O. Box 82112, Portland, Oregon 97282
503.653.8108 • www.amatobooks.com

Photographs by the author unless otherwise noted.
Cover Illustration by Ron Jenkins.
Illustrations by Ron Jenkins unless otherwise noted.
Fly Plate Photos by Jim Schollmeyer

Book and Cover Design: Kathy Johnson

Printed in Hong Kong
Softbound ISBN-10: 1-57188-434-3 • ISBN-13: 978-1-57188-434-3 • UPC: 0-81127-00268-9
Hardbound ISBN-10: 1-57188-422-X • ISBN-13: 978-1-57188-422-0 • UPC: 0-81127-00256-6
Limited Edition ISBN-10: 1-57188-423-8 • ISBN-13: 978-1-57188-423-7 • UPC: 0-81127-00257-3

1 3 5 7 9 10 8 6 4 2

Title Page: In autumn, coho, pink and chum salmon marshal on flats near parent streams before pushing into fresh water. These flats, found throughout Washington and British Columbia shorelines, offer easy wading and sometimes very good fishing. Anglers here are waiting at the Chico Creek estuary at Dyes Inlet, near Bremerton, Washington. (Photo by Les Johnson)

Table of Contents

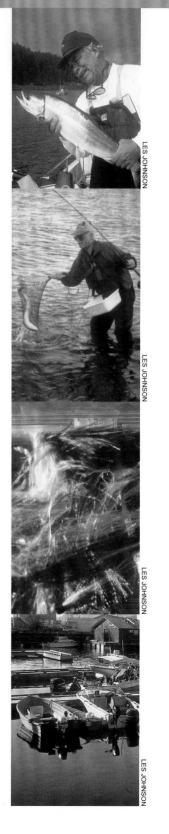

LES JOHNSON

LES JOHNSON

LES JOHNSON

LES JOHNSON

Dedication

Dedicated to Bill Nelson
1928 –

If Bill Nelson of Eugene, Oregon had done nothing more in his life than become one of the most noted salmon fly-fishing guides in British Columbia it would have been enough to put him on a short list to be placed on the Dedication page of this book. However, during his career as a salmon fishing guide Bill concentrated primarily on catching feeding salmon on the fly—in saltwater—and continued forward to develop skills few others have matched. Yet this too is just a piece of an angling mosaic that makes up the complete portrait of salmon fly-fisher extraordinaire, Bill Nelson.

In the 8th grade Bill was taught how to make a fly tying vise by his shop teacher. That was the beginning of his life-long pursuit of fly tying. It wasn't long before Bill was tying flies for the local Sears Roebuck sporting goods department for $1.20 per dozen. Sears Roebuck supplied the hooks and Bill received feathers from an employee of the Everett Zoo who saved peacock feathers for him from molted birds. He also received feathers, again from molted birds from local farmers. His dad provided him with pheasant and duck feathers. Bill recalls his early flies as crude but said that, "they did pretty well at catching fish."

At Everett High School Bill and a few of his buddies began fishing the mouth of the Skykomish River. They also began working the tidewater of the Snohomish River that emptied into Puget Sound just north of downtown Everett where they caught pink, coho and chum salmon in the fall. Chums at the time were almost universally called "dog salmon". The fly that worked for them was bright red, tied by Bill.

Bill served a hitch in the U.S. Navy during World War II, spending much of his enlistment at the Montana School of Mines training for the V-5 program which included taking many college courses. Upon being discharged at Bremerton, Washington Bill immediately enrolled at Washington State University where he continued his education.

In 1949 Bill went to work for U.S. Rubber Company. During this period Bill traveled around Oregon, sometimes hauling a cartopper boat on the roof of his car. Along with serving customers he managed to test nearly every stream in western Oregon. After several moves around Oregon with the company Bill accepted a position with Armstrong Rubber Company located in Seattle. He moved his wife Audrey and their children Craig and Pam to Lynnwood, just north of Seattle. In addition to building up his new territory Bill joined the Evergreen Fly-fishing Club in Everett where he soon was elected president.

In 1964, after four years in Lynnwood, Bill purchased Eugene Tire Patch Company located outside of Eugene, Oregon. The business included a small house and enough acreage to purchase a gentle horse for daughter Pam and a few sheep to keep the place mowed. Bill soon discovered that there was no fly-fishing organization in Eugene, so he put an ad in the local paper to see if anyone would be interested in joining. There was interest and Bill was elected president of the McKenzie Flyfishers at the first meeting.

It was not long after accepting the reins as president of McKenzie Flyfishers that Bill and friends from Eugene and Everett began formulating the idea of a national fly-fishing federation that would serve as an umbrella organization for all known fly-fishing clubs in the United States. With his usual energy Bill began contacting people around the country about his idea.

At the 1965 Oregon Conclave of Flyfishers Bill and fellow members of the McKenzie Club pulled together a Who's Who in the fly-fishing world. Guidance and participation from the Evergreen club also contributed greatly to the success of the program. This gathering of forward-thinking fly-fishing notables included Ted Trueblood, Ed Zern, Jim Green, Polly Rosborough, Gene Anderegg, and Gordy Young to name a few; an elite group highlighted by the attendance of Lee Wulff. Thanks to Bill's vision and effort the Conclave concluded with the formation of the Federation of Fly-Fishers; a landmark event in the American history of fly-fishing.

Though a great many prominent fly-fishers were actively involved in creating the Federation of Fly-Fishers, Lee Wulff, in a letter dated June 30, 1983 gave Bill credit as the person more than any other who was responsible for its founding. On the 25th anniversary of the Federation of Fly-Fishers Bill was given the organization's highest award, "The Order of the Lapis Lazuli".

For a number of years Bill had sampled and been fascinated with the saltwater salmon fly-fishing available near Campbell River, British Columbia on Vancouver Island. In 1978 Bill sold his business and moved with Audrey to Vancouver Island where they built a home near April Point Lodge on Quadra Island. April Point Lodge, owned by brothers Warren and Eric Peterson became Bill's headquarters for the next eleven years.

As a guide for April Point Lodge he developed and refined his saltwater salmon fly-fishing and bucktailing techniques. His clients ranged from folks on family vacations to anglers from around the U.S., Canada and Europe, along with an extensive list of celebrity sportsmen that included John Wayne, Ted Williams and General Norman Schwarzkopf.

Beyond all of his achievements there is an underlying decency in Bill Nelson that makes him so special in a time far too committed to the all about me way of life. Besides enjoying fly-fishing in all of its variety he has promoted a strong code of ethics and sportsmanship for those who will follow; a code which is the very foundation of The Federation of Fly-Fishers

Bill says that his lifetime dream has always been to pass on the thrill of fly-fishing to others, including his six grandchildren, five of whom have caught salmon on a fly. Through tireless effort for seven decades as a fly-fisherman Bill has realized his dream and in doing so has represented fly-fishing at its very best.

LEE WULFF PRODUCTIONS

BEAVERKILL ROAD, LEW BEACH, NEW YORK 12753   •   914-439-3798

June 30, 1983

Bill Nelson
Box 186
Quathiaski Cove
British Columbia, Canada V0P 1N0

Dear Bill:

Virginia Frank, a student at one of our recent schools, had glowing tales of fishing with you. I was glad to hear that you're still fishing and enjoying it.... and glad to get your address after these years. You are very special in my life. I feel and say that you more than anyone else is responsible for the founding of the FFF. Your reply to my letter asking if I didn't think there were enough people interested in Fly fishing to start a national group and your offer to sponsor a meeting at Eugene set the whole thing in motion. All of us should be grateful.

I get out to the Conclaves once in a while but a new group is running it. We're too busy and we feel we've pretty much done our part. This year has been a very busy one and when our last school is over in two weeks we'll head for Quebec and about a month of salmon fishing. the first real vacation we've had in a long time.

We've moved here to the Catskills, as of five years ago, to start a fly fishing school which is going well now although we take only a couple of hundred students in our season from mid-April to mid-July This is a nice section of the country and there are a lot of fishemen around... we have a lot of fishing friends.

Time goes on. Kids grow up. Things change but old friends and their memories become more valuable. Joan joins with me in sending our best wishes and we hope we can keep in touch. Should you ever be coming east be sure to let us know......

All the best,

In 1983 Bill retired as a guide at April Point Lodge and returned to Eugene where he now resides with his wife, Audrey, close to their children and grandchildren.

Bruce Ferguson
Les Johnson
Pat Trotter

Acknowledgements

A tremendous amount of cooperation and input from a long list of people was required in order for us to write our first book, *Fly Fishing for Pacific Salmon*, which was published in 1985. It has taken even more selfless, cooperative people and voluminous additional input to complete our expanded new edition, *Fly Fishing for Pacific Salmon II*.

We were fortunate in that our original volume provided timely support to fly-anglers which helped fuel the renaissance of fly-fishing for Pacific salmon. The renaissance began in freshwater and moved out onto the estuaries, saltwater bays and Pacific Ocean proper, where there was a remarkable surge of growth as anglers took their fly rods beyond local beaches and bays to far-flung reaches of the North Pacific to seek out salmon on the edge of the Continental Shelf. This growth continues today.

The increased interest in Pacific salmon fly-fishing during the past nearly thirty years provides the foundation for this book, which includes everything new we could find that has occurred since 1985 when *Fly Fishing for Pacific Salmon* was published.

We either updated or completely rewrote every chapter in the book. In addition, a chapter on the sport of bucktailing and skipflying, a unique trolling technique has been added. This method of trolling was developed in British Columbia and over time found its way to Washington and more recently to the Oregon Coast.

Once again, fly-fishing tackle manufacturers were generous with both their time and equipment, ensuring that we would not only update but improve this important chapter.

So, considering the wealth of information and fly patterns nestled between the covers of *Fly Fishing for Pacific Salmon II*, particularly all of the new material, we have an extensive list of very special people to thank.

The importance of testing the waters at distant locations in British Columbia and Alaska cannot be too strongly stated. We had a lot of help here.

We were welcomed on several occasions by Rick and Brian Grange to try our fly-fishing techniques at the West Coast Fishing Club an exquisite lodge that is set spectacularly on a promontory of Langara Island, northernmost island in the Queen Charlottes, an area that hosts all five species of Pacific salmon during the season. Rick is one of the early supporters of catch-and-release fishing for trophy salmon.

At Haa Nee Naa Lodge, located on Dundas Island, 38 miles due west of Prince Rupert, British Columbia we were guided by owner Clayton Vanier who put us over hordes of pink and coho salmon. Clayton welcomes fly-fishers and offers salt water salmon fly-fishing classes during the peak of the fly-fishing season, in August.

Clint Cameron invited us to enjoy some incredible coho salmon fly-fishing at Dolphins North Resort. His remote lodge is located on Work Channel between British Columbia and Alaska.

Shawn Bennett of Tofino on the west side of Vancouver Island, took us out after coho salmon on incredible Clayoquot Sound. It was while fishing with Shawn that we learned about skipflying.

Art Limber of Qualicum Beach, British Columbia, a premier professional fly tier sent us a selection of his beautifully dressed bucktailing patterns for inclusion in the fly chapter. He also provided us with information on bucktailing in the winter and spring for chinook salmon along with samples of his favorite magnum-size flies used for tempting these big guys.

Bill Nelson of Eugene, Oregon, to whom this book is dedicated, spent more than a decade of his working life as a fishing guide out of April Point Lodge on Quadra Island, British Columbia. During this time, he not only guided co-author Bruce Ferguson to great success out of the lodge, but has continually shared his vast knowledge of techniques and flies for feeding salmon, including the elusive sockeye. Bill gave us many of his personal insights to bucktailing and tied a selection of patterns of his own design that appear in the fly chapter.

In our quest for feeding sockeye on a cast fly, Bruce's son-in-law, Dave Carnahan, who lived on Vancouver Island at the time, discovered that the waters near Telegraph Cove offered one of the best opportunities to intercept the massive sockeye runs headed for the Fraser River. Much of the credit for our ultimate success goes to Dave and to Gordie Graham, proprietor of Telegraph Cove Resort who guided us each season over a ten-year period, using his unfailing local knowledge of the fishery to bring us triumphantly to our goal.

Cliff Olson of Vancouver, B.C., very graciously introduced us to the techniques and possibilities of fly-fishing the mighty Fraser River for its astounding numbers of pink and sockeye, as well as lesser numbers of chum and coho salmon. We are deeply indebted to him for these eye-opening experiences.

We couldn't fly-fish without fly lines and were kept up to speed on everything new from Cortland, Orvis, Rio, Scientific Anglers and Jim Teeny, Inc, who provided us with newly designed fly lines to try, some that arrived in plain brown wrappers prior to going public. Bill Reed of Cortland, John Harder of Rio and Jim Teeny, all helped us with the fly-line section.

A very special thanks however is due Bruce Richards, fly-line guru at Scientific Anglers. To say that Bruce went the extra mile is putting it lightly. He checked out every word of the fly-line section and returned detailed corrections, edits and comments, all of which were incorporated to make the chapter a great deal better and more accurate.

Bill Nash, a retired college professor from San Jose, California, and an expert on fishing knots and fly lines, added a section to the fly chapter on using LC-13, T-14 and Deep Water Express shooting heads. His clear, concise system of weighing and measuring these highly specialized lines to match various rods should take a great deal of the mystery out of building tailor-made, deep-sinking shooting heads.

Todd Vivian, rod designer at Lamiglas, Inc., provided us with several rods to try out on rivers and the salt. We also received a selection of Temple Fork Outfitters trial rods and Jim Teeny fly rods from tackle representative Dick Sagara that were used successfully on several of our excursions.

Reels that hold up under tough conditions are critical when fly-fishing for Pacific salmon. During research for this book we were fortunate to be able to place unending pressure on reels of our own, and those sent for trial by interested manufacturers.

LES JOHNSON & BRUCE FERGUSON

A great many people have been exceedingly generous in their support during our work on Pacific salmon fly-fishing from 1975 to 2007. We can't really convey how much their efforts have helped us and you, the reader. We sincerely hope that we haven't left anyone out in these Acknowledgements.

DON MCDERMID

A nice coho salmon is brought boatside to be netted.

We received trial reels from Barry Stokes of Islander Reels on Vancouver Island; John Mazurkiewicz representing Scientific Anglers of Midland, Michigan; Jerry Kelley, representing Teton Fly Reels of San Andreas, California, Bill Reed, at Cortland Line Company, Rick Pope of Temple Fork Outfitters and Tom Rosenbauer of Orvis in Manchester, Vermont.

Don Green, rod designer emeritus of Sage, wrote a sidebar on "How to Select a Fly Rod", packed with information that will help anyone get beyond the hoopla to purchase the right fly rod from any manufacturer.

Dave Lock, a long-time tackle representative from Victoria, British Columbia added a sidebar on "How to Select a Fly Reel". Following Dave's concise advice, a salmon fisher in the market for a new fly reel will be able to select one that fills the bill exactly.

Fly-fishing is really nothing without flies and we are presenting more new working patterns in the fly chapter than have ever before appeared in any salmon fishing publication that we know about; many of which have never been previously published. This chapter is filled with flies submitted by tiers and salmon fly-fishers from California to Alaska. They not only submitted flies and recipes, but wrote tier's notes on how and where to fish the flies under various conditions.

This chapter is so crammed with good information that it could have well been a stand-alone book. The fly-submitters are too numerous to list here but each has placed his or her name and home town at the end of their tier's notes.

We have the advantage of incorporating color images throughout this book, technology that was not an option in 1985. Many are from our own files but others have been sent by people who fly-fish for Pacific salmon and are also enthusiastic photographers. There is no question that supportive color images add a great deal to the book. All contributing photographers' are credited next to their photos.

Special thanks goes to all those who provided the outstanding color images, many never before published, of what salmon actually feed on in saltwater—baitfish, squid and zooplankton—the basis for "matching the hatch". They include long-time friend Bill Ludwig; Dave Roetcisoender; Lee Hendrickson; Dr. Uwe Kils, German Marine scientist of Flensburg, Germany; Valerie MacDonald, president and founder of Biologica Environmental Services, Victoria, BC and Robert

Emmett, William Peterson, Toby Auth and Nathan Mantua of National Oceanic and Atmospheric Administration (NOAA). Thanks also go to Bruce Ferguson's daughter, Christine Robinson for her persistence and talent in searching the Internet and locating additional stunningly sharp images of zooplankton used in the Salmon Feed chapter

Without the basic research on salmon feed, migration and run timing, our efforts to translate this information in to fishing techniques and appropriate flies for saltwater fly-fishing would have been of vastly longer duration. We are, therefore, enormously indebted to all those who provided this helpful data since our first edition.

In British Columbia, Terry Gjernes, now retired, was a biologist with the Department of Fisheries and Oceans and Recreational Fisheries Coordinator for the South Coast Pacific Region, British Columbia. His run-timing charts shown in Appendix IV for all salmon species throughout BC are an invaluable addition to this book. Terry calls himself a fly-fisher of ill-repute but acknowledges that he has taken all five species of feeding Pacific salmon on a cast fly—no small feat in itself.

Many others at the Pacific Biological Station, Department of Fisheries and Oceans, Canada contributed significantly to this important background information. Kees Groot, Ph.D., research scientist, ethnologist and marine biologist graciously allowed Bruce Ferguson to interview him over a long dinner in Seattle, Washington, concerning marine migration behavior variables for returning Fraser River sockeye, including magnetic directions, water temperatures, oxygen, water quality and salinity, thereby adding immeasurably to our knowledge of where to look for fish.

Richard Bailey, in conjunction with Kees Groot, prepared maps of the Telegraph Cove-Johnstone Strait pinning down likely holding sockeye holding spots to investigate with our flies.

Bob Hurst was kind enough to open up a cornucopia at Pacific Biological Fisheries and Oceans, Canada for us in our quest for salmon background knowledge. His help has been invaluable throughout the data collection phase of the book, as has his willingness to share sockeye and pink run timing and flies with us for the east side of Vancouver Island.

Jergen Westerheim generously provided pertinent publications, as well as his own expertise on euphausiid and sand lance life histories to expand on our understanding of their significant role as salmon feed.

Wayne Saito, Fraser River Division of the Pacific Salmon Commission, shared his many years of experience concerning sockeye run timing, run sizes, depth of travel and inclination to strike lures, all by different runs—key guidance for success.

Without the information provided by the above mentioned biologists of British Columbia we would have never known where and when to seek out various runs of salmon so that we could work out techniques for catching them.

In Washington, Frank Haw and Pete Bergman of Northwest Marine Technology, Inc., have provided a continuous stream of information and guidance, especially as it relates to the resident salmon program in Puget Sound. Frank's support goes back to his tenure in the Department of Fish and Wildlife when he provided valuable input for our first book.

Also in Washington, Dan Pentilla, with the Washington Department of Fish and Wildlife updated us on the life histories and spawning areas for the various species of forage fish.

Fishing companions always deserve special thanks and special mention for putting up with endless experimentation with techniques, sharing results, flies and photos. They include in addition to others previously mentioned: Bill Ludwig; Glen Graves; Tom Buckner; Randy Frisvold; Joe Uhlman, and Garry Sandstrom, owner of the Morning Hatch Fly Shop.

As usual, Preston Singletary in addition to tying his own exquisite patterns and a set of historic Washington bucktailing flies, offered feedback throughout the book when called upon, which was often. Bob Young took on the Index, a thankless challenge he swears that he enjoys. Both of these gentlemen were also regular fishing companions who can not only catch salmon but due to their years of experience, always provide insightful comments during our many talks on the beaches. Steve Rohrbach, another fishing companion also helped out by tying exquisite duplicates of the A.J. McClane series of classic coho flies and Dan Blanton's jig hook series.

The outstanding salmon identification illustrations by wildlife artist Ron Jenkins of Charlo, Montana are the best we've ever seen. They really bring out the detail needed to accurately identify each of the five species of Pacific salmon.

We have expanded the history of *Fly Fishing for Pacific Salmon II*. It is a rich, precedent-setting fly-fishing history thanks to the ingenuity of fly-fishers dating back to the 1930s and earlier, all along the Pacific Coast, but beyond doubt the ground-breakers of modern salmon fly-fishing. Photos for the history chapters were provided by Frances D. Patrick, Bob Nauheim, Russell Chatham, Art Lingren and the authors.

As you continue on through the pages of this book—and we sincerely hope you will—please bear in mind how many great salmon fly-fishers—past and present—were involved in bringing it to fruition. To each and every one who helped us with *Fly Fishing for Pacific Salmon II*, we extend a sincere thank you.

Finally, for their interminable patience and endurance throughout the creation and birth of this second edition, we extend to our wives—Jean Ferguson, Carol Ferrera and Rena Langille, our most heartfelt gratitude.

Bruce M. Ferguson
Lester F. Johnson
Patrick Trotter, PhD

Foreword

By Russell Chatham

Let's say you just moved from Denver to the Pacific Northwest. You've always enjoyed fly-fishing, but so far it's been only for trout, mostly in places around Colorado like Cheeseman Canyon. You find out your new neighbor is a fisherman too, except he has a Boston Whaler, and generously gives you a salmon now and then which he's caught in Puget Sound or out on the Pacific Ocean. One day as he's showing you his catch, you wonder out loud if there is any way to catch them by fly-fishing, and he answers absolutely not, that it's strictly a bait-and-sinker deal. He's wrong of course, but doesn't realize it.

You've read articles about steelhead fishing, and seen books on the subject, but there appears to be little about salmon. That's why the title of this book piqued your interest, and now that you're holding it, you should understand that it is one of very few in existence devoted entirely and exclusively to fly-fishing for the Pacific salmon and it is by far the most complete work. This is the revised second edition, and while the first printing in 1985 represented a watermark, this updated and expanded version really walks the cutting edge.

I remember talking to someone many years ago in California about catching striped bass on flies, and a man who was listening in asked, "Dry flies or wet flies?" And I answered "Both actually," thinking of streamers and surface poppers. To which he further inquired, "Where do you get a Royal Coachman big enough for striped bass?" (I am not a fiction writer. I didn't make this up.)

The overriding questions begging then are which flies to use, how, where, and when. Sounds simple enough on the page, but it's huge. Unless you're chronically unemployed or retired, you cannot possibly have the time to figure this out yourself. And on second thought, even if you had the time, if you can't hang on to a job you're probably not smart enough, and if retired, not energetic enough. This is rocket science on a fast track.

Fortunately for all of us, including you there who's sneaking a peak at this Foreword, these authors are the premier authorities on this subject. Moreover, they write very well, which lends to every explanation and piece of advice a crystalline clarity. There are wonderful chapters on the identification of the Pacific salmon, interesting, well-researched histories of both salt and freshwater fly-fishing, in-depth discussions about the best modern tackle, and most importantly, an outline of how these salmon feed, where, and on what.

The dictionary of complex and elaborate original fly patterns is absolutely astonishing. It was not that many years ago that practically no one knew what a euphausiid was, let alone tied a fly to imitate one. I have personally witnessed the effectiveness of Bruce Ferguson's Green and Silver, as he put on a clinic for me some years ago in Puget Sound.

One of the book's more important contributions I think, is the discussion of how to find and fish for the various species in saltwater, and on this topic, the book represents the all-time primer by the most redoubtable experts there are. Most, who fish for anadromous fish concentrate on the trout, be they brown or rainbow. For these folks, as well as those yet to taste the sea air, moving on to the more complex universe of the Pacific salmon, will indeed require a manual, and this a remarkable fund of information, instruction, and lore.

At the end of the book, Les Johnson comments on the current state of the once enormous salmon runs, pointing out that they took everything nature could throw at them for ten centuries, yet in a mere 155 years, not even a millisecond in geologic time, man has rendered them in many cases, threatened, endangered, even extinct. For our Pacific salmon to make it for another ten centuries it is going to require lots of hard work at the ground level by all of us.

Russell Chatham
Livingston, Montana
August 15, 2007

Right: Fly-fishers working along a Puget Sound beach. (Photo by Bruce Ferguson)

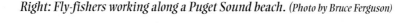

Bruce Ferguson

Bruce received the "Silver King Award," which is presented to an individual who has made "extraordinary contributions to the sport of saltwater fly-fishing over an extended period of time." Later, in 2003, at the International Fly Fishing Show and Conclave, held in Idaho Falls, Idaho, he was among those named as "Fly-fishing Legends" of the FFF. Most recently, in 2005, as part of a celebration of his 80th birthday, he was presented a special plaque by the Puget Sound Flyfishers and South Sound Flyfishers, both located in Washington's Puget Sound region, which stated: "For outstanding and devoted efforts to improve resident salmon and wild cutthroat trout fishing in Puget Sound, and for his generous contributions to fly angling through his writings, presentations, and fly patterns."

Bruce resides with his wife, Jean on the water near Gig Harbor, Washington, where he continues to pursue his prized salmon with the fly.

Bruce's lifetime passion for fly-fishing has led him to become a significant contributor in developing the sport of fly-fishing in salt water for Pacific salmon over a span of more than thirty years. At the same time, he has freely passed on this knowledge at seminars and programs throughout the Northwest. In 1985 he co-authored the first comprehensive book on the subject, *Fly Fishing for Pacific Salmon* with Les Johnson and Pat Trotter. Since then, one of his most cherished accomplishments has been to catch chinook, coho, pink, chum, and sockeye; all five salmon species available on North America's west coast, on a cast fly while they were actively feeding in salt water.

When not pursuing saltwater salmon, he has devoted considerable time to chasing tarpon and bonefish in Belize, the Bahamas, and the Florida Keys. In fresh water, he has sought out Labrador's oversize brook trout; Argentina's Tierra Del Fuego sea-run brown trout; and in the United States, from Alaska to Montana and throughout the Northwest, he has enjoyed the cornucopia of coldwater fisheries.

A life member of the Federation of Fly Fishers (FFF), he has represented this organization on many occasions at state and regional regulation hearings and forums concerning conservation and salmon fishery allocations. Bruce represented the FFF as a member of the U.S. Delegation to the U.S.-Canada Pacific Salmon Treaty negotiations in 1984. His accomplishments and commitment to the salmon resource have been recognized on numerous occasions. After receiving a number of awards from the Northwest Council, he has more recently been recognized by the National FFF. In 1996,

Les Johnson

Les has been an outdoorsman and writer for more than forty years, concentrating on fishing, hunting, fly-tying and conservation. His articles have appeared in *Field & Stream, Outdoor Life, Sports Afield, Western Outdoors, Salmon Trout Steelheader, Fly-Fishing in Salt Waters, Fly Fisherman* and *Fly Tyer.* His books include: *The Sea-Run Cutthroat Trout, (four editions); Fly Fishing for Pacific Salmon* (co-authored with Bruce Ferguson and Pat Trotter), and *Tube Flies* (co-authored with Mark Mandell). *Fly-Fishing Coastal Cutthroat Trout,*

published in 2004 is his latest completely new work on his favorite trout. Les was founding editor of *Western Fly Tying* magazine, which he later expanded to into *Flyfishing & Tying Journal* and was a founding board member of Greatlodge.com, a national hunting and fishing website.

In addition to writing about his fishing adventures, Les has been a tireless advocate for the protection of salmon, steelhead and coastal cutthroat trout.

In 2000, the Washington Fly-fishing Club presented him its Tommy Brayshaw Award for his continued contributions to conservation efforts and conservation-oriented legislation. In that same year, together with a group of like-thinking individuals, he helped to found the Wild Steelhead Coalition, an advocacy group dedicated to saving wild steelhead in Washington. In 2002 he was presented the Dawn Holbrook Memorial Award by the Northwest Fly-anglers for lifetime achievement in teaching others to grow in the art and science of fly-fishing.

Les lives in Redmond, Washington with his wife and fishing partner, Carol.

Pat Trotter

A native of the State of Washington, Pat has been an ardent fly-fisherman and fly tier since childhood. His column, "From the Fly Book" appeared regularly in *Salmon Trout Steelheader* magazine for many years, and other article of his on fly-fishing and fly-tying subjects were published in *Fly Fisherman* and *Flyfishing* magazines. Pat is also author of the book, *Cutthroat: Native Trout of the West*. Originally published in 1987, it is now on tap for a second revised and updated edition. Pat is a member of the Federation of Fly Fishers and was honored by the Washington Council of those organizations as "Federator of the Year" in 1991. He is also a member of Trout Unlimited and Washington Trout. Pat belongs to two professional organizations, the American Fisheries Society and Society for Conservation Biology.

A consulting fisheries biologist by profession, Pat specializes in the conservation biology of our rare, threatened and endangered coldwater fishes.

Pat lives in Seattle, Washington with his wife, Rena Langille.

Russell Chatham

Russell Chatham has been painting and writing for close to fifty years. His work has been exhibited in hundreds of exhibitions around the country, and he has been published in every periodical devoted to fishing. And although he has fished extensively throughout the world, his first love is the Pacific salmon. Russell lives in Livingston, Montana.

Ron Jenkins

Ron is known as the Dean of Montana Wildlife Artists and has been described as a 'fisherman's artist' for his fine illustrations of trout and salmon. A few of Ron's honors as an artist include the winning design for the 1964-65 Federal Duck Stamp competition, and the 1980 Montana Bird Stamp. His work has appeared in the prestigious Yawkey Woodson Exhibits, he painted the Pennsylvania Trout Stamp in 1991, a New Brunswick, Canada conservation stamp and the first-ever trout stamp for Rhode Island.

Introduction

When we embarked on the project of writing our first book on fly-fishing for Pacific salmon more than twenty years ago, the sport was not widely pursued in either fresh or salt water. We soon discovered however that it was a sport with a broad scattering of champions. When, after considerable resolve we decided to write a book on the subject, we discovered that it didn't take much urging to begin receiving information on the sport from San Francisco to Anchorage, and points between. Being far more enthusiastic than experienced we did not make a concerted effort to sort out information that came in. We just folded it all into the mix. In retrospect this proved to be exactly the thing to do; offer interested fly-anglers every bit of information we could come up with regardless of its eventual importance.

The result, *Fly Fishing for Pacific Salmon"*, became a primer for contemporary fly-fishers on the Pacific coast. In addition, fly-fishers from Maine to New Jersey embraced the book and adapted much of the information to fishing for striped bass since ours was one of the first volumes available on fly-fishing in cold northern marine waters—on either coast. The greatest interest though was to those of us who pursue our salmon with the fly in the marine waters of Washington State and British Columbia. The initial result was a successful book, for which we remain grateful. The early interest that occurred during the first five or six years of its time on the shelves brought about an even more important result in that many of us who had taken up the fly rod to fish Pacific salmon were soon exchanging ideas, fly-line preferences and perhaps most important, flies in numbers and patterns that ranged from downright comical to new, accurate renditions of sand lance, herring anchovy, squid, plus euphausiids and other krill. It was the beginning of a selfless exchange of ideas that continues today.

Back then we were sure that we stood on the brink of a real advance; a new and exciting fly-rod sport, particularly in salt water. The information compiled from other salmon fly-fishers and our own fishing expeditions throughout the range of the Pacific salmon for the twenty years after *Fly Fishing for Pacific Salmon* was published seemed to bear this out.

However, as research for the history chapters on Pacific salmon fly-fishing for our new book was melded with information from the first volume, we realized that we had not been riding the wave of a fly-fishing breakthrough at all. We were in fact witnessing a reawakening.

Fly-fishing for salmon in fresh water had been going on since the 1930s along coastal rivers from Northern California to British Columbia and became quite popular. It was also pursued by smaller corps of saltwater anglers in Washington and British Columbia in the 1930s until the end of World War II. Then it appeared to lose followers to the outstanding steelhead fishing being enjoyed all along the Pacific Coast. However, the pioneers of the period had made serious breakthroughs in fishing techniques and fly patterns that led the way for the renaissance that was rekindled by our first book.

Today there is little question that fly-fishing for Pacific salmon is a sport that is not only here to stay but is growing in popularity with each new season. Anglers swing stout conventional fly rods and long two-handers to search for every species of salmon that enter our coastal rivers. Along our miles of open beaches and from boats growing numbers are working the marine waters.

There have been salmon lodges set near great salmon rivers in Alaska and British Columbia that attracted fly-fishers dating back to the 1950s. Today many of these lodges showcase the tremendous salmon fly-fishing that they offer.

Salmon lodges on saltwater locations are often small relaxed operations hosting perhaps a dozen anglers per week. There are also spectacular establishments; veritable fishing versions of the elegant Empress Hotel in Victoria, British Columbia or the Fairmont in San Francisco, California. Many of these luxury resorts feature boats rigged to suit fly-fishers and offer guides well versed in the art of saltwater fly-fishing. In addition, less glitzy but no-less functional charter

Bruce Ferguson (left) and his brother Gordon on an early fly-fishing trip to Bristol Bay Lodge, Alaska. Circa 1980.

operations are available to fly-fishers fishing Puget Sound or the marine waters of Vancouver Island.

It is fair to say that fly-fishing for Pacific salmon has enjoyed a rebirth that its pioneers probably did not envision so many years ago. It is our hope that we treat this rebirth with respect and make every effort to ensure that our quest for these great anadromous fish is ethical, with minimal impact on the resource.

Fly-rod anglers who have been fundamentally involved in the renaissance have in large measure treated the sport with respect; making it more than a self-important game of numbers caught. It is our sincere hope that all those who pick up the fly rod to search for Pacific salmon in fresh water or salt, will embrace the entire fishery; its history, its pioneers, its literature and its future. Fly-fishing for Pacific salmon is a grand sport that should not be reduced to just another vehicle for those who are self-impressed by piscatorial body counts.

We should strive to make fly-fishing for Pacific salmon the world-class sport that it deserves to be in every regard. In a nutshell it should be about the fishing and all it entails, not just catching fish.

In concluding the introduction to the original *Fly Fishing for Pacific Salmon* we wrote; "It is our hope that all who read this book will look upon it as a beginning". Once again, even with all we've learned since 1985 that has been packed into the chapters herein, we know that *Fly Fishing for Pacific Salmon II* is not a complete and definitive work. There remains much to learn. Once again we hope that our effort will serve to move the sport forward technically and ethically, all the while developing a clear vision for ensuring the Pacific salmons' long-term survival.

Les Johnson
Bruce M. Ferguson
Patrick Trotter, PhD

CHAPTER ONE

Salmon Life Histories and Identification

By Bruce Ferguson

Illustrations by Ron Jenkins

At first glance, the five species of Pacific salmon native to the Pacific Coast of North America look very much alike—and they are. Their spawning, feeding and migratory habits are similar as well. It is, nonetheless, important for the fly-fisher to understand the unique differences that exist between the species—and the major strains within each species—in order to pursue this great sport fish successfully. It is also crucial so that the fly-fisher may participate intelligently in decisions that will ensure the future of the resource. This chapter encompasses the important points in detail enough to provide a general understanding of each of our Pacific salmon. It is not intended to be an in-depth, scientifically probing analysis.

The most widely accepted theory on the origin of present-day species of Pacific salmon goes back to pre-glacial times when the genus *Salmo* was distributed around the entire northern section of the northern hemisphere. The best evidence now suggests that development of the genus *Oncorhynchus* from the original *Salmo* stock took place in what is now the Sea of Japan about six million years ago. The parent *Salmo* was an anadromous fish, meaning that it migrated to fresh water at maturity in order to spawn successfully. The newly evolved *Oncorhynchus* was also anadromous. Its evolution into the several species now known and the distribution of these species into what is now thought to be their native range is believed to have occurred during the subsequent periods of fluctuating glaciations. These glacial periods are known as the Pleistocene Epoch.

All Pacific salmon die upon completion of spawning, perhaps an evolutionary survival trait to provide nutrients to the rather sterile nursery streams for sustaining the development of baby fish prior to their ocean migration. Steelhead trout of the Pacific Coast, Atlantic salmon and sea-run versions of other trout species are also anadromous, but do not all die following spawning. Why the difference? No one really knows.

Pacific Salmon Life Cycles

All Pacific salmon have comparable life cycles. Spawning adults travel to freshwater spawning beds located anywhere from just above tidewater to several hundred of miles inland. The homing instinct of salmon remains one of nature's greatest marvels with most fish returning to the identical sections of gravel from which they themselves were born. Still, considerable straying does occur, a characteristic that undoubtedly greatly aided colonization in new river systems following glaciations. Depending on species and particular strain, the majority of salmon arrive from July through April, with most stocks of all species spawning in the fall.

Each salmon species has its own preferred spawning habitat. Some use small gravel, some large; some spawn in fast, relatively deep water, others in shallow, relatively slow-moving water. Even lake beaches are commonly used, especially by sockeye salmon. The one consistency is that all salmon require clean, well-oxygenated water and unsilted gravel to facilitate successful spawning.

The Spawning Ritual

Pairing occurs when aggressive males begin circling a ripe female. While she waits patiently, males commence fighting for her favor; first bumping and pushing, then locking their grotesquely-kyped jaws, to twist and thrash and roil the pool, until one dominant male remains. Vanquished suitors limp off, sometimes to await another opportunity with the female just lost; or to go in search of a new prospective mate. With a bit of luck a deposed male will usually find another likely female in short order; preferably one that isn't already being guarded by a cruiser-class swain.

Once a male salmon has won his mate, the chosen female begins using her tail to scoop out a depression in the gravel to clear away silt, sand and small gravel until a shallow, saucer-shaped trough is created. Positioning herself so that her vent is directly over the nest or redd, she waits for the male to move in beside her. The two then release their eggs and sperm together. The sperm, having performed its job, is swept downstream in the current, while the orange-reddish eggs settle down into the bottom of the redd. The female then moves upstream from the redd and again, using her tail, loosens the gravel which drifts down into the redd to cover the eggs. This ritual is repeated until all of her eggs have been deposited and safely covered.

With her eggs covered, the female, weak and nearing death, guards the redd until she can no longer maintain her position in the current. As the last of her energy ebbs away she will slowly drift downstream, struggling valiantly to remain upright but finally keeling over onto her side and settling down onto the gravel, her gills moving slower and slower. Within a few hours, or days at the most, she along with the other members of her spawning run will be dead. Their decomposing carcasses will deliver important nutrients back into the river to complete the cycle. The entire spawning process, once mating has begun, lasts about two weeks.

Up From the Gravel

After wintering in the gravel, the newly born salmon, called alevins, sustain themselves for a time by absorbing their egg sacs. When the nutrients from the egg sac have been used, the alevins become fry that wiggle free of their gravel sanctuary to begin swimming freely and feeding independently in their parent waters. Only five to ten percent survive to this point. Freshwater life for these juveniles varies by species from a few days to three years. During this time they feed on a variety of organic matter and grow rather slowly.

Their positioning in the stream is in large measure determined by their body size, and a definite pecking order exists in any given stretch of water. As would be expected, the larger species and larger individuals occupy the best food-producing runs.

As their length increases to about two inches, the salmon become known as fingerlings, or parr. They have become stronger, more mobile and feed aggressively. Eventually, the time arrives for the fingerlings to descend their creeks

Trey Combs with a bright chum salmon taken in the Queen Charlotte Islands.
Even chromers like this one sometimes carry a hint of calico markings just below the silvery sheen of their skin.

Sockeye salmon saltwater colors.

BRUCE FERGUSON

Chinook salmon saltwater colors. Note black gum line.

BRUCE FERGUSON

Coho salmon saltwater colors.

BRUCE FERGUSON

and rivers and move out into the estuaries and salt water proper. This outmigration occurs in the spring, during which they undergo yet another physiological change.

The dark backs and barred sides or parr markings give way to a greenish back and silvery flanks, felt to be another survival adaptation to make the fish less conspicuous to predators upon reaching salt water. While working their way downstream and undergoing these changes the salmon are called smolts.

After spending a few weeks in the rich estuarine feeding area and adapting to salt water, the salmon, which have received a surge of growth from the abundant food available, embark on their ocean migration. Generally, they move northward, traveling within 25 miles of shore until they reach their favorite feeding grounds in the Gulf of Alaska where they spread out and mingle with other salmon stocks in the ocean feeding pastures. Depending on species, with some variation within a species, they spend from a few months to several years in this environment, gaining weight rapidly. Their movement is generally counterclockwise, following the prevailing Pacific Ocean currents.

There are some strains of Pacific salmon that do not follow this pattern however. Many stocks important to fishermen from California to Washington move south, sometimes a thousand miles or more to develop into mature fish. Other strains are satisfied to call the inland sea areas from Puget Sound through the Inland Waterway in Alaska as home for their entire saltwater existence. Most of these strains are believed to migrate only short distances from their particular part of this "inland" ocean. This latter group is unusually important to the fly-fisherman as it allows a year-round fishery that is relatively protected from offshore weather.

The feeding habits of salmon in salt water vary somewhat by species in regard to the size of food they require to sustain themselves as they gain length and weight. Feeding will also differ with respect to geographic location and the availability of food. Generally, various behavior is tied to the presence or absence of squid, various baitfish (anchovy, herring, smelt, sand lance, sardine, etc.), and zooplankton, crab larvae, euphausiids, amphipods and copepods. Attention to the specific feeding details for each species plays an important role in aiding the angler to develop patterns and presentation methods that will attract salmon.

The foregoing presents a general overview of all Pacific salmon and their habits. A more in-depth focus on the individual species follows. Sports catch size records are from IGFA as of 2005. Species harvest numbers are from the 1999 North Pacific Anadromous Fish Commission Statistical Yearbook. These numbers were the latest published or available at the time of this writing.

Fundamental as it may seem, identifying which species of salmon is on the end of your line is perhaps the most important first step in fly-fishing for Pacific salmon. Species identification is relatively easy when fish are in their spawning colors. When feeding in salt water, recognition becomes much more difficult. At the same time, fishing regulations specifying minimum lengths, retention restrictions and closed seasons by species are now an integral part of today's conservation-oriented fishing scene. It is, therefore, essential to learn how to make a positive identification before harvesting a salmon. To this end each species description is preceded by a detailed illustration by noted wildlife artist Ron Jenkins, of the fish in ocean-phase coloration, with tips for quick identification

Pink salmon saltwater colors.

Chum salmon saltwater colors.

Chum salmon, spawning teeth barely showing.

RON JENKINS

Quick Identification, Ocean Phase
The chinook salmon has a mouthful of large, sharp teeth protruding from a black gum line. The entire inside of the mouth is not necessarily black. Numerous small spots are on the tail. The large size of a chinook also assists in identification.

Chinook salmon are also known as king, tyee, spring, black-mouth (immature), and grilse (immature less than three pounds). They are the largest of the salmon species, weighing about 18 to 20 pounds and less than 40 inches at maturity. However, chinook salmon have been taken commercially up to 126 pounds (53 inches long) in the waters off Petersburg, Alaska. A monster of 97 pounds was caught, on hook and line from the Kenai River, also in Alaska.

Chinook are the least abundant of the salmon species by a wide margin, yet they are the salmon species most sought by sport fishers. Still, the 1999 commercial and subsistence catch was 1,349,000 with an additional 594,000 sport caught for a total of 1, 943,000 chinook salmon taken in North American waters that year.

The life span of chinook salmon varies with the spread being three to eight years. Ignoring precocious males, called "jacks" which mature at two or three years, most survive four years with five-year-old chinook being common to Alaska waters.

In salt water, chinook are identified by black spotting on the back, dorsal fin and upper and lower tail. They are greenish-blue to black on the back, shading to silver on the sides. They have a blackish mouth with a black lower gum line and sharp, white teeth. The male spawner is blackish while the female is brassy to red.

Chinook spawning grounds in North America range from San Francisco Bay in California to Alaska's Wulik River, which empties into the Arctic Ocean. The bulk of chinook spawning takes place in relatively few major rivers throughout their range. For instance, in Canada, 50 percent of chinook spawning occurs in just 14 rivers, even though spawners utilize 260 Canadian rivers. In the United States, major chinook salmon production occurs in the Sacramento River (California); the Columbia River (Idaho, Oregon and Washington); and the Copper, Nushagak, and Yukon rivers (Alaska).

Chinook enter North American streams almost year around. The Columbia River has a spring run that ascends from February through May; a summer run that arrives from June through July; and a fall run that enters in August and September with some still showing well into October. The Sacramento not only has a spring and fall run but also a winter run whose advance guard passes under the Golden Gate Bridge around Thanksgiving and continues on through February. In general, the more southerly rivers host multiple runs of chinook while those further north, like the Yukon, are reduced to a single run.

Of particular interest to freshwater fly-anglers is the fact that spring and summer strains of chinook salmon generally are traveling to the headwaters of large river systems and retain much of their saltwater vigor and appearance during much of their extended upstream migration, whereas the fall runs typically begin to darken and lose their strength in their natal stream estuaries even before entering fresh water.

RON JENKINS

Spawning generally takes place from August through December, depending on run timing. Chinook spawning grounds vary from the main stem of large rivers to small tributaries, but the grounds do have certain commonalities. Of these; the stream underflowing large gravel to sand with alternating pools and riffles is most important. Spawning nests (redds) mainly occur at the lip of a pool where it becomes a riffle providing a maximum of the all-important underflow, thereby ensuring the necessary irrigation of eggs

Fry emerge in the spring, and if born close to the ocean, may spend only a few days to a few months in fresh water before smolting and migrating to salt water. These are called "ocean" type and are more characteristic in the southern range of the species. The "stream" type on the other hand, are generally born further upriver and spend a year, or longer in fresh water before smolting. This type occurs throughout the range, to the exclusion of the "ocean" type in the northern sections of the Pacific. Smolting and migration peaks for both ocean and stream types take place in the spring, but can occur anytime during the year.

Chinook smolts are three to six inches in length. They spend the summer in the estuary and with the fall freshets, head out to sea. During this time they grow to about eight inches, feeding primarily on a diet of crab larvae, insects, sand fleas and some baby fish.

At sea, chinook generally migrate north with a few significant exceptions. Generally, they remain in the coastal areas during their first year, gradually moving northward to offshore feeding grounds in the North Pacific Ocean and Bering Sea. Based on what we know at this time, chinook in their final year begin a gradual southeasterly midyear return migration back to their North American spawning rivers.

Of all the salmon species, chinook are known to occur in the greatest range of water depths. They have been taken with surface gillnets as well as commercial trawl nets working at depths of 350 feet. It is pretty well agreed upon that chinook prefer water more than 60 feet deep. This feeding characteristic makes them a more difficult fish to take on a fly in salt water, although as chinook approach their spawning rivers in coastal areas, they tend to hug the shorelines in kelp beds found at the edges of drop-offs.

Of special importance to saltwater fly-fishers is the strain of "resident" chinook which remain for their entire saltwater existence in the protected inshore waters of Puget Sound, the Georgia Basin and Alaska's Inland Waterway. Some of these are natural wild fish, while a much larger percentage, at least in Puget Sound, are hatchery-reared whose migratory instincts have been killed by being held in hatchery ponds for an extra few months before being released. In all other respects, hatchery salmon exhibit the same habits as their ocean-going relatives, although they are generally somewhat smaller at maturity. They too prefer deeper water and do most of their feeding close to the bottom.

RON JENKINS

Quick Identification, Ocean Phase
The coho salmon exhibits distinct sharp teeth protruding from a
white gum line with the rest of the inside of the mouth being darker.
Large round scales and sometimes spots on the upper lobe of
the tail complete the appearance.

Coho are also called silver, hooknose, northern, blueback and grilse (immature fish under three pounds). Adult coho average six to 12 pounds, but the largest coho salmon landed pulled from Pacific waters on sport tackle is a 31-pounder taken in 1947 off Victoria, British Columbia. Its length was a bit over 38 inches.

Coho salmon are somewhat more abundant than chinook, but not as plentiful as chum, pink or sockeye. Coho are the backbone of the sport catch. The 1999 commercial and subsistence catch of coho in North America was 5,065,000 fish. With the addition for that year of an additional 796,000 sport-caught, the total was 5,861,000 coho salmon.

The lifespan of the coho is predominately three years from British Columbia south, while in Alaska, four-year survival is common because of a freshwater juvenile residency of two years rather than one. Early sexually mature males (jacks) spawn and die a year earlier than normal.

Coho are identified by black spotting which is confined to the back and upper tail. They are metallic blue on the back, becoming bright silver on the flanks and belly. Their mouth is whitish to grayish along the lower gum line with prominent, sharp teeth. Male spawners have bright red sides with bluish-green backs and heads. Female spawners are not as brightly colored.

North American coho distribution ranges from as far north as the Nome River in western Alaska to as far south as Monterey Bay in California. They are, however most abundant from central Oregon to central Alaska. Coho spawn not only in the many tributary streams and headwaters of major rivers but also in a great variety of smaller coastal streams. They seldom spawn, though more than 150 miles inland from the Pacific Ocean or large protected waters such as Puget Sound or the Georgia Basin. An exception occurs on the Yukon River in Alaska where coho migrate upstream for more than 1,100 miles to reach parent spawning gravel.

There are early and late runs of coho. The majority will assemble in the salt water off of the mouths of parent rivers in late July and August, with small, vanguard runs that arrive in early July and others that do not show up until Thanksgiving. A few rivers in Washington and Oregon host very late runs of exceptionally large, bright coho that arrive well into December and even January. The Naselle and Satsop rivers in Washington are examples as are the Clackamas and Big Nehalem rivers in Oregon.

Coho that arrive early in the season, or that travel relatively long distances to reach spawning gravel are generally brighter fish that hold onto their silvery sheen, good body condition and vigor longer than late arriving runs. Late arriving coho conversely show spawning colors sooner, often while still in the estuaries since they are closer to spawning when they reach parent water.

RON JENKINS

Coho salmon spawn from October through January but have been documented spawning as late as March. As with other salmon species, coho select highly oxygenated water which usually occurs in riffles with a bottom that is free of silt. Following the spawning procedure previously described, the eggs incubate for 40 to 100 days, or more, depending on water temperature. Fry emerge from the gravel in about three weeks, an event that can take place from March to late July.

Initially after emerging from the gravel, coho fry tend to school close to their emergence site, but as they begin to grow, disperse and take up individual feeding stations to establish their "territories" which they guard aggressively. As a general rule, freshwater residency lasts at least a year and in the case of more northerly stocks, two years. Smolting and downstream migration takes place from April to August, depending on geographic location, smolt size, and water flow. Main migrations take place at night. Upon reaching the estuaries and tidal sloughs, the silvery, three to five-inch fish school up for a stay of several months of foraging to gain length and weight before continuing their migration. The coho's diet during this period consists of crab larvae, amphipods, euphausiids, mysids and fish larvae. When they have reached a length of about eight inches the young coho begin their journey; some travel only into the protected inland waters of Washington's Puget Sound, Georgia Basin in British Columbia and the southeast Alaska archipelago.

The migratory, or "ocean" group of coho generally works northward and may travel as far as a thousand miles before turning southward toward their home spawning streams 18 to 24 months later. While in salt water, coho grow faster than any other salmon species, with a recorded ocean growth from 1.76 pounds in April to 8.80 pounds in September of their final year, or well over a pound per month. They are reported to prefer feeding and traveling in the top 30 feet of water, resting close to the surface at night and swimming deeper during the daytime. Coho hold well out from the coast on their return trip, feeding and growing rapidly. The more northerly strains of salmon apparently leave the Gulf of Alaska, heading south in late June, and have been known to travel as far as 30 miles per day, averaging 16 over long distances. Some other major stocks remain for their entire oceanic life in coastal waters with some stocks traveling north to feed along the coast before returning to spawning rivers. Other stocks turn south for their time feeding and maturing in coastal areas.

Non-migratory coho salmon that live their saltwater lives in the protected, nearshore waters of Alaska, British Columbia and Washington provide the best opportunity for the fly-fisher. For this reason they produce the largest share of fly-caught salmon that are actively feeding rather than simply striking, as they do when feeding has ceased upon their return to parent rivers. Although resident coho salmon were once abundant based strictly on wild stocks, the majority of these fish—which are very important to the fly-fisher—are now produced artificially by holding the smolts in hatchery ponds or saltwater pens for an extended period. As in the case of resident chinook, the shorter saltwater existence and reduced feeding opportunities tend to result in smaller spawning adults, with an average weight of four to six pounds. Migrations do occur to capitalize on feeding opportunities but are confined to a relatively small arena. The coho's general use of the top 30 feet of water coincides with the fly-fisher's interest in fishing close to the surface. This fact makes the coho of particular interest as a potentially world-class sport fishery from Oregon to Alaska.

RON JENKINS

Quick Identification, Ocean Phase
The pink salmon's identifiable teeth, very small scales and most importantly, the only species with large, oval spots covering the entire tail.

Pink salmon are also known as humpbacks or *humpies*. They attain a length of 30 inches or more. Some sport-caught have weighed up to 14 pounds. However, the average fish is much smaller, between three and five pounds.

The pink is the most abundant of all the Pacific salmon, without question. Even though the bulk of the fishery is commercial, it is a readily available and becoming increasingly popular with fly-fishers as a sport fish. Major runs occur almost exclusively in odd-numbered years in Washington and western Alaska. In the remainder of Alaska and British Columbia there appears to be a more balanced run size between odd and even years. The life span of pink salmon is always two years. With the life span of the pink salmon being so short, there are no early maturing jacks. North America commercial and subsistence catch of pink salmon was 152, 380,000 in 1999. The sport catch added 348,000 for a total catch of 152,728,000.

Pinks, in their ocean phase, have metallic blue backs, shading to silver on the flanks. They have several large, oval black spots on the back and tail. Teeth are small and weak. Scales are much smaller than on other species. The spawning male develops a pronounced hump on the shoulder, hence the name *humpy* or *humpback*. Its sides and back turn brownish while its lower side and belly become very white. Spawning female pinks do not develop the hump, or hooked jaw of the males.

Pink salmon are found in North America from the Russian River in California to the McKenzie River in the Northwest Territories of Canada. The primary spawning distribution however, is from the Puyallup River in Washington's Puget Sound to the McKenzie. Spawning occurs mostly in the lower sections of rivers, sometimes even in tidewater. Conversely, there are some strains of pink salmon that spawn more than 100 miles upstream in long rivers.

Pink: *spawning pair*

RON JENKINS

Pinks enter coastal waters on their spawning migration from June through September throughout their range. Spawning takes place shortly thereafter, from July through October. Pink salmon lose their brightness very quickly upon entering fresh water since they usually spawn only a short distance above salt water.

The eggs, which are buried in clean gravel, hatch from December through February after an incubation period of 90 to 150 days. Fry emerge from the gravel in April and May and move directly downstream, traveling at night to avoid predation. If the spawning stream is short, fry may arrive in salt water the same night that they started downstream. At this point they are barely an inch in length. In the estuary, Juvenile pinks form large schools that remain together for several months, feeding on copepods, other zooplankton and fish larvae.

Beginning in July and continuing into fall, juvenile pinks migrate rapidly northward in a narrow bank along the coast, which may stretch out for nearly a thousand miles. They travel at an estimated ten miles per day during their northward migration. While wintering at sea, they continue to move and feed in a generally southerly direction in the Gulf of Alaska, turning back northward in their final spring and summer before beginning their homeward migration. Time at sea is approximately 12 months, in addition to the time they spent as juveniles in the more protected estuarine salt water.

Research conducted on the open sea indicates that pink salmon prefer surface or near-surface feeding. Most appear to feed and travel in the upper 30 feet of water but may occasionally be found down to 75 feet below the surface. The most active feeding occurs at dusk, although pinks are opportunistic and will feed any time of day if sufficient food is located.

As is the case with chinook and coho, there are some strains of pink salmon that remain as "resident" non-migratory stocks along inshore waters of Puget Sound. These resident pinks may be somewhat smaller than those that migrate northward but as a tradeoff are present on a year-around basis.

RON JENKINS

Quick Identification, Ocean Phase
The sockeye salmon is one of two species with no spots. It also has no teeth, giving it the nickname of "rubber lipped coho".

Sockeye are also known as red, or blueback salmon. A land-locked strain is known as kokanee or silver salmon. Sockeye are the most streamlined of Pacific salmon with adults normally weighing from five to seven pounds. The largest specimens can, however attain a length of 33 inches and a weight of 15 pounds. Stocks from the Columbia River are smaller, averaging only three to four pounds.

In North America waters, sockeye are the second most abundant species behind pinks, and most are taken commercially. In 1999 the commercial and subsistence take was 46,270,000. The reported sport catch was 474,000 for a total of 46,744,000 anadromous sockeye. In addition a very large sport fishery exists from California to British Columbia on the non-migratory, lake-bound form of sockeye known as kokanee.

Sockeye have a life span of from three to eight years with four and five years being most common. In salt water, sockeye are a metallic, greenish-blue on the back with fine, black specklings. There are no large spots. They have silver sides shading to white on the belly. Teeth are small and not prominent. Male spawners are a brilliant red overall, except for the head, which is olive-green. Female spawners have the same coloration, except for some runs which exhibit green and yellow blotches on their bodies.

Spawning populations of sockeye occur from the Sacramento River in California through the Yukon in Alaska. However, the bulk of the fishery occurs between the Columbia River and Bristol Bay, Alaska. Most spawning occurs in major river systems, with the Bristol Bay area the most productive and the Fraser River system in British Columbia second in importance. Other major systems are central Alaska's Cook Inlet and the Chignik, Copper and Karluck rivers, also in Alaska; British Columbia's, Rivers and Smith Inlet, as well as the Skeena and Nass rivers.

Adults enter their spawning rivers between May and October, with the bulk moving into fresh water from July through September. Some of the larger river systems have both early runs that occur in July to early August and late returning runs that arrive in parent rivers from September through October.

RON JENKINS

Spawning may take place only a mile, or so above tidewater, but mainly occurs in riffles 700 miles or more from the Pacific Ocean. In almost all cases, spawning takes place in rivers which have lakes in their headwaters. Actual spawning occurs in the gravel of feeder streams entering the lake, in gravel areas of the lakeshore that is fed by springs, or in the outlet stream to the lake.

Fry emerge from the gravel in April and May and proceed to the lake where they reside from one to four years. Most however spend from one to two years in their parent lake before smolting from April to June and traveling downstream on their seaward migration. Sockeye smolts are three to five inches long at the time of outmigration. Upon entering salt water, sockeye move along the coast in a rather narrow belt, during which they feed actively on fish larvae and crustacean zooplankton, including copepods, amphipods, euphausiids and crab larvae. However, by winter they have become widely dispersed and have moved well offshore in the North Pacific and Bering Sea. They will make feeding migrations. During their one- to four-year cycle, sockeye will make feeding migrations from north to west in the summer. In fall they migrate south and east.

At sea, sockeye can be found in depths up to 200 feet, but normally are nearer the surface in the upper 50 feet of water. As they approach the inland waters on their return trip, they travel at a rate of 30 miles per day, continuing to feeding during this time. Sockeye do not appear to linger in coastal waters on their way to parent gravel, with some major stocks completing 80 percent of their migration within 15 days. For the fly-fisherman, this necessitates the need to know individual run timing and to be there when it is occurring.

RON JENKINS

Quick Identification, Ocean Phase
The chum salmon has no spots and barely discernable teeth.
Large oval scales and upon approaching maturity, faint
irregular vertical bars along the flanks.

Of the five species of Pacific salmon in North America, chum is of average abundance. Regarded as primarily a commercial and subsistence fish, the total North American chum catch by three harvesters in 1999 was 22, 596,000. The sport catch, although growing in importance was only 34,000 fish, producing a total catch of 22, 360,000.

Chum are also known as fall, or dog salmon. Sport-caught chum have been recorded at 40 inches long and weighing up to 35 pounds. However, they are more commonly found in the 6- to 10-pound range.

The chum life span varies from two to seven years but more commonly is three to five years. In salt water they have metallic blue backs with occasional black speckling. They do not have black spots on their bodies, fins or tails. Teeth are not prominent. Spawning males develop vertical reddish or dark streaks against an olive background. Females have the same markings but not to the same degree.

Distribution of chum salmon in North America is greater than for any of the other Pacific salmon species, occurring more or less continuously from the Sacramento River in California through Oregon, Washington, British Columbia and Alaska, east to—and including—the McKenzie River in Canada's Northwest Territories. McKenzie River stocks may spawn nearly 2000 miles from the Pacific Ocean. There are both early and late runs of chum salmon, but in general, spawning occurs earlier in the northern end of the range than at the southern limits of distribution.

Because most stocks spawn so close to salt water, chum tend to lose their brightness and take on their spawning colors early, in many instances before they enter fresh water. They are, therefore they are not considered to be a prize on the fly unless nabbed when they first arrive near natal streams and are still actively feeding. A fresh-run chum is a spectacular fighter capable of extremely long, fast runs and dogged resistance at the battle's end before giving up. The later runs of chum salmon are usually larger than the early, or summer run, often weighing up to 20 pounds or more.

RON JENKINS

Spawning takes place from June through January, depending on the specific strain. Fry emerge from the spawning gravel the following spring and move downstream immediately, usually at night. When traveling long distances to salt water, chum will begin feeding on insect larvae. Regardless of river length, all chum fry reach saltwater estuaries no later than mid-summer. Most however arrive at estuaries in April and May. Other than their outmigration period to salt water, chum salmon have no freshwater residency period.

Once in salt water the young fish school and remain in coastal areas for the next several months, usually within 20 miles of shore. During this time they feed actively on copepods, amphipods, euphausiids, crustacean larvae, fish larvae and insects, a diet they retain throughout maturity. By fall and early winter, they move out to sea, at which time they are about eight inches in length.

North American stocks of chum spend the bulk of their lives in the Gulf of Alaska. They seem to inhabit deeper waters than coho, sockeye and pink salmon with offshore depths of 200 feet recorded, although they move closer to the surface at night. Later, as chum approach their spawning rivers, they are found at depths of 50 feet, or less. By July, the bulk of maturing fish are on their way from the North Pacific feeding grounds, with the exception of the very early runs which have already departed for home rivers. Since there are so many stocks and run timings, there is no mass exodus as is the case within the more concentrated runs of spawning sockeye. Growth of chum salmon is very rapid during their final migration.

Summary

It can be seen that each salmon species, as well as stocks within the species, has its own distinguishing characteristics. Salmon vary in terms of their life span, size, diet, depths at which they feed, migration routes, particularly toward maturity, run sizes and timing. These variables are all significant to the salmon fly-fisher. To be successful, it is important to learn the distinguishing traits of each.

CHAPTER TWO

Saltwater History

By Les Johnson and Pat Trotter

In 1876 a ship of the U. S. Coast and Geodetic Survey sailed into Baker's Bay at the mouth of the Columbia River and dropped anchor under the bluffs near Fort Canby, the new military post. Its mission was to chart the mouth of the river. But its captain, Cleveland Rockwell, was a fly-fisherman and coho salmon were showing in the clear, salt water of the bay. It was an opportunity he couldn't resist.

Rockwell himself later described his historic encounter in the pages of *Pacific Quarterly*, Vol. 10, No. 4, October, 1903:

> *Equipped with a good two-handed English salmon rod of ash, with a lancewood tip, one hundred yards of braided line, and the best flies, all furnished me by a valued friend, I left the vessel's side, alone in my dinghy, to try for silverside salmon.*
>
> *No salmon had ever been known before to take a fly…and I had very little hope of success. I had but a few hundred yards to pull from the vessel before arriving near the steep and rocky shore of the bay, and, laying in the oars, I took my rod and commenced casting. Though an old hand with an eight-ounce trout rod, I found a two-handed rod an awkward thing. However, I soon succeeded in making a cast far enough from the boat to hook a salmon. What a thrill of excitement accompanied striking the hook into the solid tongue of that first salmon—and how my heart rushed up into my throat as the alarmed fish made his first frantic rush for liberty!…*
>
> *The salmon and I fought it out…all around the harbor, and half the military post was down on the shore to see the fun; and when I finally thrust the gaff into its shining belly and lifted it into the boat, a cheer went up…which, with the salmon thrashing around in the boat, made me feel quite proud of the adventure. He weighed twenty-five pounds.*

> *The genial and enthusiastic lighthouse keeper at the Cape became much excited and expressed the profoundest regret that he had lived there ten years and never knew that salmon could be caught with a fly. He came aboard and examined my tackle, and I supplied him with a few flies.*
>
> *In a week every rooster on the military post presented a most forlorn appearance; necks and tails had both been plucked to make salmon flies.*
>
> *Many a salmon have I taken from the sparkling bay under Cape Disappointment since that day, but the lively adventure with my first salmon remains an episode of supreme pleasure.*

Rockwell's account indicates that for a time the residents of the bay at the mouth of the Columbia River enjoyed the fly-casting sport. But it didn't last. Gradually the more serious

DAN BERGLUND

Les Johnson testing out tackle and flies in Washington's South Puget Sound. This early saltwater fishing was hit-and-miss at first but became more productive as fly patterns and techniques improved. Circa 1975

business of making a living and putting food on the table prevailed. Pacific salmon had been taken for food and commerce since the first settlers arrived, and by the Native Americans before that. The fly rod gave way once again to nets and baits.

Beyond this account, the saltwater history of fly for Pacific salmon is largely defined within the area from the southernmost point in Washington's Puget Sound, north to the Strait of Georgia in British Columbia along the mainland to Lund and from Victoria to Campbell River on the east side of Vancouver Island. This vast marine environment is broken up with seemingly endless miles of islands large and small that offer bays, oyster-strewn beaches and inlets of protected water that do not exist along the Oregon and California coastline. Alaska also has protected salt water in its southeast region but historically, few if any Alaska sport anglers bothered with fly-fishing in salt water because salmon by the hundreds could be so easily taken from river estuaries. Washington and British Columbia fly-fishers led the way because the myriad saltwater bays, and broad river estuaries could be negotiated in relative safety in small boats.

At the turn of the century, fly-fishing was largely a game for gentleman-sportsmen, those few individuals who could afford the time and expenditure for equipment and to travel long distances in pursuit of their sport. Such individuals visited the Northwest from time to time, most of them heading for the east coast of Vancouver Island, and left accounts of their exploits in libraries and letters.

Sir Bryan Leighton was one such visitor. In a letter dated December 31, 1905 and quoted in Hodgson's *Salmon Fishing*, Sir Bryan wrote, "of salmon on the Pacific coast we find six varieties—the king or spring salmon, the coho, the steelhead, the humpback, the dog salmon, and the sockeye. Only the first three will take a lure, and I have caught the coho on the fly only." He went on to say, "The coho I have many times caught on a fly in the estuary of a river. I found that coho took any silver bodied fly and that no. 4 or no. 5 was the best."

Another early writer was Sir John Rogers, who came all the way from Egypt to troll for kings at Campbell River. But often for a change of pace he would anchor his boat off a point where he knew the fish would pass and cast a fly for coho. He took a great many fish in this way and was copied by other anglers who saw the success he was having.

Thus, by 1919, when A. Bryan Williams published his book, *Rod & Creel in British Columbia*, it was a "pretty well acknowledged fact that the coho salmon will take the fly readily and the spring salmon occasionally if it is presented to them properly."

The way to do it, Williams wrote, was to "choose shallow water, or even anchor your boat out on the line of a run of cohos when they are swimming in schools near the surface," or place yourself off the mouth of any small creek up which the fish go to spawn."

Charlie Stroulger (right) shown here with a huge 22 1/2-pound coho salmon taken on the fly, grew up on the Cowichan Bay hillside where his family lived for most of the 20th century. During the 1930s and into the 1960s, Charlie and his brother Jack saw the best of the Cowichan Bay coho fishing and it was on this bay that bucktailing became the way to catch the scrappy coho. Charlie was regarded as Vancouver Island's premier bucktail fly tier. His flies were a must if you wanted to increase your chances of success with the lively coho and his legacy to the sport is his Grey Ghost bucktail.

"Use a double-handed fourteen foot rod at least," Williams recommended. Then he added, "It need not be an expensive split cane; a good greenheart will do quite well. For salt water a plain enameled line is good enough, as you seldom need to make long casts and salt water soon ruins a silk line. Most of your flies should be tied on 5/0 hooks. Few patterns are needed; the Jock Scott, Silver Doctor, Silver Wilkinson, and Durham Ranger are as good as any."

Williams observed, in 1919, that while a few men always used a fly and others did occasionally, the sport had not really been followed up as it should. The idea of the salmon as anything but a food fish, to be boated in the most efficient manner possible and hauled off to a table, was a hard one to get across. And nothing had changed 15 years later when Roderick Haig-Brown published *The Western Angler*. Haig-Brown wrote that "while quite a few fishermen could claim a long-time habit of spending September and October with a fly rod in some bay where the cohos school and feed, the development of the sport had been quite slow." About the only change to be noted was that fishermen had largely put aside

Vancouver Island fly-fishers working the beach for coho salmon. Fishing from the beaches actually began in British Columbia in the 1930s and in Washington in the 1940s. Circa 1970.

the standard Atlantic salmon flies in favor of patterns with silver bodies and various combinations of white, red, yellow, and brown bucktail. These flies were usually tied on 2/0 hooks and had nearly uniform two-inch-long wings.

About 1935 or 1936 there was a tremendous improvement in coho flies as anglers became more aware of the candlefish, herring, and other baitfish that salmon actually feed on, and they tried to tie flies to match. Polar bear hair was now commonly substituted for bucktail and the wing was extended to three or more inches. These new, longer flies proved themselves quickly.

Roderick Haig-Brown lauded the change. "The old bucktail fly was a dead, ugly creature, dull of color, without luster or any illusion of translucency," he wrote. "Polar bear hair is superior in every way....There is very little doubt that in nearly all conditions it is more attractive to the fish than is bucktail."

By this time American anglers had spread the sport to the Puget Sound country. Places such as Possession Bar, Bush Point, Point No Point, Steamboat Island, Double Bluff, and Elliott Bay came to be as well-known among the Washington fly-fishing fraternity as Campbell River, Nanaimo, Sooke and Cowichan Bay was to the Canadians.

Fishing the salt water was not actually necessary for Washington and British Columbia fly-fishers in the 1930s when they first pushed out into the marine environment near their homes because the rivers draining into Broughton Strait, the Strait of Georgia, Hood Canal and Puget Sound

were also stiff with salmon, steelhead and coastal cutthroat that could be caught readily from summer through late fall. What made the fly-fishers of Washington and British Columbia unique was an insatiable curiosity fired by their love of fly-fishing. Enos Bradner, Roy Patrick and Letcher Lambuth of Washington; Roderick Haig-Brown, Tommy Brayshaw and W.A. "Bill" MacDonald of British Columbia to name just a scant few, were cutting edge fly-fishers constantly searching for the opportunity to take their fly rods to what we call today, *the next level.*

With so much salt water available and easily accessible—and with salmon leaping along the shoreline from spring through fall it was inevitable that fly-fishers would eventually trek the beaches, or motor their skiffs along tide rips to cast for salmon. Accounts written about fishing Pacific salt water for salmon began appearing in articles and books in the late 1930s and continued on through the 1950s with most of it being accomplished with floating lines (which were all that were available at the time) and big bucktail and polar bear hair flies dressed on large, long-shank hooks, up to 5/0,

FRANCIS D. PATRICK

Roy Patrick holds up a nice coho salmon taken casting in the salt of Puget Sound. Circa 1960.

designed to imitate mature herring and sand lance. A further addition to salmon streamers was a small spinner that barely covered the head of the fly. Anglers swore that using a coho fly without the added attraction of a tiny spinner reduced its effectiveness by at least ten percent. There is no record of who factored this percentage, or how it was arrived at.

The first ventures into salt water by the pioneers of fly-fishing in the Pacific salt were in large measure an extension of the fishing method that anglers with conventional tackle employed; trolling. Few did much casting. It did not take long however for fly-fishers to discover that when salmon, especially coho, were working on or near the surface that casting the big polar bear streamers could be very effective. Most Northwest fly-fishers used their heavy, finely crafted split cane steelhead rods made by Hardy, Granger, Montague and Orvis; stout and well up to the task of dealing with aerial-minded coho or hard-pulling pink salmon. Anglers who took their trout outfits to the salt discovered, usually when they shattered prized rods while trying to handle a mature coho that stouter tackle was called for.

One well-respected Washington angler, Wesley Drain, did not subscribe to either the spinner-enhanced fly, or trolling. He was quoted on this subject in *Streamer Fly Tying and Fishing* by Joseph D. Bates, Jr.

"I cast to my fish the same way you would cover a rise in a lake or pool," said Drain, "and have never felt the need or urge to attach a spinner to these patterns."

While stout, split-cane fly rods held up quite well, adjustable spring-and-pawl drags on the largest Hardy reels of the day did not put up much resistance when an angler was joined in a monumental struggle with a wild, fresh-run coho. With only a left-side palming plate to press against on the Hardy Perfect or sticking one's fingers into the whirling spool of a St. John for drag, slowing the blistering runs of a large, northern coho was a hit-and-miss proposition when working from a rocking skiff. A bit too much manually-applied drag pressure often abruptly terminated the contest when the angler's leader would part with a loud, demoralizing *snap!*

Since fishing for salmon with the fly rods of those early days was so challenging, many Washington and British Columbia anglers opted to troll their flies with little or no added weight using standard steelhead rods and level-wind reels loaded with 200 yards of 12-pound-test braided line. On the end a small barrel swivel and an additional 4 feet of gut leader was tied on to which the big polar bear streamer was attached. One popular reel of the day for trolling coho flies was the Pflueger Rocket, geared for a fast retrieve and with an adjustable star drag that would stem the blazing runs of coho, or on occasion, even larger chinook salmon.

At the end of World War II in 1945, fiberglass rods came onto the market. Lighter, stronger and more durable than bamboo, fiberglass caught on quickly with fly-fishers, many of whom were more than happy to discard their conventional steelhead rods and level-wind reels. Armed with fly rods that would send a big, 3/0 streamer to good distances and with backbone enough to set a heavy hook and handle a crazed coho, the fly-rod again became a working tool for the front line saltwater fly-rod anglers of Washington and British Columbia.

Washington salmon fly-anglers who ventured out to the remote coastal fishing villages of La Push, Neah Bay and Sekiu after World War II immediately noticed that conventional gear anglers were trolling a new type of streamer called

FRANCIS D. PATRICK

Roy Patrick, founding owner of Patrick's Fly Shop, the center of the Seattle fly-fishing universe from 1946 through the 1970s, with a limit of wild, resident coho salmon taken by him and a friend in August 1947.

a tube fly. The tube fly, designed by Lloyd Peters of Port Angeles, Washington in 1946 was trolled right in the outboard motor wake at a very fast clip, sometimes skipping completely out of the water. This fast troll was emulated by fly-fishers trolling polar bear streamers on size A level, floating fly lines. Coho salmon had to work hard to catch the wildly skipping fly which brought about some spectacular strikes.

Roderick Haig-Brown tied his Coho Golden and Coho Blue, as incredibly beautiful as any Atlantic salmon patterns, for use in the Campbell River estuary and further out into the salt. Both patterns were successful. For larger patterns, Haig-Brown used streamers, preferring polar bear to bucktail. He continued to experiment though, not completely convinced that polar bear was the best material for a saltwater salmon fly.

British Columbia, fly-fishers were developing their own saltwater tactics, pulling their big polar bear streamers with stout fiberglass fly rods. The fly line was substituted with 100 yards of 10- to 12-pound-test monofilament on top of another 100 yards of stout, braided backing. The fly was usually fished with no weight but at times they would add a very light crescent sinker of about one-half ounce ahead of the fly. The method became known as bucktailing (See Chapter 8, "The Fine Sport of Bucktailing") and continues to grow in popularity.

Polar bear, which accepted Veniard's dyes much better than bucktail, inspired anglers in Washington and British Columbia to begin experimenting with colors that would accurately imitate the two primary forage fish of Pacific salmon; herring and sand lance. Two of the favorite patterns developed were called the Herring and Candlefish developed by Letcher Lambuth of Seattle. A third popular dressing was the Coronation, a Roy Patrick pattern.

Roy Patrick of Seattle established Patrick's Fly Shop in 1946. The little shop that is still in business on Eastlake Avenue in Seattle under the ownership of Jimmy LeMert

Early years of spring fishing had anglers scaling back to trout tackle to catch these young-of-the-year coho salmon.

quickly became the gathering place for serious local fly-fishers. Patrick, in addition to being a fine fly-fisher, was one of the premier fly dressers of the period and the person who tracked the progress of the fly-fishers of Washington and British Columbia who were pushing ahead in saltwater fly-fishing. Patrick did not record or write in the journalistic style of Enos Bradner, Roderick Haig-Brown, Bill MacDonald or A.J. McClane. He was instead a recorder of the flies. In addition, Patrick and his wife, Fay mastered the art of the unique dyeing process and color blending that went on in the never-ending effort to emulate the subtle tones of a herring or candlefish as closely as possible. Patrick wrote two self-published books, *Tie your Own Flies* a concise, well-organized volume that went through several printings and the first of its kind to be written by a Northwest author. His most important work however was *Fly Patterns of the Pacific Northwest*, an uncomplicated recipe book with Roy's sketches and annotations dropped in here and there. This book also enjoyed several printings from 1954 through 1970 and captured all the patterns of the early Northwest coho flies, including his popular Coronation. For all he contributed to the sport of saltwater fly-fishing during its formative years in Washington however, Patrick was not one to shower credit on himself. More than once he was heard to say that he was the person who kept a finger on the pulse of what was evolving in the development of Northwest salmon flies; giving most of the recognition in pattern development to his friend and contemporary, Letcher Lambuth.

Letcher Lambuth was an incredibly gifted inventor, amateur scientist, fly-tier, fly-fisher, and builder of exquisite bamboo fly-rods that were the equal of any created throughout the United States. He was a man of immense curiosity with meticulous attention to detail, attributes that are clearly

evident by the manner in which he set forth to tie a polar bear streamer that would accurately match the colors of herring and candlefish. This was during the period when polar bear streamers were carrying the day for saltwater fly-fishers and tiers in Washington and British Columbia and they all had their own ideas as to what made a *good* coho fly. Lambuth was determined to find out what it would take to make a perfect coho fly. The following description is taken verbatim from Enos Bradner's book, *Northwest Angling.*

> He [Lambuth] constructed a tank in the basement of his home, of one cubic foot capacity, with a mirror bottom and glass sides. Covering the top of the tank with a tin cone, he placed a 200-watt electric light bulb inside and closed the bottom with a green gelatin filter which simulated underwater illumination. The tank was then filled with salt water containing sufficient plankton to give the water the same optical values as that in which the cohos would normally feed. The salt water was obtained on a cloudy day when the plankton were near the surface. Candlefish were then placed in this aerated tank.

What Lambuth discovered was that the candlefish (eulachon), which has a gray back, pale green median line and white belly, looked markedly different in the tank with its specially filtered light. The back changed to an iridescent gray, the median line a deep red and the belly an iridescent white.

Using bundles of polar bear hair, each individually dyed to his specifications by Fay Patrick who formulated each color, Lambuth set about designing a candlefish streamer that carried the coloration of the actual baitfish under water, the way a coho salmon would see it. His efforts were immediately successful. He followed the candlefish with the herring pattern. Both flies became standards that are still used by saltwater fly-fishers and remain highly popular with British Columbia anglers.

Fly-fishing for mature coho salmon became an increasingly important segment of the Washington and British Columbia saltwater fishery from the 1930s until the post World War II years. That is the period when literally hundreds of regional resorts were established at good fishing spots and they bustled with sport fishermen from spring through fall. The small, utilitarian cabins and boat launches were a far cry from the expansive and elegant fishing lodges that dot the North Pacific region today. These homey little vacation resorts catered to entire families and were fully booked from summer through fall allowing Washingtonians and British Columbians to easily reach both resident and migrating salmon from rented skiffs. At spots like the Point No Point Resort on Bainbridge Island in Washington children could play on the sandy beach with their buckets and shovels while watching their folk's fish along the rip line for salmon not far offshore.

During this period a fishery began for immature resident coho salmon. Sport fishing for immature salmon has continued to grow continually since its inception into an enormously popular sport that accounts for tens of thousands of small, local salmon every year. Today, most of this fishery is targeted at hatchery-reared salmon, primarily coho. In the earlier days a highly extractive sport fishery was waged on the then abundant resident native salmon; aggressive, fast-growing feeders that bit eagerly. Although this sport was popular from the start, it was looked upon from different perspectives by anglers and writers of the day.

In *The Western Angler (1939)*, Roderick Haig-Brown wrote about the commercial fishing impact on local coho salmon stocks from 1920 through 1933 and how the catch

This is an old Field & Stream *Honor Badge awarded to Les Johnson in 1962 for landing an actively feeding 31-pound chinook salmon near Skagway Rocks, Neah Bay, Washington.*

Bruce Ferguson checking out tackle and flies in south Puget Sound. At this early juncture, almost everything was an experiment based on old volumes by Roderick Haig-Brown, Enos Bradner, Joseph Bates, Jr. and other writers who chronicled the early days of fly-fishing for Pacific salmon. Circa 1975.

escalated through 1936. In 1937 the catch dropped sharply due to overfishing in 1934 and floods in 1935. Haig-Brown also chastised sport fishermen who engaged in fishing for immature coho salmon that Canadians called salmon trout or bluebacks, stating that they too had to share the blame in depleting coho salmon populations by taking so many fish before they had a chance to grow to maturity and spawn. The fishery continued though, with reckless abandon, for several more years until coho stocks throughout the Georgia Basin began systematically tumbling like dominoes. This is when hatchery programs were implemented to boost runs, rather than taking the avenue of conservation by placing reasonable restrictions on the fishery. During one period in fact, catch limits were entirely removed from coho salmon allowing sport anglers to take all they wanted.

Enos Bradner in his book, *Western Angling* (1950) wrote that the resident coho salmon was the "family fish of the year-around anglers of the Puget Sound country." These "silvers", as they were commonly called in Washington at that time, were taken virtually every month of the year with a slack period only in the mid-winter months. In Bradner's view, there was no problem with an intensive sport fishery on resident coho salmon. With nearly every small creek entering Puget Sound hosting a bountiful run of coho in those days, Bradner's viewpoint is easy to understand.

On the Outdoor Writers Association of America website, under *OWAA Legends*, there is an article posted by Robert J. Jones entitled, "Remembering W.A. 'Bill' MacDonald". In the article, Jones relates that MacDonald, a highly respected British Columbia writer and filmmaker, was working with *Field & Stream* magazine on an outdoor film series. Several of the films were made with A.J. McClane, popular fishing editor of *Field & Stream* magazine. One of these exceptional movies was "Coho on the Fly" which was filmed in 1948. MacDonald and McClane fished Discovery Passage from open

Martin James, BBC radio and television fishing and hunting celebrity, visited Washington and fished with Les Johnson. James landed several resident coho salmon like this chunky three-pounder. Martin vowed to try for Atlantic salmon along his UK beaches upon returning home. (Les Johnson)

Bill MacDonald and A.J McClane had, however, taken the lid off of a little-known, though outstanding sport fishery and shown it to the world.

A resurgence in fly-fishing for salmon along the beaches and estuaries of Washington and British Columbia took place. A resurgence in fly-fishing for salmon along the shore began in about 1975. In part this may have been a sport-fishing by-catch enjoyed by cutthroat fishermen who had been fishing along the beaches for years. Increased angling pressure on salmon may also have been due to a dip in steelhead runs that occurred at about that time. Saltwater net-pen rearing of coho salmon by both the Washington Fish and Wildlife Department and treaty Indian tribes sharply increased the numbers of coho salmon that remained residents in Puget Sound rather than migrating to the Pacific Ocean due to a delayed release program. Holding back the release of young of some of the salmon for several weeks beyond the time they would normally migrate inhibited their urge to leave Puget Sound. Some of Washington's pen-reared coho did migrate however, to Barkley Sound and Clayoquot Sound on the west side of Vancouver Island.

skiffs, casting to huge northern coho salmon with a bucktail called the Discovery Optic, a fly McClane had tied especially for coho in saltwater. The film enjoyed great popularity and is now considered a classic.

After working with McClane, MacDonald continued making films and writing articles for *BC Outdoors* and other periodicals until the early 1990s. One of his greatest assignments was to cover the demolition of hazardous Ripple Rock in the Seymour Narrows of British Columbia in 1958. MacDonald's voice was heard throughout the free world as he counted down for the largest non-nuclear explosion in history.

McClane, destined to become one of the all-time greats among fishing journalists, continued to make regular visits to Washington and British Columbia throughout his long, illustrious career, particularly enjoying the great steelhead fishing on Vancouver Island and the Olympic Peninsula. On his trips to the west coast, McClane frequented local fishing shops to exchange ideas with Roy Patrick, Bill Loherer, Clarence Shoff and other forward-thinking Puget Sound area fly-fishing notables of the period.

McClane, also an epicure and excellent chef, wrote in one of his articles that during his trips through Seattle he never missed going to the Athenian Café at Pike Place Market where he could get *a plate of razor clam hash and a good cup of coffee.*

In the May 1950 issue of *Field & Stream*, McClane wrote "Cohoe on the Fly." In the article which, like the 1947 *Field & Stream* film, took place on the waters of Discovery Passage, McClane recounted taking coho salmon upwards of 20 pounds on his Discovery Optic bucktail. The article created a bit of interest and spurred a modest pilgrimage of fly-rod anglers to Campbell River, British Columbia but not in numbers that could be considered a ground swell.

Judee Stearn landed this big chum salmon while fishing at the Chico Creek estuary near Bremerton, Washington in October. The chum grabbed a size 6 green Flashabou Comet.

This increased population of resident coho quickly created a banner sport fishery for boaters—and anglers who walked the beaches—to catch limits within a reasonable cast from shore. The fishery continued from late winter through the following autumn when the coho were fat 3- to 6-pounders reaching spawning readiness. These resident coho salmon were joined in the fall by runs of big, mature northern coho of 7 to 14 pounds that were returning from the Pacific Ocean. From 1975 through 1991 this was a phenomenal sport fishery before it too began slipping into decline.

The decline of coho salmon in Puget Sound was caused by a combination of commercial overfishing, increased

Les Johnson holds up the first two coho salmon he caught on cast flies in salt water. Using a fiberglass rod, Pflueger Medalist reel and a shooting head made from a level sinking line, he landed these feeding coho at Neah Bay, Washington. Circa 1962.

FRED BOITANO

pressure by sport fishers, unfavorable ocean conditions, habitat degradation and the sharp cutback of resident pen-rearing programs by the Washington Department of Fish and Wildlife.

As local salmon populations throughout Puget Sound and the Strait of Georgia continued to struggle, even with extensive hatchery support, fly-fishers began looking further out along the horizon at the many saltwater fishing lodges located along the British Columbia mainland, Vancouver Island, the Queen Charlotte Islands and Prince of Wales Island in southeast Alaska. It was not long before fly-fishers began joining gear fishermen at these deluxe fishing hostelries to chase salmon far out into the Pacific salt.

For all its growth there appears to be ample room for even more fly-fishers to explore beaches, inlets, estuaries and the vast offshore waters of the Pacific region from Puget Sound to Southeast Alaska. The question is, will there be enough suitable habitat for the well-being of wild fish, and will hatcheries be managed carefully to supplement wild runs rather than overwhelm them.

CHAPTER THREE

FRESHWATER HISTORY

By Les Johnson

The pursuit of fishing for Pacific salmon with a fly in fresh water had its beginnings on the streams of Southern Oregon, Northern California and to a lesser extent in Washington and British Columbia, established by anglers more intent on catching steelhead and sea-run cutthroat trout than salmon. With the exception of Humboldt and San Francisco bays, Californians did not have the expanses of protected salt water within reasonably easy reach of available transportation that Washington and British Columbia anglers enjoyed for salmon fishing. Similar constraints faced Oregon anglers. This made the protected estuaries and tide pools of rivers along the coastline the first spots where Oregon and California anglers could effectively fly-fish for salmon. While fly-fishermen looking for trout did hook the occasional salmon, and a handful of anglers pursued them with Atlantic salmon rods, the sport was considered to be best left to heavy casting rods, conventional reels, stout braided lines and either spoons, spinners or bait. In fact, most fly-anglers considered hooking salmon, which would roil a good pool and scatter the trout before breaking off, more of an annoyance than anything else.

One of the earliest reports of purposely fishing for salmon on a fly in fresh water is datelined Sacramento City, February 3, 1850, just five years after Captain Gordon's disparaging remarks about the Pacific Northwest, *"where the salmon will not take the fly!"*

Although anglers were taking salmon from Northern California rivers in the early to mid 1800s, the first sport fishery of real importance dates to the period of 1860 through 1870 when the Western Pacific Railroad started a line of service up the Sacramento River Valley. With this transportation spur opened, it wasn't long before resorts were established in small towns along the way to serve vacationing San Franciscans who arrived to enjoy the pleasant interior valley weather and the excellent fishing along the Sacramento River and its many productive tributaries. In those early days the Yuba and Feather rivers, Battle Creek and other feeder streams were

Legendary salmon fly fisherman, Bill Schaadt with a huge chinook salmon taken from the Smith River in Northern California. Circa 1960.

fished with fly tackle for trout and steelhead while the main Sacramento was worked with lures and bait for salmon.

The prestigious California Anglers Association was formed in San Francisco in 1890. It was made up primarily of transplanted East Coast American or immigrant European fly-fishermen who favored Mill Creek, San Rafael Creek, Laguinitas (Papermill) Creek, San Mateo Creek and many other small streams within range of the limited transportation of the day. Their catch consisted mainly of salmon and steelhead smolts, erroneously called, trout. While all of these streams hosted strong runs of coho salmon, the fish of importance were the small, highly energetic steelhead that arrived in good numbers from late winter through spring.

On the northern coast at Humboldt Bay, the town of Eureka was already a bustling logging town on its way to becoming the lumbering center of California. It was also on the verge of becoming an important fishing destination. Logging companies cut skid roads along the edges of the Eel River which entered the Pacific Ocean just south of Humboldt Bay. These roads allowed loggers to reach the immense stands of giant redwoods. They also provided access for local anglers to reach breathtakingly pristine runs and pools of the upper river that had previously been unreachable. They found the Eel's formerly untapped reaches fairly teeming with steelhead, sea-run cutthroat, coho and chinook salmon.

Ironically, all the while those anglers were able to fish the upper reaches of the Eel by following the logging roads, the transport of timber to sawmills was occurring over these same rutted roads. Cutting down the huge redwoods was hard and dangerous and skidding out the logs with horse and mule teams was slow and tedious. The growing habitat damage that was steadily diminishing the great Eel River runs of salmon went unnoticed. The timber business was thriving, people were working and there seemed to be an endless wealth of fish. Everybody was happy.

When word of this superb fishing reached the San Francisco angling gentry, the first trips to the Eel River were hastily planned. It was no small task to travel to the Eel River from San Francisco in those days. By stagecoach, the first stop was Sherwood, then northward another 105 miles to Dyerville on the Eel, where there were a few boat liveries and lodgings for the infrequent vacationing anglers from San Francisco. When steamship lines started the San Francisco to Eureka run some years later, the trip became considerably less adventurous, if not less nauseating. Travelers, with their imaginations fired by tales of the spectacular salmon, steelhead and sea-run cutthroat fly-fishing that awaited them, accepted every mile of crooked, furrowed road or retching bout of seasickness with stoic resolve.

John Benn was among the first anglers to make the trip to the Eel River during the summer of 1890. Smitten by the beauty of the area and the fishing, Benn, upon his return to San Francisco promptly sold his business and holdings, went back to the Eel and purchased a home near the hamlet of Scotia, south of Eureka. It was here that Benn learned the fly-tying art and became the first of many great Eel River tiers. Though his patterns were specifically dressed for steelhead and sea-run cutthroat, he soon discovered that these same patterns would also take coho salmon and even hook the occasional chinook. If there is a time to pinpoint conception of the viability of fly-fishing for Pacific salmon in fresh water, it would have to be during the years John Benn spent on the Eel. Prior to Benn's success with flies, common opinion was held that Pacific salmon could be taken efficiently only with spinners or bait.

As Benn's legend grew, attracting ever-increasing numbers of fly-fishermen to the Eel, the primary fish sought were the summer steelhead and sea-run cutthroat. Only anglers using stout casting tackle would go after the chinook and coho that began showing in the pools in early September. Fly-fishermen of the day, still under the influence of European trout angling techniques usually fished steelhead with small, brightly dressed wet flies. It must have been a sight to behold when a gentleman angler would suddenly find himself hooked up to a 40-pound chinook salmon that grabbed his number 10 Professor and went chugging off across the pool. Most of these chance encounters were pulse-quickening and lively, but of short duration, ending abruptly when the salmon would part the knotted gut taper with a casual shake of its head, leaving the angler with an accelerated heart rate and no fly. Such experiences would cause some anglers to carefully avoid pools that might hold salmon. Others though, while staring at snapped leaders and broken rods were flushed by the experience and pondered the strength of tackle they would need to actually bring such huge salmon to hand.

The angling camps in the wilds of Northern California were well established and approaching world acclaim on the Eel, Klamath and Trinity rivers by the early 1920s when word began leaking out about Oregon's Rogue and Umpqua further north. Fishing these swift, remote Oregon streams proved to be an even more formidable angling challenge than the rivers of California.

The Rogue's salmon pools—which, during these early years held runs of bright chinook salmon in the spring, summer and fall—started a few miles above the town of Gold Beach, situated on the shore of the Pacific Ocean. The first good fly-fishing lies—loaded with steelhead from June through September—began on the swift slicks downstream from the settlement of Agness, near the mouth of the Illinois River, a major Rogue tributary. Marvelous angling water, most of which is still best fished by boat, continued upstream to pools well beyond Grant's Pass to the hamlets of Shady Cove and Prospect. It was on the Rogue that author and sportsman Zane Grey landed his first Rogue River steelhead in 1925. He wrote passionately about the steelhead of the Rogue in his 1928 book, *Tales of Freshwater Fishing* but made little mention of its salmon runs.

Francis H. Ames, a respected and accomplished Oregon journalist, wrote extensively on Pacific Coast fishing from the late 1920s through the 1960s in newspaper columns, magazine articles and books. In his excellent book, *Fishing the Oregon Country*, 1966, The Caxton Press, Ames told of his salmon fly-fishing experiences on the Rogue River. In 1932, Ames, during a morning of fishing, used a 5-ounce cane fly-rod and a red, feathered spinner to hook eight spring chinook salmon. Ames noted that, *"Some took me to town. Others I was able to land."* Although Ames was an expert angler who employed all types of gear for his salmon fishing, he was convinced that *a whippy rod, like fly rod*, weighing not more than 6 ounces (which probably corresponds to a 9- or 10-weight), would beat a big salmon more efficiently than a stiffer rod.

Vancouver Island was home \for two of British Columbia's best-known fly fishermen, General Noel Money, shown here in a 1920 photo, and his protégé Roderick Haig-Brown. The General, as he was fondly called by local fishermen, was acclaimed for his service to king and country and for years, the British Columbia government honored him with auto license plate no. 1. Noel Money was passionate about his fly-fishing and after he returned from World War I, his car with its tell-tale license plate would be seen parked at his beloved cabin on the Stamp River where he could be found casting his flies to steelhead. Or, he was often seen near Island estuaries casting for cutthroat and coho salmon. Haig-Brown valued his friendship with Money very highly, dedicating The Western Angler *(1939) "to General Money of Qualicum Beach, finest of western anglers."*

He kept his salmon fishing simple, using red flies for chinook and yellow for coho. Ames' salmon flies were unique, tied with an inch, or so of bead chain ahead of the fly to enhance their sink-rate in swift, deep, coastal rivers.

The North Fork Umpqua River, like the Rogue, attracted a devoted following of anglers who annually made the pilgrimage to Major Mott's fishing camp across from the mouth of Steamboat Creek to fish for steelhead and salmon. When camp broke for the 1929 season, Mott penned an article, *Umpqua Steelheads*, which appeared in the July 1930 issue of *Forest and Stream.*

While angling success for steelhead and sea-run cutthroat continued to improve during the early years along the Pacific Coast rivers, coho and chinook salmon remained enigmatic. Anglers fly-fishing specifically for salmon often played out an exercise in frustration as they watched their deftly cast patterns treated with indifference, if not downright disdain, as they drifted through schools of bright, ocean-fresh salmon finning calmly in the depths of clear pools. Fortunately, some of those early anglers got lucky every now and then. From these rare but valuable successes however, techniques for hooking salmon were developed and served to sustain their tireless efforts. If, in those days, a few fish had not been hooked from time to time, it is not difficult to imagine the entire Pacific Coast salmon fly-fishery being defunct by the 1930s. Enough fly-fishermen, then as now though, persevered and every successful landing of a bright, Pacific salmon would add to their growing knowledge on how to take these big, powerful fish with flies to keep them casting diligently for weeks.

Unlike their angling brethren on the Rogue and Umpqua, Eel River fly-fishermen were not content to fish solely for summer and early autumn steelhead. By 1930 they were working the Eel's pools and drifts into November and December. If summer-run steelhead would take a fly, they contended that so would the larger late-fall and winter steelhead. Their assumptions proved to be correct as heavy, fast-sinking, bucktails began accounting for impressive numbers of big, winter-run steelhead. Not only did deeply drifted patterns take steelhead, but also attracted coho and fall chinook with increasing regularity, making the years from 1930 to 1940 pivotal in the history of fly-fishing for Pacific salmon.

Just as anglers of the late 1800s and early 1900s blazed trails to the banks of Pacific Coast streams in quest of steelhead, the angling brigade of the 1930s was responsible for moving the Pacific salmon fly-fishery forward a long way toward the sport we are familiar with today. Many of the anglers of this period became icons of fly-fishing having written important angling literature, developed angling techniques and accurately scoped the baseline of tackle requirements and development of flies that remain valid to this day on all West Coast rivers.

Young Roderick Haig-Brown hiked rivers on Vancouver Island and Washington's Puget Sound as a young logger, always with his fly rod along. The knowledge he accumulated from his travels would eventually fill the pages of several classic books that we still read today.

Clarence Shoff, owner of Shoff's Sporting Goods in Kent, Washington developed his Polar Shrimp for steelhead but it too became a standard among salmon fly-fishers along the Pacific Coast.

By 1940, Eel River anglers were fishing for chinook and coho salmon in earnest. Sparsely dressed fly patterns tied on heavy hooks to sink quickly in deep, swift water were designed to hold big salmon. Comet flies credited to Grant King were tied with bead-chain eyes; Jim Prey's optic series with large, painted brass bead heads and the flies of Peter Schwab, slender and neatly dressed with bodies of brass wire quickly gained favor among California anglers and are still used for working the bottom gravel in deep, plunging pools of big West Coast rivers for salmon.

The next important development in freshwater fly-fishing for steelhead and salmon is credited to Ken McLeod of Washington and Californian, Myron Gregory. Independent of each other, they were working on splicing short sections of heavy fly line to smaller-diameter running lines. Gregory's focus was on creating the right combination to attain record distances from the platform during fly-casting competitions held at the famed Golden Gate Park casting ponds. McLeod

was intent on designing a line that would drive a fly across the wide, swift western Washington rivers he fished. Both McLeod and Gregory were successful in their endeavors. Gregory, who was also a great fly-fisherman, became a tournament casting champion and McLeod placed many winners in the fly division of the annual *Field & Stream* fishing contest records.

The 1940s and early 1950s saw most serious West Coast salmon and steelhead fly-fishermen outfitted with high-quality tackle. They had discovered early on that cheap cane rods soon took dreadful sets and often splintered under the pressure of a big salmon. Horror stories about reels exploding into a diffusion of screws, springs and spindles under the strain of a hard-running salmon became commonplace when told over a dram of whiskey by anglers sitting around an evening campfire. Stout, exquisitely crafted, split-bamboo rods from Orvis, Leonard, Powell, Winston, Granger and Heddon became the order of the day. These rods, 9 to 11 feet in length, were powerful single-handed tools that would drive heavy lines and carry weighted flies long distances, or negotiate a shot-laden leader through a deep pool. Reels by Pflueger, Bronson, Ocean City, Shakespeare, J.W. Young and

Roderick Haig-Brown's home, on the banks of the Campbell River on Vancouver Island, British Columbia which he named, Above Tide. It is now a bed-and-breakfast and a great place to stay and breathe in history.

Farlow were used on these big, robust fish but it was the Hardy Model Perfect 3-7/8 inch that captured the fancy of these anglers. Its strong, three-piece construction, left side palming plate and beautiful whining song when checking a running fish all contributed to its popularity. Out of production for many years, original Model Perfect 3 7/8-inch reels are only available through collectable tackle dealers or occasionally on E-Bay these days. The introduction in the last several years of superb reels by Islander, Orvis, Scientific Anglers, Jurasek, TFO and other present day manufacturers have supplanted the Perfect as a salmon and steelhead reel. Even

VALERIE HAIG-BROWN

Our rivers are not as bountiful as they were in earlier decades when they were walked and waded by Roderick Haig-Brown. The future well-being of salmon fishing in fresh water will depend on our ability to reduce our catch and to embrace the total fishing experience.

today though, an original Perfect in good condition—a symbol of what fly-fishing once was on the West Coast—still commands a handsome sum from almost any veteran angler who has the opportunity to bid on it.

The single remaining problem for salmon fly-fishermen was that even bead-head optic patterns or flies heavily weighted with fuse wire could not always be counted on to swing deeply enough through the pools to get in front of bottom-hugging fish, especially chinook, with regularity. Just about every stratagem was tested in an effort to overcome this particularly troubling facet of the sport.

Silk lines were soaked overnight, or impregnated with red lead, so they would sink readily but consequently weighed a ton and cast miserably, putting undue strain on prized bamboo rods. Fly-line manufacturers braided silk fly lines over lead wire cores, creating lines that would indeed sink. They proved to be unsuccessful though as the wire would break from casting stress and began poking through the braided surface after minimal use. Braided silk lines were cut into shooting heads and varnished in another attempt to add sinking weight. For all practical purposes, none of these methods worked very well and angling proficiency for Pacific salmon remained limited by the fly lines available—lines which simply weren't adequate for the West Coast angler's task at hand.

It was about this time that California anglers began cutting lead-core trolling line into short lengths to drive flies into the depths of a salmon pool. Lead core did the job. Lead core was not the most user-friendly solution at first, but they did make it work and in doing so, began the movement toward fly lines that were designed and manufactured

almost entirely to serve the needs of innovative and strong-armed Pacific Coast fly-anglers.

For the most part, the evolution of salmon fly-angling on Pacific Coast rivers was slow and steady from the 1870s through about 1950. During this period the pioneering spirit and visionary nature of the anglers was the primary driving force. They stretched the demographics of the sport, probing most of the accessible rivers from British Columbia to Northern California. But for 75 years there was little progress in equipment for taking salmon. Then fiberglass became readily available as a rod-making material after World War II.

Fiberglass was strong, lighter than cane, would not take a set (the curse of many cane rods), cast well and in the heavier rods, had the tremendous lifting power that was vital in fighting and landing large salmon. Early fiberglass rod manufacturers included Garcia-Conlan, Harnell, St. Croix and Wright & McGill to name a few. The rods that became household names among West Coast salmon anglers though were made by Fenwick, J. Kennedy Fisher and R. L Winston. Blanks and rods built by these manufacturers reflected the input of West Coast salmon and steelhead anglers who needed rods nine feet and longer with power enough to belt out 90-foot casts. It was the casting properties of fiberglass rods that allowed the practical application of lead-core shooting heads weighing upwards of 400 grains. Although they still took some getting used to, lead-core shooting heads were much easier to deliver with the new fiberglass fly rods and made dredging the deep, green pools of Pacific coastal rivers a reality.

Then, in 1953, a small fly-line company named Scientific Anglers, Inc., located in Midland, Michigan, undertook development of a fly line made of polyvinylchloride formed over a solid braided core. Under the guidance of Leon Martuch, the company, Scientific Anglers, soon announced the Air Cel, a

LES JOHNSON

Precocious salmon that return after a year at sea are called jacks. This one came from the Elk River in Southern Oregon. Jacks provide excellent sport on light tackle.

The late Bob Nauheim, one of California's most celebrated salmon fly-fishers, was a contemporary of Russell Chatham, Bill Schaadt, Michael Fong and other notable fly-fishers who fished the Eel and Smith rivers in the 1960s. Bob is holding up a Smith River chinook salmon that was truly, "as long as his leg." Circa 1975.

fly line with excellent casting properties that would float all day long without ever needing an application of floatant.

An event of even more significance to West Coast anglers came when Scientific Anglers introduced the Wet Cel, a line that would sink readily, not by soaking up water but by having a greater specific gravity than water. In addition, it could be cast as easily as a floating line. Viewing the Pacific Coast as one of the prime places to experiment with the new sinking lines, Martuch rallied a team of angling notables. This team of Western veterans included Ken and George McLeod, Enos Bradner, Myron Gregory, Karl Mausser and Forrest Powell to name a few. With these heavyweights of West Coast fly-fishing in the Scientific Anglers camp, a landmark field test was launched. The results proved to be dramatic as the sinking lines enabled fly-fishermen to swing their flies down into places on coastal streams that were previously restricted to lead-core heads or conventional tackle. Operating quickly on the field testers' feedback on the new lines, Scientific Anglers brought out 30-foot shooting tapers in even faster sinking rates. After many years of slow, steady progress, fly-fishing success for steelhead and salmon on West Coast rivers

made a quantum leap forward. Salmon anglers from the Eel in California to the Skeena in British Columbia finally had lines that would cast easily and sink fast and deep. There was no place in the West that the sinking lines made more of an impact among salmon fly-fishers than along the banks of the scenic Smith River in Northern California, which was on the brink of becoming legendary.

The Smith River is a cold, clear stream that cuts through solid bedrock, bordered by basalt cliffs in its upper reaches then slows and widens as it meanders through magnificent stands of redwood along the Northern California coast to meet the Pacific Ocean just a few miles south of the Oregon border. The remote Smith, in addition to its exquisite natural beauty, holds a fall run of huge, muscular chinook salmon that rival the size and strength of chinook salmon anywhere on the Pacific coast. These magnificent chinook salmon enter the Smith from September through February. In the 1950s through the mid-1970s, they arrived in extraordinary numbers and a vanguard band of dedicated fishermen began gathering every autumn under the shelter of the huge redwoods in Jedediah Smith State Park to meet them.

It was along the banks of the Smith River that fly-fishing for Pacific salmon in fresh water began to receive the attention that had previously been spotlighted on the glamorous steelhead. Slowly, word got out about the giant chinook of the Smith River and as it did, the anglers who marshaled along the river banks each autumn to challenge them became icons to those of us who read about their accounts in the pages of national outdoor journals. Myron Gregory, Bob Tusken, Russell Chatham, Bob Nauheim, Jack Geib, Frank Bertainia, Larry Green, Dan Blanton and the most legendary of them all, Bill Schaadt, were just a few of the many who became devoted to the Smith River. Armed with fiberglass rods and fast-sinking Wet Cel or lead-core shooting heads they developed angling techniques, honing every nuance of the cast, the mend, the drift of the fly and the retrieve to a fine edge while testing the mettle of bright, powerful salmon of 30 to 50 pounds and more. The techniques developed and refined by this dedicated Smith River corps of fly-fishermen expanded to anglers on the Eel, Redwood Creek, the Matole and other coastal California rivers.

We owe a special thanks to Russell Chatham for capturing this important salmon fly-fishing era in his collection of essays, *The Angler's Coast*, first printed in 1976. When he expanded, updated and reissued the book in 1990 Chatham searched out a selection of wonderful black & white photos of the Smith River's halcyon days and many of its fishermen. It is a book that belongs in the library of every serious salmon fly-angler who cares about the history of the sport.

Inspired by the success of the fly-fishermen on the Smith River, anglers up and down the West Coast began pursuing salmon on a fly in earnest, taking chinook and coho from the deep holding pools of the great pacific Coast streams that flow directly into the sea like Oregon's Chetco, Washington's Sol Duc and British Columbia's Skeena.

From the 1950s to the present there has been a continuous series of breakthroughs in equipment and technology that makes the fly-fisherman of the New Millennium a real force; a *Robo Angler* of sorts. His clothing makes him nearly omnipotent against cold, wet weather; he casts light, fast-action graphite rods and plays salmon on precision-crafted fly reels with silk-smooth disk drags. Remote salmon populations in wild, faraway places no longer enjoy the protection of isolation. All it takes is money to utilize ultra-invasive transportation systems consisting of jet liners, float planes, helicopters and powerful river sleds to bring the world's most obscure niches of wilderness fishing water and fragile runs of big, wild salmon within easy reach to be coveted as never before. Today, no river is too deep or swift for the well-equipped salmon fly-fisherman and there is no more sleeping in leaky Forest Service cabins or tents. Today, deluxe lodges at the farthest flung destinations indulge us in comfort that borders on hedonism.

Sadly, though, technology hasn't done much to protect the salmon, especially chinook and coho stocks, the most coveted of fly-rod salmon which, due to over-harvest and environmental degradation have been diminished through much of their historic range. To demonstrate this point, a scant ten years ago chum salmon were not seriously pursued by anglers and received only passing attention in the first volume of *Fly Fishing for Pacific Salmon*. Today, with chinook and coho stocks receiving increased protection from both the commercial and sport fishery and many stocks living under the under the umbrella of the Endangered Species Act, the abundant chum salmon has become a prime target species. Now it too has recently suffered signs of decline in some of its populations, a victim of heavy angling pressure, habitat loss and excessive harvest.

Even as runs shrink from environmental impact and over-harvest, our efficiency at taking salmon on commercial gear, conventional tackle—or the fly—becomes more finely tuned each season, beyond anything we even dreamed of fifty years ago. We need to be watchful to ensure that the efficiency of science and technology do not finally ravage this marvelous resource once and for all in the name of *maximum sustained harvest* or *fishing opportunity*. What the salmon needs is science and technology that is applied with vision and a long -erm plan that is best for the salmon. A plan that is best for the salmon will over time be best for all of us. A successful salmon plan will have to deal with the formidable challenge of improving its habitat, and increasing its numbers, rather than being satisfied to simply slow its decline. Anything less and we will all too soon be writing the final chapter in the freshwater history of the Pacific salmon.

Fly-fishers from the Bay Area of California line up on the Chetco River just above the Highway 101 bridge near Brookings, Oregon. This fishery has been going on in Northern California and Southern Oregon since the 1950s.

CHAPTER FOUR

Salmon Feed

By Bruce Ferguson

In the years prior to the 1985 publication of the first edition of *Fly Fishing for Pacific Salmon*, most saltwater fly-fishers relied on the old adage, "Salmon eat baitfish patterns that have silver tinsel bodies and dark backs—and they will strike at something brightly colored out of anger." Letcher Lambuth, Roderick Haig-Brown and others of the Pacific Coast avant-garde tiers had worked on realistic baitfish imitations prior to this time but not many followed their lead. Since those years we have learned a lot. Today, there is agreement among most experienced Pacific salmon fly-fishers that in order to ever be efficient at the sport one must first become familiar with the various food forms that salmon eat.

It is important to remember that salmon may travel through a few to several habitats during their lives; from purely fresh water in parent streams, to pure, ocean salt water. Between these extremes salmon spend time in estuarine water, and the water of protected bays, all of which can vary greatly and host different types of salmon feed. The information in this chapter has been compiled from extensive stomach analyses which were performed to identify the fish and organisms that each species of salmon feeds upon and how these food forms look and act while alive in the water. These are the factors of primary importance to the fly-fisher who not only wants to identify the different baitfish, squid, or zooplankton but also tie effective flies that will match this diverse salmonid bill of fare.

For example, salmon from southern Puget Sound in Washington go through the entire range of possible habitats from purely fresh water to ocean salt water as they migrate out to the Pacific Ocean. Conversely, salmon born in a coastal creek would migrate through only a small marine estuary before entering directly into the Pacific Ocean. Some salmon, called resident strains, are purely *inside* fish that spend their entire lives in Hood Canal, Puget Sound or Georgia Basin in British Columbia.

The graphics on page 49 show the varied habitats that salmon can migrate through as they move out of natal rivers and back into them on their spawning run.

BRUCE FERGUSON

Matching the hatch is often far more successful when fishing for actively feeding salmon. Over the years, author Ferguson has carefully compared his flies to the actual baitfish while fishing throughout Washington and British Columbia waters.

Summary of Salmon Feeding Habits

Salmon of catchable size feed in all saltwater habitats, depending on time of day, time of year and location of prey. They tend to feed in the habitats listed. As they grow larger, salmon obviously need more nourishment to sustain them. This translates into their consuming greater quantities of zooplankton (krill) and larger fare such as squid or baitfish; the three basic categories of food for Pacific salmon. It is important for the fly-fisher to know which food forms salmon concentrate on whether they are resident, *inside* salmon or if they travel through several habitats during their life cycle. The important food forms are listed here for each species of Pacific salmon in the various marine or estuarine venues that they may pass through.

MARINE TRANSITION ZONES

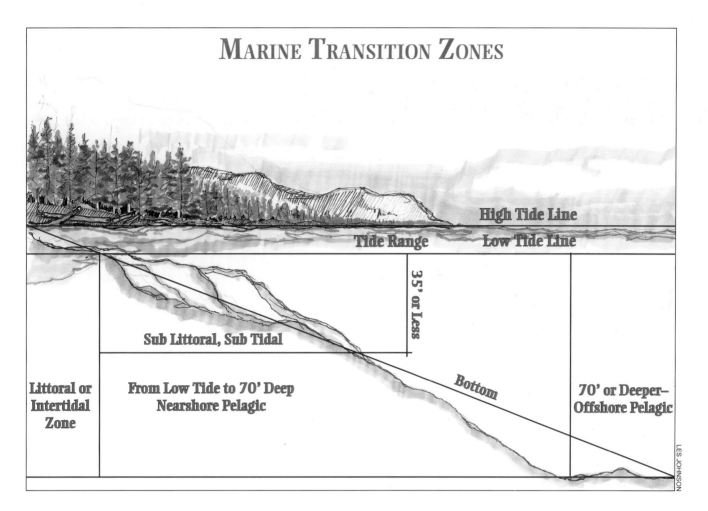

High Tide Line

Tide Range   Low Tide Line

35' or Less

Sub Littoral, Sub Tidal

Bottom

Littoral or Intertidal Zone

From Low Tide to 70' Deep Nearshore Pelagic

70' or Deeper– Offshore Pelagic

LES JOHNSON

Chinook
Marine Transition Zone

Shallow Sublittoral (May-September): Crab larvae, Insects, Fish, Gammarid amphipods

Nearshore Pelagic (May-September): Crab larvae, Insects, Fish, Gammarid amphipods

Offshore Pelagic (Year-around): Fish (herring), Euphausiids, Hyperiid amphipods, Squid

Suboceanic (May-September): Fish (herring, sand lance or candlefish, smelt), Insects, Crab larvae, Amphipods, Shrimp larvae

Oceanic (Year-around): Fish (anchovy, herring, smelt, sand lance or candlefish, pilchards), Euphausiids, Crab larvae, Squid, Pelagic amphipods (Hyperiid)

Coho
Marine Transition Zone

Shallow Sublittoral (April-July): Crab larvae, Amphipods, Fish eggs and larvae, Mysids

Nearshore Pelagic (April-July): Crab larvae, Euphausiids, Amphipods, Fish

Offshore Pelagic (Year-around): Fish (herring, sand lance, or candlefish), Euphausiids, Crab larvae, Amphipods

Suboceanic (April-August): Fish (herring, sand lance), Amphipods, Crab larvae, Mysids, Isopods, Insects, Euphausiids

Oceanic (Year-around): Fish (herring, sand lance, pilchard, anchovy, smelt), Euphausiids, Squid.

Pink
Marine Transition Zone

Shallow Sublittoral (February-June): Calanoids, Harpacticoids

Nearshore Sublittoral (March-July): Calanoids, Harpacticoids

Offshore Pelagic (March-August): Amphipods, Crab larvae, Euphausiids, Larvacea

Suboceanic (March-September): Calanoids, Harpacticoids, Gammarid amphipods, Barnacle larvae, Larvacea, Insects, Fish eggs

Oceanic (Year-around): Fish, Euphausiids, Hyperiid amphipods, Squid, Copepods

Sockeye
Marine Transition Zone

Sublittoral: Not commonly found in this habitat

Nearshore Pelagic (April-September): Euphausiids, Shrimp, Fish larvae, Calanoid copepods

Offshore Pelagic (May-September): Insects, Amphipods, Crab larvae, Euphausiids
Suboceanic: Data not available
Oceanic (Year-around): Copepods, Euphausiids, Hyperiid amphipods, Crustacean larvae, Fish, Squid, Crab larvae

Chum
Marine Transition Zone

Shallow Sublittoral (March-July): Harpacticoids, Larvacea, Calanoids, Euphausiids, Amphipods
Nearshore Pelagic (March-July): Calanoids, Euphausiids, Amphipods, Larvacea, Crab larvae, Harpacticoids
Offshore Pelagic (May-August): Amphipods, Euphausiids, Crab larvae, Fish, Copepods
Suboceanic (April-September): Harpacticoids, Gammarid amphipods, Calanoids, Crab larvae, Mysids, Insects, Fish eggs and larvae
Oceanic (Year-around): Fish, Euphausiids, Hyperiid amphipods, Copepods, Squid, Pteropods, Crustaceans

BAITFISH

The shapes and sizes of baitfish that salmon forage on range from moderately deep (herring); to moderately slender (various smelts, sardines and anchovies); to very slender (sand lance). Nearly all baitfish exhibit prominent pearly eyes with black pupils. They have dark bluish-greenish, or brownish to black backs shading to silver on the sides and bellies. The post larval length of these baitfish varies from about two to 12 inches with most being in the three to nine-inch category.

Baitfish comprises the bulk of the diet for chinook and coho salmon but comprise only a limited amount of the diet for pink, chum and sockeye.

Herring
Pacific Herring: *Clupea harengus pallasi*

Pacific herring are bluish-green to olive on the dorsal surface, shading to silver on the sides and belly. They have a prominent, pearl-colored eye featuring a black pupil. Sexually mature specimens are from six to 12 inches long.

They spawn in shallow water, generally from February to June. Herring travel in large schools, with the juveniles (about 1 1/2 to 4 inches) living in relatively shallow water from May to October before moving into deeper water in the fall.

Herring have a lifetime aversion to light and are found near the surface only at dusk, night and daybreak unless they are forced to the surface in "balls" by predatory diving birds or foraging salmon.

Common from San Diego, California to northwestern Alaska, herring are a major source of food in the diet of chinook and coho salmon, particularly as one- to five-inch juveniles.

Herring tend to swim in large, fairly tight, schools spreading out only to feed. When under attack from the side or below, juveniles jump and scatter. When frightened they all dart simultaneously at the same speed without pausing, anywhere from a few feet to 30 feet away from the perceived danger. This quick movement creates a hole in the school but actually creates a more concentrated school. When the danger passes, the hole fills back in. When crippled by attacking predators, or sick, herring become prime salmon prey, as they swim aimlessly, flutter erratically, rising and then sinking as they struggle along.

Anchovy
Northern Anchovy: *Engraulis mordax*

Northern anchovy are a metallic bluish-green on the dorsal surface and silver on the sides and belly, although some Puget Sound stocks feature a dark brown back. They have a pronounced pearl eye with black pupil, a very large mouth and silver gillcovers that flair out as they swim. From above, a school of anchovy's gillcovers flash and twinkle like a huge handful of new dimes that has been thrown into the water. Anchovy range in length from four to five inches with a maximum at maturity of nine inches.

Spawning in inlets or offshore in surface waters year-around, anchovy move offshore in winter and return to the nearshore in the spring. Very light sensitive, anchovy prefer the bottom in the daytime and surface at night.

Anchovy occur from Cape San Incas in Baja, California to the Queen Charlotte Islands in British Columbia. They, like the herring, are preferred food in the diet of chinook and coho salmon.

Anchovy also exhibit a strong schooling tendency whether in open water or along beaches where they are seen near the surface during daylight hours. The silver flash of their gills as they feed in unison is unmistakable. When alarmed, these baitfish dart away and down, leaving an open area commensurate with the size of the attack. The darting motion covers at least three feet and is incredibly fast. When feeding, the individual motion of the anchovy is one of pronounced undulation like that of a belly dancer and involves the entire body.

Sardine
Pilchard or Sardine: *Sardinops sagax*

Sardines have a dark metallic blue or green dorsal surface shading to silver on the sides and belly. Round, black spots occur on the upper part of the sides. The eyes are large and silvery with a black pupil. Sardines are slender fish and rarely exceed a foot in length. They spawn 100 to 300 miles offshore and the young move inshore where they tend to school near beach areas. Sardine migrate north in summer and south again in the fall, with the oldest fish migrating the farthest north to the west coast of Vancouver Island. Smaller fish move north to Washington and Oregon. Sardine are a good source of food for chinook and coho salmon when available, although the numbers of this once abundant baitfish have declined sharply since heavy overfishing in the mid-1940s.

Smelt
Surf Smelt: *Hypomesus pretiosus*

The dorsal area of the smelt is light olive-green to brownish with sides and belly silvery and iridescent with a bright reflecting band along the side. The eye is large and pearly with a black pupil. These are slim fish that attain a length of up to 12 inches in California waters but rarely exceed eight inches in British Columbia. They spawn on moist beaches most of the year. Three- to five-inch immature smelt have been taken in the Strait of Georgia in April and June. Smelt occur from Long Beach, California to Prince William Sound in Alaska and are among the preferred food items in the diet of chinook salmon.

Smelt are straight-line swimmers when under attack. They leave the area at high speed, essentially utilizing their tails only for movement. They do not ball up or school tightly when under attack but scatter as individuals. Smelt are seen in shallow water only during spawning runs at high tide.

Whitebait Smelt: *Allosmerus elongatus*

These baitfish are pale greenish to almost colorless with a sharply defined silver stripe along each side. The eye is distinct with a pearly eye and black pupil. Whitebait smelt grow to a length of nine inches, spawn in the ocean and the juveniles remain translucent until they are three inches long. Whitebait smelt are found from San Francisco, California to southern Vancouver Island, British Columbia along the Strait of Juan de Fuca.

Sand Lance, Pacific Sand Lance, Candlefish or Needlefish
Pacific Sand Lance: *Ammodytes hexapterus*

The back of these slender baitfish is gray or green with iridescent sides and a silver belly. The sand lance is a very slender baitfish ranging from immature specimens of four inches to adults of eight to ten inches. Immature sand lance frequent kelp beds where they are an important forage fish for chinook, coho and maturing pink salmon. This is an offshore fish as well; important  to the conventional angler as it is to fly-fishers. Distribution is from Southern California to Alaska's Bering Sea. When

One swipe through a sand lance ball produced this bucketful of bait. When bait is available in this abundance, salmon are usually not far away.

available, the sand lance is a frequent food item for chinook and coho salmon.

Sand lance travel in loosely-knit schools with two to three fish per cubic foot. They are usually observed feeding along shorelines. Feeding sand lance swim in a corkscrew motion, moving two to three feet at a time. When under attack or otherwise frightened sand lance will dive downward at a 45-degree angle and bury themselves in the sand.

Size comparision of (top to bottom): herring, sardine and surf smelt.

Capelin
Capelin: *Mallotus villosus*
These baitfish have olive-green backs merging to silver on the sides and belly. Slim-bodied, the capelin achieve a length of five inches in the southern reach of its range and up to eight inches in the northern extreme. It has prominent silvery eyes with a black pupil. Spawning occurs on fine gravel beaches in September and early October. Capelin are found in North America from the Strait of Juan de Fuca, British Columbia north throughout Alaska.

Eulachon
Eulachon, Candlefish or Columbia River Smelt: *Theleichthys pacificus*
Blue to bluish-brown on the dorsal area, with silver sides and belly, these slender baitfish have small, pearly eyes with black pupils. They range from a mature size of ten inches

with immature specimens being about four to six inches. Eulachon spawn from March to May in fresh water from the Russian River in California to the eastern Bering Sea in Alaska. The name "candlefish" was given to these coastal baitfish as they were used extensively by coastal Indians as a source of oil. Dried and with a wick added, eulachon were burned as candles.

SQUID

Squid come in a great variety of species from very small to the giant squid of maritime legend. Obviously, in order to be considered feed for salmon, they have to be small enough for salmon to eat and not the other way around. Therefore, when considering squid as an important food item for salmon, we are discussing either those species under about eight inches in length, or the juveniles of larger species when the juveniles are of an edible size for consumption by salmon.

Squid occur throughout the entire range of feeding salmon, with some species found at very great depths, while others are more surface oriented. However, most species tend to approach the surface at night. Sockeye, pink, chum, chinook and coho all include squid in their oceanic diet, as do toothed whales, porpoises, sea lions, seals, sea birds and many other kinds of fish, not to mention man. Squid feed on other mollusks, crustaceans and fish, depending on their tentacles to bring it to their mouth, which is a strong, horny beak. Food is torn into small pieces before being eaten. Squid grow rapidly, have short life spans and die after spawning.

Of special interest to the fly-fisher is the squid's rather unusual means of locomotion. All squid swim by water-jet propulsion. They are able to swim in either direction with equal ease and amazing speed, matching that achieved by the most active fish. Its two fins or wings allow the squid to hover or glide by slow undulation. When frightened, the wings and jet combined can produce dazzling speed in a straight line for a considerable distance. There appears to be no pulsating action, but rather one of smooth and if necessary, rapid acceleration.

Another point of interest is the squid's ability to change color rapidly by means of chromatophores imbedded in its skin. They can lighten or darken the hue, or change color completely to match the background, or as a reaction to various stimuli. The basic color of squid is translucent grayish-white with dots of this color scattered across the body; like all members of their family, they have the disarming ability to eject a black, inky cloud when frightened—the original "smoke screen". In all, this ancient marine animal is fascinatingly different from what is normally seen in salt water and worth observing in its own right. Being a favored food item for salmon, squid are well worth developing as flies. Sport and commercial salmon trollers both inshore and offshore have used the familiar, squid-imitating Hootchies, with their long, rubbery tentacles in various colors as a mainstay for taking salmon.

Squid: *Loligo opalescens*

BILL LUDWIG

This squid has a maximum total length of under 14 inches, with the largest specimens in British Columbia not over eight inches. The body is a tube-like mantle with a large, stabilizing fin on one end and a pair of prominent, pearly eyes with black pupils on the other, beyond which extend a number of short tentacles. The eye cover is iridescent, greenish-yellow on top. Body color is milky translucent with a faint bluish tone and brown spots. These can change within seconds to darker colors, or when the animal is excited, to completely different coloring in small, iridescent spots of red, brown, orange, yellow or mottled gold.

The *Loligo* is the second most important squid in world commercial operations and distributed from Cedros Island, Mexico to the southern part of the Gulf of Alaska on the Pacific Coast of North America. It spawns at ages one to four, but is typically three at sexual maturity. Spawning takes place in ten to 115 feet of water in protected bays throughout the year, but usually occurs from April through July with spawning in the northern end of the range earlier in the year and into winter in the southern end. Death usually occurs after spawning.

The colorless young are dispersed by the ocean currents. Juvenile growth in shallow water is rapid, where they become an important salmon food. Young squid feed primarily during daylight hours in 60 to 150 feet of water. However, in collecting live specimens to photograph for this book, squid were taken on an overcast day no more than 50 feet from shore in less than ten feet of water along a beach in Puget Sound, Washington. As evening approaches, squid move toward the surface and feed actively on moonlight nights. They are definitely attracted to light at night.

Swimming behavior is the same as that described for all squid. Because of the *Loligo's* affinity for living relatively close to shore in protected, shallow water and its importance in salmon diet, this species is especially important to imitate in fly patterns and retrieves.

ZOOPLANKTON

This broad group of salmon prey is defined as "passively floating or weak swimming minute animal life." Individuals range from 1/16 of an inch to two inches with most between 1/8 and 3/4 inch. Characteristically, they have prominent, dark purple to blac eyes and translucent bodies with a variety of tints depending upon species and background. These hues range from milky white to pink along with some specimens being pink, yellow, orange, red, green, gray, brown and shades of purple. Many species collect in tide rips and eddies in large numbers, so tightly massed that they appear to be—and are in fact called "swarms". At other times they may appear as well-separated individuals.

FRANK HAW

Salmon feed heavily on zooplankton, particularly during their first year in the salt. This is the stomach content of a young coho salmon caught in the Tacoma Narrows, South Puget Sound.

For some zooplankton species, preferred habitat is close to shore between the kelp or eel-grass and the intertidal zone. Most however, dwell in the offshore environment in the top 25 feet of water and just under the surface at night and early morning. Since zooplankton generally dislike bright light, they tend to descend to lower levels during daylight hours. They are primarily small crustaceans but include the larval forms of large crustaceans and fish.

Crustaceans

The zooplankton that are discussed here comprise a large part, but far from all the varieties that suit the palate of Pacific salmon. These "beneath notice" diminutive animals form the bulk of the diet for chum, pink and sockeye salmon. In fact chum, pink and sockeye do not have prominent teeth since there is minimal need for them to grip larger prey. Zooplankton is also a preferred diet for coho when they are available in sufficient quantities to make them an easy meal. Only chinook salmon feed on zooplankton to a lesser degree. However, even chinook, taken by sport fishers trolling plug-cut herring, have occasionally been found to be jam-packed full of zooplankton.

Salmon are opportunistic, usually looking for the most food for the least effort. Because of this, free-floating zooplankton, especially when massed in large swarms, presents an attractive food choice that salmon seem to prefer over other available food.

Feeding salmon are known to show a mysterious preference for black flies at certain times. Shown here are the stomach contents of a small coho salmon that had ingested several black feathers along with zooplankton.

Nothing is more exciting to me than sight-fishing for surface-feeding salmon, casting zooplankton flies. Although I've witnessed this phenomenon many times, the frosting on the cake is when both herring and salmon are sighted feeding alongside each other on a swarm of densely packed euphausiids It is awe inspiring to see this occur miles offshore in the open Pacific Ocean.

One episode immediately comes to mind. It was mid-August in 2003. Pink salmon runs occur in large numbers only in odd numbered years in our Washington waters, so we were hoping for both coho and pink on this particular expedition out of Neah Bay. My fishing companions, Bill Ludwig and Glen Graves and I could hardly wait to reach our destination—Swiftsure Bank, miles away and close to the Canadian border. We had done this successfully for the past two years and were looking for a repeat of our amazing good luck in these waters. Screaming sea birds alerted us to the presence of our quarry. Then in the dim light of a fog-mantled dawn, we spotted what we had hoped for; acres of feeding fish—salmon and herring—gorging on euphausiids.

Here in our view were herring so thick that you could even smell them, right along with pink and coho salmon, all shoulder-to-shoulder nosing the surface. Regardless of the numbers of feeding herring in evidence, the salmon were also focused on the euphausiids.

Bill and Glen were rigged with the recommended deep-sinking lines and 3- to 4-inch Flash Tail Clousers in chartreuse and white. As always, I wanted to experience the joy of taking salmon on the surface with my diminutive one-inch-long euphausiid pattern fished on a floating line. The outfit seemed out of place for such wide-open ocean conditions; however, much to my satisfaction I quickly had a husky pink salmon throbbing against my bent rod as it ripped off my fly line and a length of backing. In short order I hooked and released several 4- to 6-pound pink salmon, keeping one to take home.

Then, the fog lifted and the show was over, as the euphausiids sought deeper water to avoid the bright morning sunlight.

I had observed that none of the salmon even took notice of the abundant herring swimming in their midst. Since herring are a major food item for both pink and coho salmon it was obvious that they preferred the euphausiids. This was born out when we cleaned the pinks and fin-clipped hatchery coho that we'd dropped into the fish box. These included the ones kept by Bill and Glen on their deep-water Clousers. Almost all stomachs were jam-packed with euphausiids. There was just a scattering of equally available herring.

The point of this anecdote is that either the densely packed swarms of euphausiids were easier to catch than the herring, or they just tasted better to the salmon.

Crab Larvae
Crab Larvae: *Sp. unknown*

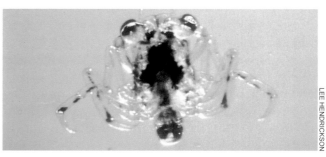

Crab larvae are basically transparent with reddish-brown to brownish cast. Eyes on stems are an iridescent bright blue and the bodies of these larvae have a roundish appearance and prickly feel. This detail can be clearly seen under a microscope.

The sixth or megalops stage of development is important as this is when the major feeding by salmon occurs. During the earlier five stages, or zoea, the organisms are only about 1/32 of an inch and perhaps not large enough to be of interest to salmon.

The free-floating megalops stage, which lasts about a month, appears from April in Oregon to September in British Columbia, within a half-mile offshore. This stage occurs in Puget Sound in late May and early June. Megalops are most abundant in the top six feet of the water column within five miles of shore. As the larvae develop into adults, they drop to the bottom where they assume "natural" crab posture, at which stage they are no longer a viable salmon food.

The swimming action of the larvae is smooth and continuous in a straight line at a rate of about six inches per second. Although the larvae of other crab species are important, the Dungeness was selected for description because it is the most commonly known and widely distributed. It ranges from the tip of the Aleutian Islands in Alaska to the southern tip of Baja California in Mexico. Dungeness larvae are a substantial source of food for both chinook and coho when available, and to a lesser extent to chum, pink and sockeye salmon.

Shrimp Larvae
Shrimp Larvae: *Pasiphaea pacifica*

DAVID ROETCISOENDER

Transparent with iridescent reddish spots, shrimp larvae can apparently change their coloring at will. Other species are also transparent but with spotting and antennae color variations including pink, yellow, brown and orange-red. To the unaided eye, these colorings give an overall pastel hue of the colors noted. In the free-swimming stage they are from one-third to one inch long with a general appearance similar to a mature shrimp with the same prominent antennae, but more slender body proportions.

Larvae are present from March through May in all species reviewed. Although research data indicates they are found at depths from 25 to 200 feet, it is our belief that they rise closer to the surface at night and early morning when light conditions are poor, and retreat to the depths noted during daylight hours. As the larvae mature, they move toward bottom, finally taking up residence there as adult shrimp.

Swimming action is slowly forward in a continuous motion. When frightened they scoot backward in short, fast jerks. As adults, coonstripe shrimp are found from Sitka, Alaska to San Francisco, California in 60 to 200 feet of water on sandy or gravelly bottoms. A number of other species have overlapping distribution and occur in generally deeper water. The larvae are an identifiable chinook salmon food.

Krill
Euphausiids

There are 11 genera and 85 species of krill which is a common name applied to all euphausiids. The largest resides in the Gulf of Alaska and measures close to four inches. The best known is the Antarctic krill, which is over two inches in length. Krill are a major food item in the diet of baleen whales of the world. It is fortunate that krill are so abundant as a single whale will eat 1.5 to four tons per day! Virtually everything in salt water preys on krill: squid, fish of all kinds, penguins, albatrosses, puffins, seals, as well as whales. And, almost anyone who has traveled on salt water at night has seen them, probably without recognizing what they were seeing, for krill are frequently observed as flashing sparkles of light as a boat cuts through the water, or as an anchor is dropped over the side. They are the lightning bugs of the sea. A number of species swarm on occasion, that is, when they form tightly grouped masses near the surface, which in general appearance looks like the Milky Way.

Of the large number of krill species, one which occurs most abundantly in the salmon range *Euphausia pacifica* is described here in more detail.

Euphausiids: *Euphausia sp.*

LEE HENDRICKSON

Individuals of this species vary in length from about 1/8 inch to a maximum of slightly less than one inch. They appear as tiny shrimp with slender bodies and more legs. They are a milky-white transparent color overall, with tiny color spores above the legs, which may give them a faint pinkish cast. They are commonly known as "shrimp spawn".

This euphausiid is distributed from Southern California to the Aleutian Islands in Alaska, and is the most abundant euphausiid species in Washington's Puget Sound. It is found in larval form in surface waters both day and night. However, the mature forms tend to react negatively to light and are found at or near the surface primarily at dusk, night and at daybreak. In Washington they have been observed on the surface during late fall and winter months in midday. Otherwise, they are reported to descend to depths of as much as 200 feet in inland waters, and more than 1000 feet in the offshore waters of California and Oregon.

Spawning takes place in California on a year-round basis with the majority occurring from May through July. Oregon coastal waters produce spawning in late summer and early fall.

The northern range of ocean spawning is in late May and June. In Puget Sound, the marine environment with which we are most familiar, spawning is at its peak in April and May, declining in summer, with a lesser resurgence in the fall. Populations decline from late fall through February. The life span is reported to be a single year throughout its range except for Alaska where it lives two years.

Euphausiids of this species glide along, head first using a rapid leg action. They can hover in place, proceed at a fast, steady pace in any direction, or move in short "darts". They are also capable of a corkscrew swimming motion with the diameter of the corkscrew from two to six inches. When frightened, they appear to snap their abdomens and scoot backward from three to eight inches, actually spraying out of the water when pursued by predators.

All five salmon species feed actively on euphausiids when they are available, both in inland and open-ocean waters. When on this feed, especially when the euphausiids are at or near the surface, salmon can be readily persuaded to take a fly.

Copepods
Copepod: *Diaptomus sp.*

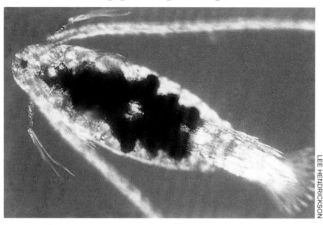

Since some of these small crustaceans are only 1/5 of an inch long as adults, it is understandable why so few outside the research field, or recent graduates of a marine biology class, are aware of the importance or even the very existence of these animals. In fact, there are some 4500 copepod species, and they form a vital link in the aquatic food chain as the initial consumers of microscopic plant life. They are reported to be the most abundant group of crustaceans and even of plankton in general. One estimate states that in a single year a little over ten cubic yards of water in the Baltic Sea produced nine billion of these organisms.

More inhabitants of the sea feed on copepods than any other animal. These range from the aforementioned baleen whales to the tiniest fishes and most certainly includes chum, pink and sockeye salmon, the primary zooplankton feeders among Pacific salmon. Coho and even chinook, especially juveniles, feed to a lesser degree on copepods.

Although, as salmon food, most attention is paid to the free-swimming, pelagic calanoids, it is worth noting that copepods have developed a number of parasitic species. Among these, the familiar sea lice are most well known. Salmon therefore cannot only eat copepods but at the same time, in a sense, can be eaten by copepods. Such is the intricacy of nature.

A generalized life history of a typical abundant species of calanoid copepod is presented here in more detail. Adult length is about 1/5 of an inch. This species, like other calanoids, has a single, very long antenna on each side of its head, in which there is a single, inconspicuous eye. The body is colorless, unless the animal has stored pigmentation from

Baitfish to fly comparison

ingested plant food in which case they pick up red, orange or gray-green coloration and easy visibility may result.

Calanus plumchrus are distributed from Oregon to the Bering Sea in Alaska. They are abundant in spring and summer as adults, in surface waters when they spawn. The developing juveniles live in deeper waters throughout the colder months, then rise to the surface again in the warmer months to feed on microscopic plant food.

They are excellent swimmers, tending to hang upright in the water, settle, then move upward in a short, body-length pulsing movement. When frightened, this copepod moves from several body lengths to several inches in any direction at a speed hard to follow with the naked eye. The overall appearance in this situation is a quick, darting motion. Their long, prominent antennae are important in facilitating either movement.

Amphipods
Gammarid Amphipod: *sp. unknown*

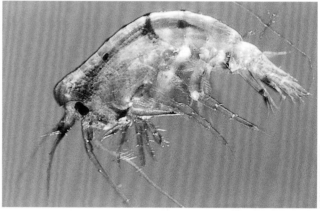

There are some 3,600 different species of amphipods. They are predominantly marine but have numerous freshwater forms as well. Some are pelagic and free-swimming, hence are of primary importance to salmon, while others, in fact most, tend to creep along the bottom, or among aquatic plants. Most are bent in shape, having curved backs and in general resemble fleas, to which they are totally unrelated. The freshwater scud, familiar to trout fishermen, is an amphipod, as is the sand hopper or sand flea of marine beaches. The largest known species is a deep water variety almost five inches long, but the bulk of marine pelagic forms are only about a tenth of an inch in length, making up for their diminutive size by their vast numbers.

Hyperiid Amphipod: *Hyperia macrocephala*

This is a typical body form of Hyperiid amphipods, featuring very prominent eyes and head.

DR. UWE KILS

Hyperiid Amphipod: *Parathemisto pacifica*

BIOLOGICA ENVIRONMENTAL SERVICES, LTD.

Rarely more than 1/2 inch in length, the *Pacifica* displays prominent eyes.

Amphipods comprise the food staple for a good many fish, and are reported as a portion of the diet of baleen whales. Herring and mackerel feed heavily on them as do tuna and Antarctic penguins.

Man rarely consumes amphipods but they have been known to save men's lives. In a recorded report, the ill-fated Greeley Expedition of the Arctic in the early 1880's was comprised of 25 men. In March of 1884, in desperation when their larder was nearly depleted, they constructed a net with an iron barrel hoop ring and a bag made from sacking. With this they snared as many amphipods as they could. Although between March and June 23rd of that year, most of the expedition died from starvation, seven were rescued and owed their lives to the amphipod diet. It was estimated that some 1,500 pounds were caught and devoured in that time period.

Of more relevance, chum, coho, pink and sockeye salmon consume amphipods as an important part of their diet.

The pelagic forms eaten by salmon are of two types: gammarid and hyperiid. Gammarids have inconspicuous eyes, while hyperiids have large heads and large, dark eyes. They are generally transparent with pastel hues of pink, orange, green and violet. Powerful back muscles can be straightened suddenly, causing a rapid hopping, or darting

motion creating a thrust that carries these animals several times their body lengths. Amphipods also "zoom" in erratic curves or circles. They commonly lie on their sides when at rest, in their characteristic "flea-like" position.

Barnacle Larvae
Barnacle Larvae: *sp. unknown*

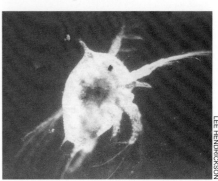

LEE HENDRICKSON

Adult barnacles that are found firmly attached to rocks along the shore, boat bottoms, sea turtle shells and even whales, as well as virtually any other underwater marine surface, go through a series of developmental stages as free-swimming larvae. It is during these stages that the larvae are a recognizable salmon food. Less than a tenth of an inch in size, these minute, three-sided colorless, transparent crustaceans are nonetheless fed on by salmon, especially pinks.

Fish Larvae
Prickly sculpin larvae: *sp. unknown*

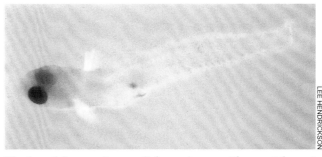

LEE HENDRICKSON

The larval forms of many fish species provide nourishment for salmon when available. They are generally colorless and transparent, with prominent dark eyes. Size is small, up to an inch, or so. The larval forms are weak swimmers, moving forward with quivering undulations, and are therefore attractive prey for all salmon species, especially as juveniles or small, immature fish.

Conclusion
The overviews of representative marine salmon prey species presented in this chapter will, we hope, provide the fly-tier with many new insights into the tremendous potential for tying patterns of interest to Pacific salmon. If nothing else, you'll turn a few heads when you report that you hooked a nice sockeye on a No. 16 hyperiid amphipod imitation in the near-pelagic zone of your favorite bay.

CHAPTER FIVE

Finding the Salmon in Salt Water

By Bruce Ferguson

You can't catch a salmon on the fly in salt water if you don't know first how to find them. In fresh water salmon tend to hold up in the same places year after year and spawning has taken place over the same gravel beds for centuries. Once located these places in a river can be counted on to produce consistently throughout the season. Over time the veteran angler will learn to pinpoint where the salmon will lie in a river and track them as fall freshets move them steadily upstream to their final destination. This is not a blueprint for success for the saltwater fly-fisher.

Professional British Columbia fly-fishing instructor, Kathy Ruddick searched for coho salmon in the Queen Charlottes and finally found this 19-pound monster coho five miles offshore cruising and feeding near the surface in 400 feet of water. She nailed it with a herring pattern.

Bruce Ferguson has spent more than thirty years studying the habits, movements, feeding and run-timing of Pacific salmon. His knowledge has been tested in every nook and cranny from Puget Sound through the Georgia Basin on up to southeast Alaska. He has put it all into this book.

Locating salmon in vast expanses of salt water is far more complex since the fish are moving constantly in quest of food and cover great distances in this pursuit. Different species of Pacific salmon prefer different depths in search of the diet items they prefer; for instance, chinook often feed more than fifty feet down while coho salmon like the upper twenty feet or so. Conversely either species can show up almost anywhere in the water column. In addition, wind, tide, time of year and time of day are all pieces of the puzzle that must be set in place in order to get one's fly in front of a salmon.

Other than certain small bays or inlets, it is not realistic to attempt to pinpoint where the salmon are in large saltwater areas like Puget Sound and Hood Canal in Washington, or

The popularity of fishing for salmon from the beaches of Washington and British Columbia has burgeoned during the last several years. Action like this is becoming commonplace.

Georgia Basin in British Columbia. The new salmon fly-fisher will enjoy success more quickly—and over time more regularly—by understanding basic water conditions and water types. And, maintaining a diary of one's fishing days by marking down pertinent information on tide, weather, or time of day in a journal. Washington saltwater fly-fishers often jot down their notes in the margins of *Walks and Hikes on the Beaches around Puget Sound* by Harvey and Penny Manning, an invaluable volume, particularly for the salmon fly-fisher who prefers casting from the beaches rather than a boat.

The Dynamics of Fishing the Salt

Fly-fishing for salmon in salt water is a game of variables and anyone who thinks that a day of chasing salmon in the salt is a leisurely day on the water has it all wrong. Fly-fishing for salmon in salt water is a fast-paced, intense, three-dimensional hunting expedition. The angler accustomed to the rather confined parameters of even a large river is sometimes overcome by the broad expanses of water upon first venturing out to the salt. Oftentimes if success is not experienced early, and this can be the case, the angler may lose confidence and head back for the comfort zone of a favorite stream. Those who hang in there, however, will soon gather snippets of knowledge that begin to form a cornerstone for fly-fishing productively for salmon in the salt. Water conditions, feeding birds, tide rips, surfacing bait—and of course—jumping salmon, begin to form a mosaic of information from which the angler can draw upon, set a strategy, choose a proper fly and hook-up with a salmon. It really isn't all that difficult, although there is a learning curve. Decisions often have to be made quickly because salmon in salt water are constantly on the move, feeding or chasing feed, swimming close to shore on one tide and hanging well beyond casting range on another. At other times salmon may jump around within a short cast of one's boat, or be easily spooked and never allow a caster to get within range. It is a dynamic fly-fishery and that is the very reason so many anglers are taking their fly rods to salt water. Anglers who relish a challenge and stick with it will soon find that the rewards are well worth the effort.

Salt water, not unlike rivers and lakes, has a character all its own. With tides and wind continually changing direction the marine environment is never quite the same two days—or even two hours—in a row. There is a mysterious, underlying elusive restlessness about it. This ever-changing nature of inlets, bays and the Pacific Ocean proper is what makes saltwater fly-fishing for Pacific salmon so compelling.

Locating salmon is never an absolute, nor, for that matter, is when they will be in any given spot. For instance a bay that may be stiff with salmon one day can be barren of salmon the next. While the search is an important and exciting element of salmon fly-fishing in salt water it can also be a frustrating aspect of the game if finding fish to present a fly to come about randomly or by accident.

My years of fishing for salmon from South Puget Sound in Washington to the Queen Charlotte Islands in British Columbia has given me some insights to locating salmon on a regular basis. In addition, I have been privileged to fish with some outstanding saltwater fly-fishers who have been extremely generous with their own experiences on finding salmon. Utilizing this information will serve to improve your salmon fishing success much more quickly than those of us who started fishing salmon by the seat of our pants in the salt thirty years ago—and those who preceded us dating back to the 1930s.

Chris Bentsen landed this nice salmon while fishing on a Vancouver Island beach. At times fishing can be outstanding but you have to be prepared to move around from one beach to another to locate fish.

BILL LUDWIG

When fishing new or big offshore water one of the best methods for locating salmon is to hire an experienced fly-fishing guide. Author Ferguson and his friends secured the services of Capt. Chris Bellows on a trip to Neah Bay, Washington. Thanks to Bellows' experience they enjoyed two days of superb fishing over feeding coho.

There are, however, places where salmon prefer to hold up for a time whether it is to rest or feed. These are the places to look for salmon when fishing the salt. It is not an absolute guarantee that there will be salmon in these selected places but it surely will improve your odds for getting a hookup.

Points of Land

Salmon, like all other beasts that survive in the wild, learn to feed themselves in the easiest possible way. Some of the favorite places for salmon to look for food are islands and points of land where the running tide forms an eddy on the downstream or "downtide" side. Feed either in the form of weak-swimming zooplankton or stronger-swimming baitfish like herring collect in these areas providing a readily available meal for foraging salmon. Baitfish and zooplankton find respite from the current on the downtide side of islands and points and do not realize that the combination of quiet water

ART LINGREN

Hooked salmon like to run under the kelp to gain freedom. Art Lingren's son Charles applies side pressure to keep the salmon clear while his pal Randall looks on. Circa 1990

walled off by a running current actually forms a trap, making them easy pickings for hungry salmon.

The tide runs in one direction past these points when it is rising and reverses when the tide is falling. The angler simply switches to the side where the eddy forms when the tide turns as the bait will also move to the other side of the point to once more find protection from the tide flow.

Tide Rips

When fishing from a boat, either in the many bays of Puget Sound or southern British Columbia, or in the Pacific Ocean proper, one of the most reliable indicators of where salmon will be (other than seeing them leaping clear of the surface)

BRUCE FERGUSON

Bill Nelson sweeps his fly along the edge of a rip line near Quadra Island, British Columbia. Baitfish become vulnerable when they are caught in a rip. Salmon are often found along the seams of rip lines feeding on baitfish and zooplankton.

is in the tide rips. A tide rip is where two or more moving currents running at different speeds will create a slower moving face that tends to concentrate zooplankton and baitfish. Tide rips most often form a line on the surface where the divergent currents meet. If there is drifting material gathered on one side of the rip the other side will be clear. It is along this clear edge that you concentrate your casting as your fly line will not gather annoying flotsam and the salmon will be there darting in and out under the debris, because as with an eddy on the downtide side of a point, they find the bait captured in rips to be extremely vulnerable prey.

It all sounds pretty inviting and unproblematic, but if you happen to be working a tide rip running in one direction and the wind whistling in from the opposite point of the compass it can quickly turn a calm surface into a serious chop. Under such conditions standing up and maintaining one's balance while attempting to cast a fly is no small trick. This is obviously not the situation we are looking for. A day of this kind of fishing with thighs pushed against the bow rail and being banged constantly can guarantee you a pair of nasty bruises across both thighs and thoroughly jarred to your teeth. The good news is that these heavy, extremely rough tide rips do not usually hold many fish. Even if there are salmon feeding in these heavy tide rips, casting and line control difficulties generally negate one's chances of many hookups.

What the fly-fisher is looking for is a relatively modest tide rip with perhaps just enough wind to allow the boat to drift along parallel to the line at a speed just right for placing casts just barely into the rough side of the rip or at the edge of any accumulated flotsam. Oftentimes swarms of zooplankton and baitfish in a less bumpy tide rip are clearly visible, a good sign that there are salmon around.

Veteran fly-fisher Garry Sandstrom releasing a beautiful coho salmon. Garry was working his fly deep next to a raft of kelp when the coho hit. Action took place at Dundas Island, British Columbia.

Kelp Beds

When the veteran salmon angler sees a kelp bed, two things come quickly to mind; fast-moving currents and drop-offs, both of which are attractive to salmon since they are beneficial in two ways; the kelp invariably will hold concentrations of baitfish and zooplankton and it provides cover for feeding salmon. A fly cast between a kelp bed and the beach, especially when bait is breaking the surface is most often productive near the high turn of the tide. The outer edge of a kelp bed, best worked from a boat, is generally most productive on the low turn of the tide.

Author Johnson releasing a nice chinook of about 20 pounds. He and Trey Combs connected with several chinook on this morning while fishing out of West Coast Fishing Club on Langara Island. This one hit a Calamarko squid pattern.

Water Depth

Both resident and migrating salmon display a strong preference for feeding and traveling along the shoreline. At times they can be seen in water hardly more than a foot deep, tearing into immature herring or sand lance—a scene that is dead certain to get an angler fumbling nervously as he eagerly makes a cast into the melee. All too often, the combination of baitfish flashing through the surface in a futile effort to live just a second or two longer, and salmon whirling and slashing through the hapless forage combines to cause most of us to botch the cast completely. These feeding frenzies right up against the shore are the exception rather than the rule. Generally salmon prefer to hold in water from six to 30 feet deep or more in these locations during daylight hours.

During my years fly-fishing Pacific salt water, I have seen incredible concentrations of bait, either visually or on the depth finder in a boat, ranging from the surface to more than a hundred feet down. I've witnessed hoards of zooplankton dimpling the surface like raindrops; baitballs on the surface that were so round, tightly packed and bright that they looked for all the world like a chandelier from a 1930s ballroom;

and enormous schools of herring on a depth finder that began on the surface and went down more than a hundred feet. Anywhere these gatherings of bait occur, more often than not there will be salmon in the vicinity.

Several years ago in South Puget Sound young herring (2 to 4 inches long) elected to jam themselves into virtually all the shallow bays in the area rather than move to deep water, which is their normal habit. Most local old-timers could not recall a similar situation in decades.

During the few weeks that the herring swarmed in the shallows, anglers bundled up in warm clothing and gloves could be found casting around piers, moored boats or just right up against any local shoreline. Fly-fishers would cast out and retrieve with little success. Finally, they observed salmon, chinook and coho, slashing through the schools of bait and then dropping down to the bottom to await the sinking cripples, where they would leisurely feed upon them. Fly-fishers switched to sinking lines and would cast out and allow their herring-imitating offerings to sink slowly to the bottom. They were soon hooking up with salmon regularly, and did so until the bait finally moved off to deeper water.

Feeding salmon, at least those within range of the fly-fisher, are usually found from the surface to 40 feet down and they seem reluctant to move up and down very far from their selected feeding level of the moment. Chinook salmon are the exception to this rule. Although chinook are often found near the surface, they are bottom-loving creatures, frequently cruising at depths well beyond the range of most fly-fishers. If you find the level where the feed is holding, you find the fish. This applies to all salmon species and it holds true for every marine area not just along the shoreline.

Surfacing Salmon

When out on the salt, salmon can be seen jumping with the occasional water-clearing leap, gently rolling, or with splashy surface rises everywhere in the vicinity. Whatever rise form the salmon presents, one thing is certain; an actively surfacing salmon will be far easier to catch than endlessly casting blind in hopes of connecting with one that has not given its position away. The new angler sometimes doesn't recognize the surface activity of salmon. Small, immature cohos and pinks will jump frequently but as they increase in size they tend to show their dorsal fins and tails more in a slow roll

CHRIS BENTSEN

This salmon hit a small, pink Clouser Minnow in the salt water not far from the mouth of the Cluxewe River on Vancouver Island.

when near the surface. When chinook and coho salmon are feeding voraciously on baitfish however, they often explode like hand grenades on the surface, an activity that is impossible to miss. In autumn, as all salmon species hold impatiently off the mouths of natal rivers, they will sporadically jump and roll while their systems adapt to the brackish, salt/sweet mix of estuarine water.

Salmon in the salt are part of an extremely dynamic environment. They move and reposition themselves as tides and currents change in order to stay within range of baitfish schools or krill swarms. If they are jumping actively, the novice fly-fisher may believe that there are far more salmon present than is actually the case. I was once informed by an experienced saltwater fly-fisher that if I saw one salmon jump that there were probably a hundred more in the school with it. His comment, combined with my stream fishing experience as a trout fisherman, where you cast directly to the rise, kept me clinging to this false premise for a good many years.

Some years later I was liberated from this ill-conceived concept by my brother Gordon, every bit as ardent and serious a fly-fisherman as me. He snapped me out of my—*if you see one salmon there are probably a hundred more around*—state of mind during a trip to the Queen Charlotte Islands. I was randomly casting an unwieldy monstrosity of a fly with a heavy, equally unwieldy fiberglass rod. Gordon was using a light spinning outfit armed with a Mepps spinner.

In the gray dawn, we were sitting in a 12-foot rental aluminum skiff that was taking in water at rate that made us both anxious, since we'd forgotten to bring along a bailing can. But we were looking at literally dozens of mint-bright, hook-nosed coho salmon leaping and swirling all around us. I continued casting with increasing frustration while Gordon sat back taking in the scene and keeping a watchful eye on the water level in our skiff.

Finally he said, "Maybe we should be casting directly in front of one of the salmon we see jumping." With that he promptly flipped his little Mepps spinner several feet ahead of a swirl the size of a wagon wheel and immediately struck into a broad-shouldered coho salmon. I thoroughly enjoyed Gordon's spirited engagement with the coho on his light spinning rod. Finally with the battle won, I carefully slipped the net under a prime 12-pounder.

After his magnificent demonstration, my brother gallantly volunteered to keep the skiff afloat while I attempted to hook a coho on the fly. While he rowed the boat, and bailed it with his boot, I continued to cast with mounting desperation but could not for the life of me break my habit of casting á la trout fishing, directly into the swirl where a coho had shown

Baitballs like this one can sometimes be seen from a long distance. Ferguson and Johnson located this one before the birds did and hit several pink and coho salmon during some very fast fishing with sinking lines.

Sea birds feeding on baitfish and zooplankton are key to locating salmon. Here baitfish were feeding on zooplankton which were in turn being eaten by sea birds and coho salmon. Author Ferguson and his fishing pals hit several salmon around this feeding frenzy.

itself. I was the poster boy of inflexibility; the classic example of a slow learner. It was years before I finally learned how important it is to think that there is only the fish you see and cast well ahead of it.

Sea Birds

Diving, circling, screaming concentrations of marine birds have long been a well-known clue to the location of pelagic game fish throughout the world. This holds true for Pacific salmon. In Washington's Puget Sound country, where I make my home, certain sea birds not only provide a great recon-

naissance service for salmon anglers; some of them are actually identified with specific types of feed.

The petite Bonaparte's gull with its black head in summer and white head with gray patch in winter is a dead giveaway to the location of zooplankton concentrations and schools of small baitfish. Their call of "ere-ere" compels you to rush over to see what is going on. Bonaparte's may be present in hundreds or even thousands if they get over a big enough swarm of zooplankton or immature baitfish. Oftentimes you can see salmon slashing through the bait below the birds, sharing in the bounty.

In winter we also experience herring balls. Here, murres, auklets and pigeon guillemots (which fly as easily under water as above) herd the ill-fated herring into huge, tightly-massed, revolving balls. These herring balls can, at times, be seen slightly above the surface, looking for all the world like a full moon rising from the ocean. Screaming glaucous-winged and other large gulls hover and dive on the balls, picking off whatever herring they can. The predominately white coloration of the gulls makes them plainly visible at long distances. Salmon are usually in close attendance under any herring ball. Be cautioned however that even though they are concentrating on devouring herring, the noisy approach of an outboard motor can spook them very quickly.

Migration Routes

On their return from ocean feeding grounds, salmon migrate back to home rivers along accustomed and predictable routes. This is when the fly-fisher will be looking for them; while they are still feeding voraciously to build a final store of energy that will carry them through the rigors of spawning. Checking with staff members at local tackle shops specializing in saltwater fly-fishing is a good first step. As your fishing experience increases it is vital to build up information in a personal diary. This data becomes increasingly valuable as the seasons roll by.

When to Look for Salmon in the Salt

Knowing when to fish is equally as important as where to fish. Without learning and acting on the when part it will definitely leave your salmon success glass half empty. Keeping a detailed personal journal of your outing experiences, carefully noting the following variables will have you with a full glass in much shorter order.

You have no trouble locating salmon when you see a lineup of anglers like this. These eager anglers were waiting for the chum salmon to move into casting range at the Hoodsport salmon hatchery on Hood Canal. Terminal fisheries like this one can get pretty crowded which doesn't always appeal to fly-fishermen.

As an example of the kind of information that is needed, and in order to improve the readers' odds of being at the right spot at the right time, we have presented several general run timing charts by species for all of British Columbia. (*See Appendix IV*). This information is particularly geared to the fly-fisher. It is the result of more than twenty interviews conducted with British Columbia Oceans and Fisheries, Canada staff members. We are especially indebted to Terry Gjernes for the extraordinary help in assembling this information. Prior to his retirement, Terry was Recreational Fisheries Coordinator for the South Coast Pacific Region of Oceans and Fisheries, Canada.

Oftentimes salmon will be feeding just a few feet offshore on beaches throughout Washington and British Columbia. Bob Young found this nice coho in knee-deep water at Lincoln Park in Seattle.

Run Timing

It does very little good to book a trip to a fancy lodge, only to arrive before the scheduled salmon runs, or after they've already passed through. Even with careful study and inquiry this can still happen.

For instance, co-author Les Johnson and I took a trip to Dundas Island out of Prince Rupert, BC for the sole purpose of catching feeding sockeye migrating to the Nass and Skeena rivers. In spite of careful planning, we missed the sockeye run entirely. Fortunately, we saved the trip by fishing the hordes of voracious pink and coho salmon that were migrating through while we were there. Over the years we have not always been so lucky.

Dolphins Fishing Resort guide Steve Shelley (right) and Bruce Ferguson check a chart during a trip to remote Work Channel on the Alaska/British Columbia border. Authors Johnson and Ferguson were investigating the fishing forty-five miles north of Prince Rupert. This area is still pretty much untouched by salmon sport fishers.

Even with this data at hand, it is still prudent to contact the lodge or fly shop in the locale where you will be fishing to obtain the most current data available. This information alone can turn a potential disaster into the trip of a lifetime.

Just as it is important to know the location of the routes that salmon follow on their way to natal streams. It is equally important to know the approximate time that they will be traveling these routes. Arrival times of salmon migrations can vary from a few days to a few weeks, depending upon ocean conditions, feeding opportunities in the salt, or water levels in their home rivers.

Ferguson has been a diligent record-keeper for the thirty-odd years that he and Johnson have fished together throughout the Pacific Coast for salmon. Here he is noting the day's fishing in his log.

Light Conditions

Many among us can still recount early, misty, fog-shrouded mornings at small boathouses all along the west coast where big breakfasts of ham and eggs were served under the smoke-yellowed illumination of small light bulbs by waitresses who kept coffee cups filled and ashtrays emptied. The morning tide and weather report, scrawled on a blackboard was discussed while we awaited enough light so that we could fire up our rented salmon skiffs and legally leave the moorage. From Prince Rupert, British Columbia to Morrow Bay, California this scene was repeated at small coastal hamlets and is still in evidence at selected major Pacific coast salmon sport-fishing ports; but the intimacy of those early pre-dawn fishing mornings has long been gone. One detail that has never changed in keeping this nostalgic memory of salmon fishing mornings alive is the never-changing need to be out on the water at the crack of dawn—or earlier—and to fish right through until pitch darkness. Anglers who aren't prepared to spend the

entire day fishing should plan to fish as early and as late in the day as possible and skip the midday hours completely.

By full sun-up, the best of the action is over. In the evening the reverse is true. You never want to come in before you need your running lights turned on. The reason for this is that zooplankton and baitfish exhibit a definite aversion to light, perhaps because they feel more vulnerable when they can be easily seen. Since bait forms are most often near the surface during low light, it should come as no surprise that foraging salmon are near the surface as well.

As the day progresses and light increases, the entire food chain seeks deeper water—in many cases deeper than the fly-fisher can efficiently present a fly. With this in mind, it logically follows that cloudy, foggy or overcast days will extend the time that zooplankton and baitfish will remain near the surface. For this reason winter fishing is, at times more productive at both ends of the day due to the light being less intense throughout the day. Summer fishing by contrast requires more discipline when arriving thirty minutes late in the morning may have cost you all of the day's action.

Since salmon will select the safest time to feed near the surface it stands to reason that during nights when there is a full moon, they will feed voraciously under cover of night but still with ample light to easily find food near the surface. Oftentimes the angler going out the following morning will have tough going as the salmon's appetite will have already been sated.

Better than a good day at work. Some excellent saltwater fly-fishing is found near metropolitan areas. Frank van Gelder landed this nice pink salmon off Brown's Point in view of downtown Tacoma, Washington.

Tides

No serious fly-fisher would think of going out on the salt without first checking his tide table, or pulling up local tides on the Internet. Tide tables listed on the Internet are recorded at many locations within a geographic region. For instance,

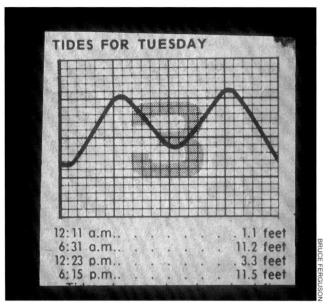

TIDES FOR TUESDAY

12:11 a.m. . . . . 1.1 feet
6:31 a.m. . . . . 11.2 feet
12:23 p.m. . . . . 3.3 feet
6:15 p.m. . . . . 11.5 feet

A tide table is one of the most important items for the fly-fisher searching for salmon in the salt. All areas are different in how they fish during various stages of the tide. Learning about each area is important to fishing success. A pocket-sized tide book with charts for each day is commonly used by veteran anglers. You can also print local tides from the Internet.

Internet tide tables for Puget Sound give the timing of tides for literally hundreds of spots throughout the Sound. This is important as rising and falling tides can change considerably from one place to another within Puget Sound. So, wherever you are planning to fish, always check out the tides the night before.

Checking out the tide is important for several reasons; it can help you to determine the best spot to fish as some places fish better than others at certain tidal times and heights; some boat ramps are easier to negotiate than others when the tide is either high or low; and some spots may bring dangerous rocks close to the surface. Hitting one can bend a prop or stove a hole in your boat at low tide. The most critical reason though is that throughout the area where the salmon fly-fisher casts flies in marine waters it is the tide; incoming, outgoing, high, low, or in the middle, that triggers salmon into feeding.

Slack water at the tide turn, either high or low, is usually not the most productive time to fish. Most veterans are in agreement that the two hours before and after the high or low tide turn will usually produce the most consistent results. Here again there is an explanation. Moving water tends to collect food in a more restricted area. This allows salmon to expend are less energy while feeding, whether it be on baitfish or zooplankton. Extreme tides however that produce heavy currents usually sweep the weak swimming forage long

distances, often scattering it so far and wide that the salmon spread out to get at it. With both bait and salmon spread out over a large area of water, fishing is not nearly as productive. However, there are exceptions to any rule.

For instance, while the turn of the tide, either incoming or outgoing, is generally considered to be the peak time for salmon in the salt, an exception exists, particularly when fishing the Pacific waters from the northern end of Puget Sound, north through the Queen Charlottes and around southeast Alaska's Prince of Wales Island. In these spots, taking feeding chinook salmon on a cast fly is often most productive on the high slack. This is the time when you can get the best herky-jerky vertical retrieve on your favorite squid pattern. With the tide at a standstill, or barely moving, your fly is moving just the way chinook like it. My co-author Les and Trey Combs discovered this trick a good many years ago

Even very small streams like Eagle Creek, shown here, should not be overlooked as they can hold substantial runs of chum salmon. Eagle Creek chum salmon show up quite bright and can be fished with floating lines on the shallow estuary flat.

around Langara Island. Bellingham fly-fisher Jim Darden made this vertical retrieve a standard for taking deep-feeding chinook more than fifteen years earlier than Les and Trey when he timed the drop of his lead-core shooting heads with a stop watch to take salmon around his favorite northern Washington waters.

In areas where the beach drops off steeply, bait will sometimes increase in concentration rather than scatter. This happened to Les and Bob Young one day at Lincoln Park in Seattle. The tide was one of the lowest of the year, dropping all the way to the flat sandy bottom at the edge of the beach curve. Although it was a sunny midday, they found salmon chasing bait right up to the end of their rod tips and had a fantastic day catching a dozen or more bright coho that had just arrived at this mile-long city park.

It is important to learn how the tide affects the various places you fish. When a spot is fishing well, it is rarely a random occurrence. Provided the salmon are around, it will almost always be the tide that puts them on the bite.

Wind

Windy days and choppy or downright rough water oftentimes present a fishing opportunity for a fisherman trolling with a downrigger. Not so for the fly-fisher. A flat surface allows much better vision making spotting surfacing salmon easier. A slightly choppy or riffled surface can be helpful when it comes to getting into casting range. A howling wind though that builds high waves makes fishing unpleasant, unproductive and sometimes dangerous as such conditions can capsize a small boat with little warning. Wind can also cause a vagrant fly to be blown off course to bury itself into the back of your head or hand with unexpected severity.

Time of Year

Coho salmon are particularly well suited to the customary modes of the fly-fisher. They exhibit accelerated growth in their final year and modify their feeding habits in order to get the most weight gain for the least effort. Until coho salmon reach about two pounds they concentrate their efforts on the abundant, slow-moving zooplankton. At this time they are

Looking straight down into the maw of a tightly packed bait ball, it's easy to see how such a mass of bait would attract salmon. If you find a bait ball, salmon will rarely be far away.

easily taken on the fly and are most visible feeding on the surface during morning and evening hours. The more abundant the food supply the faster the coho grow. As this occurs, the coho, rapidly growing larger and faster, begin to concentrate their feeding efforts on the more substantial fare of baitfish. Coho will continue to prefer baitfish for the remainder of their lives until they are ready to move into natal rivers and spawn. The single exception is when coho find dense swarms

Fly-fisherman Dan Lemaich checks out a Puget Sound beach at low tide to view the structure before pulling on his waders and stringing his fly rod. Cobbled beaches like this hold sand lance, herring, other baitfish and zooplankton, all food items favored by Pacific salmon.

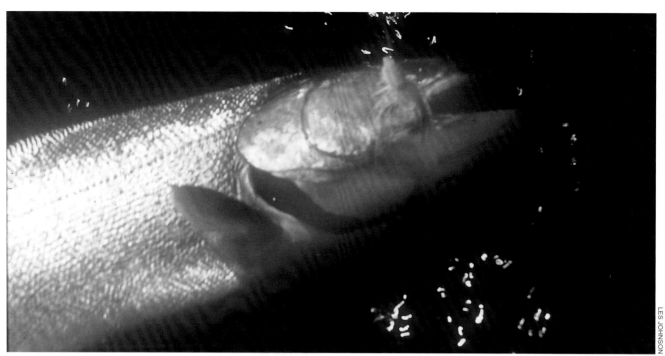

*Above: Chinook salmon are the largest of the Pacific salmon but often shy. The best time to tempt them to a fly is usually at dawn and dusk when they are feeding near the surface or over a shallow bottom. Author Johnson found this chinook while fishing along a kelp bed at first light in thirty feet of water near Langara Island in the Queen Charlotte Islands.
Below: Sometimes a break from searching for salmon can produce a catch of nice halibut like these. Ferguson and Johnson enjoyed this change-up during an afternoon break from searching for salmon.*

of euphausiids and other zooplankton available which they will feed upon as an obvious diet preference.

For resident salmon in Puget Sound, our home waters, the zooplankton-phase fishing begins in November. They continue to feed on the readily available krill until about June when they make the switchover to baitfish. Farther north, in the Straits of Georgia, the switch in feed occurs earlier due to a more abundant supply of herring, sand lance and other baitfish. From this time until spawning the baitfish diet prevails and the salmon are seen less frequently on the surface. In September and October coho salmon begin showing up at the river mouths. There is a great disparity in the timing of coho salmon arrivals at the mouths of natal rivers, as there is with all other Pacific salmon. It is a wise angler who maintains a diary to keep track of the various run arrivals at favorite rivers. If you are either too early or too late, you can miss the heart of the run and consequently will enjoy little or no action.

In summation, the time to go salmon fishing is whenever you can to a spot with ready access. But, given a choice, the more variables you can incorporate into your timing of when to go, the better your odds for being at the right spot at the right time. And that is the key to success in hooking Pacific salmon.

River Mouths and Estuaries

When various salmon runs near their natal streams there is a period of time when they must adapt themselves biologically to fresh water. Depending on species, the salmon may hold off the mouth of parent rivers awaiting fall freshets of rain to raise the river level enough that they can access their spawning beds more easily. These salmon are called "waiters" and the time they spend off the mouths of parent streams has become known to fly-fishers as the "waiting period". As salmon flush in and out of river mouths with each high tide they are slowly exchanging the salt water in their systems for fresh water. On short coastal streams salmon

Finding salmon in saltwater locations can sometimes involve some pretty exciting trips. Les Johnson and Trey Combs flew in this vintage Grumman Goose from Masset to North Island Lodge in the Queen Charlottes.
Below: On trips to far-flung destinations you might find more than just good salmon fishing. Johnson and Ferguson (shown here) photographing a native burial log, hired a Haida native to take them to this ancient village on Graham Island in the Queen Charlottes for an afternoon.

When the wind comes up on open Pacific water it can be great fishing for the fishermen trolling in a big seaworthy boat. For the fly fisher, wind can make for a long, often unproductive day.

will often change from bright silver to spawning colors very rapidly. On rivers where they must travel considerable distances to reach spawning-ground gravel, the change in coloration does not usually begin until they are well upstream and comes about more slowly. In any event, when milling around in brackish and salt water, salmon may be concentrated for a period of several days or several weeks. Their feeding urge is rapidly winding down at this point but they will still take a well-presented fly.

Fly-fishing ends for the dedicated saltwater fly-fisher at the river mouths and estuaries. Once the run has cleared the estuary and is into the river, the saltwater fly-fisher heads back to favorite saltwater bays and beaches to hope for the last of the bright fish that often don't return until the first genuinely piercing winds and driving rains of early November begin pressing in from the Pacific Ocean.

CHAPTER SIX

Finding the Salmon in Fresh Water

By Les Johnson

When my friends and I were grade school kids living at Bay City, Washington we always knew that the salmon were on the way to our favorite river when the gill netters and trollers began offloading chinook and coho salmon into big weigh-in boxes on the cannery docks at Westport from early July through early September. Those little gill-netters, decks awash from the weight of their catch meant that we could get a few hours of work each week for a month or more, icing down box after box of fish before school opened. I remember one year that a chunk of my cannery earnings were enough to cover the cost of two pairs of Lee Riders, a couple of plaid flannel shirts, a warm J.C. Penny's wool mackinaw, and, tall lace-up boots with a little pouch on the left one to hold my pocket knife. Without that

financial windfall from the salmon canneries I would have been wearing whatever hand-me-downs my older cousin, Ronald hadn't totaled out during the previous school year. Any cash I had left over was donated to the family coffers.

We also knew that not long after the commercial fishermen began bringing in their catches, first the chinook, followed by the coho, that salmon would soon be showing up in the lower reaches of our personal salmon and cutthroat stream, the Elk River. It flowed into the south arm of Grays Harbor, not far from where we lived. Since it was the only river we fished, it made for pretty uncomplicated planning. The next step was to drag out those stiff old Montague split-cane rods with dimensions like snooker cues, and Pflueger Rockets loaded with stout braided line to begin plunking egg-

Salmon will hold in the lower reaches of coastal rivers, like this emerald green pool on the Smith River in California, awaiting a surge of rain before going further upstream. In the early season when fresh fish are arriving on every high tide and the water is clear, anglers concentrate on these pools just above tide water.

Salmon move quickly from saltwater bays into parent streams when a sudden burst of rain raises flows. Guide Sid Cook took Les Johnson and Mark Mandell from Thorne Bay, Alaska, up to a tidal pool on the Thorne River when the rain hit where they connected on big bright coho salmon like this one that grabbed Johnson's red marabou streamer.

about can be had for the price of a friendly smile and a package of dyed hen hackle from the 50%-off basket.

If all of these methods seem overly laborious, one can always pull up one of the burgeoning list of fishing web sites and scan the bulletin boards for local salmon fishing dope. When someone posts the popular question, "Anyone know where the salmon are showing up?" you can count on a long list of responses pinpointing salmon hotspots on local rivers.

Return to the River

Upon entering parent streams, salmon always hold for a time in the tide pools and tide-affected pools at the top of tide thrust. Here they make the final adjustment to fresh water. With chinook salmon this can take place from early spring until winter. There are in fact runs of chinook salmon entering natal rivers from San Francisco Bay to the Bering Sea every month of the year. Coho, pink, chum and sockeye salmon arrive from early summer through late autumn with many of the runs overlapping, often putting two or three species in a river during the same period.

cluster baits on the bottom of the deep, green pools a quarter mile upstream from the mouth of the Elk. It was right at the transition area where tide changes didn't affect the water level significantly and was one of only two or three holes on the river that we fished for salmon. The season officially began when one of us would struggle mightily to bring the first big salmon, most often a chinook but sometimes a coho, flopping onto the gravel bar, bright and beautiful.

At that period of our lives, in about the sixth through eighth grade years, the inaugural salmon of the season was about the greatest thing we could imagine, since we were still some years away from acting on the hormone-fired crushes we had on some of the local girls. The season concluded when our mothers let us know that they were not going to can any more salmon so we'd better stop fishing.

Today salmon runs are reported in all local and regional newspapers; on radio and television outdoor shows; at monthly fly-fishing club meetings, and by simple word of mouth from those guys who *always* are first to know when the salmon show up in regional rivers. Let us not forget our favorite tackle shops where all the fishing news fit to gossip

Seattle angler Stacy Stratton traveled to Alaska to find this bright salmon in a river estuary.

Donna Teeny's huge sockeye salmon weighed in at 13 1/2 pounds. Donna was fishing on the Kenai River in Alaska using a green Teeny Egg Sucking Leech.

DUNCAN AND SONS OUTFITTERS

Once in fresh water, waiting to make the trip upstream to their spawning gravel, all Pacific salmon have stopped feeding. When conditions are right though, they can still be coaxed into striking spoons, spinners, plugs; live bait such as anchovy, herring, roe, or prawns—and flies. At this time salmon have become acclimated to their riverine environment with the completion of the water changeover in their bodies from salt to fresh. It has been a traumatic time for salmon that causes them to bite sporadically; hang out on bottom in a dour mood; or sometimes tear around a tide pool wildly for no apparent reason.

Finally settled into the fresh water of their parent streams, salmon, especially chinook, chum, pink and sockeye, will begin to bite pretty well. Coho salmon have the reputation of being a bit more difficult to tempt upon first entering natal rivers, but they too will succumb to the right offering. Their bodies, sleek, strong and firm from foraging in the rich

LES JOHNSON

A boat or raft allows anglers to cover more water than the angler fishing from the bank. Preston Singletary guides his raft near a row of old pilings in the lower Stillaguamish River where a school of pink salmon were holed up. Dave Essick was using a sinking-tip line to get his fly well down into the hole.

feeding grounds of the Pacific, now provide the sustenance they will need to make their final journey upstream to their home spawning beds. Here, where they were born, they will spawn and die, completing their amazing life cycle.

The Lower River

In any stream, the best fishing is over bright, energetic salmon. These are the "chromers" that all salmon fly-fishers look for early in the run. They hunt for these sleek, silvery salmon in the lower to middle reaches of the river for the most part. If retention is allowed, bright, early returning salmon are also the best eating thus are prime candidates for one's backyard barbeque, smoker, or freezer. Bright fish will continue to show up throughout the duration of the run. The preponderance of bright salmon, however show up early in the run. As the season progresses arriving salmon will show gray, rusty or red blushes of color on their flanks and by late season silvery-bright fish are far less abundant.

LES JOHNSON

Dave Essick shows a nice Stillaguamish River pink salmon that grabbed his fly. Pink salmon are best fished in the lower reaches of a river when they are fresh in from the salt. Pinks turn dark rapidly once in fresh water.

For the angler fishing on foot, the odds for finding salmon are considerably better on small to medium-size streams than on major rivers like the Columbia or Sacramento. On larger rivers working the best water is more productive from a raft, jet boat or in the estuaries of some of our largest rivers, a seaworthy ocean-going dory.

Larger rivers are also more productively fished with trolling gear and wobbling plugs, sometimes wrapped with a sardine or herring fillet. On large rivers, the bank angler has to learn where salmon hold close to shore in reasonably shallow runs within casting range. Some pools in large rivers that are extremely deep and far off can be difficult to reach with a fly. Furthermore, many of our long inland rivers in the western United States, particularly in California, Oregon and

Les Johnson fished a hole below a small feeder creek on the Skagit River to take this chum salmon. The salmon were more concentrated upstream where the anglers can be seen ganged up. The chums holding in the deeper water were not quite in full spawning colors, thus better fare for the smoker.

Washington have been dammed extensively for hydroelectric power and diverted to support extensive irrigation programs. This has severely negated the opportunity for good fishing on legendary salmon rivers like the Snake, Sacramento, or Columbia, making them almost completely dependent on massive hatchery programs to support the harvest of otherwise depressed runs of wild salmon.

As competition for angling space increases though, we are seeing more and more bank-bound fly-fishers working the edges of even very large rivers along the coast. This has proven to be creative curiosity, because there is not much doubt that when salmon fly-fishers get it into their heads to make something work they will make it work. By moving onto the banks of our largest streams we are further spreading out the angling population and a bit of extra elbow room doesn't hurt a thing.

On smaller streams of relatively short length that have not had their runs seriously reduced by overharvest, habitat damage, or has its wild fish supplemented with the sensible numbers of hatchery fish, a day of fishing allows complete coverage of many runs and pools. This can be accomplished by hiking along the river, driving from place to place, or drifting a section of river by boat or raft. Being able to move along and fish several pools on a section of a stream greatly improves one's prospects of locating concentrations of salmon.

The vast, sometimes intimidating expanses of swift, open water found in marine angling is not as evident in freshwater salmon fishing. Fishing for salmon in fresh water is not, however such a simple game that it should be approached casually. The experienced freshwater salmon angler learns where salmon will hold in a river—and where they will not knowing full well that random casting is rarely productive. Locating the heaviest-hit hotspots on a river isn't difficult. On weekends, when a salmon run is at its peak, the best fishing holes are usually lined elbow-to-elbow with anglers throwing a cornucopia of offerings; egg clusters, herring, spoons, plugs, jigs, Buzz Bombs and sometimes, flies. Fly-fishermen usually learn to avoid these casting carnivals since it is pretty difficult to stake out enough room to deliver a fly while standing in the midst of all of those big casting and spinning outfits and can be downright dangerous with big, heavy plugs, spoons and jigs sailing every which way.

Pools below small feeder creeks or sloughs often hold schools of salmon that haven't been hammered unmercifully

Finding Salmon in Fresh Water

Salmon often find respite from the current in the bottom of apparently very swift pools. Often these pools have a bottom laced with large boulders that break up and slow the current. These spots fish well but are often overlooked.

LES JOHNSON

like those holding in larger, easily accessible pools. The salmon fly-fisher who takes time to prowl riverbank trails along the tide areas of coastal rivers is eventually rewarded each season by finding a couple of new pools. This exploring may also produce an extra hole or two in his or her punch card with perhaps a dollop of serenity and solitude as a bonus.

The importance of locating these spots in the lower reaches of rivers, sometimes in the most unlikely places, was brought into clear focus for me more than twenty years ago when I was fishing with my guide the late Denny Hannah, of Elkton, Oregon, in my experience one of the best river salmon fishing guides on the West Coast, particularly on the small to medium sized rivers on the southern Oregon coast. We had been floating Oregon's Elk River with little success even though we had been putting some very dependable flies through some gorgeous salmon holding water.

Then, we rounded a bend and Denny pulled hard on the oars to stop our progress before we shot into a swift, narrow run of turbulent water about thirty yards long.

Denny quickly dug in the oars of his drift boat hard to pull up on the gravel on our right, "Whoa! We don't want to go past this spot without making a few casts. Did you bring along one of those roll-your-own shooting heads that really sink fast, Les?"

I looked at the swift, dark chute that ran right down the center of the river. "How fast?" I asked.

"Fast like lead core," he answered.

I nodded yes and began changing from a type III shooting head to one made from LC-13 lead core. Denny poured a couple half-cups of coffee while he waited. With the LC-13 looped on and a small Comet on my leader I asked, "Now what? This water is running way too fast to hold salmon. Maybe too fast to get down into, even with LC-13."

"That's what everybody thinks. In fact it's what I used to think some years ago until I found out different," Denny said. "This hole runs fast and it is about ten feet deep but along the bottom you can see the tops of some huge rocks. They break up the flow down deep giving salmon a very nice quiet place to hang out right in the middle of a run that looks better suited to whitewater kayaking than salmon fishing."

"How did you discover it?" I asked.

"I was anchored about straight out from where we are now and decided to stop and take a break with my clients before going down to the next hole which is one of my favorites."

"And....?" I urged.

"Well, one of the guys didn't reel all the way up and his eggs were bouncing just off of the bottom," Denny said, almost laughing. "Then all of a sudden his rod started dancing and darned near went overboard before he got a hold of it. The result was a 30-pound chinook."

Denny's account was good enough for me. The dense head would put the fly in around the boulders but not hang up due to the velocity of the water.

I began working my fly down through the fast run one step at a time, casting forty-five degrees downstream. All of a sudden I felt two hard yanks and came up solidly.

"Snagged!" I yelled. "Damn it."

Denny looked at the serious hoop in my old 10-weight J. Kennedy Fisher and said, "I don't think so. Look at that tip vibrating. I believe that you've picked up a chinook, Les, or vice versa."

I reared back again and this time the rod suddenly came alive. Line began peeling off my reel and fifty feet downstream a slate-flanked chinook fractured the surface with an energetic, if not classic jump. The battle was long, and for a good while didn't seem to going in my favor but I finally lead the salmon over Denny's waiting net. We weighed it in at 23 pounds. We smiled and clinked our coffee cups. Denny winked but said nothing, letting me know that I'd just received a lesson; to fish the known good spots but always be sure to look for salmon in the most unlikely places.

We fished a while longer and I caught and released a smaller salmon. When I placed my fly in the keeper I said, "Looks like we caught the only two salmon in your secret spot, Denny."

With our rods tucked safely out of the way, Denny pulled out into the current, grabbed his big steel Thermos and banged it against the side of the aluminum drift boat. The "clang" of the thermos brought the pool to life as chinook salmon—dozens of them—jumped and bucked and shot off upstream whipping the riffle to a froth.

"It appears that there were a few left down there, Les," he said with a chuckle.

Where Do You Begin?

It is always best to begin fishing at the first report of salmon in the lowest fishable reaches of a river. Usually, barring a southwester coming in from the Pacific to raise and roil the rivers, the water clarity is conducive to spotting salmon in the pools and runs. From there you should work your way to the upper tide area; lower river, then the middle section and finally the uppermost runs where the fish are still vital and not moving onto the spawning gravel. This method works throughout the season. Savvy anglers will sometimes upon arriving at the middle reaches of a river without experiencing any action, head back down to the estuary knowing that a surge of salmon will be pushing into the river on every high tide, especially during the early to middle stages of the run. Then the run slows steadily with just a few stragglers showing up at the very end of the migration. These last salmon

Tackle designer Jim Teeny holds up a beautiful sockeye salmon that he took from the lower reaches of an Alaska river using one of his rods and flies.

DAVE DUNCAN AND SONS

may, depending on the species, already display dark or bright red flanks and although they will still bite and their flesh is firm, they move through the river with urgency as they are in a more advanced stage of spawning readiness than the earlier arriving fish.

Strategy

With salmon runs moving through our rivers for a period of weeks, or months, how should we approach fishing for them? One can, of course, simply find a couple of favorite spots and pound on them all season and get lucky during times when the salmon move through. It worked for my pals and me in our school days. For anglers who wish to ply their offerings through the varied types of water from the tide pools to the upper reaches of a river though, it will require a bit of strategy. This strategy begins with fishing the river throughout its legal length and to keep close tabs on the salmon that are arriving. It can become a very intriguing pursuit. I have always preferred to begin at the lowest reaches of a river when the vanguard schools of salmon enter the tide pools.

Tide Pools

After a great many years of fishing for salmon in our West Coast rivers I still get chills up my spine when I see those first bright fish greet me with a leap through the surface of a tidal area. Just as Pacific salmon in salt water are at the pinnacle of their strength when they come back onto the Continental Shelf in the waters of southeast Alaska and the Queen Charlotte Islands, so are the salmon entering tide pools at the peak of their final phase of life in their parent rivers. They are bright and strong; in my opinion, the very best time to tempt them fairly on a fly rod in fresh water.

Tide pools vary greatly in their topographical makeup with some being much easier to negotiate—either by foot or boat—than others. There are rivers of long incline, braiding through mudflats that do not make for the best footing. The Elk River of my youth in Grays Harbor is such a river. Others

BRUCE FERGUSON

Cliff Olson working the Fraser River near Chilliwack, British Columbia. Tracking salmon runs from the time they enter the Fraser until they reach spawning gravel is the reason for Cliff's success on pink, coho and sockeye salmon.

On British Columbia's mighty Fraser River there is a series of braids and points well upstream of the mouth near the town of Chilliwack that is a favored spot of sockeye fly-fishers. We were hosted at this spot by a Canadian friend, Cliff Olson. Prior to fishing, Cliff gave us insights on where to look for sockeye. He noted that anglers work downstream, particularly off points that reach out into the current, casting into the seams that form and hold sockeye. They also watch secondary braids where sockeye may move out of the main river to seek a sanctuary of sorts. Cliff added that it is also important to wade carefully and keep a sharp eye for small schools of sockeye that are prone to move along very close to shore in knee-deep water.

Any of our Pacific salmon may hold in the tide pool or tidal-influenced lower stretch of a river for a few days, or for a week or more. It depends on the intensity of their spawning urge. Early arriving salmon in longer rivers may not be in much of a hurry. Salmon entering short coastal rivers, although sporting bright flanks, are further into spawning readiness and thus do not tarry long before reaching the water that flows over the gravel of their birth.

There is not much in this world that can beat a day on a nice tidal area of a salmon stream in the fall, particularly if it has not suffered too badly from the degradation of progress. It may be shirt-sleeve warm, brisk enough for a thick wool sweater or require a hooded rain parka. With maples and alders shedding their leaves and flocks of waterfowl flying low over the estuary further out, your rod strung and a favorite fly tied on, all you need is that advance guard of salmon swirling around to get your river season off to what you hope will be a rip-roaring start.

Know Each Pool

Each tide pool you fish has to be learned. This means that you have to understand how the current flows through it and how to get your fly placed into an under cut banks or close in to a fishy-looking root wad. You will need to take several lines of different sinking rates in order to most efficiently swing your fly through all of the likely places. And you will always have to pay attention to the tide to learn how each tide pool fishes and where the fish stack up at different stages of the tide. You will want to figure out the best places around the tide pool to land and release your salmon. With a bit of experience you will find that each tide pool takes on its own character; on a daily basis and at different periods of the season. Fly-fishers who consistently hook salmon from tide pools are those who have taken the time to learn the ins and outs of each tide pool they fish.

Tidal-Influenced Pools

Upstream from the tide pools of a river you find stretches of water that are influenced by the rise and fall of the tide. These tidal areas back up and flow slowly on an incoming tide and run lower and faster on an outgoing tide. These are

pour into large, deep tide pools with good footing from which to cast. The Garcia River and Salmon Creek in Northern California are good examples of angler-friendly tide pools.

Finally, there are rivers that wind out through a grassy estuarine plain offering nice foot paths and ample room to cast to the salmon as they come through. One ideal example of this is the Copalis River on the north Washington coast. The Copalis winds through a mile or more of grassy flat before punching out through the beach to meet the Pacific Ocean. Another example is the Union River that flows through a long, grassy field before emptying into Hood Canal near Bel Fair. Finding rivers with fairly easy access in their tide sections is imperative to getting an early crack at the salmon as they move in from the salt.

*Mark Mandell looks on as Mike Kinney uses a streamside rock as a priest to dispatch
a chum salmon that is destined to be smoked for his holiday buffet table.*

spots where salmon may hang around a while, or shoot on through to reach water that is free of tidal influence. In these pools salmon have usually settled down somewhat and are sometimes enticed by a fly with good swimming qualities.

In tidal-influenced pools and runs salmon are often prone to swim around actively. If they aren't moving around it is likely that they are holding in the comfort of an under-cut bank or in a depression that has formed below a root wad, large log or boulder. A good pair of polarized glasses will help you spot salmon almost anywhere in a pool.

Oftentimes the pools and runs in the tidal-influenced stretches of a river will be fairly long with a bend or two. If the run has a deep slot and a shallow side with a nice gravel bar to fish from, you will be able to employ all standard techniques for working your fly. You have to bear in mind however, that the easier it is to fish a spot, the more people that will be fishing it. For this reason it is imperative to learn how

to fish tide influenced runs that are not so easily mastered. The competition will almost surely be less intense.

Salmon will generally hold at the downstream end of a tide-influenced pool. On small rivers salmon can sometimes only enter a tide pool before and just after the high tide as the water may not be comfortably deep for them at low tide. Salmon may actually become trapped for several hours in the pool if there is a very low tide. If there is still enough water for the salmon to move about at all, it can be a productive time to cast to them. They will move toward the front end of the pool as the water backs up and deepens from the next incoming tide, knowing instinctively that the water will soon be deep enough to allow them to push upstream to their next holding station. When the water is clear enough you can often see the salmon scoot upstream rapidly which usually means that you should go upstream after them, or to watch for the next school to move in from the tide pool.

JERRY SIEM

JD Love, fly-fishing guide on Washington's Olympic Peninsula, with a late-season coho salmon that grabbed his deep-swinging fly in the Sol Duc River. Several Washington rivers including the Naselle, Wynoochie and Satsop are known for their big, late-arriving coho salmon.

Anglers who fish small coastal rivers often go down to the beach to watch for a fresh run of salmon to splash through the riffles and into the tide pool. This is done primarily early in the run when salmon are ascending the river on every high tide. Later in the run when the arrival of salmon has slowed considerably, fly-fishers begin concentrating more on the runs from the tidal influenced water and on upstream to the middle river.

Lower to Middle River

I like the lower to middle sections of coastal rivers, and I mean coastal rivers of strong flow, the size of the Sol Duc or Hoh, on down to easy-to-cast-across streams like the Satsop or Naselle in southwest Washington. It is easy to locate salmon in the mid-section of these rivers because there is simply not as much water for salmon to hide in as there is in larger rivers. The lower to middle stretches of our West Coast rivers are often beautiful, bordered with hillside thickets of Douglas fir, hemlock, cedar and accented with autumn-tinted alder

and maple to add a splash of color. Salmon rivers are almost always low, clear and emerald green in the autumn before the heavy rains of November have raised them into spate. And of primary importance we can still find vigorous salmon, particularly chinook and coho, in almost every pool and riffle. Since the chum will arrive a month or more later the lower to middle reaches of our salmon rivers are great places to cast our flies to chinook and coho with the prospects for good results very high.

If there is a caution in fishing this stretch of a salmon river it is that many places along the banks are guarded by nearly impenetrable stands of Douglas fir pecker poles and vine maples. Some die-hard fly-fishers who refuse to pass up a good spot just because of wader-ripping access will often pull heavy rain pants on over their breathable waders in order to make it through rugged underbrush. It helps.

Both chinook and coho prefer water that is well oxygenated, not too fast but with some depth; or a run with a riffled surface that provides overhead cover. They are usually still very active unless they have been holding in the lower to middle river for some time and we can easily spot these fish as some of them will have taken on a mosaic of spawning color.

All along the middle section of a coastal salmon river there will be deep pools that bend ninety degrees, called elbow holes. There is probably not a river on the Pacific coast that doesn't have an "Elbow Hole". Salmon can be counted on to stack in these deep bends; the ones that my old pal Denny Hannah referred to as, "big old boily holes." Chinook and coho both like to rest in these deep bends. If however, chinook and coho are in the river at the same time, the chinook will dominate these favored resting places. Coho that arrive after most of the chinook have moved upriver onto the spawning beds will readily drop into these prized resting places.

There are also fairly long runs with deep center cuts, or slots along the far bank that beg to have a swung fly dance through their depths searching out salmon.

Middle to Upper River

The middle to upper stretch of a salmon river often offers long, sleek runs spilling into deep pools. It will have a lot of places where a nice gravel bar along one side allows for easy casting into the green slot on the far side. These spots will be mindful of steelhead runs and the salmon holding here will often be antsy, busily swimming around the run. Coho, chinook, chum, pink and sockeye salmon all inhabit these runs on their way upstream to the spawning beds. Swung flies with a lot of swimming action, or very tiny offerings are often the ticket in these middle river waters.

Nearly all of the salmon you find will be displaying spawning coloration by now with very few real bright fish in the mix. They are still firm of flesh however and sometimes

Sos Ouch, owner of Xstream Fly Fishing Equipment employs one of his portable pontoon boats to drift for big salmon in the Vedder River near Chilliwack. This big chinook fell to a black fly fished on a 12-weight rod and sinking line.

very grabby. This penchant to bite is what makes salmon fishing in the middle to upper reaches of a river attractive to anglers. The window of opportunity narrows when salmon arrive at the middle to upper river as spawning readiness ramps up considerably with coloration becoming more vivid. The jaws of male salmon will have begun to twist into grotesque shapes with fighting kypes forming in advance of the battles due to be staged over the favors of ready females waiting on the spawning gravel in the upper reaches of the river.

The Upper River

Once in the upper river, salmon are looking for love and will strike savagely at lures or flies, some say to protect the females on redds. Whatever the reason the upper reaches of a coastal river is the place to leave salmon to their mission. It is their time to spawn, protect their eggs and die; their bodies decomposing and returning nutrients to the river where they were born. However, the freshwater fishing is not yet over.

Back to the Lower River

Toward season's end many anglers will return to the tide pools and lower river for a last try at late-returning salmon. In Washington and Oregon some of the biggest and brightest coho salmon arrive late in the season. Some Southern Oregon and Northern California rivers have runs of late-arriving chinook. These fish may not be numerous but they are big and some do arrive bright. In Washington there are several rivers that host large, bright coho salmon that don't enter the rivers until Thanksgiving with bright fish straggling in through Christmas. As a young man living in Aberdeen I was steelhead fishing in February on the Satsop River just above the old highway bridge at a spot called the "Twenty-Pound Hole". I was fishing with an old Granger drift rod, Pflueger Supreme knuckle-buster and cluster eggs when I hooked a big "steelhead". After a long hard fight it turned out to be a bright, fresh-run coho salmon of 19 pounds.

In these latter days of a salmon run the first harsh winds and rains of winter have begun pelting the coastline. If the rain squalls are not too heavy they will prod the last of the salmon into the tide pools. If, on the other hand, very heavy rains blow the rivers out, the salmon will shoot on upstream without the angler getting even a few passes at them.

The most determined of the fly-fishers will stake out spots on the tide pools and lower reaches of rivers that host late-run chinook, coho and chum salmon. Facing one wet, cold squall after another pushing in from the Pacific they bundle up in wool sweaters, fleece pants and rain gear, hoping to connect with even one dawdler as wind-driven sleet rips across their cheeks and numbs gloved fingers. When the last of these hard-core fly-fishers eventually abandon the tide pools and lower river, salmon fishing is over for the year.

CHAPTER SEVEN

Saltwater Fishing Techniques

By Bruce Ferguson

Locating Pacific salmon in salt water does not end the contest. In fact, this is where the real frustration begins. There are techniques that have been found to work much of the time since the first edition of this book, all wrung from countless hours of determined experimentation by dedicated fly-fishers, primarily in Washington and British Columbia. We now hook coho and pink salmon with regularity. Chinook and sockeye however remain a challenge to hook up on a regular basis in salt water. Chum have become a much more important sport species than when our first edition was published. Chum are now taken increasingly while they are feeding in open salt water, and have become very popular on estuary flats. Sockeye salmon are still difficult to hook consistently while feeding in salt water. With all of our success over the past several years, there remains much to be learned.

To the great benefit of the purveyors of fly-tying materials and finished flies, most of us suffer from a knee-jerk reaction to any situation where salmon are jumping all around us and yet refuse to display even the slightest interest in our most valiant efforts to hook them. From this we all too often conclude that it is because we don't have the right fly. This could well be the case of course, and there is considerable space in the fly chapter of this book devoted to the subject. More than likely though, it is our fishing technique that is at fault. One reason I subscribe to this thinking is that I know of a great many veteran Washington saltwater anglers, like Bob Young, Jim Koolick, and the late Al Allard, who have achieved enviable success on Pacific salmon with some pretty quickly assembled, rudimentary flies, while others with exquisite imitations of baitfish and krill do not score nearly as

When pink salmon were grabbing his flies before he could get down to the coho around Dundas Island,
Bruce switched to a prototype super-fast-sinking integrated head and quickly hooked up with a coho.

A match-the-hatch fly on gill cover of a salmon that grabbed it. The fly proved to be a good match.

Saltwater Angling Methods

Due to the constantly moving nature of Pacific salmon and the diverse environs of their immense arena, some highly specific techniques have evolved for taking them during their saltwater phase. This "saltwater phase" encompasses the time when they depart parent rivers to begin feeding in the sweet/salt mix of tidewater; when they are foraging far out in the northern reaches of the Pacific Ocean; as they weave amongst the tendrils of food-rich kelp beds that rim offshore islands; while migrating along their saltwater homing routes; or when they return again to the estuaries of natal streams.

Approaches

A high-speed approach onto the deep holding waters that chinook salmon usually haunt is rarely a matter of great concern in terms of spooking the fish. Furthermore, most savvy lure and bait fishermen swear that surface-running coho and pink salmon are attracted to the air bubbles and spinning blades

Guide Steve Shelley holds up a salmon that Johnson landed while fishing at Work Channel. He was employing what Ferguson calls the "nothing retrieve."

consistently. So, while pattern is certainly not trivial, neither is it the entire answer. The cornerstone of fishing salmon successfully in the salt with flies is technique.

Our objective is to shed some light on the best of these techniques and help you to achieve a more productive hook-up-to-cast ratio.

Carol Ferrera (left) and her sister Rose Worsfold relax on a rustic bench on the beach near the Cluxewe River estuary at the north end of Vancouver Island. Their rods are ready and waiting for coho and pink salmon to show up within casting range. There is not an easier technique for catching salmon in the salt.

of the propeller and they troll at relatively high speed with a short line to take advantage of this phenomenon. When casting to surface-feeding fish though, for some reason nothing will put them down faster than the noise and vibration of a gas or diesel engine. This is especially true when it is running at high speed in calm, shallow water. Since surfacing salmon are moving faster than you can row a boat to keep them in casting range, engine noise poses a real problem. There is however a good way to turn this problem into an opportunity.

Interception

Upon spotting a school of feeding salmon some distance away, determine their direction of travel, start your motor and granting the moving school of salmon wide berth come in well ahead and preferably upwind from them. Cut your motor and wait for the salmon to approach within casting range. If your craft is small enough to handle with oars you can fine tune your drift to best position yourself or your partner to make a good cast. Repeat the process when the salmon have passed you and are again out of casting range.

Open salt water is usually as clear as a mountain lake. A fly-fisher standing in a white, high-sided runabout may not realize how readily visible he is to his intended catch of the day. I used to own just such a boat, an 18-footer with a white canvas top to boot. In order to keep from tangling my line, I would stand on a large Igloo cooler, letting the fly line rest on top of the canvas canopy. I kept wondering why, except under very subdued light conditions, the salmon always seemed to continually surface just beyond range of my best cast. It was when I borrowed a friend's 12-foot aluminum car-topper that I suddenly seemed able to cast that extra 20 feet to drop my fly in front of the salmon. Or was it the fact that my profile was lower and I could approach the fish more closely without scaring them off? When I observed another friend casting and hooking salmon at close range while *seated* in his canoe, the answer became obvious. My casting hadn't improved. My lower profile was just less threatening to the fish.

Covering the deck of your boat or skiff with indoor/outdoor carpeting will also allow you to work more closely to feeding salmon which gives you many more viable casts

Working small zooplankton patterns along kelp beds where pink salmon are feeding can be very productive. This prime pink sipped an FJ Pink that Johnson cast on a floating line to the edge of the kelp near Bruin Bay, on Graham Island, in the Queen Charlottes.

Bill Ludwig, author Ferguson's fishing partner for many years, with a limit of coho salmon taken while throwing Clouser Minnows on fast-sinking lines.

during a day on the water as your foot sounds are considerably softened.

Keep in mind that you are attempting to get within casting range of a very skittish fish that lives in clear water which is a very efficient conduit for sound. So, use your oars or the current to get close to feeding salmon—and do everything you can to minimize the sound of squeaky oars and muffle footfalls on the deck.

Many times I've heard the comment, "there's lots of salmon jumping and rolling but they just won't take a fly."

This happens every September and October as the salmon complete their homeward saltwater migration. They are no longer feeding and have collected in small schools along shallow shorelines waiting for rain, or bellies bulging with roe and sperm to urge them in to estuaries and upriver to their fresh water spawning destinations. Make no bones about it, these salmon are a challenge, but there are ways to improve your odds for success. We've come to call them "waiting period" salmon.

LEADING THE SALMON

X

When immature coho are line feeding either along a beach or in deep water, the angler needs to determine the direction of the fish and the distance between its jumps. Then the fly is cast well ahead of, and beyond, the fish before starting a retrieve. This method works from a boat or the beach.

LES JOHNSON

Several years ago I noticed that if I went out by myself that I would tend to revel in the warm fall sunshine and drift around quietly with my rod strung and ready to go. When I would first arrive on the scene, especially using an outboard motor, the jumping and rolling salmon would quit surfacing and refuse to take my quickly presented little attractor pattern. However, if I eased my anchor over the side and sat quietly for about fifteen minutes, making no casts, surface activity would resume and a carefully cast fly dropped at the edge of the school would nearly always bring a strike on the first strip of the retrieve. On a good day I could repeat this success-story half a dozen times before permanently spooking the salmon. Since I dislike doing nothing for an extended period of time I started taking a magazine along with me. It normally took about fifteen minutes to read a short article, preferably a fishing story, so I decided to name this sneaky procedure the "magazine technique".

Conversely, I took note of the fact that anyone else approaching with their outboard running or even rowing, dropping an anchor over the side, or banging the deck of their boat would immediately put the fish down. Even if boats would troll by at a distance, the same thing would occur. In other words, being quiet on the water, including around salmon that seem to be very active, is most times essential to success.

BRUCE FERGUSON

Johnson keeps his rod tip aimed at the fly during the retrieve. It allows the angler to better feel light strikes and to make a hard strip-set before rearing back on the rod. It is the most reliable method for solid hookups when fishing baitfish imitations.

CASTS

There are several casts that have been developed by salmon anglers who fish from a boat, or walk along cobbled saltwater beaches. None of these casts are difficult to master but they are very important to one's success in actually hooking fish.

Casts From a Boat

There are two basic casts for working from a boat. One I have named the *coho cast* for putting your fly in front of salmon that are showing themselves on the surface. The other is called the *lob shot*, and is designed to launch a fast sinking shooting head, or integrated shooting head such as the Cortland Quick Descent, Teeny T-Line, Rio Striper Density Compensated, Scientific Anglers Streamer Express or Orvis Depth Charge to salmon holding deep in the water column. Since the first edition of this book fly lines have been steadily and dramatically improving, not only making these casts much easier to perform but markedly more productive.

Coho Cast

With salmon, particularly coho and pinks, being constantly on the move when feeding on or near the surface, a quick, accurate delivery is key to dropping the fly into their feeding path. This does not mean dropping your fly into the ring of the rise as you might when fishing for a spring creek trout. The coho cast is placed well ahead of the moving salmon so that your offering will cross its feeding path. Failure to do so is probably the number one reason for lack of success on surface feeding salmon.

Also, unlike trout fishing where working at distances of twenty to forty feet is often the name of the game, being able to cast at least sixty feet (and many West Coast anglers can cast much further) is often necessary in order to consistently reach moving salmon. Additionally, the saltwater caster does not have the luxury of endless false casts that the trout angler enjoys when placing a fly in front of a trout holding on a feeding station. The salmon caster has to achieve sufficient line speed within two or three false casts to fully load the rod so that the fly is quickly placed in the path of the salmon, evidenced by a spot where a salmon has either jumped or swirled.

It is important to have stretched your fly line completely before beginning to cast, even if fish are surfacing all around you. This will facilitate a long, tangle-free cast most of the time, provided you haven't inadvertently allowed one of those mysterious "moving coils" of line to crawl underfoot. Having the line pinned underfoot instantly reduces an intended 80-foot cast to an irritating 20 feet, dropping it well short of a distant moving target. Stepping on your fly line not only fouls the cast but also grinds dirt into its surface, wearing it out more quickly and diminishing its worth as a casting tool. With the cost of fly lines today requiring a

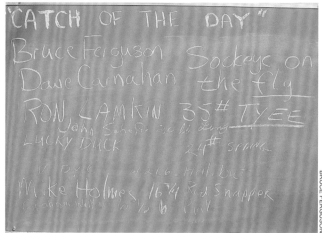

The tally board at Telegraph Cove had Bruce and his son-in-law at the top with two sockeye salmon taken on the fly. It was a first at Telegraph Cove, on northern Vancouver Island.

significant outlay of cash, it behooves the angler to get as many seasons as possible from each one; and the complete salmon angler needs several.

Lob Shot

Salmon fishermen have become increasingly skilled at taking salmon from very deep water by use of a wide variety of lines from the many high-density sinking lines to super-fast sinking LC-13, T-14 and Deep Water Express shooting heads that will transport a fly down 50 feet or more, where salmon often feed on baitfish or zooplankton under the right tidal conditions, current speed and bottom structure.

Integrated shooting heads such as the Cortland Quick Descent, Orvis Depth Charge, Rio Striper, Scientific Anglers Streamer Express, or Teeny T lines are made to order for Pacific salmon in the salt. These lines make it easy to work a fly at depth and are available in a range of weights from 150 grains to more than 600 grains. With this broad weight selection anglers can fish a fly deep with everything from a 6-weight to a 12-weight rod depending upon the size and depth of the quarry and the water conditions. All of these lines are made to order for the lob shot.

The lob shot is nothing more than the cast developed to launch these often heavy and always front-loaded lines efficiently. Shooting tapers can be backed up with Amnesia monofilament shooting line which has been popular for thirty-odd years. More often today a thin-diameter intermediate-sink fly line of about .024 to .030 inches is used behind heads designed for fishing deep. It handles easily while giving up very little in distance to Amnesia or other monofilament shooting lines.

The lob shot, for throwing a deep-sinking line or lead-core head, first developed in California for taking salmon holding in deep river pools, was adapted for Pacific salmon saltwater fishing more than twenty-five years ago by Jim Darden, a fly-fisher from Bellingham, Washington. It is one of the best chinook salmon areas in Puget Sound with resident coho salmon less abundant. With these salmon often feeding very deep, this fishery was primarily the domain of downrigger anglers working their flashers and Hootchies or cut-plug herring over bottoms 60 to 100 feet deep.

Darden, a dedicated fly-fisher, determined that if the tide was either slack or not running hard, and he could sink a fly as deep as the downrigger fishermen, he could take chinook salmon on a fly. To accomplish this he built a super-fast sinking Cortland LC-13 lead-core head backed up with Amnesia monofilament shooting line. Stretching out the Amnesia to relax it, he would make his back cast, allowing the lead-core head to barely touch the water behind him. An immediate forward cast "water loaded" the rod so he could easily shoot his line forward. With an open loop to keep the lead core from cracking him in the back of the head, he simply launched it very high, allowing the weight of the head to pull the Amnesia quickly from the deck of his pram. Then it became a waiting game.

Darden would watch his fish finder to note the depth of the feeding salmon and time the drop of his shooting head with a stop watch. When his fly arrived at the depth of the fish he would begin a retrieve. In the event you do not have a fish finder on board, you can locate the salmon by using a countdown system, letting the fly sink for a ten-second count before beginning your retrieve, then twenty, thirty, and so on until you either hit bottom or begin connecting with salmon. By remembering how long it takes your fly to reach the strike zone you can duplicate the specific cast until the fish move out.

Our current selection of modern integrated heads or shooting heads cast very well without water loading, particularly when cast with one of our new-generation graphite rods that has the strength to do the job. With these new lines, reaching the depths is much easier than when Darden developed the method. The open loop cast is still utilized with the heaviest integrated heads but they are so well balanced that casting them is mastered without difficulty.

Water loading is still sometimes needed in order to launch LC-13 and tungsten-coated T-14 or Deep Water Express, the very heaviest and fastest sinking of the head systems. Combined with a high release of the forward cast, the lob shot has turned dense, heavy, super-fast-sinking heads into standard tools among salt water salmon casters when it comes to cutting through swift currents to reach deep lies. To facilitate the lob shot on these very heavy heads many saltwater fly-fishers have begun to use heavier fly rods in the 10- to 12-weight range, particularly when fishing over very large chinook salmon in the marine waters of Alaska, Vancouver Island and the Queen Charlotte Islands.

The merits of the lob shot and fast-sinking heads were plainly illustrated in 2003 on a trip to Haa Nee Naa Lodge on Dundas Island, west of Prince Rupert, B.C. Les Johnson and I had the opportunity to use prototype clear camo integrated sinking lines with extra-fast-sinking integrated heads and intermediate-sinking running sections. We had been picking up pink salmon on the surface using our regular clear intermediate-sinking lines. However, we were failing to get past the voracious pinks to reach some big, newly arrived coho that nearby gear fishermen were catching. Fishing near a brace of roundish, rather prosaic rocks named "One-Lump and Two-Lump", we switched to the extra-fast-sinking 300-grain, lines (which have since been placed on the market as Quick Descent, for all to enjoy). Utilizing the standard lob shot, we let our flies sink rapidly down through the huge school of near-surface pink salmon to about the 40-foot level where we began nailing big northern coho almost at will and greatly reduced hook-ups from the marauding schools of pinks.

Directing the Cast

When a salmon jumps or rolls the angler begins the cast. With one, two or three false casts at the most, using a double-haul to quickly achieve optimum line speed, the fly is shot toward the targeted salmon. When a fish breaks the surface the angler notes one of four indicators that dictate fly placement.

1. If the salmon shows a dark back it is headed away.
2. If it shows a white belly it is headed toward the angler.
3. If it leans to the left it is most likely moving in that direction.
4. If it leans to the right it is most likely moving to the right.

Wherever the salmon is heading, the angler should attempt to place the fly at least ten feet in front of the spot where it surfaced. If the cast fails, the angler needs to make a strong roll cast, lift the line and quickly direct the fly 20 feet ahead of the salmon's path. If this cast fails, look for another target because that salmon is long gone.

One last word on casting from a boat is that salmon at times will surprise you by appearing quite near to the boat. So, while being a good distance caster is certainly important, you must also be ready to drop a quick cast to a fish that shows at very close range. It is also important when retrieving to watch for a salmon following your fly from the far end of a long cast almost to the boat gunwale or beach before suddenly darting forward to take it. This trait occurs with some regularity so always fish out every cast right up to the line/leader junction.

The clear floating or clear and clear camo intermediate slow-sinking lines that were developed since the first edition of this book have made a huge impact on fishing for

Current rips hold bait which in turn attract salmon. When fishing from a boat, drift parallel to the rip line and cast next to, or directly into it. If the salmon are around, you'll know quickly.

LES JOHNSON

surface-feeding salmon. Salmon very often prefer a fly pulled just beneath the surface, even though they are showing themselves while feeding by jumping, swirling or finning on the surface. For this fishing the full-sinking intermediate line has become preferred over the sinking-tip. That said, the intermediate-sinking line is also used to advantage on shallow flats or estuaries when fishing for waiting period coho or chum salmon

However, it is not the complete answer. When fishing offshore in Blackfish Sound and the Queen Charlotte Strait off of northeast Vancouver Island, pink, coho and sockeye are frequently seen on the surface, feeding on swarms of euphausiids Under these conditions the shortcomings of some of the new, clear intermediate lines become evident. Though rated as intermediate or type 1, they sink at a rate that I would consider more of a type 2. This irksome sinking rate variance in all sinking lines is due to the fact that there is no industry standard numbering system to establish the sink rate of sinking lines. One manufacturer's line sinking rating of IV (four) might be another's rating of V (five). I have observed repeatedly on bright, sunny, calm days that the line would pull the fly down too quickly and it would pass under the salmon, not by much, but enough that they didn't see the fly. I made a note to myself to be the first one through the fly shop door if a clear, floating, memory-free line is ever designed and placed

on the market. As of yet, to my knowledge, this line has still not been developed.

So, in summary, with these two basic casts and the variety of lines available, an angler working flies from a boat can cover every situation that will ever present itself.

Casting From the Beach

Anglers fishing from the beach use the same intermediate lines and shooting tapers but more often rely on a floating line than the angler fishing from a boat; the difference being that the beach angler is bringing the fly toward shore into very shallow water where there is little need to put a fly down much below the surface for a salmon to spot it. Some beach fishing, for waiting period chum or coho salmon on estuary flats as an example, involves casting to fish swimming in water only a foot, or two deep. Pink salmon returning to natal rivers also run very close to shore within easy reach of an average cast.

Although the beach angler does not have the mobility of the boat fisherman, he or she will often find salmon showing at much closer range than will the boat angler. Salmon like to feed near shore. While the boat angler is casting *toward* the beach, reaching for the salmon, the beach-bound angler is casting *away* from, at an oblique angle, angling or parallel to the beach often hooking salmon on casts of 30 feet or less. When the fish are in very close this can be an advantage.

When, on the other hand the salmon are feeding well off shore the mobility of a boat offers a distinct advantage.

Oftentimes the beach angler will actually chase salmon that are moving parallel to the beach in order to gain a position ahead of them. Once the angler is well ahead of the fish a cast is made to intercept their path of travel. If the cast does not produce, the angler may take off again to get in front of them. Sometimes, persistence and strong legs prevail and the caster is rewarded with a hookup.

Increasing numbers of beach casters, whether using a standard fly line or shooting head, employ a stripping basket, a unique portable casting platform that was invented by west coast fly-fishers decades ago for steelhead fishing. With the line completely stretched, resting in coils in the basket the angler can deliver the fly quickly to a moving salmon achieving long distances as the line uncoils from the basket and shoots out through the rod guides with amazing ease. Here again, a clean fly line is important in reaching maximum casting distances.

Although the beach angler relies less on a fast-sinking line, whether a shooting head or integrated head, there are places where they can be used to advantage. Fishing from rocky ledges into deep, water where getting the fly down is important, a fast-sinking shooting head or integrated head works very well. This type of shooting head is also valuable when working a beach that has a fairly steep incline as it allows the angler to get the fly down into the depths and amongst the rocky structure where salmon may be feeding, particularly on a very bright, sunny day.

BRUCE FERGUSON

Lessons learned. Ferguson's grandson Ben Carnahan catches on fast. During a trip with granddad, Ben spotted a school of pink salmon jumping along a stretch of Vancouver Island shoreline. He quickly grabbed his rod, cast out and promptly hooked up. Circa 1994.

Casting in Windy Conditions

The saltwater salmon fly-fisher must learn to embrace wind as a constant companion. It is important to learn to place your cast where you want it to go, in spite of the wind's gusty bursts that seem to come from every direction.

From a drifting boat, a cast with the wind at one's back can effortlessly carry a fly the full length of the line; a true

*Beach veterans, from the left, are Preston Singletary,
Les Johnson, Bob Young and John Thompson. Between them they have about ninety years of
fishing experience from beaches in Washington and British Columbia. Beach fishing has been going on since the 1930s.*

The late Al Allard was one of the most innovative of the anglers probing the Puget Sound salt with a fly dating back to the 1970s. Al is credited with developing the simple but effective waiting-period flies, the Allard Yellow and Allard Orange.

BRUCE FERGUSON

ego builder. With this cast, the downside is that your boat will drift rapidly over your line. In this situation, no matter how fast you retrieve, you have little ability to control your line which usually means that you will not be able to get any action on the fly and therefore attract no fish. For this reason it is better to cast at right angles to the wind, or even directly into the wind.

Casting into the wind with a floating or intermediate-sinking line requires high line speed and a tight casting loop. This can be achieved by learning the double-haul, an essential cast if you are going to be successful when casting during windy conditions on salt water.

Many veteran anglers who have mastered the double-haul to achieve high line speed will fire casts out sidearm, very close to the water, thus getting *under* the wind to some extent. Remember that in order to come to terms with casting in windy conditions you have to practice, practice, practice.

Wind and the Beach Caster

Casting from the beach either into or with the wind poses challenges similar to those of the boat angler. On a day when wind is in the forecast it is a good idea to bump up a rod weight or two. If you usually use a 5-weight for small young, immature coho salmon, take your 7-weight along. It will be a much better tool for driving a line into a blustery onshore

wind. The 7-weight rod should be loaded with a line designed for these conditions. Orvis offers its Salmon/Steelhead Taper, Rio has a Steelhead and Atlantic Salmon Taper, Teeny has its Long Shot and Scientific Anglers features its Steelhead Taper. All of these lines cast well with excellent properties for quickly picking up the line and directing your fly to another salmon. These are cold-water lines, designed for the job.

If the wind is at the beach caster's back, a very high back-cast, actually driving the line nearly straight up will, on the forward cast carry the entire line straight out over the water. This can work to the advantage of the beach caster as the wind generally holds the line straight, allowing for a long retrieve, putting the fly in front of the most possible fish. Now all you have to do is develop all of the retrieves needed to work your fly seductively.

Retrieves
Think Like a Salmon

To consistently catch salmon on flies you must first begin thinking like a salmon. What triggers a strike? How will zooplankton and baitfish react when they are either frightened or crippled? How do you make your fly behave to match the movement of the bait? Some of the answers to these questions are found in the salmon feed chapter, and even more can be discovered by close observation on the water. What you have to do is visualize your fly under the water as you retrieve, even though you cannot see it; manipulating your line and rod tip to imitate the actions that tease, infuriate, or trick the salmon into striking.

Successful saltwater salmon fly-fishers pay close attention to the action they put on the fly as they retrieve. Bob Young, a California expatriate and veteran of Puget Sound beaches, can launch a shooting head into the next county, a skill learned during his years fishing striped bass on San Francisco Bay. In addition, Bob is keenly attuned to how he retrieves every cast—and different types of patterns.

Bob says, "I'm not a great fly tier so I usually opt for very simple dressings. My technique is to make long casts in order to achieve the longest possible retrieve while paying close attention to how I manipulate the action on my fly. I use everything from long strips to short erratic tugs to give my fly a lifelike action. If the salmon are around I'll usually catch my share."

Zooplankton Retrieves

For my part, I have spent years observing the live behavior of zooplankton and baitfish, both in the open salt water and in a specially designed aquarium. What seems to trigger most strikes by salmon is action out of the ordinary. Either the prey appears to be escaping and needs to be eaten promptly,

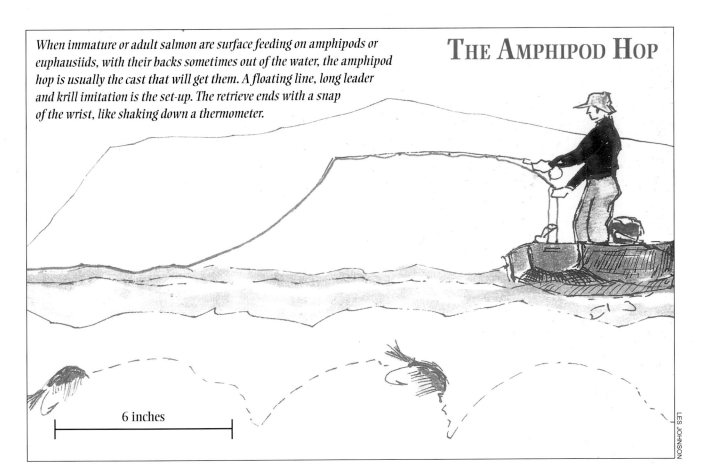

When immature or adult salmon are surface feeding on amphipods or euphausiids, with their backs sometimes out of the water, the amphipod hop is usually the cast that will get them. A floating line, long leader and krill imitation is the set-up. The retrieve ends with a snap of the wrist, like shaking down a thermometer.

6 inches

LES JOHNSON

or crippled and becoming an easy, leisurely meal. Retrieves that simulate these conditions have the best chance of being rewarded with a strike. It takes a real focus on what your fly is doing to create favorable odds for success.

When salmon are either actively feeding on zooplankton in winter and spring, or are in their "waiting period" off the river mouths in the fall, they seem particularly susceptible to the same type of retrieve. This has been fine-tuned over time but its "birth" seemed more like a short series of revelations for me.

The first of these came several years ago on a splendid October day when I was out fishing for waiting-period coho salmon with my good friend, exceptionally innovative fly-fisher, and one of the pioneers of Washington's saltwater fly-fishing renaissance, the late Al Allard. Al had anchored his boat in knee-deep water off a shallow river mouth in south Puget Sound with adult coho salmon swirling and rolling all over the broad, flat estuary. We were standing side-by-side in his boat, just at the edge of the outgoing current. I was watching Al out of the corner of my eye, trying to learn something about his retrieve. He was using his usual floating line and an off-the-shelf, 9-foot leader with a 6-pound tippet to which was knotted a Royal Coachman with an extremely long, sparse, white bucktail wing. I was using a shorter winged Polar Shrimp. Otherwise our outfits were identical. Aside from that something was dreadfully wrong. Al was consistently

hooking salmon after salmon while I was unable to tempt my first fish to strike.

The Amphipod Hop

Finally, in utter frustration I said, "Al, you've caught enough salmon for the day. How about cutting off that fly and letting me use it?" Al, always a gracious and generous man, snipped the fly from his tippet and handed it to me. I quickly replaced my Polar Shrimp with Al's Royal Coachman and began casting his "killer" fly in anticipation of hooking a fish—but it didn't happen. I continued presenting and retrieving the fly for several minutes but could not connect. Once again I was forced to eat humble pie.

"Al," I said, "I'm not doing something that you were doing. Watch my retrieve and tell me where I'm going wrong." So, I cast again and Al began watching my efforts.

"Shorten up your strip to six inches to a foot in length." Al suggested. "And give it a little added move at the end of the stroke. These waiting-period salmon like a fast-moving fly."

I had obviously been doing things very wrong because once I got the hang of Al's retrieve I hooked six big coho salmon before the bite was over. Thereafter I experienced great success with Al's retrieve, but had a difficult time accurately describing it to others.

Then, one evening I was fishing with biologist Frank Haw, who conceived, developed and launched Washington's

LES JOHNSON

Bruce Ferguson with his grand slam salmon taken in salt water. Johnson eased their boat along a rip line where chum salmon were rolling on the surface. One cast put Bruce into this chum, his first taken in salt water. It gave Bruce the distinction of taking all five species of Pacific salmon feeding in salt water.

resident coho salmon program, and his wife Angela. I was trying to describe the retrieve, but was not doing so very well.

Angela, a registered nurse said, "Frank, it's just like shaking down a thermometer." Never have I heard it described better because that is exactly the move needed at the end of the retrieve; a short snap of the wrist, just like shaking down a thermometer.

Al's original amphipod hop retrieve generally brings strikes within a few to several strips of line. When his usually deadly retrieve does not bring a quick strike response, I have added a couple of variations.

Twitch-the-Tip Amphipod Hop

When I see a salmon closely trailing my fly as it nears the boat, I have developed a "desperation retrieve" that I utilize with some success. By twitching the rod tip from side-to-side as I continue the same amphipod hop, an action is added to the fly that closely imitates the hopping and jiggling swimming action of amphipods I watched in a saltwater aquarium. Oftentimes when retrieving I'll feel light tugs on the fly indicating that a salmon is nipping at the wing or nudging the fly. When this occurs, adding a sideways twitching action to the amphipod hop very often provokes a curious, cautious or seemingly indifferent salmon, into suddenly slamming into the fly with a punishing hit.

Slow-and-Easy Amphipod Hop

This variation of the original retrieve is especially good when visibility is poor, such as in roily water; at daybreak; or just before nightfall. During such times, salmon can usually be seen jumping or finning but won't take a fast-moving fly. The answer, many times is to make several strips of line using the amphipod hop, then pause, allowing the fly to settle. Then the retrieve is repeated. This works equally well for both the boat and beach caster.

Fishing the Amphipod from the Beach

When casting from the beach the tide is very often running to the angler's left or right. The beach angler will make a long cast and actually mend the line like a river angler and begin alternately stripping with the amphipod hop and then allowing the fly to swing and settle into the current with no action before starting the retrieve again. The fly can also simply be allowed to drift with the current between short strips. The beach angler generally feels a firm but not hard tug, tug, tug, on the fly when a salmon takes it.

Preston Singletary, a long-time Puget Sound beach regular, considers this retrieve one of the most important to coax strikes from salmon especially early and late in the day, when they are feeding in the rip lines but reluctant to grab his pattern.

The success of this pause in the amphipod hop actually makes perfect sense when you think about it. During the low light of morning and evening salmon cannot see the fly as well when it is moving rapidly, especially a small, pale amphipod or euphausiid imitation. To a feeding salmon though, the slower movement of the fly drifting in the current in the midst of all of those real crustaceans, looks like a helpless hearty hors d'oeuvre.

Les and I have found that at times, pink salmon feeding along a kelp line nibbling euphausiids can be taken with a very gently presented cast on a long leader and a close imitation of an amphipod or euphausiid. At Langara Island, near Connehaw Rock on the northern end of British Columbia's Queen Charlotte Islands, we were drifting slowly toward a huge school of pinks that were unhurriedly sipping the little krill. When we were close enough, Les cast our mutually-designed FJ Pink on a long, light leader at the edge of kelp where the salmon were feeding. He stripped it ever so slowly in twitching, one-inch pulls. Suddenly it was taken in a hammering jolt and he set the hook. The result was a big-shouldered, 8-pound pink brought to net.

The Change-Up

There are times the most realistically crafted fly can actually become lost in a huge swarm of krill, and be summarily ignored unless taken by sheer luck. This is when employing the same retrieve with a change-up pattern sometimes does the trick. An example of this phenomenon occurred when Les and his wife, Carol were fishing along the beach bordering Bioughton Strait at Cluxewe Resort on Vancouver Island in the fall of 2003. Pink salmon were rolling and finning everywhere but regular krill patterns, including the reliable Pink Cigar or FJ Pink didn't faze them.

A local angler who was sitting on one of the rustic driftwood benches, enjoying an evening Scotch and watching the action, offered Carol one of his Hurst Handlebar patterns. It was the same size and general shape as a Pink Cigar or FJ Pink but tied with fluorescent red Edgebrite plastic. The little Handlebar glowed in the afternoon sun when Carol cast it out into a crowd of feeding salmon. Within a few strips of line she set up on a nice bright pink. The lesson here, and it cannot be too strongly stated is, always keep a large selection of change-up patterns in your box for such situations.

Baitfish Retrieves

Important as zooplankton is in salmon diets, there is no substitute for baitfish when it comes to getting a real mouthful of protein and putting on weight. Chinook salmon spend most of their saltwater life in the pursuit and capture of small fish for feed while other species, in varying degrees use baitfish to fill themselves out as they close in on maturity. For coho and pink salmon this occurs at around the two- to three-pound mark.

Barry Stokes connected with this nice pink in knee-deep water while fishing from a southern Vancouver Island beach.

PAULINE LOOS

Baitfish of all kinds can move with amazing speed in short bursts when frightened. This speed, combined with an incredible ability to dodge, twist and turn makes it logical for salmon go after the slowest and weakest members of a school; those that are either stunned or crippled. Therefore, the retrieve that is going to work needs to emphasize the irregular and erratic movement of a wounded baitfish rather than relying on a steady, rhythmic retrieve that imitates a healthy specimen that may be a difficult meal to catch.

Fishing with baitfish imitations, contrary to some ill-conceived notions, is not a one-size-fits-all technique, either with tackle or pattern. Like other fish, herring, sand lance, or anchovies, all favored items on the salmon bill of fare, grow steadily throughout the season. So, from spring through fall, salmon anglers are casting flies to match a variety of bait sizes, all of which must be retrieved in different ways—and depths—due to their size or location in the water column.

Another thing to keep in mind is that there are often several age groups of baitfish in an area at the same time in a range of sizes. This occurs throughout the season. For this reason you should always carry a selection of baitfish patterns to match the color and size of the available forage, time of year not withstanding.

Shallow-Water Retrieve

In June and July it is common to see recently hatched herring and sand lance one to three inches long schooling along the shorelines of Puget Sound, Hood Canal and along the coastline from British Columbia through southeast Alaska. At dawn and dusk salmon locate these schools and charge into them in water little more than a foot deep. It is exhilarating to see and a rush to be able to cast into this visible feast. One might think that any cast with any fly will do the trick in this situation, but this isn't the case.

There are two different approaches that have proven effective over time. The first is confined to the shallows where the salmon are spraying bait.

Surprisingly, salmon can be easily spooked by the noisy fall of a heavy fly line and will rarely hit an imitation that does not closely match the size of the baitfish. In shallow water, the importance of a delicate delivery also comes into play.

A slow-sinking shooting head or full-sinking intermediate line is called for here combined with a long leader tapered to 6- or 8-pound test. From a boat the angler works along slowly casting ahead of the bait schools and salmon, dropping the fly into the melee as gently as possible. The retrieve is a series of four- to six-inch strips alternated with a slight pause after the strips. Strikes usually come when you again commence the retrieve, which adds a bit of life to a fly, giving it the look of a crippled herring or sand lance.

This coho salmon was taken from two feet of water on a saltwater flat. It was waiting to go upstream when it hit a waiting-period pattern. The beaches near estuaries are where tried-and-true saltwater devotees do their last fishing of the season.

The angler working from the beach when the salmon are feeding little more than a rod's length away from shore, finds that it is quite often productive to cast either parallel to, or on an oblique from the beach. This keeps the fly in the strike zone for the longest possible time.

As fruitful as this method is, many is the time when there is no response at all. If the shoreline presents a shallow beach area that drops off steeply, and salmon are breaking on the bait in the shallows, close inspections shows that the salmon are not staying along the exposed beach line. Rather, they are roaring up from deep water, grabbing a baitfish meal,

The late David Hurn of Victoria, British Columbia was a member of the Roderick Haig-Brown Fly Fishing Association and one of the first fly-fishermen to target feeding salmon in the salt water around Victoria. Hurn was a highly respected provincial fisheries biologist and one of the most willing persons to ask information of and very generous with the information and expertise he had accumulated.
The Roderick Haig-Brown Club has an award in David Hurn's name given annually to the member who has contributed the most to conservation.

turning and retreating to the safety of depths. Here, a second approach works better. A #3 or #4 sinking fly line cast into the deep-water edge and allowed to sink before retrieving will often turn the trip from totally frustrating to bountiful.

Crippled Herring Retrieve

This retrieve, was first described to me by the late Dave Hurn, of British Columbia who was an astute observer of bait in relationship to salmon. It does the job when salmon are feeding from below on a thick, widely spread school, or schools of herring that at times, cover up to an acre of water.

"Casual observation," Hurn told me, "suggests that when salmon, cruising at depth, encounter a group of herring, they take up an attack pattern, slash through the bait and then move on. Closer study has convinced me this is not the case. I believe that for every salmon attacking the herring, there are at least five more waiting below." That, according to Hurn is where the action is.

The attacking salmon slash into the schools of herring in swift, violent, twisting thrusts, driving them to the surface, where hundreds of screaming gulls, terns and diving birds await the bounty. Herring that are stunned and crippled spin downward out of the main schools, arcing and whirling helplessly into the jaws of hungry salmon that are leisurely awaiting an easy meal.

For the novice, there is an urge to cast out and make fast "bucktailing" retrieves across the surface through the panicky herring. This may work on occasion but with a relatively few salmon slashing up and down through the herring schools there are usually too many real fish to allow your imitation to be grabbed with any degree of regularity.

Hurn recommended an extra-fast sinking line for this work. The line could be an extra-fast sinking integrated shooting head of 27-30 feet in length, or a similarly fast-sinking shooting head. An LC-13, T-14 or Deep Water Express shooting head might be called for if the current is really moving along. When a boil of surfacing herring is spotted within casting range the angler casts to either edge of it and feeds out line to allow the head to quickly carry the fly down under the school. When the fly is pulling tightly downward the angler begins a retrieve of short, erratic pulls, using only the first finger of the line hand, followed by pauses to allow the fly to flutter downward like a wounded herring. The rod tip should be keep pointed at the fly with the tip actually under the surface.

Since the salmon holding deep are in a rather docile feeding mode the take will not usually be the smashing strike we have come to expect from a hefty coho. It will often be a subtle tightening of the line, or a gentle, tug, tug, tug. At this time the angler draws up the slack and when there is solid tension, sets the hook hard and the battle is on. The quarry may prove to be a coho but could be a feeder chinook, chum or pink salmon; or it may be a nice lingcod which are famous for joining one of these coho feeding sessions.

Although Dave Hurn conceived this deep coho retrieve many years ago, it remains an effective technique. Be ready to use it any time slashing coho are driving bait to the surface.

Bruce Ferguson with a sockeye (left) and a pink salmon taken on the fly. It took several years for Bruce to figure out the elusive sockeye but on this trip he and his son-in-law Dave connected.

The Deep Swing Retrieve

Many times, especially in open water, if the tide is starting to run or the wind picks up it is difficult to get the fly down deep enough to reach the level where fish are feeding, no matter how hard you try. The solution to this problem is really quite straightforward. Named the "deep swing retrieve," it has rescued many an otherwise fruitless day on the water. A compelling example of this occurred at the end of July, 2002.

I had been invited to join long-time fishing companions and good friends, Bill Ludwig and Glen Graves on a trip offshore from Neah Bay Washington. We met Captain Chris Bellows, of Topwater Charters at daybreak at his 24-foot boat which is especially fitted out for open-ocean salmon fly-fishing. This particular day stands out in my memory. First of all, Neah Bay is situated at the mouth of the Strait of Juan de Fuca where it meets the Pacific Ocean. It is rarely flat calm out there. The first day there were three- to five-foot ground swells.

The big interest to the fly-fisher is the fact that this is a major feeding ground for salmon prior to their migration inshore to their spawning rivers. They are still in prime condition and possessing their most feisty attitude. In the waters we would be fishing, some 15 miles offshore in the open Pacific Ocean our quarry would be coho salmon.

Captain Chris soon noticed birds working the surface and altered our course to check out the activity. What we came upon was an incredible concentration of ocean life. Acres of euphausiids were just under the surface with sea birds—Sooty, Shearwaters, Sabine Gulls, Northern Fulmars and a Black-footed Albatross with a spectacular seven-foot wingspread-feeding on the bounty. From under the krill, schools of large herring broke the surface with coho salmon interspersed. Two humpback whales sounded with flukes high. We listened to them "blowing" somewhere in the fog, unseen. Later, a single humpback swam right under the boat in plain view. Being the only boat in sight, its 24-foot length seemed mighty puny compared to the 40-foot whale—definitely a National Geographic moment. Even with all of this natural grandeur spread out in front of us, we were anxious to connect with the coho. After coaxing a few of the surfacing salmon with a clear floating line and patterns like the Hurst Handlebar, Pink Cigar and Sandstrom Euphausiid, we decided to go after the deeper feeding, and we hoped, larger coho in the area.

Captain Chris located salmon on his fish finder at considerable depth. I switched to a prototype Cortland 555 sinking integrated line with a 30-foot extra-fast-sinking 300-grain head and an .031-inch shooting line. With virtually no memory it was a pleasure to cast the recommended 3- to 4-inch, chartreuse-and-white Flashtail Clousers. I made a cast parallel to and ahead of the drifting boat, feeding additional line and allowing the slack to swing deep as we passed over it with the boat, pointing the rod tip straight at the fly. When the slack pulled tight I started a medium-fast retrieve of six inches to one foot accentuated with a downward snap of my wrist at the end of each strip. Now able to feel even the slightest tug on the fly, it wasn't long before I was fast to a silvery bright coho.

If the action slowed, or I felt tugs but no grabs, I would go to a "twitch the tip" amphipod hop and was soon in business again. Using this retrieve we were all into what could only be described as crazy fishing. By noon we had to rest our arms, cramped from continuously casting and fighting salmon. The count was an almost unbelievable 75 coho landed between the three of us, with probably that many more hooked and lost. There is no question of the merits of the "deep swing retrieve."

If you don't have a fish-finder aboard to tell you where the salmon are and there is no surface indication of feeding salmon other than the occasional jumper, there are often times when even a subtle tide rip will provide a clue to a possible salmon concentration. These rip lines are usually easily spotted as they will be clean and clear on one side and piled up with kelp and a mosaic of other floating debris on the other side. These rips can be close to shore, or miles offshore when the tide is moving but not yet running full bore.

The drill is to position yourself on the clean side of the rip line and parallel. Using a full-sinking line, your cast is made on the clean side and parallel, well ahead of the boat in the direction of the drift. Either baitfish or zooplankton flies will work equally well, depending on what the salmon are feeding on at the moment, so you want to be prepared for anything. Feeding salmon of all five species succumb to the "deep swing retrieve" so be sure to make it part of your standard casting repertoire.

The Saltwater Down-Tide Cast and Retrieve

Bill Nelson, an Oregon native and charter member of the Federation of Fly Fishers, was a saltwater fly-fishing guide at April Point Lodge on Quadra Island for eleven years. He was one of the first guides to develop fly-fishing techniques for feeding salmon in open salt water, rather than fishing for salmon milling in estuaries, and continues to hone his skills today. Early in his guiding career, Bill learned to use the swift, swirling tidal currents that swept down Discovery Passage to his advantage.

Bill developed a technique that began by rigging up a fast-sinking shooting head and a six- to ten-foot leader with a 10-pound tippet. His flies were four inches long, tied on 2/0 and 3/0 hooks. Through trial and error he learned to modify his retrieves to fit the situation.

"I learned to anchor up to a big kelp frond that was just inside of the main current. I make a cast out into the current and slightly downstream, just like fishing in a river. As the

LES JOHNSON

On her first trip to the salt, Carol Ferrera landed this chum near the Hoodsport hatchery on Hood Canal. Chum salmon offer new fly-fishers the opportunity to hone their skills on big, hard-fighting fish that arrive in huge numbers and are eager biters.

line swings with the current I mend it and when it straightens out, give a few good strips to get the salmon's attention," Bill recalls. "I discovered that if there is zooplankton around that a slow, erratic retrieve would trigger strikes. If there are a lot of herring showing, a faster strip bringing the fly back steadily against the current would prompt grabs from coho and feeder chinook."

I was fortunate enough to enjoy a grand day with Bill and April Point Lodge owner Warren Peterson a number of years ago. Using Bill's technique, we caught good-sized coho and feeder chinook for an entire tide. To this day I remember the most important note I jotted down:

"A day on the water in their company is worth five years of fishing on your own."

Cruising Salmon Retrieve

Errol Champion is another of the founding members on my list of contemporary saltwater Pacific salmon fly-fishing legends. A former president of the Federation of Fly Fishers, Champion, who now resides in Alaska, fishes the fly in the salt water around Juneau from June through September for maturing coho, pinks and sockeye salmon. In many of the bays and inlets, Champion finds feeding coho, pink and sometimes sockeye salmon cruising along the shore prior to moving into estuaries and their waiting period.

Champion fishes at depths of three to 15 feet with a fast-sinking line or shooting head and a leader of just 4 feet tapered to 10-pound test. His flies are tied on size-4 to 1/0 hooks. He allows his fly to sink to the desired depth before beginning a retrieve. For coho and pink salmon, his most frequent catch, Champion employs as fast, erratic strip. For sockeye salmon he changes to a dead drift interspersed with short, three-inch strips. Champion's uses a standard baitfish bucktail for coho and pinks while he prefers a small hot pink pattern with a white wing for sockeye.

Deep Retrieve

Fishing 30, 50 or even more than a hundred feet down in salt water began in earnest about twenty years ago in the waters around Bellingham, Washington. That is when Jim Darden, who introduced the lob shot cast to Puget Sound, decided that he'd prefer to go after feeding chinook salmon with his fly rather than mooching with heavy lead and a fresh herring. He was not deterred by the deep water where bait-fishermen found chinook, or that wisdom of the day dictated that chinook salmon in the salt would only eat bait.

To reach chinook salmon holding in deep water, Jim would simply lob the head out, and allow the mono shooting line to follow it into the depths. He used a stop watch to time the drop of his fly into various strike zones that he located with a fish finder. When Darden's fly reached the desired depth, he allowed the line to tighten, then began a slow, steady retrieve up through the water column. After retrieving perhaps thirty or forty feet of line, he would allow the fly to drop back and retrieve again through the salmon zone. If feeding chinook, feeling secure in the depths, are around, they are not hesitant to grab the fly.

Refining his retrieves for this technique, it was not long before he hooked the first of what turned out to be dozens of chinook salmon over the next few years. Jim's catches included mature feeders of nearly 20 pounds.

"It was not only an unpopular method when I began," Darden noted recently. "I still can't find many people around Bellingham to take the method seriously. They may now that we are seeing a resurgence of chinook salmon in north Puget Sound."

Another angler who has a thirty-year history of going after feeding chinook salmon on the fly is Garry Sandstrom, owner of The Morning Hatch Fly Shop in Tacoma, Washington. A notable success for Garry occurred in August 2001. He was fishing out of Haa-Nee-Haa Lodge, 38 miles due west of Prince Rupert British Columbia on Dundas Island. Garry was fishing with lodge owner Clayton Vanier on a windless afternoon with the tide at high slack.

As Garry described it, "I made a short cast, stripped out all 90 feet of Rio Deep VII line and waited for it to sink and straighten. After taking several slow, foot-long strips with my 3-inch white Clouser Minnow, a heavy salmon grabbed the fly. A prolonged fight finally brought an 18-pound chinook over Clayton's waiting net. It was a thrill."

Using this method in extreme depths can sometimes produce unexpected results. On the same trip Garry was fishing a 12-weight rod fitted out with a 1000-grain shooting head backed up with 150 feet of Cortland Type VI sinking trolling line. He was fishing a 7-inch-long Clouser Minnow. According to his fish-finder, Garry was in 185 feet of water, his objective; halibut. Instead, after hooking up on the bottom several times with the big fly he hooked and landed a solid 11-pound northern coho!

On another occasion on Clarence Straight, between Ketchikan and Prince of Wales Island, Les and Mark Mandell were showing lodge owner and guide Sid Cook a few things about fishing deep for coho in salt water. When they arrived at Shipwreck Island, boats were taking coho salmon by trolling deep with flashers and Hootchies. Sid really didn't want to put his small bucktail down more than about forty feet. Mandell finally pulled out one of his weighted ".38 Special" Calamarko Squid patterns and tied it to Sid's line. Mark then made a long cast with the fast-sinking line and shook the rest of the sinking line from the reel.

"Now don't do a thing until the line straightens out." Mark advised. Sid was skeptical but after the fly was hanging more than a hundred feet straight down, the big glow-in-the-dark Calamarko was grabbed with authority. Sid fought the fish to the surface—a fat 10-pound coho.

The Nothing Retrieve

The final retrieve is unusual but has proven to be consistently productive over many years. It is called the nothing retrieve for very good reason. It has been saved for last as a reminder that we all need to have our egos deflated from time to time. The point is that it occurs often enough to be used as a retrieval technique in its own right. The concept is that you present the fly in the right place, at the right time of the tide and anywhere from the surface to 100 feet or more down in the depths. Then, you do nothing, absolutely nothing but sit there and be patient. The only motion on the fly is imparted by wave action and wind jostling the boat.

Perhaps the most rewarding experience with this retrieve occurred three years into what turned out to be a decade-long marathon quest focused on taking the "impossible" feeding sockeye salmon in on a cast fly in salt water. My son-in-law, Dave Carnahan and I were fishing under the guidance of legendary fisherman Gordy Graham, proprietor of Telegraph Cove Resort on northern Vancouver Island. The time was August 1993. The Fraser River sockeye run was in full swing heading for its spawning river 300 miles to the south. It was just one of those glorious late-summer mornings; bright sunshine and no wind. The large tide had produced a good upwelling and a soft rip line in the Queen Charlotte Straits. Both Dave and I were casting parallel to, and on the clear side of the rip with full-sinking, type V lines, allowing them to settle to a 45-degree angle before starting our retrieves.

It was clearly time for Dave's cigar break after hours of fruitless casting, following a pre-dawn departure from the dock. Dave was standing, his cigar half-smoked, holding his rod pretty much motionless, thoroughly enjoying the interlude. By this time his fly line was hanging vertically in the water. More time elapsed. Suddenly he received a hard strike on Bill Nelson's version of the Hurst Handlebar. Dave set up on the fish solidly and it almost instantly rocketed through the surface from the 30- to 40-foot depth where it had taken the fly. In a totally reflex response Dave spit out his cigar rather than swallow it and for once, "Heavy-handed Carnahan" applied light pressure to the reel, eventually leading the fish alongside and into the waiting net. We checked closely to be sure of the species and then did a high-five for landing our first ever feeding sockeye salmon on a fly. Mission accomplished, three years after launching the quest! And, as luck would have it, I picked up my own first sockeye later on the same day—using much the same technique.

Another hilarious and instructive incident occurred while fishing out of Dolphin Resort North in northern British Columbia within sight of southeast Alaska. It was September 1, 1996 and time for the big northern coho to show up. We had a long day on the water without much success, but our intrepid fly-fishing guide, Steve Shelley was not going to give up easily. He relocated on the edge of a trash-filled rip while Les knotted on a purple, blue and white Waslick Sea Bait dressed on a tube and cast it out. He sat down in the boat and kind of dozed off, his type V fly line drifting down to about 50 feet on a 60-degree angle. The only movement imparted to the fly was from Les's heavy breathing as he enjoyed his nap. All of a sudden he awakened to a couple of bumps followed by a serious grab. He was into a coho that came straight at him, leaped high, careened off of the outboard motor hood and splashed back into Work Channel. After several leaps and a couple of sizzling runs the 8-pound coho was led over Shelley's landing net. The "nothing retrieve" had scored again!

You don't even have to be in a boat to have the nothing retrieve prompt a strike from a salmon. On another occasion, while wading a shoreline on northern Vancouver Island, I encountered a large school of 3- to 6-pound pink salmon feeding voraciously on a mass of terrified 4- to 5-inch juvenile herring. The beach was littered with dead and dying herring that had chosen to end their lives stranded on dry land rather than face the teeth of the pinks. I waded out until the water reach to mid-thigh on my waders. My herring fly

Garry Sandstrom with a fine 18-pound chinook taken fishing deep at Haa Nee Naa Lodge, August, 2001

inadvertently dangled straight off the end of my rod in the water as I watched the scene unfolding before my eyes. The screech of my reel brought me back into sharp focus as a lively pink grabbed my fly and sped off for deeper water. This episode reoccurred all afternoon as we repeated the nothing retrieve to make sure that it wasn't an accident. So, when all else fails, or just for kicks, when feeding salmon are in the area in good numbers, remember to try the nothing retrieve.

Dawn and Dark Chinook Retrieve

Les began seriously seeking chinook salmon in 1990 when he fished at Little Langara Island in the Queen Charlottes with Trey Combs, who was working on his book, *Bluewater Fly-fishing* at the time. They arrived at North Island Lodge when coho, pink and chum salmon were around in droves and they caught them nearly nonstop for four straight days. They did not, however catch a single chinook.

Les and Trey finally determined that chinook, being the shyest members of the Pacific salmon family might be more attracted to an artificial fly very early or late in the day, when all of the sport trollers fishing bait were off the water. They put in for an extra-early wake-up call and readied reels loaded with fast sinking lines and shooting heads.

The next morning at the crack of dawn they were drifting along near Little Coho Point with not another sport boat in sight. Johnson was rigged with a Calamarko tube fly and Combs with a thick-bodied bucktail. Without much ado, they began casting, allowing their flies to drop down forty feet onto a ledge at the edge of a huge kelp bed. They began retrieving their patterns with a variety of pulls, pauses and drop backs. Before long, Les connected with a 19-pound chinook. Combs followed suit a few moments later with one a bit larger. That morning Johnson and Combs landed three more nice chinook salmon before the trollers arrived, which effectively terminated their action.

"Since that time I've caught chinook on several trips to the Queen Charlotte Islands and a few around home on Puget Sound," Les noted during our planning for this book. "It has almost always been early and late; usually just before and after high slack tide over bottoms of thirty to fifty feet. My best pattern, by far, has been Mark Mandell's Calamarko Squid, a tube fly dressed with fluorescent materials, perhaps because it glows so brightly."

Fishing the Surface Popper

Anglers have been playing around with surface poppers for Pacific salmon for years off and on, with varying degrees of success. My introduction to surface flies for salmon came in early 1992 when a fishing buddy, Dick Kamrar of Gig Harbor, Washington showed me two experimental floating flies; a standard herring baitfish and a euphausiid zooplankton pattern. At the head of each fly he had tied a piece of shaped packing foam, sufficient to float the fly. Dick, a dedicated

Leland Miyawaki caught this big northern coho in the Queen Charlotte Islands on his Beach Popper. Although saltwater fly-fishing for salmon has been going on for decades, surface fishing with poppers and gurglers has recently become popular.

dry-fly trout fisherman, just wanted to see if feeding salmon would react the same way to a properly presented surface fly. Subsequently, he located a commercial popper head that was an improvement over his hand-shaped foam heads.

Dick had observed that a stunned herring or sand lance thrown out onto the water would flutter on the surface, generally swimming in circles. Duplicating this action with the "twitch-the-tip" amphipod hop retrieve produced some spectacular strikes when fished along the edges of kelp beds. Tested in South Puget Sound and along the northern shores of Vancouver Island, this exciting technique belongs in every saltwater fly-fisher's bag of tricks.

To a more limited degree, fishing with floating zooplankton flies is also a productive and rewarding procedure. When salmon are surface feeding heavily on amphipods or euphausiids, the zooplankton popper is cast ahead of the action and allowed to drift with the tide, or give a slight twitch. This is best done with a light riffle on the water. The salmon sucks in the fly rather than slashing it as is the case with a baitfish pattern.

Popularizing the surface popper in Washington however has to be credited in large measure to Leland Miyawaki of Kent, Washington, a salmon fly-fisher who haunts the beaches of Puget Sound year-around, fishing exclusively with his Miyawaki Beach Popper. While Miyawaki admits that salmon miss his popper nearly as often as they connect with it, just seeing them go crazy trying to grab it is a real kick. And make no mistake, salmon do connect with it, often in spectacular fashion.

"I usually find that casting the popper out either straight-away, or on an oblique angle from shore and bringing it back in long, smooth strips works best," said Miyawaki. "I never try to make a big disturbance with it."

Leland tied a few of his poppers for Les and I to take on a saltwater trip to British Columbia. With pink salmon all around the boat, our casts and retrieves with the poppers brought salmon swarming to the surface, knocking the lightweight popper all over like a badminton bird. Although we didn't have Miyawaki's technique down pat, we managed to hook several pink salmon and a few coho. There is no question that a popper works very well when salmon are feeding near the surface; it is also a lot of fun.

Fishing Waiting-Period Salmon

The time comes when salmon move near to their parent streams with their roe skeins and egg sacs growing so full and ripe that their digestive tracts atrophy and they quit feeding. When this occurs they may still be bright as a new dime, or beginning to take on the first hint of spawning color. In either case they are still hard-fighting fish, firm and muscular. When salmon wait at the mouths of rivers or along adjacent beaches, but are not yet ready to ascend to their spawning areas, fly-fishers call it the "waiting period". For the tried-and-true saltwater salmon fly-fisher, this period from late summer through late fall is their last hurrah.

Waiting period salmon have essentially lost interest in the normal baitfish, squid or zooplankton flies but they will often eagerly slam small, bright attractor patterns.

Fishing for waiting-period salmon is not a particularly sophisticated game as the fish can, at times, be jamming beaches near estuaries in huge numbers, chum salmon being a case in point.

When salmon begin to marshal off their parent rivers, fly-fishers can be seen spread out along the nearby beaches or at the mouths of small creeks, wading out onto the gently sloping saltwater flats where the salmon are rolling and jumping. Anglers in boats will also move in and anchor as the tide rises. Since most of these places tend to be shallow, hooked salmon, even relatively small pinks can make astonishing runs, especially when pulling against a rod too light for the task.

There are times when a floating line and long leader will work just fine for waiting-period salmon, particularly if there is no wind chop on the water. A better bet is a clear intermediate sinking line that will work on flat water, or if there is wind chop as it won't get blown around and is easier to control. Rarely is a deep-sinking line required for this fishing but it never hurts to have one in your gear bag, just in case.

The most popular rods for waiting-period salmon, chum, coho or pinks is a fast-action 7- or 8-weight. Pinks however can be handled on a 6-weight. There are areas in Alaska where mature chinook are taken at the mouths of rivers, veteran anglers use nothing lighter than a 10-weight.

When waiting-period fish begin to school up just off the river mouth a great many of them are illegally snagged either by fly-fishers using large, heavily weighted flies, or conventional casters using Buzz Bombs, large jigs or heavy spoons. Waiting-period salmon tend to go for small offerings, generally from size 2 through 10, tied sparse but stout. Salmon that are beginning to sprout spawning teeth are tough on small flies.

Casting to waiting-period salmon is not difficult as they are always on the move in singles, small schools, or sometimes quite large schools. While singles and small schools of salmon aren't quite as exciting to see, when cast to they tend to take the fly fairly. Casting into large, thrashing schools of salmon will often cause you to inadvertently snag a fish.

Waiting-period salmon can be spotted when they jump, of course but just as often you will see what we call "nervous water", ripples caused by the fish moving along just under the surface. With your fly at the ready you want to cast about ten feet ahead of the moving salmon and about 10 feet beyond them and then begin an immediate retrieve of short strips with a snap of your wrist at the end. The take will be solid but not always a hard pull. When it happens, set the hook and then hang on as they realize their situation pretty quickly and beeline for deeper water. Play them firmly but not too tight. The hook, even a very small one, will usually hold provided you don't horse the salmon. Boat fishers net the salmon without lifting it from the water while removing the hook. The beach angler slides the salmon gently into the shallows at the edge of the beach to remove the hook, then revive and release it. When large salmon are present many beach anglers carry a long handled net rather than chance losing a large fish to last-minute gyrations in the shallows that can snap a leader.

Waiting-period flies are generally pretty simple and one would think that any old fly will work—and sometimes this is true. However, a lot of very effective flies have been developed over the years by experienced anglers specifically for waiting-period salmon, particularly chum, coho and pinks. The list of waiting-period patterns grows with each new season. Fly shops on Vancouver Island carry several trays of flies for the waiting period which are called "beach flies" in BC.

Since we don't know what may trigger a waiting-period salmon into striking, it pays to carry a large selection of patterns ranging from large to small and somber to bright. As we've written so many times, don't count on a few patterns to do the job.

Les and Carol were fishing at Tofino in September, 2005 with our mutual friend, Don McDermid of Campbell River, over waiting-period salmon that were well up into the bay. Cast as they might the coho were resolutely zipper-lipped.

Shooting-head systems are still popular and functional for getting down into chinook salmon territory. Jim Darden, shown here when he first started using heads for taking chinook 25 years ago, still uses shooting-head systems.

POINTS OF LAND
➡ Current Direction
⚬ Zooplankton
⚬ Baitfish

Veteran beachbound anglers always take advantage of points of land. When the tide sweeps past such places bait tends to move into the calm side where the current isn't so fast. This attracts salmon. As the tide changes, anglers move to the opposite side of the point.

LES JOHNSON

Finally, Don who had been pouring through his four large boxes of flies came up with an old chartreuse-and-white Clouser with a pink centerline.

"This sparse little Clouser worked well on these tight-lipped fish several years ago. I may as well try it since nothing else is working." He tied on the fly and promptly connected with two coho in short order. If Don had not carried such a large inventory of waiting-period patterns they would probably not have hooked a salmon that day. If your waiting-period box becomes jammed full, don't weed it out; buy another box and keep on collecting these unique attractors. You cannot have too many numerically or by pattern.

So, when the season begins to wane in the salt water proper, watch your local fishing reports and be prepared to hit the nearest waiting period beach. You'll be glad you did.

Putting It All Together
Having read through all of the casts, retrieves and detailed descriptions from anglers who have fished the fly for many years in the salt, it is time to put all of this information together. And, there is a ton of information in this chapter, much of it focused on certain species of salmon in different situations. Many techniques have been developed for a certain species of salmon. While working well for the intended species these techniques are not limited specifically to chinook, or chum, or coho, as examples. Do not lose sight of

the fact that all of the casts and retrieves will work for all Pacific salmon species at one time or another. The angler who succeeds on a regular basis is one who will utilize any of the casts or retrieves when the feeding situation presents itself, no matter what species of salmon is the quarry. Remember, all salmon will feed near the surface; deeper under a school of herring; or near bottom in food-rich kelp forests.

A Few Tips on Fly-Fishing for Different Salmon Species
Although all Pacific salmon will eat many of the same feed and haunt the same waters, they are different in many respects and knowing a few tricks of the trade definitely narrows the odds of catching them. Here are a few tidbits that should prove useful to the new saltwater salmon fly-fisher.

Chinook
There is not much question that feeding chinook salmon in salt water are tough to entice and land on a fly. This is in part due to their tendency to be wary; preference for deep water; and well-deserved reputation as finicky biters. For all of these reasons, setting up tackle for chinook should never be a casual endeavor, because once hooked, a mature chinook becomes a real load against even a very stout fly rod. This is the case whether you are after relatively small resident chinook in Puget Sound or the Georgia Basin weighing 7 to perhaps 20

pounds or the big northern lunkers that haunt the waters of the Queen Charlotte Islands and southeast Alaska.

Feeder chinook salmon in the 6- to 10-pound range that roam along the Pacific Coast from Monterey Bay, California to southeast Alaska can be pretty well handled with a fast-action, 8-weight outfit, a good reel with an adjustable drag and capacity for 200 yards of 20-pound-test backing under a fly line or shooting-head system. This outfit will handle flies three to five inches long, tied on size 2 to 2/0 hooks. Most anglers who fish for steelhead or on coastal salt water have an outfit that fills this niche.

Before you even consider setting up tackle for big, off-shore chinook salmon in the 40- to 50-pound class, you are well advised to get into shape for long sessions of casting a 9- to 12-weight fly rod, using sinking heads from 400 to 600 grains and flies that weigh as much as a 7mm Remington Magnum slug. You don't want to already be worm to a frazzle when your long-anticipated battle is finally joined.

One of the best places to find a trophy-size chinook salmon is in the waters around Langara Island, northern landmark of the Queen Charlotte Islands archipelago. Salmon begin showing here in June and filter through until mid-September. June and July is when they marshal in these feed-rich grounds, gorging for days or weeks, to pack on pounds before continuing their journey to natal streams—and when they are most susceptible to the fly. The West Coast Fishing Club at Langara Island provides superb accommodations and has guides knowledgeable in putting their clients on top of chinook salmon. During the 2002 season at the West Coast Fishing Club there were 101 chinook salmon weighing from

Mark Wickline holds up a nice chum salmon that grabbed a small green fly near Chico Creek estuary. Washington has dozens of creeks and rivers that host runs of chum salmon from October through early December. With the present decline in coho numbers the chum has become an important game fish.

40 to 69 pounds caught and released. There were many hundreds more caught and retained. While nearly all of these huge chinook salmon were taken by trolling with bait, the sheer numbers of big fish landed make the waters around Langara Island a top prospect for the trophy fly-fisher.

Peregrine Lodge located on Graham Island in Naden Harbor also has great chinook water that has yet to be really worked hard for chinook salmon. Just outside the harbor entrance there are vast kelp beds, rich with bait that hold chinook from June through September.

Fly-rods from 9- to 12-weight are the order of the day for trophy chinook salmon. Saltwater reels with full-disk, adjustable drags and capacity for an honest 200 yards of 30-pound-test braided backing under a sinking line or shooting head. Leaders tapered to 16 pounds will turn over the big, bulky, 5- to 7-inch bucktails required to imitate full-grown sand lance or herring. Although big chinook are sometimes taken near the surface, you will need either an extra-fast sinking integrated heads, or full-sinking line.

A large, mature chinook feeding in salt water is unquestionably the most highly prized Pacific salmon trophy in every respect. You may fish for days, weeks or (heaven forbid) years, before hooking one. You want all possible advantages on your side when it happens.

Tim Tullis waited until the coho season was winding down in British Columbia to take this thick-bodied 17-pound coho. The largest salmon of the year are often caught near the end of the season.

Chum

Primarily zooplankton feeders, chum salmon should really be classified as "opportunistic" in their approach to feeding since they will chomp down on sand lance, herring or squid in addition to zooplankton if it is readily available. Les and I have taken a limited number of chum salmon in offshore Pacific waters and the majority of them hit 4- to 5-inch-long bucktails and squid imitations, since that was the dominant forage in the area at that time. This does not mean however that if you happen onto a school of chum salmon feeding on zooplankton that you shouldn't quickly gear up with a little FJ Pink, Pink Cigar or Hurst Handlebar and begin casting with a long leader. It just might get you the ride of a lifetime from a very fast salmon. The 8-weight outfit that you would use for feeder chinook will double nicely on chum salmon.

When fishing chums at estuaries during the waiting period the water may often be little more than three feet deep. Usually a floating line will do the job. However there are times when an intermediate-sinking line will take the fly just a bit deeper, which is helpful on a bright day. Les usually

Resident coho can provide a potentially great fishery throughout British Columbia and Washington. Once a wild salmon fishery, it is currently made up primarily of hatchery salmon. Peter Caverhill, retired B.C. Department of Fisheries biologist caught this one while fishing with long-time friend, Don McDermid.

Pauline Loos releasing a nice pink salmon while fishing near Victoria, British Columbia.

uses an intermediate or type II sinking shooting taper with an intermediate shooting line for chums. A few spare heads, from floating to various sinking rates, tucked into a pocket gives him an easily carried range of options.

Coho

The aerobatic display of a coho hooked in salt water is what makes it the most popular Pacific salmon among dedicated fly-rodders. When hooked, a coho of any size from yearling to mature northern slab invariably takes to the air at least a few times during the battle. In addition, coho are very often within easy reach of our modern lines and exceedingly vulnerable to the fly in salt water.

The same 7- and 8-weight outfits and lines that serve for feeder chinook and chum salmon will handle coho salmon as well. Adult coho feed extensively on anchovies, sardines, sand lance and herring. They are also partial to small squid.

Juvenile coho taken in Washington's Puget Sound and Georgia Basin in British Columbia feed heavily on euphausiids and amphipods from the time they are about a foot long until they reach 18 to 20 inches when they switch over to more substantive baitfish. A fast-action 6-weight trout rod is the ticket for these smaller salmon. You will want spools with floating, intermediate sinking and a deep-sinking or a shooting-head system which is available even for this light outfit.

Outstanding spots for the fly-rod angler to seek mature, feeding coho salmon in the salt include; Washington's Neah Bay at the entrance of the Strait of Juan de Fuca, Tofino on the west side of Vancouver Island. Quadra Island is another. Langara Island of the Queen Charlottes also gets good runs of coho as does Dundas Island and Douglas Channel on the northern British Columbia mainland. In southeast Alaska coho are found in the salt around the Baranoff Islands, Prince of Wales Island in Thorne Bay and in Ketchikan near Shipwreck Island on Clarence Strait. These are but a small sampling of the more popular hotspots for coho on the fly in salt water.

Clayton Vanier, owner of Haa Nee Naa Lodge on Dundas Island, with a prized feeding sockeye salmon taken in the salt. Vanier has spent several seasons pursuing sockeye with his fly rod.

Pinks

Pink salmon don't come into range of the saltwater fly-fisher until they are mature fish of 3 to 8 pounds. One of the pleasures of fly-fishing for pink salmon is their astonishing numbers and aggressive approach to any fly that lands in their view. From Alaska to Washington, the summer months see large schools of pink salmon moving down the beach lines as they seek out their parent rivers. Chrome bright and eager to grab a small euphausiid pattern, or sparsely dressed streamer or Clouser, a silvery-sided, pink salmon taken in prime condition from the salt is a beautiful creature. It is difficult to believe that after only a relatively few days in its parent stream that the pink starts to take on its eventual dark purplish coloration, with the males' backs deformed and their jaws twisted into grotesque, toothy fighting tools. It is then that the beautiful pink salmon becomes the *humpy*.

Although pinks can be handled on light gear like a 6-weight trout outfit, they are sometimes in the company of larger coho salmon, especially in northern offshore waters. Casting to a small school of pinks only to have a 14-pound northern coho crash the party can be disastrous. One is better off to rely on the 7- or 8-weight to dispatch pinks quickly (so you can hook up another) and to give you a good chance of landing that big-shouldered northern coho that just might decide to compete for your fly. In Washington a 5- or 6-weight is often employed for pinks in the salt and estuaries.

Pink salmon feed on zooplankton or baitfish; whatever is readily available. During our trip to Haa Nee Naa Lodge on Dundas Island, Les and I changed flies often during heavy pink salmon bites just to see if there was something that they *wouldn't* take. They grabbed them all; baitfish, squid,

euphausiid imitations—and surface poppers. There are times however when they can be frustratingly selective.

Sockeye

Almost exclusively zooplankton eaters, especially focusing on euphausiids and amphipods, and averaging 5 to 7 pounds in weight, the sockeye salmon has been throughout history regarded as a fish to be caught commercially in purse seines, gill nets and by trolling. Although there exists an increasing recreational troll fishery taking feeding sockeye on a cast fly has been viewed as a near impossibility. Those fly-anglers who have caught four feeding species in salt water, chinook, chum, coho and pink, consider the elusive sockeye to be the "Holy Grail". Sockeye make up for their modest size with

Ben Carnahan takes it easy after landing a pink salmon on a fly while casting from a Vancouver Island beach under the guidance of granddad, Bruce Ferguson. The pink was taken on a 1994 fishing trip.

a fierce fighting spirit and spectacular airborne gyrations when fighting the hook. The 7- and 8-weight rods used for other Pacific salmon will perform equally well on sockeye. Fly lines from floating through extra-fast sinking are needed to probe the right depths to locate this pinnacle of saltwater salmon fly-casting.

Zooplankton flies that work especially well tend to be hot red-orange or pink and about an inch long. Bill Nelson's version of the Hurst Handlebar and Garry Sandstrom's Angel Hair Euphausiid are two of the best. Key to success is the retrieve which should be S-L-O-W. Use a chironomid retrieve with little or no action, or a very slow short twitch followed by a short, slow methodical pull with no "pop" at the end. Pause in between pulls to let the fly to settle slightly. This is best accomplished with no wind and at the tag end of a big, out tide, along the edge of a soft rip or in a back eddy.

To catch sockeye on the surface you pretty much have to see them working there. They can readily be identified as they move faster than either pinks or coho. A floating hot pink chenille fly with a pink deer-hair wing on a number 6 saltwater hook has proven effective for Bill Nelson who fished dead-drift at the end of an out tide. Bill has been one of the most successful fly-fishers on feeding sockeye with some three dozen to his credit over a seven-year period. Clearly, this pursuit is not for the impatient.

Some suggested spots to try for sockeye are from Telegraph Cove Resort and other lodges tributary to the Queen Charlotte Strait; and through the Johnstone Strait and down to Quadra Island on Vancouver Island's east side. From these locations you would be intercepting the large Fraser River runs.

For those with a pioneering spirit, try Dundas Island at Haa Nee Naa Lodge where you would be focusing on the Nass and Skeena river runs. These are British Columbia's semi-protected marine waters. Careful attention to run timing is essential at any location.

Catch and Release

Salmon are delicious food fish and most of us keep several each season for eating fresh, or to serve up as a splendid alder-smoked fillet for the holiday table. Many times though a salmon will need to be released after capture. This can be for a variety of reasons; there are minimum and maximum sizes

When salmon become picky, the same flies and tactics can be employed to take feisty black rockfish which are located around rocky points and kelp beds. At times rockfish will grab flies from the surface.

LES JOHNSON

imposed on some species; seasons on certain salmon species may be closed; or the angler may choose to release a salmon just for the pleasure of the experience and not put any in the box. Whatever the reason, it is important to practice release methods that will ensure a maximum survival rate.

It is also essential that the fly-fisher realize that there is always some hooking mortality no matter how careful he or she may be. If the angler is keeping the fish, only those that are bleeding, have been hooked through an eye, or have taken the fly down into the gills or throat should be retained. This should be the norm for all catch-and-release fishing, rather than sorting out the biggest and brightest with which to awe family and friends. By adhering to the following points, you will ensure that more salmon survive the release process to fight another day, or make it to the spawning grounds.

Release Procedures

Always use a rod and leader tippet that will allow you to land your fish promptly. This way you can release the fish before exhaustion limits its chances for survival.

Don't bring the fish into the boat or even touch it, if possible. Shore fishers should never pull the salmon up onto the beach. This means leaving it in the water. A net, especially one with rigid plastic webbing, will not only remove a lot of scales but will damage the eyes of the fish.

Bring the salmon alongside your boat, reach over and with a pair of needle-nose pliers grasp the hook and turn it over. This will release the fish.

Another method was developed some years ago by members of the Washington Department of Fish and Wildlife. An ordinary teacup hanger is screwed into the end of a length of doweling (which can be cut to a length matching the prevailing minimum length legal size of the salmon in your area).

When the salmon is ready to release, simply loop the teacup hanger through the bend of the hook, lift up on the dowel and, at the same time, pull down on the leader. The fish will drop off immediately without ever being touched. The procedure is simple, safe and fast. Shore fishers can use this same dowel-and-teacup hook tool very nicely.

Reviving Exhausted Salmon

If a salmon is so exhausted that it cannot swim away readily, in lively condition, revival is required. Hold the salmon gently under the stomach away from the gills with one hand and by the wrist of its tail with the other. Move the salmon gently back and forth to work water through its gills. Usually it will begin to move in your hands and then scoot quickly off into deeper water.

Stretching the supply of salmon by reducing handling mortality is an increasingly important factor in maintaining our sport.

CHAPTER EIGHT

The Fine Sport of Bucktailing and Skipflying

By Les Johnson

When we wrote *Fly Fishing for Pacific Salmon* in 1985 we did not include bucktailing. The Canadian term "bucktailing" is a method of trolling large bucktail flies and we rather sanctimoniously determined that a book on Fly Fishing for Pacific Salmon should only include techniques that involved a cast fly. Upon updating the history chapters of this volume, we realized that trolling a bucktail fly in salt water was the precursor to actually casting flies for salmon in both Washington and British Columbia. We had both taken salmon by trolling and casting flies at Sekiu and Neah Bay over the years before we met to become friends and co-authors. Furthermore we knew that

bucktailing is a salmon-fishing technique that continues to increase in popularity with each new season. Many dedicated bucktailers ply their beautiful trolling flies using the same high-quality rods and reels that are employed by conventional fly-fishers. Bucktailing is a serious pursuit.

Skipflying is a slightly different method of bucktailing where the flies are trolled extremely slowly just on either side and slightly aft of the outboard motor. This has become popular at Tofino, BC and other places and can really raise one's blood pressure when a coho salmon comes right up next to the boat to slam the fly.

To give bucktailing and skipflying the space they deserve, we elected to dedicate a chapter to the methods. We were fortunate to obtain a wealth of information from three top professionals in the fine sport of bucktailing, who combined have compiled a King Tut's treasure of experience: Bill Nelson, Shawn Bennett and Art Limber.

Bill Nelson, a long-time friend of Bruce Ferguson, lives in Eugene, Oregon but was for several years a highly-sought salmon-fishing guide out of April Point Lodge on Quadra Island, British Columbia. Bill spent years working the productive salmon water around Quadra Island. He now stays closer to home and is enlightening anglers on the Oregon coast to the finer points of bucktailing.

Shawn Bennett guides out of Tofino, on the west side of Vancouver Island, perhaps the most popular fly-fishing location for coho and chinook salmon on all of our Pacific marine waters, at least in recent years. In addition to conventional fly-fishing, Bennett is an early proponent of skipflying, a variation of bucktailing that works exceptionally well on Clayoquot Sound where the town of Tofino is located.

Art Limber, who lives at Qualicum Beach on Vancouver Island, is one of the premier professional tiers of bucktailing flies in British Columbia. His polar bear hair streamers are beautifully dressed but tied for durability and long, hard use. His other salmon patterns, used for casting, are equally handsome and effective. Art is also an expert at bucktailing, through the winter, working his exquisite bucktails for big,

APRIL POINT LODGE

Guide Bill Nelson (right) with a very special client, Gen. Norman "Stormin' Norman" Schwarzkopf of Desert Storm fame. The general handled his light fly rod very well and landed this big chinook salmon near Quadra Island, British Columbia.

Pauline Loos holds up this nice coho salmon that smacked her fly when she was bucktailing at Clayoquot Sound at Tofino.

resident chinook salmon after most other anglers have quit for the season.

Nelson ties flies primarily for his own use. Bennett was at one time a professional fly tier but had to give it up when he took over as Operations Manager at Weigh West. Shawn now purchases most of his flies from Art Limber although he still makes up some of his special Clouser variations for casting to coho. Limber is a full-time professional fly tier who has perfected his casting and bucktailing patterns over the years on the coho and chinook salmon in the waters around Vancouver Island

Bucktailing

Bucktailing is a method of salmon fishing that began simply as trolling big streamer or bucktail flies, with little or no added weight behind small, outboard skiffs, primarily to catch foraging coho; aggressive saltwater feeders that like to work the surface during feeding binges. While it is indeed trolling, bucktailing has been fined-tuned for a fly-rod that is strung with either monofilament or fly-line, combined with a range of throttle settings to give the fly the right action to spur the strike response of coho feeding near the surface.

Early on it was discovered that employing a fairly fast troll and keeping the fly not more than 30 feet, or so behind the boat, right in the prop wash was the key to goading strikes from coho. Sometimes the fly was trolled just fast enough to run barely under the surface. At other times it would be pulled at a higher speed to cause a ruckus on the surface and even jump out of the water from time to time. Strikes were often so hard that the hook was set solidly into the salmon's jaw before the angler could rear back on the rod. This method of bucktailing has grown through the years and is one

of the most popular methods of fly-fishing for coho salmon throughout the marine waters of British Columbia.

Skipflying

Skipflying for coho salmon is a fairly recent offshoot of bucktailing and is also a trolling technique but one that is both similar, and very different, from bucktailing. In skipflying the bucktail is trolled very slowly, barely beyond the motor with only a few feet of fly line and a long leader extended from the rod tip. The rod is then set into a sturdy rod holder with the tip low, pointed at the fly. Under a slow, sometimes ultra-slow, troll, the fly cruises along the top, leaving just the slightest "V" wake but nothing more. Upon first witnessing skipflying, I wondered how a fly trolled so closely—and

Barry Stokes, production manager at Islander Reels, holds up a hefty coho salmon taken while bucktailing at Tofino, British Columbia.

slowly—almost near enough to reach out and grab, could tempt a coho salmon. Well, it can; and it does.

Bill Nelson on Bucktailing

Bill Nelson is one of the early champions of bucktailing and certainly one of the most well-known guides around Quadra Island. Retired from guiding now, Nelson credits his introduction to bucktailing or skipflying to Rob Bell-Irving and Joe Watson of Campbell River, British Columbia in the early 1970s. "They called it 'fishing Qualicum style'", Bill said of his indoctrination to the sport.

When Bill began fishing in British Columbia, he liked the fishing, and the place, so well that he sold his business in Eugene, built a home on Quadra Island and became a professional fishing guide.

"It was a nice home," Nelson recalls. "About a half-mile from April Point Lodge. It was a wonderful setting with the beach in front and the water all the way north to 'The Narrows'. My wife Audrey and I loved the spot. We watched huge

Shawn Bennett is the fly-fishing manager at Weigh West Marine Resort in Tofino, British Columbia. Shawn is one of the most accomplished guide/fly-fishers working on the waters of Clayoquot Sound. He specializes in skipflying.

STEVE PROBASCO

cruise ships pass through and all of the wildlife come and go with the seasons. And the sunsets...well, they were about as good as it gets."

From 1977 through 1989 Bill worked closely with Warren Peterson and his brother Eric, co-owners of April Point Lodge. Together Bill and Warren perfected bucktailing in the waters around Quadra Island.

During his guiding career, Bill also spent some winters in New Zealand. In December 1983 and January 1984 he and Audrey did a stint in the filmmaking business when they worked with Geof Thomas who was directing a film for Air New Zealand. For one segment of this film Nelson fly-fished for trout in some of the freshwater rivers. Billy Pate made a saltwater segment and Jim Drury—who starred in the television series, "The Virginian"—was featured in a separate segment.

Bill and Audrey have since returned to Eugene to renew and enjoy family ties. However, Bill still finds time to enlighten anglers on the Oregon coast to the finer points of bucktailing. During his years as a guide, Nelson developed a series of flies specifically for bucktailing around Quadra Island. He now employs the same flies and skills fishing the waters off of the Oregon Coast where they have proven to be equally productive.

For bucktailing, Bill employs what he calls "skipflying tackle" for all of his bucktailing and skipflying.

"I use 9-foot, 8-weight fly rods and Hardy Marquis #1 reels loaded with about 200 yards of 15-pound-test monofilament," Bill noted. "I have found that longer rods are more difficult to use in a boat and for working the fish in close to

the net. At one time I used 6-weight rods but have found that they are too light for anglers who are not experienced at handling fish like coho salmon on light gear."

Nelson ties a barrel swivel to the end of his main line and adds 9 feet of leader to the fly. "When trolling, I usually vary the distance of the fly behind the boat. Sixteen pulls, or about 30 to 35 feet is normal but sometimes the flies can be only ten feet from the stern when using the slower-moving skipflying technique. I generally connect everything with improved clinch knots and have found them to work just fine, even holding the large chinook salmon that we often hook," Nelson said. "On occasion I will tie a riffling hitch on a small fly to make it wake better," He also noted that he rarely employs spinners in front of his flies.

"I've enjoyed some good company guiding people from near and far to help them catch salmon by bucktailing," Nelson added. "Some of my clients include Sammy Snead, the golfer, General Norman Schwarzkopf, and Ted Williams who was a terrific angler."

Nelson could have added that those clients were also in very good company.

Shawn Bennett on Skipflying

I introduced Carol to bucktailing and the fine sport of Skipflying for coho salmon when we fished with Shawn Bennett out of Weigh West Resort at Tofino. I had done a fair amount of bucktailing for coho salmon years earlier with my mother, Annite Mae Johnson out of Redondo, Washington. Now, more than forty years later we were with Shawn who was piloting a 17-foot center-console skiff, with a forward casting platform especially designed for fly-fishing. The clean design had unsullied rails that don't grab at one's fly line and under-gunwale rod racks that hold spare fly-rods safely out of the way. After guiding us through a tricky series of channels, around islets adorned by storm-sculpted evergreens and over barely submerged reefs, Shawn throttled down at Monk Rock out some distance from the conifer-covered southwest slope of the Cat Face Mountains on spectacular Clayoquot Sound.

Clayoquot Sound is a large protected bay broken up by small islands, massive rocks and raft after raft of kelp. In July and August it can be absolutely alive with wild northern coho salmon.

"Welcome to 'Coho Central'," Shawn said with a sweep of his arm across the tree-bordered horizon. "It is what I call Clayoquot Sound."

In the clear, slowly rolling water we could see schools of chrome-bright coho salmon swarming into the sound on the rising tide, some not more than a rod's length from the boat.

"It is one of the best places that I know of for catching coho and chinook as well, by either casting with Clousers and other baitfish patterns, or skipflying. We're going to start this morning by introducing you to a bit of skipflying. It is

Carol Ferrera with a prime coho salmon taken while bucktailing out of Tofino on Clayoquot Sound with husband Les Johnson and guide Shawn Bennett. When the bucktailing on Clayoquot Sound is hot the action can be tremendous. For first-timers with their own boats heading out to Clayoquot Sound it is advisable to follow an experienced fishmaster.

similar to bucktailing except that we move along very slowly with the flies even closer to the boat."

Shawn handed us two Art Limber bucktails, beautifully dressed from dyed polar bear hair; each embellished with a number 2 silver Indiana spinner blade at the nose, and showed us how to set them out just beyond the prop wash of the motor. We had no more gotten the flies into position and were watching them skim very slowly along the surface with the miniature spinners twirling when the excitement began.

"Look!" Carol exclaimed. "A salmon came right up under my fly. There's another one. There's a whole school of them!" A few seconds later Carol was showered with salt water as her fly disappeared in a big, foamy boil and line began peeling from her reel. She grabbed her throbbing fly-rod from the holder, set up on the streaking salmon and shouted, "I've got him!"

The coho responded with a series of skywalking leaps as it ran out all of her fly line and a respectable length of backing. After a lively give-and-take battle during which Carol saw her backing splice come and go through the tip top two

more times, she at last eased the coho over Shawn's waiting net and our first salmon of the day, a chunky 10-pounder, was dropped into the ice box. It was a fine start that turned out to be a banner day of skipflying.

Art Limber on Winter Bucktailing for Chinook Salmon

Bucktailing, Limber discovered years ago, is not restricted to coho salmon, although the coho is most intensely sought by bucktailers. However, the waters around Campbell River on Vancouver Island offer excellent winter fishing for local chinook salmon. This winter fishery begins in December and goes on until the herring spawn in March.

Large flies in herring colors are the order of the day for winter chinook bucktailing, as mature herring are the primary feed during this period. An all-white polar bear streamer is also effective during times when large schools of squid are present. When fishing for chinook salmon in the winter months, Limber likes to have his 16-foot skiff on the water at

Whether working at his tying table dressing his beautiful and popular bucktailing flies, or fishing them, Art Limber is one of the very best in the game. His flies have become legendary among British Columbia bucktailers and are being used with increasing regularity by U.S. anglers.

the crack of dawn, as that is when schools of herring will be feeding near the surface.

Since some chinook in the winter season can easily top 30 pounds, stout tackle is recommended. Limber uses a 10'6" fiberglass mooching rod for winter bucktailing that can take a beating and will not nick and weaken as easily as graphite rods if the going gets tough. A large-diameter single-action reel loaded with 25-pound-test monofilament, a 9-foot, 20-pound-test leader and one of his magnificent polar bear bucktails running behind a size 2 or 4 Colorado spinner rounds out Art's tackle.

Art generally runs his fly 40 to 60 feet behind his boat, usually with no additional weight. If a strong current is running, he will add a 3/8- to 5/8-ounce crescent sinker between the main line and leader. He is adamant about color selection for winter chinook salmon fishing. When there are shrimp, plankton blooms and spawn in evidence, Limber uses small, 3-inch flies in pink and orange, or gray and pink. Olive, purple, dark green and gray patterns are best for imitating herring or needlefish. Sometimes a pink Art's Special does the trick as a change-up.

"I prefer polar bear for my salmon flies as it has a beautiful sheen and takes dye colors well." However, he concedes that bucktail, yak hair, and mountain goat are also good materials for bucktailing flies as is FisHair, SuperHair and other synthetics.

A final bit of advice from a master of the craft is, "If you decide to attempt your own dying, I recommend that you keep your colors on the light side as they will appear darker when wet."

Flies for Bucktailing

One can go bucktailing with just about any streamer fly. The earliest patterns for bucktailing, back when it was still in its infancy, were dressed on 2/0 to 5/0, long-shank, extra-stout Mustad, Partridge, or Sealy streamer hooks. All were 3X to 5X stout with a limerick bend. These evolved into the flies we use today, which employ smaller hooks, a tandem-hook rig, or a single trailing hook. These modern hook systems seem to be particularly efficient at hooking coho salmon and are less damaging to a fish that is going to be released alive. Bucktailing flies, also called coho flies, are dressed on tubes by some anglers but trailing-hook or tandem-hook patterns, as tied by Nelson, Bennett and Limber are the most popular styles and have been for several years. A selection of flies by these three innovative and talented tiers appears in the fly chapter.

Bucktailing With Mom

It was in the mid-1950s, about a year after I had returned from my hitch in the U.S. Marine Corps that I first tried bucktailing, under rather unusual circumstances. I was going to college at the time, and every autumn, usually just after Labor Day, hordes of northern coho salmon would arrive in

Author Johnson and his mother, Annite Mae Johnson were trolling bucktail flies together for the first time out of the old Redondo, Washington boathouse when she landed this 15-pound coho. Ms. Johnson never fished another herring during the rest of her salmon fishing career. Circa 1955.

Les Johnson with a nice Clayoquot Sound coho that hit one of Art Limber's famous bucktailing flies, the Orange and Pink.

Puget Sound. My parent's home was situated on the Puget Sound waterfront at the community of Redondo, between Seattle and Tacoma. I always knew exactly when the coho arrived at Redondo because my mother, Annite Johnson, would call me and say, "Lester, the silvers are here!" That was my cue to head south from Seattle to take her fishing. Mom loved fishing for silver salmon, as coho were commonly called in Washington at the time, and always insisted that I guide her throughout the fall season.

We would meet at her place for coffee. Then I would go down to the old Redondo Boathouse to rent a boat and secure my Evinrude 4-horse outboard to the transom. I'd pick up a scoop of live herring and cruise up to the beach in front of mom's where she would be waiting. Whenever possible we would begin fishing a couple of hours after the low tide turn. She was convinced that silvers always hit better on an incoming tide.

I had our rods strung with 2-ounce crescent sinkers and 5-foot-long herring leaders rigged with two-hook gangs of Mustad Octopus hooks. Although mom dearly loved to hang into those big silvers, she was always aghast when I would take a lively herring from the bait bucket, hold it down on a short pine cutting board and unceremoniously slice off its head at an angle to create a cut-plug. She seemed to get over

it once the bait was in the water spinning nicely and was ecstatic when a silver would smack it and sail end-over-end into the air. The issue of hurting those little herring however, always bothered her, although it bothered her not in the least when I would conk a big silver on the head and throw it into the fish box.

Sacrificing live herring with my fillet knife reached a critical point one morning when mom arrived at the boat carrying two tiny pillows she had sewn up, each about the size of a package of Lucky Strikes. They were, she explained, for pressing against each side of a herring's head in order to smother it painlessly before I cut it into a plug bait. Her experiment proved to be a dismal failure because even after an interminable time struggling between the pillows before finally calming down, the herring would invariably bounce back to life and flop around frantically to avoid its inevitable decapitation.

Then one day I met mom at the beach with the rods rigged and no herring on board. "Where is our bait, Son?" She asked looking around the boat. "How are we supposed to catch salmon without bait?" I pointed to the two 4-inch bucktail flies with spinners on their noses that were tied on in place of the herring rigs.

"We're going to troll bucktail flies for silvers today, mom," I said. "I bought these at Foote's Sporting Goods and Jay gave me a few tips on how to fish them. No herring to smother or cut, and Jay said that these flies really work." She appeared a bit skeptical but was game to try anything that would allow her to catch silver salmon, especially if it didn't involve executing any more of those little herring.

My strategy couldn't have worked better, that is once I convinced mom that she should only have her fly out about thirty feet behind the boat; and that it was supposed to bounce around in the prop wash. It was an overcast morning with silver salmon breaking the calm Redondo Bay surface everywhere. Ahead of us anglers in two boats were working on hookups with silvers. We had pulled our flies little more than a hundred yards when her rod was nearly yanked from her delicate hands and her old Penn reel began wailing as the line ran out.

The first time the silver cleared the surface mom exclaimed, "Oh my God! It's a huge one!"

Mom was no slouch at playing salmon though, and in a short time we pulled a fifteen-pound silver into the boat. She was absolutely beaming as she carefully washed and preened the green-and-white bucktail back into shape. Mom and I fished together for several more years out of Redondo, and at least once each season on the Washington coast at Sekiu or Neah Bay and we caught a lot of silver salmon but we didn't kill another herring. The moment that big silver latched onto her green-and-white bucktail fly at Redondo, mom became a full-fledged bucktailer; and she never looked back.

CHAPTER NINE

Freshwater Fishing Techinques

By Les Johnson

There have been a great many Pacific salmon on the end of my fly line during the past four decades. I've been fortunate enough to hook them up from the Eel River in California, the Elk River in Southern Oregon, the Skeena in British Columbia, the Thorne River on Prince of Wales Island in Alaska, and the Sol Duc in Washington. There has also been a long list of Pacific Coast rivers and tributary streams in between where one of my flies has intercepted a salmon.

Despite the fact that the roots of Fly Fishing for Pacific Salmon were planted some 125 years ago and that a fresh-run salmon of any size is a noble adversary when taken fairly on a fly rod, a lingering notion has remained among many anglers that taking these fish on a fly is a less dignified pursuit than taking an Atlantic salmon or Pacific steelhead. This may have something to do with the fact that all Pacific salmon die upon spawning. Or, it may be that they may not hold their bright sheen quite as long once they enter fresh water. Who knows? What I do know is that a big, bright northern coho blasting through the surface of a river with my fly in its jaw and cartwheeling a couple of times before coming back down to rip 50 yards of line from my reel is pretty heady stuff. In his fine volume, *The Well Tempered Angler*, 1959, Arnold Gingrich, founding father of *Esquire* magazine and a superb fly-fisher, wrote; "*And when I say salmon I include,*

A beautiful northern coho salmon landed in the Kasix River in northern British Columbia by Marty Leith. The coho was being revived for release by guide Dustin Kovacvich while Leith took the photo.

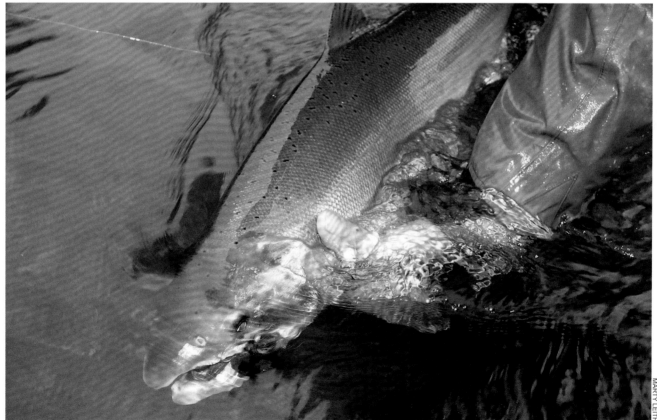

MARTY LEITH

Bob Young of Seattle was fishing the Situk River in Alaska when he connected with this fine coho. Bob changed shooting heads several times before he found the one that presented his fly at the right depth.

of course, grilse and sea trout, sea-run browns, brooks or salters and rainbows and steelhead, but excluding Pacific salmon, which as far as this form of fishing (fly-fishing) is concerned is something that comes in cans." This quote appeared in the first edition of *Fly Fishing for Pacific Salmon* and I believe that it is worth repeating twenty years later. Although I hold Arnold Gingrich in the highest regard as a brilliant angler, writer and editor, and have all of his books including his only work of fiction, *Cast Down the Laurel,* that particular statement of his was well off the mark in 1985. With all due respect to Mr. Gingrich, with the increased interest in fly-fishing for Pacific salmon we are enjoying today, his statement presently misses the entire target by a country mile.

Carol Ferrera used an intermediate sink-tip six-weight line and a size-8 Flashabou Comet to tempt this Stillaguamish River pink salmon on a foggy September morning. Small flies are usually superior to large, weighted patterns that tend to snag more fish than they fair hook.

The slow but steady change in attitude toward Pacific salmon is probably due in part, at least, to the fact that so many runs of Atlantic salmon and Pacific Coast steelhead have been clinging to tenuous survival under the protection of the Endangered Species Act. Pacific salmon have also suffered from overharvest and habitat degradation, which has pushed many strains onto their own list of threatened or endangered populations. Today many rivers are subjected to severely restricted bag limits, catch-and-release status or have been closed to all sport fishing for Pacific salmon.

In numerous West Coast rivers though, Pacific salmon are still around in healthy enough numbers to offer the fly-rodder a decent, and on some rivers, a very productive sport fishery. Certain populations that have been in decline are in fact, stabilizing. With more people in quest of fewer and fewer Atlantic salmon and west coast steelhead, fly-fishers who once viewed Pacific salmon with disdain have become enlightened to the fact that a chinook, coho, chum, pink or

This nice four-pound pink is about average for the Stillaguamish and other Puget Sound rivers. Further north in British Columbia pinks run considerably larger.

sockeye, fresh from the salt, can provide all the thrills of a steelhead—and that the odds of hooking several salmon during the season are a whole lot better than catching even half as many steelhead.

Finding the Salmon

Finding salmon in a river really isn't difficult but many anglers miss the best of fishing for salmon in fresh water since

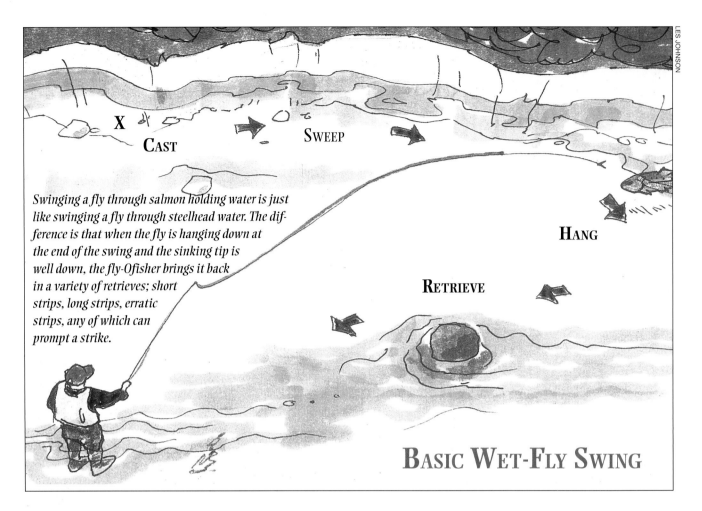

X
CAST
SWEEP

Swinging a fly through salmon holding water is just like swinging a fly through steelhead water. The difference is that when the fly is hanging down at the end of the swing and the sinking tip is well down, the fly-Ofisher brings it back in a variety of retrieves; short strips, long strips, erratic strips, any of which can prompt a strike.

HANG

RETRIEVE

BASIC WET-FLY SWING

they get pretty well stuck as to where they look for them. What most of us search for are salmon that have moved into the river recently and are still bright and strong, perhaps just showing the first blush of spawning color. Most salmon in excellent condition and full of vigor are found in the lower to middle reaches of the river. Further upstream, salmon that have arrived earlier are displaying spawning colors and feeling an urge in their loins to pair up and spawn. In the uppermost reaches of a river, males are more interested in fighting over the favor of a female resting on a redd than slugging it out against a heavy fly-rod.

The type of run that salmon are holding in; the condition of the salmon; and the species of salmon also have to be taken into consideration when casting to them. While Pacific salmon have essentially the same life cycle, each species has its differences. The angler who takes time to learn to present the right fly properly under all conditions to each of the five species of Pacific salmon is the one who will, over time bring the most salmon to hand.

One of the methods for effectively taking Pacific salmon "on the fly" is by using extremely heavy, lead-weighted flies. When these offerings are tossed in amongst a school of salmon, a "hookup" is almost ensured, all too often in the dorsal fin, flank or tail of the fish. Some anglers are happy with this method

and brag to no end at taking 10, 20 or 30 salmon in a day, most of which have been foul-hooked. It is indeed fishing with a fly-rod. Whether it is fly-fishing or not is open to question.

One foggy September morning on the lower Stillaguamish River below the town of Arlington, Washington, a run of fresh pink salmon was moving through a public recreation area called Blue Stilly Park. My wife Carol and I watched an angler who had waded across the river to join a couple of others who were using heavily weighted flies to snag one pink salmon after another from a spot where the fish were stacking up. His wife who couldn't wade across remained on our side respectfully upstream of us, catching nothing. Carol and I were using 6-weight fly-rods, floating lines with intermediate sinking tips and size-8 pearl pink Flashabou comet flies. We were away from the huge crowd of salmon, preferring to fish a run, about five feet deep, closer to our side of the river where we could see the pinks moving up through the tailout into the pool directly in front of us

We weren't "hooking" quite as many pinks as the guys across the river with the lead-embellished offerings, but we were doing just fine with all of our salmon hooked squarely in the jaw and providing a brisk fight against our light rods. At Carol's urging I walked up, introduced us and rigged the lady's leader with one of our flies. Then I invited her to move closer to where we were fishing so she could get a good cast over the pinks. She whooped with joy only moments later when she hooked her first pink salmon fair and square on a wet-fly swing. Upon catching her next pink salmon she exclaimed, loud enough for her husband to hear, "There's another one hooked right in the jaw." When her husband asked her if she needed any help she answered, "That's okay. Les and Carol are helping me." She then continued casting and before long she was hooked up again. We had made a convert.

Using a fly-rod to purposely foul-hook salmon after salmon as a measure of fly-fishing success is not a method that will be discussed in this chapter. Most of the time, all Pacific salmon can be taken fairly on a cast fly, with snagging kept to an absolute minimum, and always unintentional. Learn the casting techniques and under the right situation in which to apply them and you will take most of your salmon fairly hooked on a proper fly, minimally weighted or with no added weight that is worthy of a place in your fly box.

The Wet-Fly Swing

The wet-fly swing is the cornerstone of all our wet-fly fishing techniques for trout, steelhead or salmon. It is the same cast that I employed to hook my first chinook salmon many years ago in the Quillayute River on Washington's Olympic Peninsula. The importance of mastering this cast cannot be too strongly stated. The successful salmon angler will use the wet-fly swing as the basis for many angling situations. This basic cast can be easily modified, depending on current speed and water depth to put one's fly in front of the salmon wherever they are holding in a pool. The classic wet-fly swing is made by casting across and slightly downstream, followed by an upstream mend of the line and then tracking the fly through its arc with the rod tip. When the swing has slowed and the fly is hanging down in the lower end of the pool, a slow retrieve of the fly for several feet is usually employed. This additional movement of the fly can stir a salmon into grabbing. The wet-fly swing is the guts of the game in fishing salmon in rivers and it can be accomplished with a floating line, sinking tip or sinking shooting head depending upon the depth and speed of the river and mood of the salmon. And, there are going to be times when you will want to have all three types of lines on hand to meet various situations.

Atlantic salmon or steelhead sometimes rise willingly to a dry or damp fly that is riding on top, in the film or creating a wake on the surface. Pacific salmon are not as prone to rise (although we have discovered that coho and pink salmon will grab a floating or near-surface offering readily under the right conditions) so the most effective wet-fly presentation is to have your fly swinging in an arc, on a tight line, a few feet above the river floor. You want your fly to ride slightly above the eye level of the salmon. Like other fish, salmon look up, not down; hence a fly drifting below a fish is not likely to be seen and taken fairly but often becomes an inadvertent snagging lure.

With a concentration of salmon located, begin fishing upstream of their position whenever possible. If you have the opportunity, start at the very top of a run or pool and work downstream plying your fly over every inch all the way to the tailout. On a small river with relatively shallow holding pools, a 15-foot sinking tip of moderate sinking speed might be the right line. On a big river with very deep salmon pools and heavy current, an extra-fast-sinking 24-foot sink-tip or 30-foot sinking shooting head may be the answer.

If the water is clear, I like to begin with something like a small comet, spun marabou or a rabbit-strip fly in red, orange or black. When fishing a fairly heavy flow I combine a sink tip or shooting head of the right sinking speed and a leader of not more than four feet in length to keep my fly near the bottom.

From the top of a pool or run, begin with a short cast quartered down stream. Throw an upstream mend, and allow the fly to swing through the pool. Follow the line with a low rod tip to minimize slack and maintain contact with the fly for maximum feel, which is crucial, especially if you happen to be working through a pool full of finicky biters that may only alert you with the faintest tug on your fly. From your original position, lengthen each subsequent cast in two-foot increments, until you have worked out the longest length of line you can cast efficiently.

Begin moving downstream, one step at a time, after each two or three casts, continuing to use your longest comfortable cast. Always allow the fly to swing completely through the pool until it is riding directly below you and let it hang in the current for several seconds before retrieving it back slowly. Using this methodical approach, you will cover every inch of a pool—or in the case of a large, wide river—all of the water that you are able to reach when fishing from shore.

When your fly is swinging just right you will feel it ticking an occasional rock at the end of its arc through the pool. If you are not getting the fly down deeply enough, mend your line a second time as it swings downstream, to further slow its speed, so that it has additional time to sink. Controlling the speed of your fly line by mending it as needed during a cast, align your fly straight and true as it swings through the strike zone. Having the line pulling straight from the rod tip to the fly will give you the optimum contact with your fly so that you can detect even a light take.

If more than a couple of mends is not putting your fly down deeply enough, switching to a faster-sinking tip or shooting head is generally required. On the contrary, if you find your fly line hanging up or dragging, stop fishing and change to a slower sinking tip or shooting head. Sometimes a floating line with a long leader may be required.

Your first complete pass through the pool may not produce a salmon. This is not uncommon. When you have worked your way down through the pool, and if there is enough elbow

Carefully releasing a spent salmon is critical to its survival. The late Denny Hannah, one of the finest salmon guides on the southern Oregon coast, and a long-time friend of author Johnson, gently releases a chinook back into the Elk River.

room, go back to the top, change flies, and repeat the systematic, step-by-step sweep of the fly down through the pool. Getting a hookup may require several passes, even if the pool is chock-full of salmon. Utilizing a well-controlled wet-fly swing to probe every nook and cranny of the pool is the key to putting your fly in front of a salmon that is spoiling for a fight.

When you are sharing the water with other anglers, move down along a pool while fishing and then walk back to the top. This gives all anglers a chance to work their flies through the pool. It is a civilized way to fish.

Beginning at the top of a pool and working down to the bottom and then walking back to the top was at one time standard form on all Pacific Coast rivers, and is still alive and well along most Canadian rivers, particularly among fly-fishers. In recent years, on U.S. streams there is a tendency to stake out a spot and stick with it rather than move. There is also considerably less concern about crowding in on another angler than there was in years past. This is an example of the "all about me" generation, the result of our teaching some of the younger folks how to catch fish with a fly-rod but failing to include respect and principles in the lesson.

The Downstream Drift

A downstream, slack-line cast has always been a deadly method for sneaking a dry fly into a cagey trout's feeding lane—and it can be equally effective as a wet-fly presentation when salmon fishing—under low, clear water conditions when the salmon are hunkered down. Over the years I have found that using a downstream drift and letting the fly simply hang in the current right in front of a spooky salmon's nose is sometimes the only way to promote a strike. The downstream drift is a technique I have learned to count on when fishing over picky chinook salmon in low water situations. I first used it on salmon successfully more than twenty years ago while fishing just above tidewater on the Sixes River, a small, southern Oregon coastal stream noted for its big, late-run chinook salmon with Denny Hannah.

"We've got a good salmon spot coming up, Les," Denny noted, "but swirls form during low water that makes it tough to get a good swing with your fly."

As we rounded the bend I saw the swirling hole downstream of a large old water-polished cedar log that had become securely imbedded into the bank during a long past spring flood. The hole appeared to have enough depth and current to attract salmon but the exposed end of the log caused the slow moving water to bounce back upstream forming the pesky swirl where the fly should be presented.

"Pull in above the log and drop the anchor, Denny," I said. "I'll try casting short and just let a fly drift down along the log and hang in the hole to let the current move it around. We'll see what happens." Denny quickly had his drift boat set up above the hole, the anchor secured and the oars shipped. I stripped off a length of line and cast a number-8 comet-style pattern called a Rusty Squirrel toward the water just outside of the log and the swirl. I had planned to cast slightly outside of the swirl so the fly would be sucked down under the log toward the lower end where Denny figured the salmon to be holding. I overshot the cast slightly and when the fly hit the water the surface exploded like a depth charge going off but the fly wasn't taken.

I turned to Denny and nodded. He smiled and wiggled his red eyebrows up and down in response. My next cast was on the mark, hitting just upstream and outside of the log. I let the fly drift down into the hole like a tumbling nymph until all the slack was pulled out of the line. A salmon boiled just under the surface, below the fly but either refused it, or missed.

"Make that cast again and let the fly hang in there like you did before and maybe just twitch it a few times, Les," Denny advised. "That was a nice chinook and he might take again if your bug still aggravates him. But be sure to let him eat it. Don't take it away from him."

I made the cast and when it settled into the hole, twitched it a couple of times and after a moment the line began to slowly tighten. I could tell that the salmon had picked up the fly. Over my shoulder I could hear Denny whisper, *"Wait...wait...wait"*. I waited until the rod started to develop a distinct hoop, then slammed back hard to set the hook solidly. The salmon turned, thrashed to the surface and tore downstream. Then, rather than leave the pool, it turned toward the far bank and after fighting stubbornly for about 15 minutes, was brought to net. It was a fat chinook, shiny as a new dime and looked to be a solid 18 pounds. Denny removed the hook and gently pushed the salmon back and forth in the current until its silver sides began a slow, even breathing rhythm—and let it swim from his grasp. Two more Sixes River chinook fell to the downstream drift that day as we fished every spot deep enough to provide comfort for a salmon.

More recently I was fishing during the fall on a favorite stretch of the Sol Duc River that flows out of Olympic National Park. The Sol Duc was very low and clear and a school of chinook salmon was holding at the far side of a green pool under a rock overhang. Try as I might I couldn't get the fly close enough to provoke a strike. Time after time I would swim a fly past them but they were not about to leave the shelter of the sheer rock ledge

Finally, I walked upstream and waded across a shallow place in the riffle that fed the pool to reach the other side of the river. From this vantage point I was looking almost straight down along the rock overhang and could see the chinook stacked along the pool wall. I made a test cast to see where the current would pull my fly. The cast was too far out so I set out a second cast a bit closer to the overhang. As the fly swung into the shade I saw the flash of a chinook's flank that may have indicated a pass at my fly. I lengthened the line a bit and made the same cast. When nothing happened I lengthened the line a bit more. Still nothing after perhaps a dozen or more casts, each a bit further down the pool, I watched the fly disappear from sight.

When the line pulled the fly well under the overhang I almost immediately felt a gentle *tug..tug..tug*. Dropping the tip I slowly reeled the slack line onto the reel. As the tip began to nod down under tension I set the hook hard.

Talk about salmon going everywhere! My hooked salmon boiled onto the surface and at least thirty others swirled around the pool and jumped with several shooting noisily up the shallow riffle on my right into the next run throwing water in every direction. I kept the line tight and was thankful that the chinook was not intrigued with the prospect of heading downstream. It fought stubbornly but the hook held and within several minutes I slid a beautiful chinook of probably 20 pounds ashore.

Once the downstream drift is mastered—and it isn't a difficult cast—even a light take of the fly can usually be detected. The take is not, however always the same. As the fly line tightens and the fly begins to undulate slowly, a salmon may move up, grab it then swing back into its holding position. If most of the slack is out of the fly line, the signal is a gentle *tug-tug-tug*.

If the line still has some slack and the fly is drifting when it is taken, there will be a tightening, or distinct drag on the line, not unlike a trout taking a nymph. Don't panic at this moment because striking too quickly is apt to pull the fly out of the salmon's mouth. A salmon will usually hold the fly in its mouth as it returns to its station. At this moment you simply lower the rod tip and take all the slack out of the fly line before reefing back to set the hook.

If the planets should happen to align, the slack will have cleared and the line will be tight so that the salmon will take the fly with one helluva yank that sets the hook and joins the contest in one euphoric instant.

Although the downstream drift is often most easily accomplished from a boat, it is also a good technique for the bank angler to employ in some situations. When your only option is to fish from the deep side of a river with the salmon holding in water right against the bank where you are standing, it is sometimes the only viable cast.

When you are in a position where casting room is very confined, simply roll cast and shake out a length of slack line in a series of lazy, serpentine bends. This is an invaluable technique when using the downstream drift to present a fly to salmon that are holding in a place that doesn't allow you room for a back cast.

The Downstream Cast and Retrieve

A unique method of utilizing the downstream cast and retrieve is employed by fishing from a pram tied to a hawser that has been stretched across the river. With the pram secured to the hawser, called a "hog line" with a slip knot, the angler casts directly downstream into an estuary hole or tide pool, and then slowly inches the fly back just above the bottom, through a school of salmon. This method was developed in the 1950s by California anglers belonging to members of San Francisco and Monterey area fishing clubs who utilized it on the tide pools of the Smith and Eel rivers.

As the Smith and Eel became increasingly popular, the California salmon fly-casters soon migrated across the border into Oregon where they joined Oregon anglers who line up for salmon bank-to-bank on the Chetco River just upstream of the Highway 101 bridge near the town of Brookings. Standing in their prams (most of which are tricked out with everything but a portable chemical toilet), anglers anchor up, or in some places tie up, to a hog line that has been stretched across the river at the top of productive salmon holes. Employing fast-sinking shooting tapers of Deep Water Express, T-14 or LC-13 to make long, downstream casts, they then let their flies sink deep before beginning a slow retrieve back through the pool. When an angler hooks up, the anchor is raised or the tether rope is released, allowing the pram to drift clear of other anglers' lines while the fish is being fought. I've seen some big chinook salmon taken by this method. I've also seen prams drifting a long, long way downstream before the outcome was decided. Since hog-line fishing is most often a

A big chum salmon hit Mark Mandell's swinging tube fly in the wintry waters of Washington's North Fork Stillaguamish River. Mark was using a 10-foot, 8-weight rod to handle the hard-running chum.

one-person operation, fighting a big chinook salmon and bringing it to net from an 8-foot pram can be a pretty good trick.

On a smaller stream an angler can often wade out near midstream in a pool and utilize the downstream cast and retrieve. When the fall chinook show up in the little Naselle River in southwest Washington this is a technique that has served me well on many occasions. One spot that rarely fails me is coincidently called the "Johnson Hole".

I use a slow-sinking line in the soft current and low water, wading out nearly to the center of the Naselle to make a long downstream cast mended toward the far bank. When the line settles and straightens below my position as the current pulls downstream I begin my retrieve.

Sometimes the Johnson Hole fails me but if the salmon are there I am usually rewarded with a hard take on a slow, erratic retrieve. If the chinook is 20 pounds or smaller I can usually handle it with an 8-weight outfit. A big chinook though, and there are some brutes in the Naselle, can end the battle in short order on tackle too light.

There are hundreds of salmon pools throughout our smaller coastal streams from northern California to Alaska. In any one of them the downstream cast and retrieve can be used to advantage.

Short Lining

If I am unable to fish from the side of a river where I can work a wet-fly swing, fishing from the deep side of the run is called for. Working the deep side of a salmon hole, where the holding slot is tight against the bank, often requires roll casting and feeding out line in order to put the fly down into the depths or in under a cut bank. The method is called short lining. In this situation, shaky footing can cause a misstep and will take you from knee-deep to over your head into a situation that can get you soaked at best and drowned at worst. Ensuring that I've taken the steadiest possible position, I make a roll cast slightly upstream, make a big mend and feed out slack. As the head drifts downstream, straightening and sinking to fishing depth I lower the tip and begin a slow retrieve. This method swings the fly right in against the bank where you hope there are some salmon holding.

Some years ago Mark Mandell of Port Townsend and I spent a week on Prince of Wales Island fishing for coho salmon in Clarence Straight, Thorne Bay and in the Thorne River. It was the day after Mark had shown our host Sid Cook how to take feeding coho salmon from eighty feet straight down in the salty depths of Clarence Straight near Shipwreck Island with a super-fast sinking head and one of his Calamarko tube flies.

An overnight rain had urged most of the coho in Thorne Bay a mile up the Thorne River where Sid figured we should go. Sid's usual spots could not be reached due to the raised river level so we got back into his van and drove another half-mile upstream to try a place where Sid noted that we could fish from the deep side.

As we neared the bank of the rain-swollen Thorne through the high, wet grass Sid was saying, "Watch out along here as you never know when you might go through into a backwater slough that has been covered by the grass." And that is exactly what he did, his left leg went hip-deep into a short, narrow slough that was camouflaged by the rain-beaten grass. We pulled him out little the worse for wear, letting him know what a great guide he was for demonstrating what we shouldn't do.

I poked along carefully with my wading staff the final ten yards to the river, located solid footing and tied a hot red spun marabou streamer onto a 5-foot leader. My roll cast set the fly out a short distance into the Thorne. I made a hard mend as it pulled downstream and sank. The line had no sooner tightened and swung in under the cut bank when I found myself eyeball-to-eyeball with a big, bright coho salmon that sailed a full five feet out of the river with my marabou streamer stuck in its nose. It was a big, hot salmon that ripped a good 30 yards of line from my reel before I could turn it back upstream. Eventually I worked it in close where Sid had found a spot to kneel down and net it without doing a header into the river. It was a handsome male of about 15 pounds.

We fished for a couple of hours making our herky-jerky roll casts over the high grass; casts that worked a whole lot better than they looked on style points. After catching several coho with this method we headed back to Sid's Deer Creek Cottage where we were staying. We had four nice fish on ice for the trip home.

Interception Cast and Retrieve

I have spent many an autumn day beating paths through estuary marshes and bushwhacking to reach backwaters and sloughs in the lower reaches of Pacific coastal rivers during fall salmon runs. It was my passion as a young man when I fished the Satsop and lower Wynoochie rivers near Aberdeen, Washington every fall for big coho salmon.

I look for salmon that have entered calm side channels and back eddies on their way upstream. Slack-water sloughs, or even quite, primary river pools during low, clear water are often passed over by anglers working the spots more commonly known to be productive and easier to reach.

Settling into quiet waters for a time before moving upstream is a trait demonstrated by nearly all Pacific salmon that return early in the run, when they are still weeks away from spawning. These salmon usually range from silver to slightly rosy along the flanks and are robust and full of vigor.

When holding up in these slow, deep places—perhaps because of the quiescence of the water—salmon, particularly coho, often become quite active, at times clearly visible, creating torpedo-like wakes as they move about just beneath the surface. Watching pairs and small schools of coho salmon swimming along, creating wakes is pretty exhilarating stuff.

Mark Mandell displays the testy chum before releasing it.

This is similar to the behavior we sometimes witness when salmon gather in the estuary of a river before pushing on into the tide pools.

Oftentimes, the toughest part of fishing over these productive slack-water environs is locating a decent position from which to cast. Backwaters and sloughs along coastal rivers can be banded with thickets of willows intermingled with tangles of berry vines, and sometimes barriers of devil's club. These are places that test the stoutest multi-layered leg fronts of the best breathable waders and quickly reduce the bargain basement variety to tatters. The reward however is sometimes worth the gamble of ventilating one's waders in order to stake out a spot from which to exercise even an abbreviated backcast. At other times, you may be fortunate enough to find a beautiful, clear pool with ample back casting room that is filled with active salmon.

A long-time friend, Bob Young, and I stumbled onto such a situation one recent October on a small coastal Washington river. We got into our waders, strung our rods and struck out down the trail bordered with evergreen vines and willows. The day was sunny and warm. Yellow leaves falling from tall alders were grabbed by the gentle breeze and scattered along

Working a very deep, slow salmon pool requires a sinking tip or head and a floating running line. The cast is made at least 45 degrees downstream. This will get the fly well down into the pool but will not hang up on rocks as readily as a full-sinking line. Retrieve is just like the standard wet-fly swing.

CASTING TO SCHOOLS IN A DEEP POOL

the ground. Due to a prolonged period of low water, there was just one angler on this particular pool and he was leaving as we arrived. He shrugged as he went by but said nothing.

The pool was low and crystal clear and nearly still except for the patchwork quilt of surface wakes stirred up by a school of frisky coho salmon or a big swirl near the tailout. We had planned to try for late-season summer steelhead. Then a handsome 10-pound coho cleared the surface, displaying its big shoulders and slightly bronze flanks.

With these coho around and feeling so lively, the steelhead have all probably been run off into the riffles to hide out," I said to Bob. "Coho dominate steelhead when they are parr-size and they dominate them at maturity."

"Maybe we can hook a couple of coho," Bob replied. "What do they like?"

"When they are active like this, something small and sparse, retrieved just under the surface on a floating line will sometimes tempt them. And, I may have just the fly." I dug into my vest and pulled out a box of summer steelhead flies. "Here we go, a couple of Silver Browns, a pattern designed by Roderick Haig-Brown many years ago just for situations like this. He wrote that it works on sea-run cutthroat, steelhead and salmon. Try one. Use a floating line, cast ahead of moving fish and strip it across their bow."

Bob accepted the number-8 Silver Brown and waded across the tailout of the pool, scattering several coho. Once

in position he tied the Silver Brown onto his leader and began casting. The salmon were swimming and rolling everywhere making it difficult to direct a cast that would intercept a fish. After watching for a minute, Bob repositioned himself behind a sunken log and made a short cast out over it. Before I could get my leader lengthened and my fly tied on, Bob whooped.

"Got one," he chortled, his rod was bent over and his old Medalist reel wheezing as the coho ripped off across the pool. "He took it just like a trout but is pulling a whole lot harder."

Bob played the coho into the shallows where he hand tailed it. It was a muscular, male of about eight pounds, showing color but still firm and strong. In typical coho fashion, it had twisted and turned during the fight, hitching several loops of leader around its nose. Bob worked out the barbless hook and held the coho gently, moving it back and forth in the cool flow. Within a couple of minutes it was breathing evenly and slipped free of Bob's gentle grip quickly disappearing into the jade green depths of the pool. A short time later I hooked up with a coho, a bit smaller than Bob's but equally feisty. The battle was brief and spirited. Within a few minutes I revived and released a firm, six-pound hen. It was a great way to start off the day. We then departed the pool to leave the salmon alone and hiked off upstream to find a steelhead or two.

The interception cast and retrieve is simple, accomplished most often with a floating line, long leader and almost always, a small, sparse fly. Over the years I have seen salmon take the fly pulled across its nose then continue straight ahead before realizing that it is hooked. I have watched a single salmon turn from a small pod to grab a swimming fly, then turn again to rejoin its pals before the hook has fully tightened into the corner of its jaw.

Whenever I am working a river for salmon it is more often than not with a shooting head system. I always have a selection of small, sparsely dressed flies on hand for such situations as Bob and I experienced. I also carry a spare spool with a floating line along. When coho are grabbing flies stripped along the surface it is a refreshing change from casting and retrieving a deeply sunken line through the depths of a salmon pool.

Casting to Schools In a Deep Pool

During the fall we often find schools of salmon holding up in deep pools that have a rather modest current. This is particularly common with pink salmon prior to their impending love-in that will take place further upstream on the spawning gravel. Anglers often surround these pools casting everything from heavily weighted spoons and yarn-draped buoyant lures to flies of every description. Salmon are routinely snagged in these situations when they stack up.

They can all however be taken on the fly by working it with an integrated head or shooting head. A small Comet,

Hubert Humpy, Horner Shrimp or even a saltwater krill pattern like the FJ Pink will provoke strikes. It is a simple game. Using a line of the right sinking rate, cast in any direction where you have room to set out your line. Allow the fly to sink well down into the pool and begin a retrieve of 6-inch pulls. Strikes can come anywhere during the retrieve.

The Milling Salmon Tangent Cast

The first time I witnessed chinook salmon milling in a pool was one fall day on the Quillayute River many years ago. At the time I was unfamiliar with the phenomenon and really did not know what I was witnessing. That day I accidentally experienced a short, violent hookup with a big chinook that I cast to casually with my little 7-foot Phillipson fiberglass 5-weight and hooked it. The short fierce struggle was no contest.

I have since seen chinook salmon milling around in pools of coastal rivers from California to Washington. These elongated routes can take place in the short space of 20 feet, or from the head to the tailout of a long pool. Salmon fly-fishers have learned that salmon exhibiting this behavior will strike a fly quite readily. The trick is to present the fly the way the salmon want it. The technique for goading milling salmon was told to me by an old friend, writer and gifted fly-fisher, the late Mike Fong of San Francisco, California.

LES JOHNSON

There are times when salmon mill in a pool turning at various points along the route. They will most often strike a fly when it forms a tangent with their turning point. It is a tricky but productive technique developed by the late Mike Fong of San Francisco, California.

MILLING SALMON

This milling activity was once thought to be a low-water trait. It may be, however that we are only able to observe the phenomenon when the water is reasonably low and clear. In any event, After a lot of observation and endless casting, Mike noticed that when salmon are milling, they will strike a fly just as they turn but rarely while swimming on the straightway. This gives the angler several spots along each milling route when the salmon are prone to strike, so regardless of the configuration of the pool, there is almost always going to be a vantage point from which to place an effective cast.

Prompting a milling salmon to strike requires accurate casting so that as the fly swings through the current, its arc forms a tangent with the turning arc of the salmon. Since salmon usually mill in a loose formation of singles, pairs and groups of up to six or more along their route, the more casts that can be placed across the turning radii of the fish, the better the odds of hooking up. Ideally, to get a strike, the fly has to be traveling at the same depth, or a bit shallower than the milling salmon are swimming. A salmon will, at times, move up to take a fly when milling but will almost never move deeper. You have to experiment with the angle of your cast and mend it to adjust the depth of the fly. If controlling your cast doesn't get your fly lined up with the salmon, change to a faster or slower sinking line. When you figure out the right combination of line sink rate and casting angle, the take of a milling salmon will usually be for it to simply take the fly softly on the turn and continue swimming along. As the line tightens the fly will be drawn into the corner of the salmon's mouth where it can be solidly set.

Fishing the Surface Fly

There are times when salmon, most notably coho, will take a fly that is creating a disturbance on the surface. This unique angling opportunity usually occurs just above the estuary where the salmon, just moved in from the salt, are actively cruising over a fairly shallow bottom. The technique of fishing a surface-disturbing fly is quite simple. The offering is cast out and retrieved in an erratic manner that causes it to form a groove in the surface when stripped with steady pulls to create a very slight wake as it comes back to you. You don't need a lot of commotion to make this technique work. Since the water is shallow a surface fly is easily seen and heard by the salmon. Interested salmon will swirl around this strange, noisy creature and eventually one will grab it, usually with a startling and explosive take. This method of fly-fishing has been practiced for several years on the Pacific Coast in fresh, estuarine and salt water.

I have had the good fortune to coax coho and cutthroat to the surface on a Miyawaki Popper in salt water around Puget Sound and along the beaches of Vancouver Island for several years thanks primarily to fishing with my friend, Leland Miyawaki. My first coho in fresh water though came to a Bulkley

Mouse that I was skating across a low, clear pool on the Skykomish River downstream from the hamlet of Sultan.

There were a lot of coho present and I'd hooked a couple on a wet-fly swing before putting my fly in the hook keeper to sit back and watch the action which was pretty brisk. Most of the salmon were in the middle or head of the pool but the fish moving around the shallower tailout weren't getting much attention, probably because there were fewer numbers of them and they were more difficult for the conventional tackle fishermen to address with spoons, spinners or Corkies. I decided to give them a try on the surface where the current picked up before flowing into a long riffle. I changed to my floating line and tied on a Bulkley Mouse. It is a pattern that has been a favorite of mine since I was introduced to it by Canadian guide Andre La Porte years ago on the Bulkley River near Telkwa, British Columbia.

I tied on a black Bulkley Mouse, dressed it and began casting it above the tailout and letting it swing rapidly on a downstream mended line. I don't believe that I made more than three or four casts before a coho got interested; swirling under the Mouse that was pushing a miniature Tsunami as it swept across the current. Within a few more casts the little Mouse was absolutely pasted by a big, red-sided buck coho that instantly tightened my line and departed over the tailout for the next pool downstream. Needless to say, the coho and the Bulkley Mouse were both gone in an explosive leap.

Since that day I've coaxed up chum and pink salmon in addition to coho. Using any of the surface poppers listed in the fly chapter of this book, or one of your own design is a worthwhile effort and a whole lot of fun.

At times salmon will smack a surface fly as it swings and at others will take it on a slow retrieve at the end of the swing. That is about all there is to fishing a surface fly. It is an uncomplicated method.

All of the basic casts and retrieves detailed in this chapter—or some variation of them—will work on any West Coast salmon stream from the Kenai in Alaska to the Russian in California. To make them work it is vital that we learn to handle our tackle well and understand the intricacies and dynamics of the streams we fish. Our purpose is to present a pattern to the salmon at the right depth, speed and angle. Executing these basic casts and retrieves competently is the first step to productive salmon fly-fishing on Pacific Coast rivers. After a while, learning when to employ the right cast will become almost instinctive.

Salmon Traits in Fresh Water

Upon arriving in fresh water, salmon provide us with signals or clues such as jumping, rolling or milling in a pool. These signals, when correctly deciphered, are helpful in determining just exactly how we should present our fly to them. For instance, during fluctuating water levels caused by rain, or some-

LES JOHNSON

The Bulkley Mouse is a relatively little-known surface fly invented for steelhead. It also works very well for coho, pink and chum salmon. Just a pile of deer hair with a large head on a size-8 hook, but it makes a big commotion on the surface.

times drought, salmon are predictable in their movements upstream, allowing us to calculate where we should be stationed from one day to the next for the best opportunity to intercept them.

Rolling and Jumping Salmon

The most important aspect of seeing salmon rolling or jumping in a pool is that we know for certain that they are present. Salmon will invariable show themselves in this manner anywhere from tide pools to spawning gravel. If fish are jumping all over a pool, it is a near certainty that they are present in significant numbers. This always enhances our chances of getting a few hookups. When salmon get crowded together, they become territorial and tend to strike more readily. If only a few salmon are showing, or are showing in a localized spot in a pool, it is most likely a small pod of fish holding almost directly under the area where they are jumping. In either case, the salmon are more prone to take a fly fished deep than one aimed at the surface activity.

Whether you are fortunate enough to have located a motherlode of salmon, or even just a few, pay close attention to the activity for a while. When you have the movement of the salmon scoped out, put on the right sink-tip or head and your fly of choice, then use any of the casts appropriate for the water conditions, pool configuration and the temperament of the fish. By first planning your attack you will have a much better chance of hooking a salmon.

The Individual Salmon

There are times when we'll happen upon a lone salmon, usually a chinook or coho and sometimes an exceptionally large one, that is holding away from the rest of the school. This one-on-one challenge is too much to pass up for most of us, but it can be very tough to get a big, loner to grab the fly. First and foremost, study the water carefully, figuring out the current before ever making a cast. Tossing a splashy, random cast at a big, solitary salmon may only serve to anger it into a state of lockjaw or send it swimming away.

If you can employ it, the downstream swing is the best method for presenting your fly to a large, lone salmon. If your first cast or two doesn't annoy the salmon, causing it move away from your fly, the odds for getting it to strike improve considerably. Large, weighted flies used in this situation often snag a lone salmon as readily as hook it. For this reason a small fly lightly weighted with small bead chain, or without additional weight, presented on a short leader, is generally a better bet for a fair hookup. If a bright fly isn't the answer, change to a somber pattern. If the wet-fly swing alone won't bring a grab, combine it with a retrieve back across the big guy's nose. If the salmon gets aggravated, fins flared, the strike is more than likely imminent. And, when the salmon takes, even if it should break you off in a single surge, the effort has been worthwhile.

An important qualifier to working an individual salmon is when the fish has become red-flanked and hook-jawed, is very near spawning and holding in the gravel riffles in the upper reaches of a river. Near-spawning male salmon become extremely territorial and will strike savagely at almost any intruding fly or lure, particularly when females are in the area digging out redds. The glory of making several hookups in short order is offset by the fact that these fish are very near completion of their life cycle, drawing on remnant reserves of strength and are better left alone.

Salmon Movement By Tide
and Water Level Fluctuation

When working the lower reaches of a small to medium size river, specifically the tide pools and the first few lies upstream of tidal influence, an up-to-date tide book of the local area is every bit as important as a good rod and reel. It will tell you the time and height of the tide which in turn tells you what time to be at the river.

Fishing estuary and tide pools of small rivers is usually best when there has been a high tide the previous night, allowing schools of salmon to move in from the salt water under cover of darkness. They will be found hunkered down in the estuary and tide pools at low tide the following morning awaiting the next incoming tide. Fishing is most productive from the top of the tide until the low turn. When the tide begins to rise again, salmon begin moving upstream and the bite usually falls off quickly. The high-tide-at-night rule applies accurately only during periods of low to normal flow and is most reliable in small streams.

On larger rivers there is often sufficient water volume and depth, even at low tide, to allow salmon to move through the estuary. The best fishing will still occur when the tide begins to fall due to the salmon's natural tendency to hold up and settle into the deepest reaches of a tidal pool when the incoming tide peaks and begins to run out. When substantial rains hit West Coast rivers, the increased water volume and turbidity allows salmon to enter estuaries and tide pools any time of the day or night.

During such periods, salmon can make undetected runs for the pools above tidal influence where the water is not as roily. As the water drops, experienced fly-fishers head for these upriver places, knowing that the salmon are often stacked up and ready to bite. If the water is high enough to knock the river out of fishing condition, the only recourse is to wait until the water drops and clears and then search for salmon from mid-river downstream to the tidal pools.

Fish On! Playing a Salmon

Anyone who has been accustomed to playing trout, bass and panfish on fly tackle will quickly discover that life with an energetic adult salmon on the other end one's line is a completely different experience. A fresh-run salmon, at full strength and aware of every snag in the river, is a formidable adversary. The savvy a salmon displays for utilizing the current combined with its tenacious lust for freedom gives you all the ingredients for epic, tackle-testing struggles that often end in favor of the salmon. This is a game where attention to leader knots, backing loops and drag tension is critical. Handling a large salmon in a river is also a game of patience. A mature salmon, be it chinook, chum or coho, can only be beaten with steady rod pressure, time and patience. Attempting to force a salmon quickly to net will invariably result in a break off, if not a broken rod. Even when playing a precocious jack of 16 inches to 5 pounds, a heavy hand can cause the hook to pull out or a knot to fail when the fish gains a tight purchase on your leader tippet.

Salmon are often hooked around down-timber, sweeper logs and sunken root wads. A hooked salmon will instinctively attempt to crochet your line through these submerged snarls in order to gain leverage and break free. Pulling against a salmon that is driving into such cover usually results in a broken leader or hook pullout. You pull away from the snag and the salmon will pull toward the snag. It is better to move to another position so that you will apply pressure toward the snag, so that your salmon will pull away, which gives you a much better chance of landing it.

Art Lingren with a Dean River chinook salmon that took his black fly when he was swinging for steelhead with his two-handed rod.

There is an old bugaboo about not allowing a salmon to get any slack line in the belief that it can throw the hook more easily. This usually applies more to conventional tackle fishing with heavy spoons and plugs swinging back and forth on a leader than it does to fly-fishing. A fly, even a weighted one, being very light compared to a spoon or plug, is difficult for a salmon to throw on a slack line. For this reason you should drop the rod tip slightly whenever a big salmon makes a head-shaking jump to put a bit of slack in your line. When the salmon falls back into the water, immediately bring the rod tip up and take a turn or two on the reel to regain maximum rod pressure.

Another use of a slack line is when a salmon is downstream and you cannot get it turned around. Feeding out several yards of slack will cause the line to loop into the current below the salmon creating pressure against the salmon's jaw from downstream. This will sometimes cause the fish to take off upstream toward you. It doesn't always work but when it does, be prepared to reel fast to regain all the line you can.

Chinook

These big guys have to be treated with respect and fought with patience and a no-holds-barred attitude. If allowed to sulk in one spot, or fin sideways in the current, you can count on a long, drawn-out battle with a large chinook and odds are, it will end with the fish winning its freedom. Campfire lore is rich in stories about enormous chinook salmon from the Smith, Rogue, Hoh or Skeena rivers that were played for five or six hours before reaching down for one last surge of energy and breaking off. While chinook salmon can reach Herculean dimensions and possess extraordinary strength, the outcome of a battle should never carry on for several hours.

When a stubborn chinook salmon is sulking downstream from the angler's position, using the current to its advantage, it can be almost impossible to budge the critter, even with a 10-, 11- or 12-weight rod. If feeding slack doesn't work and the terrain allows, the angler should attempt to gain a position downstream of the salmon, all the while maintaining rod pressure. Usually, when firm rod pressure is applied from a downstream position, a chinook will most often respond with an upstream run, forced to fight both rod pressure and current. This will usually wear the salmon down, except in the case of a behemoth possessing incredible strength. Many a large chinook salmon has reduced even the most stouthearted angler to tears by simply driving off upstream, steadily pulling out backing until it hits the arbor knot, stretches the line bow-string tight, then snaps the leader with a final powerful surge of its tail.

If a big chinook salmon cannot be coerced into heading upstream, it can sometimes be aggravated enough to move—in one direction or another—by thumping on the rod grip several times. If this fails, a last resort is to throw a couple of large rocks in the direction of the salmon to startle it into moving. A word of caution is in order if one decides to initiate this ploy; a well-placed rock may panic a big fish into an uncontrollable, reel-screaming run that results in a break

A chum salmon shown here in full spawning colors with sunlight glinting from its spawning teeth is pound-for-pound as tough a fighter as exists in the Pacific or Atlantic Ocean; a knock-down, drag-out slugger with no quit. This Skagit River chum gave Mike Kinney's two-handed rod a workout before coming to hand. The chum salmon is deserving of the title, 'last great junkyard dog.'

LES JOHNSON

off. Secondly, if a companion angler is assigned the chore of chucking a hunk of streamside granite at the sulking chinook and does not merely drop it near the fish but directly onto the line or leader, the response from the muscle-tight angler when his line goes limp is probably not going to be in the form of a heartfelt thank you.

It is very important to have stout enough equipment when handling big chinook salmon. True, a chinook of 25 or 30 pounds *can* be landed on a 7- or 8-weight outfit, but the battle is often so long and laborious that the salmon cannot be revived if your intentions are to release it. It is better to use a 10-weight, or heavier when fishing rivers known to host extremely large chinook. The battle will be equally spirited and the fish can be landed faster with a better chance of releasing it alive.

When the battle with a chinook salmon nears the end, the angler is arm-weary and tired and the salmon is leaning against a short line, nearly worn out but saving a tiny reserve of strength; it will still hold a few trump cards to draw upon if there should be a mere instant of error on the angler's part. A leader that has been stretched until is has no elasticity can be snapped by a hard shake of the salmon's head; the hook, having opened a hole in the salmon's jaw so that it does not have nearly the firm hold as when the clash began allows a seemingly innocuous move to let it come away. This is a critical time—a time when many trophy-size chinook salmon gain their freedom.

Chinook is considered by many to be the New York cut of salmon. Up to 20 pounds it can be steaked-out from behind the gill covers to the end of the rib cage and then filleted on each side from there to the tail. Salmon of 30 pounds and more can be steaked but the resulting steaks are usually cut in half to form a normal dinner portion.

Coho

Taken fairly, on the fly in fresh water a bright coho salmon will provide all the aerial acrobatics of a steelhead and can be every bit as tough to land. Averaging 8 to 12 pounds with exceptional fish hitting 20 pounds or more, the coho is made to order for the steelheader who wishes to extend the scope of a 7- or 8-weight fly rod or a two-handed rod to salmon fishing. A few coho in a pool can be pretty frustrating since they are sometimes difficult to provoke into a strike. When the pool is stacked, however it is a different story. Crowded coho become aggravated and will hit flies more readily than those with a lot of room to roam a pool. Also, a coho will not like to leave the pool when hooked. Once established in an upstream pool, a coho isn't inclined to go back downstream, preferring to make its fight on the spot. The caveat here is that a coho that has just moved up into the tailout of a pool and is hooked right there may very well turn and head back downstream like a runaway locomotive.

Baked, grilled or smoked, coho salmon are held in high esteem by anglers who like to put a few away for the smoker every season.

Chum

The chum salmon, at one time held in low regard, has finally earned respect as the last great junkyard dog. An aggressive biter in fresh water and the fastest swimmer of all the salmon, the chum will pull harder than any coho and pound-for-pound will give you a tougher battle than a prime chinook. The chum salmon is losing its silvery sheen before it ever reaches fresh water, displaying the lavender, green and red coat that accounts for one of its nicknames, calico salmon.

Regardless of its color, the chum retains astonishing strength and stamina right up until it is on the spawning gravel. Male chum salmon also develop some serious teeth near spawning time, one of the reasons that they are also known as dog salmon. Veteran chum salmon river anglers often employ 9- or 10-weight rods and many go with powerful two-handed outfits up to 15 feet long on large rivers like the Skagit in Washington or the Harrison, a major tributary of the Fraser River in British Columbia. Run timing for chum salmon varies greatly from one river to the next. They arrive in July in British Columbia rivers.

In Washington chum salmon enter some South Puget Sound rivers shortly after Labor Day, while in other rivers they arrive after Thanksgiving. The wild chum salmon that enter the Nisqually River in South Puget Sound arrive silvery bright with only the faintest hint of color on their sides; and they sometimes don't show up until Christmastime.

Chum salmon crowd together in favorite holes, sometimes so thick that it is nearly impossible to avoid snagging them from time to time. You can keep away from most snagging problems with chum salmon by staying around the edges of large schools rather than casting your fly right into the middle of the melee.

Chum salmon are not popular on the barbeque by most folks. It is however a great fish for the smoker. And, it arrives late in the season, with good runs arriving just before Thanksgiving in Washington and Oregon; just in time to be smoked and served as a holiday treat.

Sockeye

The sockeye, as a freshwater fly-rod adversary, is one very tough customer known for slashing strikes, high leaps and finding your backing knot with stunning speed. It has been fished in several Alaska rivers for a good many years, mostly by local anglers. More recently the sockeye has attracted concentrated attention from British Columbia fly-fishers on the Frazer River system. Friends of ours, Cliff Olson, Don McDermid and Peter Caverhill have developed techniques to

Riverkeeper and tackle designer, Mike Kinney was using one of his custom-made shooting heads to hook up this Skagit River salmon on a two-handed rod.

tempt this most elusive of Pacific salmon with steadily improving results.

Bruce Ferguson and I were hosted by Cliff Olson for a trip on the Fraser River near Chilliwack. Cliff took us to a spot he called "the braids" where several shallow channels made it possible to work the vast Fraser as if it were a much smaller river.

"In this water we'll see the occasional sockeye jump but most of the jumpers will be pinks," Cliff advised. He then handed us each a couple of size-8 flies from his box filled with small handlebar, pink cigar and other bright patterns much like we use on the beaches.

"I haven't named it yet but I'm sure that it will work," Cliff said. "Use about an 8-pound-test leader with a swing and strip action. With this shallow water an intermediate sinking line will be the best bet. On higher water we use faster sinking lines."

The sockeye were a bit picky on this particular day, but the pinks couldn't stay away from Cliff's new fly. We all caught several pinks; and then it happened.

I made a nice long reach cast with the intermediate line and began following the fly with my rod tip. The grab was a vicious yank that took my slack and set my reel to wailing all at once.

"Sockeye!" Cliff exclaimed. "And it's a good one."

It was a good one alright that was taking backing with no apparent sign of stopping and boosted by the Fraser's significant flow, going as fast as any salmon I'd ever hooked. My 7-weight rod suddenly seemed too light for the job as it took on a deep, throbbing hoop. I followed the silver torpedo downstream for a hundred yards or more and was beginning to regain line when the fish jumped, turned and set off downstream again. Only this time it had pulled the hook free.

This is a fishery that I plan on doing more of in the next few seasons. The sockeye could well become my favorite salmon on a fly, especially when taken low in a river system when they are still bright with their rockets fully loaded. I've been told that the fishing is great during catch-and-release season, but can be extremely crowded when the run size is determined to be large enough for the retention of sockeye, highly favored for its rich, red flesh.

Pink

Small in size, but an aggressive biter and stubborn fighter, the pink, or humpback, salmon (also called humpy and pinkie) has become an increasingly important player in the Pacific salmon angling mix during the past few years. The reason being, pink salmon populations are still quite healthy throughout its range from Alaska to northern Washington.

Anglers still utilize hog lines, like this one on the Chetco River in southern Oregon, to spread out across a wide expanse of water in order to reach productive salmon lies. The method allows the anglers to cast downstream and retrieve their flies back through a productive salmon hole.

Pinks deteriorate quickly in fresh water, hence are best fished in the tidal and lower reaches of their natal rivers when they are still silver-sided or just beginning to take on a gray coloration. Fly-anglers who have taken pink salmon to heart, fish for the spunky little gamesters with fast-action, 5- and 6-weight trout outfits. The pink is the only salmon that, at maturity, can honestly be called a light-tackle opponent. And on your light gear, the pink salmon becomes a real handful. All standard freshwater salmon fishing techniques work for the pink salmon.

Although the pink salmon is not considered great table fare due to its mild flavor and light-colored flesh, it is outstanding when smoked. During a pink year we always keep several to be smoked for the holiday hors d'oeuvres table.

Netting a Salmon

Any salmon up to about fifteen pounds can be beached by leading it into the shallows then backing up to the beach, with the rod tip low and line tight while the salmon kicks its way out of the water. Larger salmon can be landed in a similar manner if a fishing partner is ready to grab the wrist of the fish's tail, giving it an additional boost onto the gravel. For a very large chinook salmon your trump card is a big landing net with a deep bag.

When a salmon is tired enough to be lead, it should be brought to net head-first with the net handler holding the net at a 45-degree angle in the water *downstream from the fish*. When the salmon's head and shoulders are over the net hoop, the angler releases rod pressure allowing the salmon to dive, head-first into the bag. At this time the net handler raises the net handle straight up to secure the catch.

Releasing a Salmon

If you are planning on releasing a salmon, it should be kept cradled in the water—in the net—while the hook is removed and its physical condition evaluated. Some salmon fight so hard and long that they are very near death upon netting and may not respond to revival techniques.

To revive a salmon for release, take it carefully from the net and cradle it upright, facing the current, with one hand supporting its belly and the other firmly grasping the wrist of the tail. Gently move the salmon back and forth, forcing water through its gills to replenish its oxygen supply. If a salmon is going to recover, it will regain voluntary gill action before very long. Within a few minutes, a revived salmon will swim from the angler's grasp and scoot out of sight into the sanctuary of deep water. If, after several minutes of revival effort, a salmon appears to have only a marginal chance to recover, or does not respond to resuscitation, it should be quickly dispatched (provided you are in a kill-fishery area) and noted on your anglers catch record card.

Final Thoughts on Angling Techniques

It would be easy to stretch a chapter on salmon angling—however laboriously—into a complete book. It doesn't seem necessary since most people reading *Fly Fishing for Pacific Salmon II* most likely have some knowledge of angling, and many are highly proficient. By building on that knowledge with the information contained here, most will be pretty well prepared to counter the stunts a salmon can perform. If a hooked salmon brings a few new wrinkles to the contest, so much the better; it can only add another element of excitement to the sport. Salmon fishing with a fly is tough and thrilling and full of surprises. This is how it should remain. Heaven forbid that we ever turn salmon fly-fishing into the next perfect science.

CHAPTER TEN

Flies for Pacific Salmon

By Les Johnson with Pat Trotter

During fifty-odd years of fly-fishing for Pacific salmon in fresh and salt water we have seen these beautiful beasts of the Pacific Ocean grab flies of just about every stripe at one time or another. This would lead one to believe that any fly can be used at any time with a good chance of hooking up a chinook, coho, chum, pink or sockeye salmon. Some of the time this is true, but not always.

When it comes to taking a fly, each of our five species of Pacific salmon can be the most exasperating creatures to ever swim in sea or stream. The aggravation of taunting a salmon into eating a fly goes back a long time, but, through the years, the frustration has gradually lessened due to the persistence of fly tiers up and down the Pacific Coast who have constantly refined existing patterns and developed new ones. Today we are blessed with an extensive assortment of fine offerings that will trigger a salmon to strike in fresh or salt water. It is far less of a crapshoot than it used to be.

Since our first book, *Fly Fishing for Pacific Salmon*, was published in 1985 we have witnessed an astonishing growth of fly-tying anglers who seek Pacific salmon. They have

Cecilia "Pudge" Kleinkauf is a well-known Alaska fly-fishing guide, owner of Women's Fly Fishing and an author who tied most of the Alaska flies in this chapter. She displays a hefty coho salmon taken from an Alaska river estuary. Teaching women to fly-fish, tie flies and enjoy the outdoors through her organization, 'Women's Fly Fishing', is a passion for which she has earned well-deserved acclaim.

Seattle fly-fisher Steve Rohrbach caught this 15-pound, late-season coho on one of his waiting-period patterns.

blended information gleaned from historical records dating back to the 1930s with present-day knowledge and personal observation to create flies that will work in wide-ranging water conditions to hook salmon in varying stages of physical condition or feeding attitude. This revitalization in the development of Pacific salmon flies is a continuance of the foundation created for us by the avant-garde tiers and fly-fishers many years ago. Much of it passed on either by the written word, an evening at the tying desk, conversations around a campfire or in the back booth of a favorite beer parlor. Tying flies for Pacific salmon has a great tradition, something that has not received a proper measure of acclaim outside of the

A comparison of fly to baitfish.

Pacific coast. Flies that have been designed to tempt Pacific salmon during this period of rebirth run the gamut in both style and taste. Inspired tiers of exceptional skill adorn hooks exquisitely with feathers, hair, fur and silk to create flies that not only catch salmon but are worthy of display in an elegant shadow box. On the other end of the spectrum there has been developed a rather large number of gaff-hook-sized monstrosities festooned with garish chenille bodies wrapped over lead-wire-covered hook shanks, fluorescent nylon wings and topped off with barbell eyes so heavy that the resulting flies would be most efficiently cast with a stout spinning rod. Within these extremes of highly crafted patterns and over-weight hooking devices we have become rich in well thought out, handsome, highly efficient and, in large measure, easily tied flies that have become reliable salmon offerings.

Freshwater fly-fishers have continued to use the Comet series, General Practitioner, Silver Brown, Horner Shrimp, Polar Shrimp, Thor and other classic patterns that can still be counted on to carry the day when called upon. There has also been countless hours spent developing new freshwater patterns, like Bjorn's Super Prawn, Chief Fat Dog and Spun Marabou streamer to mention just a few.

Polar bear hair, a favored material, particularly for coho flies, is not legal to purchase in the United States. It is how-ever legal to buy and own polar bear hair in Canada where it remains popular. Many fly tiers in the United States, particu-larly on the Pacific Coast, still have treasured, remnant sup-plies of polar bear that was imported prior to 1972, before it was declared illegal to transport across the Canada/United States border. We don't advise anyone to seek out a black market supplier of polar bear hair as long as a good substitute will work.

Many of the Canadian flies contributed to this chapter still call out polar bear and the only changes we made were to add legally available substitutes such as bucktail, yak, Islan-dic sheep or synthetics.

The most notable advances have made by innovative tiers who have developed a cornucopia of superb saltwater pat-terns that imitate all important baitfish and most forms of zooplankton. Simply stated, whether one chooses to fish Pa-cific salmon in saltwater or brackish estuaries; whether they are feeding on herring, sand lance or euphausiids, there is a growing representative selection of flies available to do the job.

Bucktail was originally the common name for flies tied with the tail hair of a whitetail deer. In Washington and Brit-ish Columbia, however, bucktail also refers to flies designed early on either from bucktail or polar bear hair, specifically for a distinctive salmon fishing technique called "bucktail-ing", a method of trolling. This salmon fishing method is so popular that its followers purchase high-end fly-fishing tackle strictly to pursue the sport, rarely making many seri-ous casts to salmon.

Many of the superb vintage bucktail patterns like Letcher Lambuth's Herring and Candlefish; Roy Patrick's Coronation or the Coho Fly series are still in use. A.J. McClane's Discov-ery Optic, one of the first saltwater coho flies to be featured nationally appeared in his *Field & Stream* fishing column (May 1950). The Discovery Optic is no longer used extensively,

Veteran salmon fly-fishing guide and fly tier, Bill Nelson shows the crowd how he ties his unique salmon patterns at an Oregon FFF Fly Tying Expo.

Bruce Ferguson adds a bit of emphasis as he dresses one of his saltwater salmon flies at the Oregon FFF Fly Tying Expo.

but is still an effective pattern. Some of these dressings dating back sixty years or more remain popular because they work as effectively today as they did when first designed. They have become the fine old wine of Pacific salmon flies.

Flies for what has become commonly known as the "waiting period" continue to be developed in great numbers and can be the difference in success or failure during the last days that salmon spend in salt water before moving into the lower tidal pools of parent streams. During the "waiting period" one never knows what fly might nudge a salmon into grabbing since it has stopped actively feeding and most likely has a completely empty digestive tract. This is the motivation to keep tying a never-ending assortment of new patterns trying them during the waiting period in the Pacific salmons' life cycle.

Attractor patterns for tempting salmon that have moved inside the estuaries and further upriver into freshwater pools above tidal influence have not changed so markedly but here too there are new flies in relative abundance to go along with the old standbys. As with effective saltwater patterns, the most productive flies for freshwater fishing are carefully assembled to flash, swing and swim enticingly enough to provoke the strike of salmon that have entered parent rivers.

Many of the flies that appeared in our first book, *Fly Fishing for Pacific Salmon*, have not been carried over into this volume because they were either rarely used or did not stand the test of time. Each of the flies that appear in this chapter, regardless of their vintage, are patterns that have established a solid reputation for tempting Pacific salmon at certain times, depending on the situation. The flies have been divided into four categories: Saltwater Feeding, Saltwater Attractors, Saltwater Waiting Period, and Freshwater Attractors. A great many of these flies contributed by anglers up and down the Pacific Coast have not previously been published.

Specific materials are called for in most of the patterns, many of which are synthetics that have been introduced to fly tiers since the publication of our first book. This seemingly endless array of new materials and colors showing up on fly-shop pegs every season is available in a dazzling pallet of colors and textures which has allowed fly tiers to develop flashier or more accurate imitations than ever before. Some of these materials, distributed under various names are identical or nearly so. Wherever the tier has specified a color, type and specific brand of material in his or her recipe, we have called it out. It is also possible that some materials may be discontinued by manufacturers and others introduced that are similar. If you cannot locate the material specifically called out for some of the patterns in this chapter there is almost certainly a suitable substitute available at your local fly shop or in a fly-tying materials catalog.

Bruce Ferguson's long-time friend Randy Frisvold is one of Puget Sound's most successful fly-fishers for all salmon species, particularly chinook.

Preston Singletary tying flies at an Oregon Council
FFF 2007 Fly Tying Expo in Albany, Oregon.

Saltwater Feeding-Period Flies

Zooplankton

Zooplankton flies depict the small, non-fish creatures that salmon feed on early in their salt water feeding cycle. Young, trout-size salmon of 11 to 15 inches gorge on zooplankton from late fall through early May. There are several categories of zooplankton with those of major importance being; euphausiids, amphipods, copepods, crab larvae and shrimp.

The color of zooplankton, collectively called "krill" can vary greatly depending upon where they live and what they eat. Usually the colors range from almost clear, to pink, orange or red.

All of these important salmon food forms are shown and described in detail in the "Salmon Feed" chapter. Many of the patterns listed under the zooplankton category can be used interchangeably. A euphausiid pattern for instance may serve equally well during an amphipod swarm and vice versa. Since euphausiids inhabit Pacific marine waters year around, most anglers have at least a basic selection in their fly boxes all of the time. You just never know when a salmon is going to develop a hankering for zooplankton.

When similar or nearly identical patterns were submitted we made no effort to see which fly was designed first. We simply trusted the integrity of each submitter regarding ownership and origin of the flies and recorded them in the order that they were received.

You can't tell a fly-fisher by the condition of his fly box—or flies. This tangle of well-used flies belongs to Jim Koolick one of the veteran salmon fly-casters along Washington's beaches.

Euphausiids

Antron Euphausiid

Originators: Brian Thielicke and Garry Sandstrom
Tier: Brian Thielicke

Hook: Mustad 34007 or equivalent, size 6
Thread: Gudebrod 6/0, white
Body: Pearl Flashabou #6905
Underwing: A few strands of pearl Flashabou
Overwing: Sparse white Antron
Eyes: Small black plastic, or Spirit River small bead chain
Tier's Note: "This pattern is also based on the ACE. It is a good pattern for both resident and northern silver salmon feeding near the surface."

—Brian Thielicke
Bonney Lake, Washington

California Neil (Original)

Originator: Neil Light
Tier: Barry Stokes

Hook: Mustad 34011, size 4-6; Tiemco 9394, size 6-10;
Partridge CS 11, size 4-8
Thread: Danville 6/0 chartreuse
Tail: Grizzly hackle tips
Body: Pale green Frostbite
Hackle: Grizzly palmered from bend to head
Finish: Any durable head cement
Tier's Note: "The original California Neil gained popularity in the Tofino area some years back. I don't know much about the history or development other than it was first tied by a visiting angler, Neil Light of California. The original and variations have

since become standard in many saltwater fly-fishers' boxes on Vancouver Island."

—Barry Stokes
Victoria, British Columbia

California Neil (Lazer Neil)

Originator: Neil Light
Tier: Barry Stokes

Hook: Mustad 34011, size 4-6; Tiemco 9394, size 6-10;
Partridge CS 11, size 4-8
Thread: Danville 6/0, red
Tail: Chartreuse polar bear and chartreuse Krystal Flash
Body: Green Laser Wrap (Edge Brite) over silver mylar tinsel. Lazer Wrap is wound on with slight spaces between wraps. Palmered grizzly is wound between wraps for added strength.
Hackle: Grizzly
Head: Red thread with high-gloss finish
Tier's Note: "There have been several variations of Neil Light's original California Neil dressed by Vancouver Island anglers but this one has been most effective for me. I don't know who should get credit for it but I have used the Lazer Neil successfully in the open Pacific Ocean and along the beaches for both feeding and staging salmon."

—Barry Stokes

Chartreuse Flashabou

Originator and Tier: Ted Pearson

Hook: Mustad 3407, size 8
Thread: Black 6/0
Tail: About six strands of pearl Flashabou

Body: Medium chartreuse chenille

Legs: About 15 strands of pearl Flashabou tied in as a throat, extending to the hook point

Head: Build up with black thread

Tier's Note: "I developed this pattern in 1984 when the resident coho salmon net-pen program was at its peak around Fox Island in South Puget Sound. At the time the pattern of choice was Bruce Ferguson's Green and Silver. I thought that perhaps a smaller pattern might be a better choice when the coho were eating krill on the surface. I wound up keeping only the chartreuse chenille from Bruce's pattern and added the Flashabou tail and legs. It worked well and continues to be my first choice when fishing over surface-feeding coho."

—Ted Pearson

McLaughlin's Euphausiid

Originator: Bob McLaughlin
Tier: Preston Singletary

Hook: Size 6-8 Mustad 3675, 34007, or equivalent

Thread: Black UNI-Thread, 6/0

Body: large white, pale pink or pale orange Estaz or Cactus chenille wrapped forward from hook bend and tied off at head. Trim top and sides leaving bottom fibers full length to represent legs.

Head: Black thread

Tier's Note: "The late Bob McLaughlin, longtime member of the Washington Fly-fishing Club, developed this euphausiid imitation in the early 1990s and used it extensively in South Puget Sound, in the bays and inlets around Fox Island and near Longbranch, his favorite areas to fish for resident coho salmon. Bob's original pattern utilized a head built up from black tying thread to represent the eye of a euphausiid. I often tie it instead, with a pair of small black plastic dumbbell eyes, or anodized black mini-bead chain, in which case I substitute fine clear monofilament for the black thread."

—Preston Singletary
Seattle, Washington

FJ Pink

Originators: Bruce Ferguson and Les Johnson
Tier: Les Johnson

Hook: Size 6 and 8, Gamakatsu SS15, or equivalent

Thread: Clear monofilament, fine

Tail: A few strands of Krystal Flash (to match dubbing)

Underbody: Spirit River Pseudo Seal dubbing (shrimp pink, fluorescent orange, neon pink, marmalade or polar bear)

Shellback: Scud Back, clear or to match dubbing

Rib: Mini Larva Lace clear, or to match dubbing

Thorax: Spirit River Pseudo Seal dubbing to match natural euphausiid

Eyes: Smallest size of black or blue Spirit River bead chain

Feelers and Legs: Several strands of Krystal Flash (to match dubbing). Tied in at the hook bend and taken forward to be pulled down and tied as legs

Tier's Note: "The FJ Pink was designed for casting to surface-feeding pink and sockeye salmon. I tied several versions, working from enlarged scientific images that Bruce acquired through the University of Washington College of Fisheries. Our goal was to create a realistic euphausiid imitation. After several tries I finally tied a sample that met with Bruce's approval. We named it the FJ (for Ferguson/Johnson), and Pink since that was going to be our inaugural target species at Langara Island while fishing out of the West Coast Fishing Club.

On our first morning, near the Bruin Bay kelp bed, I hooked and landed a feeding pink salmon that plucked the FJ Pink from the surface film as neatly as any Henry's Fork rainbow trout slurping a Quigley Cripple. The FJ Pink tied in the colors listed is a good match for euphausiids. The brightest colors work best when we want more of an attractor effect. Polar Bear white should be kept on hand for times when pale, nearly clear euphausiids are showing."

—Les Johnson
Redmond, Washington

Flashabou Euphausiid

Originator: Gary Strodtz
Tier: Les Johnson

Hook: Size 6 and 8, Gamakatsu SL11-3H, or equivalent

Thread: Fine monofilament and Danville black

Underbody: Silver Mylar tinsel

Tail, Body and Throat: Several strands of pearl Flashabou tied in at hook bend leaving stubs as a tail, wrapped forward and pulled down to form legs

Head: Black thread

Tier's Note: "This is a pattern first used in South Puget Sound. Gary Strodtz developed this no-nonsense euphausiid around 1980. It works well at matching feed that is nearly colorless."

—Les Johnson

Hallis Euphausiid

Originator: Norm Hallis
Tier: Les Johnson

Hook: Size 12, Gamakatsu SS15, or equivalent

Thread: White

Tail: White hackle tip, tied flat and squared off

Body: White marabou spun in dubbing loop and trimmed on top and sides. Bottom marabou strands left as legs

Head: White with black dot on each side as an eye

Tier's Note: "Norm Hallis, member of the Puget Sound Flyfishers developed this pattern for use on South Puget Sound coho."

—Les Johnson

Pink Candy

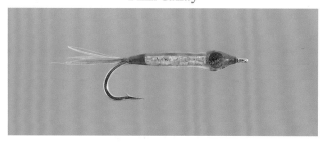

Originator and Tier: Art Limber

Hook: Tiemco 9394, size 8 and 10

Thread: Ultra 140 D, fluorescent red

Body: 10 strands of rainbow Krystal Flash

Back: Bubblegum pink feather fibers

Eyes: 1.2mm red with black pupils, stick-on

Finish: Epoxy the entire fly except for the extended tail

Tier's Note: "This is one of my two top patterns for beach coho. The other being the Olive Wizzard. The Pink Candy is the only fly that I have taken all five species of Pacific salmon on in salt water. A fast strip is best for coho, pinks and sea-run cutthroat. I fish it very slowly for sockeye, chum and chinook."

—Art Limber
Qualicum Beach, British Columbia

The "Nothing" Euphausiid

Originators: Bruce Ferguson and Randy Frisvold
Tier: Bruce Ferguson

Hook: TMC 9394, size 10

Thread: Black monocord, 3/0

Tail: None

Wing: White polar bear hair or other translucent hair or synthetic material.

Topping: Several strands of pearl Crystal Hair

Eyes: None

Tier's Note: "This result of several years of experimentation, this simple fly provides a solution to taking coho in the spring when euphausiids are swarming on the surface. Presentation is important. Using a floating or clear intermediate line, quietly cast well ahead of approaching fish and allow the fly to sit. Start with a short, popping retrieve just as the coho catch up with the fly's position. With luck you'll be into a fish instantly. A long leader with several feet of 5- or 6-pound-test fluorocarbon tippet improves your odds significantly."

—Bruce Ferguson
Gig Harbor, Washington
Randy Frisvold
Olympia, Washington

Pink Cigar

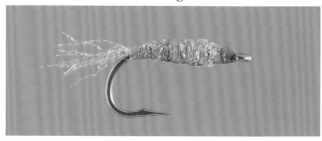

Originator and Tier: Cliff Olson

Hook: Size 6 and 8 Mustad 34007

Thread: Gudebrod floss, pink, 3/0

Underbody: Danville pink flat floss, four strands, cigar shape

Tail/Body: Dragonfly pink Krystal Flash #10

Protection from teeth: Cover head and body with Angler's Choice, water-based Soft Body

Tier's Note:"I originated the Pink Cigar to fish for pink salmon in fresh water. It has however proven to be effective on pink and coho salmon in both fresh and salt water. I generally like this fly best in size 8 but at times the size 6 is a better producer, so I always have them both in my fly box. Bruce Ferguson also has experienced success with the Pink Cigar while fishing for pink salmon out of Telegraph Cove on northern Vancouver Island."

—Cliff Olson
New Westminster, British Columbia

Sandstrom Angel Hair Euphausiid

Originator and Tier: Garry Sandstrom

Hook: Mustad 3407 or equivalent, size 12-8
Thread: Danville shell pink
Body: Angel Hair, electric pink, AHH-140
Wing: Electric pink Angel Hair
Head: Gudebrod 6/0, BCS 118

Tier's Note: "I developed this pattern originally to create a lively and translucent fly that was easy to tie. As it turns out, in order to make it effective, care must be taken to not overdress it. Too much Angel Hair and the fly will lose translucency and movement. After prolonged use in saltwater the Angel Hair color will lighten quite a bit but does not seem to lower its effectiveness. I fish this euphausiid imitation on a floating or intermediate line with a slow, two-inch strip retrieve between long pauses. Another method is to cast ahead of rising fish and swing the fly into them on tight line with no retrieve."

—Garry Sandstrom
University Place, Washington

Sandstrom Euphausiid

Originator and Tier: Garry Sandstrom

Hook: TMC 9394, size 10

Thread: Gudebrod 6/0; Clear #BCS 93
Tail: 1/8" wide clear Scud Back
Abdomen: Scintilla dubbing, blended. Mix 2/3 #06 Pale Creamy Shrimp and 1/3 #32 Vivid Red
Back: Clear 1/8" Scud Back
Rib: Gudebrod 6/0 clear #BCS 93
Thorax: Scintilla, mixed dubbing same as abdomen
Eyes: Small black mono eyes
Legs: Pick out dubbing along bottom of fly
Antennae: Stripped apricot saddle hackle stems
Mouth: Webby hackle fibers, apricot

Tier's Note:"This fly was tied from a photograph of live euphausiids of the genus Thysanoessa *provided by my friend, Bruce Ferguson. He wanted me to develop a realistic imitation of this important salmon food item, typically found from Neah Bay, Washington, north through British Columbia."*

—Garry Sandstrom

South Sound Euphausiid

Originator and Tier: Vern Jeremica

Hook: Size 6-10, sproat, tinned or stainless
Thread: White or cream Danville 6/0
Tail: Four strands of pink or pearlescent Krystal Flash
Veiling: Dyed red or orange golden pheasant tippet
Butt: White or cream Tri-Lobal dubbing
Body: Light brown/cream dubbing ribbed with two strands of Pearl Flashabou twisted together. Pick out dubbing on bottom and sides
Throat: Four strands pearl green Flashabou
Eyes: Black plastic mono eyes

Tier's Note:"I have great luck with this little euphausiid imitation during the winter months in South Puget Sound. I fish it along rip lines, drop-offs and prominent points where upwelling occurs. Bonaparte gulls are often a tip-off to a euphausiid swarm which is almost always a big attraction for coho. I fish the fly slowly because euphausiids are not fast swimmers. The South Sound Euphausiid has also worked on chum salmon."

— Vern Jeremica
Issaquah, Washington

Walkinshaw Euphausiid

Originator: Walt Walkinshaw
Tier: Les Johnson

Hook: Size 6 and 8, Gamakatsu SL11-3H, TMC 811S or
 equivalent
Thread: White
Body: Cream Antron or sparkle yarn
Throat: White or cream polar bear hairs, sparse

Tier's Note: "Walt Walkinshaw of Seattle developed this basic
euphausiid. It has proven to be particularly effective in South
Puget Sound during the winter coho fishery."

—*Les Johnson*

Amphipods

Antron Amphipod

Originators: Brian Thielicke and Garry Sandstrom
Tier: Brian Thielicke

Hook: Mustad 34007 or equivalent, size 8
Thread: Danville shell pink 6/0
Body: Pink Flashabou #6965
Underwing: Remaining Flashabou
Overwing: Darion # 11 shrimp pink
Eyes: Black mini monofilament eyes
Head: Danville shell pink thread

Tier's Note: "Garry Sandstrom and I modeled this fly after a
Pacific salmon pattern called the AFC. The blend of Antron and
Flashabou gives just the right amount of subdued sparkle. With
the plastic eyes and light materials the flies work particularly
well on near-surface-feeding fish."

—*Brian Thielicke*
Bonney Lake, Washington

Beadhead Amphipod

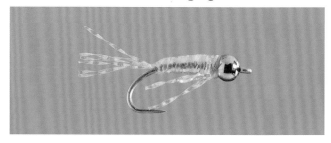

Originator and Tier: Garry Sandstrom

Hook: Size 14-18 Partridge Oliver Edwards K14ST, or
 equivalent
Thread: Gudebrod 6/0 clear BC 593
Legs, Body and Tail: Krystal Flash two strands each;
 Orange #3 and Pink #10, wrapped together and
 tapered forward.
Body Finish: Two coats of Softex.
Bead: 5/32" silver

Tier's Note: "This fly was designed to "match the hatch" in size
and color on south Puget Sound amphipods. Mixing two colors
of Krystal Flash gave me the right color. The two coats of Softex
give the fly durability and translucence. When debarbing the
Partridge hooks do not hold the hook while pinching the barb or
the point will break. A lot of anglers will feel intimidated using
a size-18 fly in Puget Sound but if you restrict your casting to
visibly rising pods of fish, your odds of hooking up are greatly
increased. My most productive setup is a floating or intermediate sink-tip line with a long leader tipped with a length of 5X
fluorocarbon. The most effective retrieve when using the Bead-
head Amphipod is a down and across swing in front of rising
pods of salmon."

—*Garry Sandstrom*

Green Amphipod

Originator: Lloyd Morrell
Tier: Les Johnson

Hook: Gamakatsu SL11-3H
Thread: Tan
Tail: Deer body hair, left untrimmed
Body: Fluorescent green chenille. Alternate bodies are
 salmon pink or white chenille
Hackle: Blue dun palmered

Back: Remaining deer body hair pulled forward over chenille
Rib: Tan thread over body and back
Head: Tan thread
Tier's Note: "This pattern, developed by Lloyd Morrell, is a take-off on the old Jameson Shrimp, a popular Washington stillwater fly from the 1960s that was a killer on rainbow trout in Jameson Lake. It was one of the first effective patterns for salmon feeding on amphipods and euphausiids."

—*Les Johnson*

RS Amphipod

Originator and Tier: Roger Stephens

Hook: Gamakatsu SC-15 size 8
Thread: Maxima Ultragreen, 2-pound-test, or fine, clear monofilament
Tail: White ostrich herl
Body: SLF dubbing, white (42) clipped on top and sides
Back: Red Deco marker topped with Softex
Eyes: Burned nylon leader and petite glass beads (1.6 grams)
Tier's Note: "The RS Amphipod is effective in the winter and spring when resident Puget Sound silvers are feeding on amphipods in the surface film. I use a floating line to dead-drift the RS Amphipod into feeding schools of juvenile resident silvers, or cast directly down current shaking out slack line to drift the fly into feeding schools. When the fly is into the school I find that a very short, periodic retrieve works best for me. The small size of the fly and numerous amphipods on the water surface make it difficult to see when a fish strikes, thus most of the time I use a strike indicator."

—*Roger Stephen*
Olympia, Washington

Singletary Amphipod

Originator and Tier: Preston Singletary

Hook: Size 16, Gamakatsu C12U, or equivalent
Thread: White UNI-Thread, 8/0

Body: Cream dubbing, picked out underneath
Shellback: 8 to 10 strands of orange Krystal Flash
Tier's Note: "This extremely simple pattern was tied to imitate one of the most common amphipods found in Puget Sound during the winter and early spring months. Resident coho salmon can often be seen feeding on them at or near the surface, rather like trout taking emerging mayflies. At such times I fish this little amphipod on a floating line, allowing it to swing in the tidal flow with no action except an occasional very gentle twitch. It can also be tied with purple or olive Krystal Flash to 'match the hatch' but orange seems to be effective under most circumstances."

—*Preston Singletary*

Swanson Harbor Amphipod

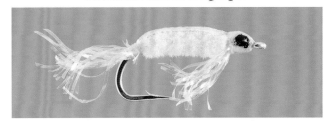

Originator: Gary Price
Tier: Les Johnson

Hook: Size 6 and 8 Gamakatsu SL11-3H, Mustad 3407 or 34007
Thread: White
Tail: Strands from Mylar tubing overbody
Feelers: Strands from Mylar tubing overbody
Body: Underbody: White fine chenille or floss with a stripe of red thread or floss back to front
Overbody: Pearl Mylar tubing tied in at tail and head
Head: White thread with small black eyes painted on each side
Tier's Note: "Gary Price of Auke Bay, Alaska came up with this amphipod pattern; simple to tie, durable and effective."

—*Les Johnson*

Shrimp

Tyler Shrimp

Originator: Unknown
Tier: Brian Thielicke

Hook: Mustad 34007 or equivalent, size 6
Thread: Danville shell pink, 6/0

Antennae: Saap Wing-Fiber, fluorescent orange
Shellback and Throat: Pink Krystal Flash #KF04
Legs: Pink Krystal Flash
Eyes: Small black plastic, or Spirit River black mini bead-chain

Tier's Note: Garry Sandstrom and I took an existing pattern and changed the color to closely match the pelagic amphipods found in South Puget Sound waters during winter and early spring. The pattern tied on a number-8 hook seems about right. A light touch of Softex on the shellback increases the durability of the fly without adding significant weight."

—Brian Thielicke

Easy Shrimp

Tier and Originator: Tim Tullis

Hook: Mustad 34007, size 6
Thread: UNI, 6/0 pink
Tail: Purple Krystal Flash
Body: Silver Mylar under pink Edgebright
Hackle: Purple Krystal Flash tied as beard
Finish: Head cement, Softex, Hard Head, or equivalent

Tier's Note: "This pink salmon fly was developed for beach fishing on the north end of Vancouver Island. It is usually fished with a floating line and a long leader using a slow retrieve. Results have been exceptional."

—Tim Tullis
Qualicum Beach, British Columbia

Frank's MVP

Originator and Tier: Frank van Gelder

Hook: Daiichi 2441, size 2
Thread: Gudebrod, orange, 6/0
Tail: Orange hackle tips trimmed to simulate tail
Body: Orange floss

Ribbing: Orange thread
Legs: Orange hen hackle
Head: Wrapped peacock herl
Eyes: Melted 20-pound-test monofilament
Antennae: Two matching moose body hairs and two strands of pearl Krystal Flash

Tier's Note: "I named this fly Frank's MVP because it is my number one fly when salmon are keying on shrimp—and because MVP are the initials of my favorite beach, Marine View Park, where the fly was developed. The idea came to me after seeing people catch shrimp off the dock in Des Moines. It occurred to me that they were a major food source for the local salmon and cutthroat. I've been catching both species with this fly ever since.

The effectiveness of the MVP is in the retrieve used while fishing it. The shrimp hop retrieve simulates a shrimp hopping from rock to rock, or along a sandy bottom. I strip it quickly three or four times, followed by a rest. The strike usually occurs on the subsequent strip after the fly rests near the bottom for a second or two. Both versions work well near estuaries. When one doesn't score, the other one generally will.

The alternate cutthroat MVP dressing has a brown floss body and brown thread with a pink thread rib."

—Frank van Gelder
Tacoma, Washington

Pink Feed

Originator and Tier: Pat Trotter

Hook: English bait hook, size 12 to 4, or equivalent
Thread: White
Tail and Feelers: Wisps of dyed hackle
Body: Poly yarn, dyed to match feathers; picked out along bottom as legs
Shellback: Clear Scudback
Veins: Reddish-orange, or hot orange, thread. One strand over the center of the back and then ribbed with the same thread
Hackle: Hen hackle, dyed to match dubbing
Head: White thread finished with head cement

Tier's Note: "I developed the Pink Feed, which has been a very successful krill imitation, in 1976. The color has evolved over the years to better imitate the colors of the euphausiids and

amphipods in our local Puget Sound waters. The dye is made from 1/4 teaspoon each of fluorescent pink and fluorescent orange dye to one pint of water. You want a very pale pink color which means that you have to rinse the feathers occasionally and when the desired color is achieved, emerge them in a vinegar bath to set the color."

—Pat Trotter
Seattle, Washington

RS Sand Shrimp

Originator and Tier: Roger Stephens

Hook: Tiemco 9394, size 6
Thread: Maxima Ultragreen leader material, 2-pound, or fine monofilament
Hook: Tiemco 9394, size 6. Nickel finish
Tail: Tan marabou
Underbody: .030 wire, wrapped length of shank
Body: Riverborn golden shiner #21 dubbing, or natural seal (D48). Clip top and sides. Apply Softex to clipped top.
Eyes: Glass seed beads (4.54 grams).
Tier's Note: "My RS Sand Shrimp has been most effective in shallow water, usually less than 8 feet deep, over sandy shelves in coves for juvenile resident silvers from winter through spring. I strip it along the bottom in short erratic pulls at moderate speed using a fast-sinking fly line."

—Roger Stephens

Simple Shrimp

Originator and Tier: Ken Hanley

Hook: Size 4 to 6, TMC 7989, Mustad 34007, Gamakatsu SL11-3H, or equivalent
Thread: Pink UNI-Thread, 6/0
Tail: Flashabou, glow-in-the-dark pink #6951
Body: Hare-tron Dubbin', pink shrimp
Head: Tying thread
Tier's Note: "It couldn't be simpler. Three materials on a hook…and go catch some pink salmon. My first choice for

feeding pink salmon is . . . pink! I use this pattern when I sight-cast to salmon in open water and on estuary flats. An intermediate line or type 4 shooting head are typically the outfits I work with since this is definitely a surface-oriented game."

—Ken Hanley
Fremont, California

Tachell Shrimp

Originator: Unknown
Tier: Jonathan Tachell

Hook: Size 2 Gamakatsu SC-15, or size 8 Daiichi 2546
Thread: Gudebrod, fluorescent orange 3/0
Tail: Fluorescent orange saddle hackle fibers
Body: Built up fluorescent orange thread covered with hot glue or epoxy
Legs: Fluorescent orange saddle hackle
Eyes: Size 18-24 black Larva Lace tied into two close knots.
Rib: Fine copper wire
Finish: Softex, Dave's Flexament, or other similar finish.
Tier's Note: "I have used this shrimp pattern successfully for resident silvers and returning adults in South Puget Sound. I prefer to fish it with a clear, intermediate sinking line using quick, 4- to 6-inch strips and an occasional pause. Salmon usually pick up the fly while it is falling. This is an excellent fly for sight-fishing, or if you know that salmon are concentrated in one area. It is less effective as a searching fly.

—Jonathan Tachell
Tacoma, Washington

Spawn Flies

Hale's Pinkie

Originator: Carl Stroud
Tier: Les Johnson

Hook: Size 6 to 10, Gamakatsu SL11-3H
Thread: White
Body: Alternate wraps of pink and white chenille

Throat: White bucktail, polar bear or calf tail, sparse
Head: White with silver bead-chain eyes
Tier's Note: "*Carl Stroud developed this pattern for use in South Puget Sound. It has proven effective during May and June when salmon are feeding on zooplankton or crab spawn. Stroud named the fly after Hale's Passage the waterway between Fox Island and the mainland, a popular angling area with coho fly-fishers. The Hale's Pinkie remains a good fly that is worthy of a couple of spaces in any well-stocked fly box*"

—*Les Johnson*

Surface Spawn Fly

Originator and Tier: Bill Nelson

Hook: Mustad 34007, size 4 or 6; most often a 4
Thread: Clear fine monofilament or white flat waxed nylon
Body: Pink bucktail or long, pink deer hair tied tight at the front and spread like a Muddler
Tail: Pink bucktail
Wing: Orange FisHair on top and sides.
Tier's Note: "*After checking out a pail filled with the actual critters and looking over the gunwale of my boat at swarms of crab and shrimp spawn I developed this pattern to use as a general imitation of crab or shrimp spawn. It works when spawn swarms are in back eddies with just enough tide movement to concentrate them near the surface. This seems to occur mostly on the flood. When coho, pinks or sockeye are feeding on surface riding spawn, commercial fishermen say that the salmon are "nodding". I use a floating line and long leader for this fishing and move the fly slowly. If the fly sinks a bit I don't worry. I just keep on retrieving slowly. When salmon are on crab or shrimp spawn this fly works well for me.*"

—*Bill Nelson*
Eugene Oregon

Baitfish

Sometime in May or June, depending upon the area of the Pacific Coast, young salmon begin to switch off from zooplankton to a diet consisting primarily of baitfish. Squid also become part of the menu at this time, especially with the chinook salmon that often feed quite deep in the water column. Early in the season baitfish may not be more than 1 or 2 inches long. As the season progresses they grow and your flies should be tied increasingly larger to imitate the actual baits. Keep in mind however that you should always carry a selection of sizes in your baitfish pattern selection. At times an off-size pattern will appeal to the whims of finicky salmon.

Sardine (or Pilchard)

Dark metallic blue or green on the back, shading to silver on the sides and belly. They spawn 100 to 300 miles offshore. Length at maturity rarely exceeds a foot in length. Sardines migrate north in summer and south in the fall with the largest and oldest fish migrating the farthest north to the west coast of Vancouver Island. Once abundant, sardines have declined steeply and not recovered since heavy overfishing in the mid-1940s.

Llama Sardine

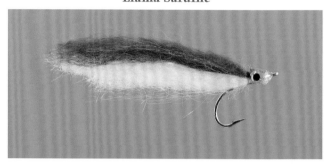

Originator and Tier: Tim Tullis

Hook: Eagle Claw Seaguard 1067U, size 2-2/0
Thread: UNI Monofilament, fine
Body: Dark blue llama over Kelly green llama over white llama
Lateral Line: Ice Wing Fiber, pearl with green hue
Head: Epoxied medium Mylar cord
Eyes: 1/8" Silver Witchcraft stick-on, holographic
Tier's Note: "*This is a Clayoquot Sound fly that could be called either first choice, or last resort. The combination of blue over green usually fishes well on cloudy days or during low light. Larger size dressings should use more material and larger stick-on eyes.*"

—*Tim Tullis*

Anchovy

The northern anchovy is distinguished by its prominent silvery gill covers. When a school of anchovies is startled and move quickly it has been likened to a handful of shiny new nickels and dimes tossed into the water column. The gill covers of the anchovies flash and sparkle with each darting turn. This important feature of a slender baitfish with a large mouth and oversized, perfectly smooth gill plates can be imitated in many ways; from building Mylar cheeks to sliding braided silver Mylar over the head of a fly to emulate the shiny gills. Seeing these flashing gill covers in the water is your signal to change to an anchovy pattern. Anchovy flies have been developed by salmon fishers on the Pacific coast over the years but there is still plenty of room to experiment

Llama Anchovy

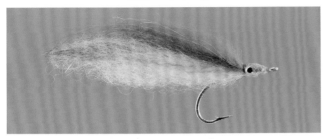

Originator and Tier: Tim Tullis

Hook: Eagle Claw Seaguard LO67U, size 2-1/0
Thread: UNI Monofilament, fine
Body: Purple llama over Kelly green llama over white llama. Add sparse bunch of Pearl Ice Wing Fiber UV hue to the white and purple llama hair
Lateral Line: Pearl green Ice Wing Fiber
Head: Epoxied medium Mylar cord
Eyes: 3/8" silver Witchcraft holographic stick-on
Tier's Note: "This fly was developed to imitate the anchovies found along the surf line in Clayoquot Sound. The pattern produced a 'once in a lifetime' experience on coho the first day it was used and has become a very solid producer since. All of the llama hair patterns fish well along rock walls, kelp beds and wash rocks."

—Tim Tullis

Waslick Sea Bait (Anchovy)

Originator: Mark Waslick
Tier: Brian Thielicke

Hook: Mustad 34007, Tiemco 811S, or equivalent; size 1/0 and 2/0
Thread: Gudebrod BCS 93 monofilament
Underwing: Fine bucktail, three to four inches long mixed with pearl Flashabou and topped with pearl Krystal Flash
Overwing: Royal blue over chartreuse bucktail mixed with corresponding Flashabou
Topping: Peacock Krystal Flash
Gill Plates: Silver Flashabou, sides only
Head: Pearl Mylar tubing slipped over built up head
Eyes: 4.5 Spirit River Tape eyes, silver
Finish: 30-minute Z-Poxy over head and eyes

Sand Lance and Sand Lance Fry

This common baitfish found in foreshore waters along the north Pacific Coast is the Pacific Sand lance, *Ammodytes hexapterus*. Common names given to this baitfish are needle-fish and (erroneously) candlefish. Long, slender and eel-like in appearance and are usually no thicker than a common pencil, even though they can grow up to 8 inches in length. Anyone poking around the sheltered bays and inlets in their quest for salmon is sure to encounter schools of them. Even chinook salmon, noted for being deep feeders will chase Sand lance up into the shallows on occasion.

Articulated Candlefish (Sand Lance)

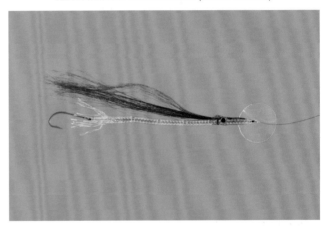

Originator and Tier: Mike Croft

Hook: Eagle Claw LO54SS, size 2-4
Thread: Gudebrod clear monofilament
Body: Braided Mylar over 1/8"OD clear tubing. Super glue in place before applying epoxy and cutting into 1/2-inch segments
Wing: FisHair, dark olive over golden olive
Head: Use one tubing segment to tie on the wing, red gills and stick-on eyes. Epoxy over all. When fishing, slip a 3/4-inch plastic disk down the leader, crimped to make it slightly cup shaped
Tier's Note: "This fly dates back to 1992 when I was searching for a fly that I could troll on days that the salmon just wouldn't show on the surface. I slip the plastic disk onto the leader (an old damselfly trick) to make it wiggle naturally as it is stripped in or trolled. I make my disks using a 3/4-inch hole punch and drill it in the middle for stringing it on the leader. The fly really wiggles. This fly wiggles so naturally that it is almost unfair. On July days when I usually could not buy a fish along the kelp beds the Articulated Candlefish brought at least six coho to hand on four straight Saturdays. I now use it when fishing with my kids, or when I'm fishing with a guy who really needs to get into a salmon."

—Mike Croft
Tacoma, Washington

Candy Fry

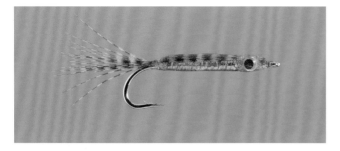

Originator and Tier: Art Limber

Hook: Tiemco 9394, size 6-10
Thread: Flymaster, olive. Clear, fine monofilament for head
Tail: Extension of back
Body: 10 strands of rainbow Krystal Hair
Back: Teal or mallard flank feather dyed moss green
Head: Clear monofilament
Eyes: 1.5 mm silver stick-on eyes
Finish: Epoxy entire fly except for tail
Tier's Note: "The Candy Fry is an excellent all-season beach pattern for coho throughout Vancouver Island. It is also great for early season cutthroat. Strip it fast."

—Art Limber

Epoxy Sand Lance

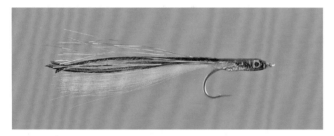

Originator and Tier: Jim Williamson

Hook: TMC 811S, Mustad 34007, or equivalent, size 4-8
Thread: Fine monofilament
Hook Shank: Two layers of silver Mylar, eye to bend
Body: Mother-of-pearl Fluoro Fibre, 10 to 12 strands, olive Lazer Flash
Wing: Three peacock herls
Head: Wrap with 10-12 strands olive Lazer Flash
Eyes: Prismatic stick-on eyes, secured with mono thread
Finish: Two coats, 5-minute epoxy
Tier's Note: "This pattern is very effective for both coho and chinook salmon on the inside waters of Puget Sound when fished from or near beaches where sand lance are found. The fly can be tied in different lengths to match the size of the local sand lance population at different times during the year. Based on the style of Bob Popovics' Surf Candy, the Epoxy Sand Lance rarely fouls around the hook."

—Jim Williamson
Bainbridge Island, Washington

Ferguson's Sand Lance (Dark) and (Light)

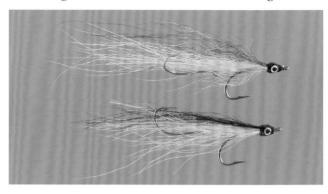

Originator and Tier: Bruce M. Ferguson

Hook: Tandem. Front hook: Mustad 34007, size 2-4. Trailer: Mustad 2553S, size 4
Thread: Black monocord, 3/0 black
Underwing: White polar bear or bucktail
Topwing: Dark olive brown polar bear hair or bucktail for the dark phase. A gray-green topwing is used for the light phase
Sides: Pearl Flashabou or Fly Flash
Eyes: Spirit River Prism Tape eyes, 1.5 silver
Tier's Note: "This fly was developed to imitate the yearling sand lance appearing in shallow northwestern coastal waters—a favorite salmon food. It is tied in two color phases, a dark brown-olive back and a gray-green back. As is true with most baitfish, sand lance can change back color depending on light conditions. It is, therefore, useful to carry both colorations of this tried and proven pattern in your fly box."

—Bruce M. Ferguson

Flashy Glow

Originator: Shawn Bennett

Hook: Mustad, size 1, 34011
Thread: Fine UNI, clear monofilament
Body: Green Sparkle Braid, or Diamond Braid
Wing: Green over yellow Everglow Flashabou
Lateral Line: Metallic green Flashabou
Head/Overbody: Pearlescent piping over head and picked out
Finish: Epoxy
Tier's Note: "This fly is a dependable producer on many species of saltwater fish but primarily coho. The idea for this pattern

was spawned from a pattern called the Flashy Lady by the late Joe Butorac a creative and respected professional fly tier from Arlington, Washington. He tied his Flashy Lady quite sparse, using bucktail. I tie the Flashy Glow with glow-in-the-dark materials, making it highly visible as it sinks down through the murky water created by algae blooms in the summer and tea-colored runoff in the fall. Early and late in the day simply hit the Flashy Glow with a flashlight or camera flash to make it really show up. I fish this pattern like other sand lance imitations using a steep retrieve up from the bottom. I also tie the Flashy Glow in pink Everglow Flashabou over a white glow belly."

—Shawn Bennett
Parksville, British Columbia

Floating Baitfish

Originator and Tier: Dick Kamrar

Hook: Mustad 34007 to tie on with size-2 Octopus bait hook trailer. Front hook can be cut off when fly is completed

Thread: Brown monocord, 3/0 waxed

Underbody: White polar bear hair or bucktail

Median Line: A few strands of red polar bear hair or bucktail topped with a few strands of pearl Flashabou

Topwing: Olive brown polar bear hair or bucktail

Head: Slip-on Edgewater Chugger Component, #6 white

Tier's Note: "The key to this style of surface fly is the chugger head. It will work for any baitfish pattern of a size that the head will float. It is especially good along the edge of kelp beds at daybreak for feeder chinook. I recommend a fly of a bit more than 3 inches with the chugger head to give visibility and surface disturbance. The Edgewater heads can be purchased in several sizes and colors."

—Dick Kamrar
Gig Harbor, Washington

FT Sand Lance

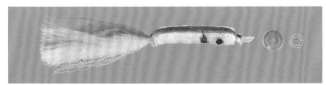

Originator and Tier: Roger Stephens

Hook: Gamakatsu size 4, SC 15

Thread: Danville clear monofilament, fine

Sequin: 5 and 8mm, pearl, found in most craft stores

Tail: White Darlon or similar synthetic or bucktail mixed with pearl Krystal Flash

Body: HMH small plastic tube, cut diagonally on the front
Closed-foam underbody covered with pearl Krystal Flash

Topping: Olive Darlon or similar synthetic

Eyes: Black on silver stick-on eyes

Finish: Softex

Tier's Note: "The front of the tube is trimmed at a 45-degree angle. When no sequin is used the FT Sand Lance (FT for 'floating tube') will skate on the surface. If a 5mm sequin is used the FT Sand Lance will have a subtle popper action. With an 8mm sequin it will have a significant popper action.

I use the FT Sand Lance for resident coho all through the winter when there are schools of jumping fish around. When adult coho are chasing sand lance up to the surface they will usually strike this pattern aggressively. I cast the FT Sand Lance at a 45- to 90-degree angle down current and skate or pop it with the current using short pauses as it swings. When it is straight down current the up current retrieve can be skated and popped continuously, or with a 1- to 2-second pause between strips. One or the other of these retrieves will take fish."

—Roger Stephens

Lambuth Candlefish (Sand Lance)

Originator: Letcher Lambuth
Tier: Preston Singletary

Hook: Daiichi X472, size 2/0

Thread: Danville black

Body: Flat silver tinsel or embossed silver tinsel

Rib: Oval silver tinsel over flat tinsel body. No rib with embossed tinsel or brightly tinned hook

Wing: Bunches of polar bear, bucktail, yak hair or synthetic
Underwing: Pale green and blue, mixed. Median line: red, thin. Topwing: French blue and olive, mixed

Head: Build up with black thread

Eyes: Spirit River stick-on eyes covered with Softex or Hard

Tier's Note: "This is a pattern by legendary Pacific Northwest fly tier, rod builder and inventor, Letcher Lambuth. The name is something of a misnomer as it represents a sand lance not a Columbia River smelt which is called 'candlefish'. He selected the colors after examining live sand lance in a saltwater tank that he invented and built. The Lambuth Candlefish is an outstanding saltwater fly that is still used in its original bucktail style. It has also become popular for casting to coho salmon in a Clouser Minnow configuration at Tofino and Neah Bay. Although it is most popular in larger sizes, the Lambuth Candlefish should not be overlooked by beach casters as it is highly effective at times when dressed on small hooks to imitate immature sand lance."

—Preston Singletary

Llama Needlefish (sand lance)

Originator and Tier: Tim Tullis

Hook: Eagle Claw Seaguard LO67U
Thread: UNI clear monofilament, fine
Body: Olive Llama hair over white llama hair
Lateral Line: Gold Polar Flash
Head: Epoxied medium pearl Mylar cord
Eyes: 1/8" silver holographic Witchcraft stick-on
Tiers' Note: "The idea of using llama hair for baitfish patterns came from Brad Root of Campbell River, BC. A good friend, Bob Jones, outdoor writer from Courtenay, BC, got us together because of our common pursuit of better baitfish patterns. At one time Brad was in the business of marketing llama as a fly-tying material and experimented with baitfish patterns. He sent some patterns to try and I was hooked on the fantastic real-life movement of the material. To give the patterns even more movement and a realistic look I added an epoxied Mylar cord head and holographic eyes. The epoxy head adds weight in front of the fly to make it swim with movement and add flash. For best results, fish the fly with a very slow retrieve. The current will give it plenty of movement. I recommend that a hook that will dissolve should be used as we have found that salmon frequently inhale the fly and can only be released by snipping the leader and leaving the fly in the fish. The Llama Needlefish is effective for chinook and coho. We first tested the pattern in Clayoquot Sound on the west side of Vancouver Island with incredible results."

—Tim Tullis

Marabou Candlefish (Sand Lance)

Originator and Tier: Mike Croft

Hook: Eagle Claw LO54SS, size 6
Thread: Gudebrod clear monofilament
Wing: Top to bottom: 1/4 olive or dark olive marabou; 1/4 damsel green or yellow ochre marabou
Flash: A few strands of silver Flashabou between damsel green and olive
Gills: Red thread around all but the top color
Eyes: Mylar stick-on
Head: Epoxy over eyes and gills
Tier's Note: "In 1993 during a lunch break on the beach, my fishing partner Mike Hamlin, mentioned that he had not seen many saltwater flies that were dressed with marabou. That night I went home and made this pattern. I have used it with great success in all of the Pacific Northwest waters, both salt and fresh.

It looks a bit fluffy when it is dry but wet it looks so much like a natural that you can swim it alongside a school of live Sand lance and they hardly notice. In recent years Capt. Tom Wolf, the South Sound saltwater fly-fishing guide, has made a Clouser variation of this fly and used it successfully. I also use it in attractor colors like pink and white; or chartreuse and white both of which are excellent changeup dressings."

—Mike Croft

Miyawaki Popper

Originator and Tier: Leland Miyawaki
Hook: Stinger, #2 or 4 Gamakatsu Octopus (barbless) secured in a doubled loop of 25-pound-test Maxima leader

Front hook: #8 Mustad 3407. Snip off point and bend of the Mustad hook when fly is completed

Thread: 3/0, any color

Head: Edgewater Dink component, size 4 or 6

Wing/Body: Matched grizzly or pink hackles; four strands of holographic tinsel; four strands of pearl Krystal Flash; small bunch of polar bear, calf tail or substitute; small bunch of olive streamer (Yak) hair and two peacock herls

Tier's Note: "Ten years ago I saw marauding coho slashing through a school of baitfish at Bush Point. Later, when I mentioned it to my friend, Richard Kamrar he showed me a floating candlefish he had been working on. I really liked the idea and began experimenting with—and modifying—Richard's original concept until I arrived at this design which I use almost exclusively for my salmon fishing.

Retrieve the Miyawaki Popper with short, quick jerks making sure that you leave a v-wake. If you get a follow or hit, either play dead then twitch, change direction with your rod tip, or retrieve twice as fast in short strokes to provoke the salmon into taking the fly. Vary your retrieves. Strip slowly, fast, smooth, or herky-jerky. Try placing the rod under your armpit and retrieve with both hands in long, steady pulls as it tracks over the water. Do not try to switch hands to set the hook or rush to get on the reel at the boil. Believe me, I learned this the hard way."

—Leland Miyawaki
Kent, Washington

Mouseback

Originator: Dick Kamrar
Tier: Bruce Ferguson

Hook: Mustad 34011, size 6

Thread: Fine monofilament

Body: Gold Diamond Braid

Underwing: White polar bear hair or bucktail, sparse

Median Line: Red polar bear hair or bucktail, sparse topped with a few strands of pearl Crystal Hair

Topwing: Golden brown polar bear hair or fine bucktail, sparse

Finish: Clear head cement

Tier's Note: "This is a general baitfish pattern. Observation of recently regurgitated fry, eaten by a concentrated pod of sea-run cutthroat and coho at daybreak provided the basis for this new fly-color scheme. Key to the pattern is the pale golden olive back

with a very sparse red median line, giving a translucent effect. Most effective when tied sparse and fished close to and parallel to the beach whenever fry are present."*

—Bruce Ferguson

Puget Sound Sand Lance (PSSL)

Originator and Tier: Richard Embry

Hook: Mustad 34007, or equivalent

Thread: Gudebrod fine clear monofilament

Body/Tail: White bucktail, clear Super Hair, peacock Angel Hair

Overwrap: Flat pearl braid, coated with Devcon 2-ton epoxy.

Highlights: Black Magic Marker on top of braid. Fine red marker for gills

Eyes: Silver stick-on coated with epoxy

Tier's Notes: "This pattern is realistic, durable and easy to tie. The overwrapping is a technique shown to me by Shawn Bennett, of Tofino, one of the most experienced saltwater fly-fishing guides in the business. The PSSI, as I call it, has been very effective for me throughout British Columbia and Washington marine waters."

—Richard Embry
Seattle, Washington

SB Dart

Originator and Tier: Shawn Bennett

Hook: Mustad 34007, size 2

Tail: White Ultra Hair, *Body:* Silver or pearl Diamond Braid over tail

Dorsal: Green or olive Antron and Krystal Flash

Eyes: Stick-on eyes

Finish: Add red gills and cover entire fly body with epoxy for sheen and durability

Tier's Note: "The sleek, narrow profile of the SB Dart imitates the Pacific sand lance, a favorite food of salmon along the

Pacific Coast. In Clayoquot Sound on the west side of Vancouver Island, I have success stripping this fly erratically from the bottom to the top like a terrified sand lance attempting to escape the jaws of a feeding coho."

—Shawn Bennett

Thorne River Emerger

Originators: Les Johnson and Dan Lemaich
Tier: Les Johnson

Hook: Size 6 to 10, Gamakatsu SL11-3H
Thread: Clear monofilament. Black thread for head
Body: Silver Mylar tinsel, criss-crossed with monofilament
Wing: Sparse Superhair, olive over pink over white
Topping: Four strands of peacock herl
Eyes: Black Spirit River small bead-chain
Tier's Note: "This fly was designed one evening over a couple of glasses of Bushmills at Boardwalk Wilderness Lodge on Prince of Wales Island, Alaska where Dan Lemaich and I were staying. It was designed to imitate pink and chum salmon fry emerging from the gravel. It proved to be a killer on cutthroat and Dolly Varden. We have since found that the Thorne River Emerger is also an effective emerging sand lance, or out-migrating pink and chum fry imitation along Puget Sound beaches.

—Les Johnson

Tibbs Minnow

Originator and Tier: Bill Pollard

Hook: Mustad 34007, size 1/0-2
Thread: Dark 3/0 and clear monofilament
Wing: Two strands of Ribbon Floss, combed out over white llama hair; emerald green or blue and green mixed topping on the variation
Sides: Purple and pearl Flashabou, mixed, sparse
Head: Pearl Mylar
Eyes: Green or gold prismatic
Finish: Epoxy over head only

Tier's Note: "Tim Tullis introduced me to this style of fly and I have taken his ideas and developed a minnow pattern with more flash and different materials. The Tibbs Minnow has been a very successful coho pattern on the west side of Vancouver Island, particularly in the Tofino area in August and September. It has been effective when used with a fast-sinking line, even when the salmon are showing on the surface. One nice quality of the llama hair is that it has a lot of action during any speed of retrieve. If one variation isn't working, switch to the other."

—Bill Pollard
Nanoose Bay, British Columbia

Tim's Blue Needlefish (sand lance)

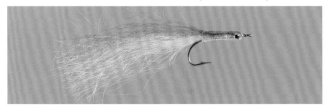

Originator and Tier: Tim Tullis

Hook: Mustad 34007, size 2, 1 and 1/0
Thread: Clear monofilament UNI, Danville, Orvis or equivalent
Body: Blue polar bear hair over UV Krystal Flash over white polar bear
Head: Pearl Mylar piping cord
Eyes: Silver Witchcraft stick-on
Finish: Cover entire area of Mylar cord with epoxy, Hard Head or Softex

Tier's Note: "The blue phase of my Tim's Needlefish is often productive on overcast days and in low light conditions in the morning and evening."

—Tim Tullis

Tim's Olive Needlefish (sand lance)

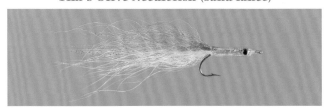

Originator and Tier: Tim Tullis

Hook: Mustad 34007, size 2, 1, and 1/0
Thread: Clear monofilament, UNI, Danville, Orvis or equivalent
Body: Olive polar bear over UV Hue Krystal Flash over white polar bear
Head: Epoxied medium pearl Mylar cord shaped with mono thread
Eyes: Silver #2 Witchcraft stick-on
Finish: Cover entire area of Mylar cord with epoxy, Hard Head or Softex

Tier's Note: "I developed this fly to imitate the abundant needle-fish or sand lance found in Clayoquot Sound on the west coast of Vancouver Island. I usually fish the fly with a high-speed, high-density sinking line or a 300- to 500-grain head. I let the fly sink close to the bottom and use a slow retrieve to fish it nearly straight up to the surface. It is important to fish the fly all the way to the surface as coho will often follow the Olive Needlefish right to the boat before taking it."

—Tim Tullis
Parksville, British Columbia

Williams Point Sand Lance

Originator and Tier: Les Johnson

Hook: Gamakatsu L11S-3H, size 2-8

Thread: Clear monofilament

Body: Bucktail, yak hair or polar bear. Top, black or olive; Bottom, white

Median Flash: Lateral scale Saltwater Flashabou, red or silver, one strand along each side

Head: Wrap the head area completely with flat pearl ribbon (found at most fabric shops)

Topping: Peacock or black Krystal Flash or Flashabou a bit longer than the hair to match top of body

Eyes: Spirit River stick-on eyes, small, well forward

Finish: High-gloss head cement

Tier's Note: "This is a basic sand lance, easy to tie and effective from south Puget Sound to the Queen Charlotte Islands. I've tweaked the pattern many times over the years most often to simplify it. I tie it from 2 to 5 inches long. The L11S hook is stout enough to hold large salmon even in the smallest size. I use the red and silver lateral line interchangeably on either the olive or black version. In certain light sand lance will display either a vivid red/vermillion or silver band along the flanks. If one doesn't work the other usually will."

—Les Johnson

Candlefish and Candlefish Fry

The eulachon *Thaleichthys pacificus* is properly called the candlefish because in the old days, coastal Indians dried and burned them for candles. Those of us who grew up in southwest Washington near the confluence of the Cowlitz and Columbia rivers knew this fish as the smelt, which ran up the Cowlitz each spring to spawn. This is another baitfish with a slender form that should guide your fly selection and tying.

The term candlefish was, years back often the name given our Pacific sand lance and many still do use the name interchangeably with the sand lance. The only reference we had to actual candlefish being imitated has been in some of A.J. McClane's early articles on fishing for coho salmon in the British Columbia salt. These too may have actually been sand lance. However, in respect to McClane, one of our greatest fishing journalists, we are leaving his three patterns listed under candlefish.

Discovery Optic #1

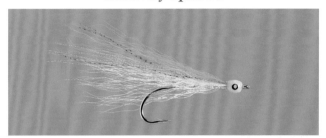

Originator: A.J. McClane
Tier: Steve Rohrbach

Hook: Daiichi X472, size 2/0

Thread: White

Body: Flat silver tinsel over padding, ribbed with oval silver tinsel

Wing: Pale blue over white bucktail, polar bear, yak, llama or synthetic materials

Flash: Sparse green Krystal Flash mixed into blue hair

Head: Built up with thread, covered with Sparkle Body

Eyes: Painted black with yellow pupils or small Witchcraft stick-on eyes

Discovery Optic #2

Hook and Body: Same as pattern #1

Wing: Orange over white bucktail, polar bear, Yak, llama or synthetic materials

Flash: Sparse yellow Krystal Flash mixed into orange hair

Head: Same as #1

Discovery Optic #3

Hook: Same as #1

Body: Flat gold tinsel padded, ribbed with oval gold tinsel

Wing: Scarlet over yellow over white bucktail, polar bear, yak, llama or synthetic material

Flash: Sparse red Krystal Flash mixed into scarlet hair

Head: Same as #1

Eyes: Same as #1

Tier's Note: "The Discovery Optic in the three dressings shown was designed by noted Field & Stream *fishing editor A.J. Mc-Clane in the late 1940s for use in Discovery Passage, near Campbell River, British Columbia. It was originally dressed with polar bear hair.*

Although the Discovery Optic still has a few remaining champions, it is no longer in wide use. Dressings 1 and 2 were used along current rips and at the edges of kelp beds. The #3 dressing was designed to imitate a wounded baitfish fluttering around herring and sand lance schools when coho are foraging heavily. The addition of Krystal Flash topping is recent, replacing the original dyed nylon fibers that McClane used for added attraction."

—Steve Rohrbach
Seattle, Washington

Herring and Herring Fry Patterns

Beach Bum

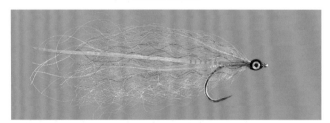

Originator and Tier: **Jimmy LeMert**

Hook: Gamakatsu SC-15, size 2-1/0

Thread: Danville 3/0 monocord, black

Overwing: Flash 'n Slinky (camo, chartreuse, rust or blue)

Underwing: White Slinky Fiber

Side Stripe: Lateral Scale Flashabou, pearl

Eyes: Pearl, stick-on eyes, 2.0. Cover with epoxy

Tier's Note: "The Beach Bum is a basic baitfish tied with Flash 'n Slinky and Slinky fiber, durable materials that have

translucence not unlike real polar bear hair. When the coho begin feeding on herring along the Puget Sound beaches the Beach Bum is the fly I always tie on first."

Jimmy LeMert
Seattle, Washington

Catface Streamer

Originator and Tier: Shawn Bennett

Hook: Size 1/0-2 Mustad 34011

Thread: Fine UNI clear monofilament

Body: Pearl Diamond Braid

Hackle: Dyed green grizzly hackle as a lateral line

Wing: Chartreuse over white polar, bucktail or equivalent

Topping: Herl from eye of peacock tail feather

Throat: Red calf tail or Flashabou tied as beard

Eyes: 2mm Mylar stick-on eyes

Finish: Epoxy

Tier's Note: "This fly has a rather broad profile which I believe is sometimes taken for a young perch or shiner, a bait sporadically found in the stomach contents of coho salmon that have been feeding in shallow sandy bays. I fish the fly along the base of the Catface Mountain range at the edge of Clayoquot Sound, British Columbia. It produces in most similar waters all along the north Pacific Coast. While chartreuse/lime with a bit of red are a common theme for many saltwater streamers, I also tie the Catface with purple, olive or blue, depending upon the baitfish I'm trying to represent. I add the grizzly hackle as a lateral line which are similar to parr marks, dyed to match the overall color of the fly.*"

—Shawn Bennett
Parksville, British Columbia

Epoxy Herring (juvenile)

Originator and Tier: Shawn Bennett

Hook: Mustad 34011, size 1/0-2

Body: Bleached white Stimudent toothpick tied in under

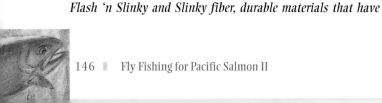

hook shank. Mark dorsal with dark blue or green permanent marker

Tail: Polar Flash, or equivalent, color to suit

Overbody: Medium pearlescent Mylar piping

Eyes: Mylar stick-on eyes, 2mm. Add gills with red permanent marker. Cover all with light coat of epoxy

Tier's Note: "This is a dead ringer for juvenile herring, called 'firecrackers' in British Columbia, a common baitfish throughout the Pacific Northwest. I like to fish this fly dead-drifted for extended periods of 8 to 10 seconds followed by a few short strips; back to the pause and then a few more short strips to mimic the motion of an injured herring. Injured herring are fluttering all around when a school of coho attack like a pack of wolves, first corralling, then smashing through the bait, finally gobbling up the struggling injured. It is not surprising that this fly is particularly effective around herring bait balls. I cast into the ball, let the fly sink down through it and wait for the strike."

—*Shawn Bennett*

Fat Head

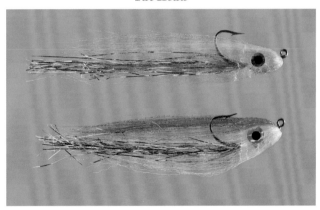

Originator and Tier: John Ryzanych

Hook: Jig-style Mustad 34185S or Eagle Claw 413, sizes 2/0-5/0

Thread: Nymo A, Danville Flymaster Plus or equivalent strong white thread

Weight: Fuse wire as needed to match the size and required weight of completed fly

Tinsel: Medium to fine silver or gold Mylar, tied forward and folded back

Body: Super Hair, or other similar synthetic fibers, tied forward and folded back

Note: Use a child's spring-loaded hair clip to hold all fibers back in fish shape while applying Softex to put a skin over the material, only at the head. This shapes the Fat Head*Eyes:* Witchcraft stick-on eyes, covered with Softex

Finish: Softex over the head and eyes

Tier's Note: "The Fat Head grew out of my need for a baitfish imitation that addressed the aspects of representation and animation more closely than existing patterns I could find. The

result is a large silhouette fly that presents the bulky shape of a herring, anchovy or other baitfish.

It is a style of fly rather than a single pattern as it can be altered to imitate just about any baitfish I have found in Pacific salmon waters. I select colors to imitate herring, anchovies or other baitfish and attractor combinations like chartreuse over white to form the general shape to suit my needs. I have found that by adding or decreasing the amount of lead I apply to the keel hook I get great action with the Fat Head on various retrieves, or a realistic dying spiral when it is allowed to sink through a baitfish ball.

—*John Ryzanych*
Castro Valley, California

Ferguson's Herring

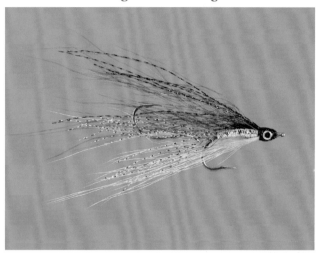

Originator and Tier: Bruce M. Ferguson

Hook: Front: Mustad 34007, size 2-6. Tandem,: Mustad 2553S, size 4 or 6

Thread: Black monocord, waxed 3/0

Body: Silver Diamond Braid

Underwing: White polar bear hair or bucktail

Topwing: Blackish green dyed polar bear hair or bucktail, topped with several strands of black Krystal Flash

Eyes: Spirit River Prism Tape, silver

Tier's Note: "Some years ago I saw pink and coho salmon chasing herring of the year on one of Vancouver Island's northern beaches. Unfortunately none of my large assortment of flies attracted attention. That night I tied a match for the herring that had jumped out onto the beach at my feet in an effort to escape the pursuing salmon. Since then, I've enjoyed great success with this pattern for feeder coho, pink and chinook salmon. The key to it effectiveness seems to be the very dark green back and "herring" profile. I have most of my polar bear and bucktail dyed to match my rather picky color requirements. You may have to search to locate just the right color of material; or begin dying your own."

—*Bruce M. Ferguson*

FF Herring

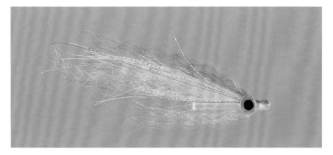

Originator and Tier: Anil Srivastava

Tube: HMH 'large' cut to desired length. Add soft tubing hook accommodator

Thread: UNI fine monofilament

Belly: White Slinky Fiber

Wing: White Slinky Fiber, Krinkle Mirror Flash and Krystal Flash

Overwing: Olive, gray and purple Slinky Fibre

Eyes: 3-D molded eyes, 'mirror', 5.0

Tier's Note: "I fish this pattern whenever herring are present. The synthetic materials absorb very little water and the fly provides a large silhouette while remaining easy to cast. In keeping with the 'large but light theme', the head is epoxied in two smaller parts; the eyes and wing are epoxied first. After they dry the overwing and belly are tied in and epoxied."

—Anil Srivastava
Tacoma, Washington

Graves' Coho Catcher

Originator and Tier: Glen Graves

Hooks: Front; Mustad 34007, size 4. Trailer; Mustad 25535, size 4

Thread: Danville white flat waxed nylon

Underbody: Four Westrim Rainbow Pearl iridescent beads strung on loop of 30-pound-test monofilament loop

Wing: White bucktail or polar bear topped with olive over pink bucktail or polar bear

Veiling: Pearl mylar piping picked out over wing and body

Head: Fluorescent green thread, floss or yarn

Tier's Note: "I developed this fly to imitate juvenile herring in south Puget Sound where it has been especially effective for winter and spring resident coho. In larger sizes it has performed

well on mature feeding coho out of Neah Bay on the Strait of Juan de Fuca."

—Glen Graves
Lakewood, Washington

Lefty's Deceiver

Originator and Tier: Bernard "Lefty" Kreh

Hook: Mustad 34007, TMC 900S, Gamakatsu SL11-3H, or equivalent

Thread: 3/0, color to match fly

Body: Six to eight long saddle hackles, four on each side tied in at hook bend

Shoulder: Bucktail, built up on each side

Back: Bucktail, color to match baitfish

Flash: A few strands of pearl Krystal Flash down each side

Throat: Red Krystal Flash, short, tied as beard

Head: Built up with thread to match fly

Eyes: Witchcraft stick-on eyes covered with Softex or Hard Head

Tier's Note: "I designed Lefty's Deceiver in the late 1950s after a trip for stripers on Chesapeake Bay with my frequent fishing companion Tom Cofield, outdoor editor of the Baltimore Post and News. We discussed what I was considering; designing a fly that would not foul and have a fish shape but could be made in almost any length. I wanted it to swim well but lift easily for the backcast. Since I was just making another pattern, I didn't really record exactly when I tied the first Deceiver, I just hoped that it would work.

I had no idea that the Deceiver would over time become a fly used all over the world, but it certainly has. It is also probably the most copied fly you will find. Many tiers have added a feather or two, made an epoxy head, or put on big eyes and given it their name. It doesn't bother me as long as people enjoy using the pattern.

The Deceiver has been effective on Pacific salmon in salt water, primarily as a herring imitation due to its large shoulder. It is regularly tied in colors to closely imitate herring but is hard to beat in white with a chartreuse back, as more of an attractor. In small sizes the Deceiver has gained a following as a good pattern for casting to salmon from Puget Sound and British Columbia beaches. Also, in recent years I've used the Deceiver in deeper water by adding a cone head. In very clear water I use synthetic materials such as Unique Hair, Super Hair or FisHair."

—Lefty Kreh
Hunt Valley, Maryland

Llama Herring

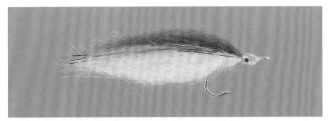

Originator and Tier: Tim Tullis

Hook: Eagle Claw Seaguard L067U, size 2-4/0
Thread: UNI monofilament, clear
Body: Baitfish green llama hair over white llama hair. Add a smattering of pearl Ice Wing Fiber in red, green, or UV Hue to the white llama hair
Lateral Line: Gold Polar Flash
Head: Medium Mylar cord, epoxied
Eyes: Stick-on holographic, 1/8"
Tier's Note: "I developed the Llama Herring for fishing around Vancouver Island. When tying larger sizes I increase the amount of llama hair to bulk up the fly and also use larger eyes. I don't use stainless-steel hooks. In case of break-offs I prefer that the hook will rust out quickly. The Llama Herring fishes well when herring are present."

—*Tim Tullis*

MT's Four O'Clock Flash

Originator and Tier: Mike Telford

Hook: Gamakatsu SP11-3L3H, or equivalent, size 1/0-2
Thread: Clear monofilament
Body: Doug's Bug Slinky Fiber, blended: white, natural misty green aquamarine and seaweed
Flash: Medium pearl Mylar tubing tied on hook and unraveled after tying on Slinky Fiber
Gills: Holographic Mylar, red, 1/64 inch
Eyes: Spirit River 3-D molded eyes, silver, 6.0
Finish: Sally Hansen's Hard-As-Nails or any other fast build-up finish
Tier's Note: "I think that the most important feature in any baitfish pattern is a balance of translucency and flash. I view the Four O'clock Flash as a style of fly that can be tied to represent almost any saltwater baitfish by changing colors and body length. The Four O'clock Flash has been productive for salmon in estuaries and open salt water"

—*Mike Telford*

Olive Wizzard

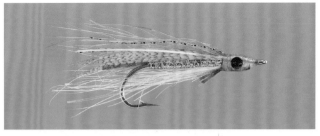

Originator and Tier: Art Limber

Hook: Mustad 34011, size 6 and 8
Thread: Fly Master, white; clear, fine mono for the head
Tail: Sparse tuft of red Fleuro Fibre
Body: 13 strands of rainbow Krystal Flash
Underwing: White polar bear topped with 4 strands of pearl Flashabou
Overwing: Olive polar bear over rolled green teal flank
Topping: 3 strands of purple Krystal Flash
Beard: Tuft of red Fleuro Fibre
Eyes: 1.5 mm red tape eyes on white thread head
Finish: Devcon 5-minute epoxy
Tier's Note:"This is one of my two favorite beach flies for coho salmon all season long on Vancouver Island beaches; the other being the Pink Candy. I strip the Wizzard fast for best results. If fish are still on the beach in November, they like a 10-second sink and slow strip. I have taken sea-run cutthroat throughout the season on the Wizzard as well."

—*Art Limber*

Pacific Herring

Originator and Tier: Chris West

Hook: Tiemco 811S, size 2-6
Thread: UNI-Mono, fine
Overbody: Black FisHair or gray FisHair, MOP Root Beer Angel Hair, electric purple Gliss N'Glow, Clear ice
Underbody: Fluoro Fibre, white
Eyes: Spirit River stick-on eyes, size 2.0
Finish: Devon 2-ton Clear Epoxy
Tier's Note: "When fishing the Pacific Herring the first approach is to separate the fly from the herring school. I like to find a position on the beach up-current of the herring so that I may

cast cross-current to the deepwater side of the herring schools. Using a slow rhythm with 15-inch strips, I also let the current swing the fly while it is being retrieved. The idea is to offer a salmon the easiest possible meal, which I hope will be my fly.

For times when casting over water devoid of herring, I use the second approach while searching for salmon. I begin with a cast the longest cast I can make, quartering up-current. This keeps the fly in the water as long as possible to extend the presentation. When the current moves my fly into a taut line position I follow it with the rod tip, down-current similar to a steelhead swing. Typically, if the fly is down-current and within five feet of the beach, I pick up and cast again. Both the dark and the gray phase take salmon depending on overhead light and water clarity."

—Chris West
Seattle, Washington

Sekiu Special

Originator and Tier: John Olson

Tube: 1/8" I.D. hard plastic tubing. Soft tubing hook accommodator can be added

Thread: Black, 3/0

Underbody: White "Glo" Flashabou

Midbody: Light blue Flashabou, sparse

Topping: Light blue Krystal Flash

Head: Build up with black thread, cover with epoxy and sprinkle with glitter. Add painted eyes when epoxy has dried

Tier's Note: "This is the first tube fly I dressed to target silvers at Sekiu. I've enjoyed good results with the Sekiu Special both casting and bucktailing. It has also worked well as a basic baitfish for inner Puget Sound."

—John Olson
Seattle, Washington

Shock & Awe

Originator and Tier: Anil Srivastava

Tube: HMH 'small' cut to length. Attach a short length of soft plastic tubing to accommodate hook

Thread: UNI fine monofilament

Belly: White Slinky Fiber

Wing: White Slinky Fiber, Krinkle Mirror Flash, Krystal Mirror Flash and UV Pearl Krystal Flash

Overwing: Royal blue, dark purple, chartreuse and orange Slinky Fiber

Cone: 3/8" nickel Crossed-Eyed Cone

Eyes: 3-D molded eyes, mirror 5.0

Tier's Note: "Shock & Awe has a nice jigging action that stimulates an aggressive response from salmon. It is my best producer in the Strait of Juan de Fuca in larger sizes. In Puget Sound smaller sizes score very well. A key to creating a smooth silhouette is to tie the belly and overwing with the fibers extending both towards the rear and out the front of the fly. The cone is then forced onto the finished fly while the front of the tube is melted flush to the front of the cone."

—Anil Srivastava

Silver Thorn

Originator: Barry Thornton
Tier: Clifford Barker

Hook: Mustad 34011, size 1/0-6

Thread: White or silver

Tail: Peacock sword mixed with pearl or pink Krystal Flash, sparse

Body: Silver metallic chenille

Throat: Red or pink hackle fibers, sparse

Wing: Peacock herl mixed with pearl Krystal Flash, sparse

Head: Peacock herl or silver thread. Painted eyes optional

Tier's Note: "Barry Thornton dressed the Silver Thorn to imitate a young herring or sand lance for coho and pink salmon. It has been very effective for several years in BC salt water."

—Clifford Barker

Sorcerer's Touch

Originator and Tier: Ken Hanley

Hook: Mustad 34011 size 1-6
Thread: Black UNI-Thread, 8/0
Optional Tag: Silver tinsel thread
Body and Underwing: Wing: Strips of silver gray Antron (5 to 8 spikes, depending on hook size). Body: Silver gray spooled Antron
Contrast Wing: Forest green Antron strips, 2 spikes. Comb out
Throat: Gray marabou
Overwing: Squirrel tail, dyed blue, sparse for size 4 hooks, full for larger hooks
Collar: 2 Chinese saddle hackles, dyed fluorescent blue
Head: Hare-tron dubbin, gray
Tier's Note: "I designed the Sorcerer's Touch for saltwater silver salmon along Baranoff Island and Chatham Straight in Southeast Alaska. My favorite technique is to use a 350-grain sink-tip line and present the fly close to the kelp beds. Depending on water clarity and current speed I typically use a 2- to 3-foot pull retrieve at a moderate tempo. I also try to work the pattern near any interface between shallow flats and deeper water."

—Ken Hanley

Ted's Swift-Sure Special

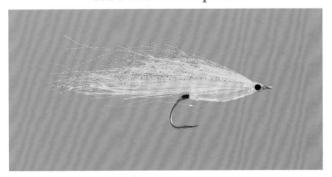

Originator and Tier: Ted A. Schultz

Hook: Eagle Claw 66S, Mustad 34011 or Tiemco 777SP, size 2
Thread: White Nymo for body, yellow Nymo for the head

Tag: Red Nymo or Danville flat waxed nylon
Body: Underbody, flat silver mylar tinsel. Overbody rainbow or pearlescent piping, lacquered for durability
Wing: Base, rainbow and luminescent mylar; white bucktail and silver Krystal Flash. Main wing, yellow bucktail or FisHair. Topping, Florescent yellow Krystal Flash
Eyes: Black
Tier's Note: "In the mid-1960s I would ride my bike down to Picnic Point north of Edmonds and fly-cast off the beach. My fishing pals and I never knew what we would catch; it could be a silver, blackmouth, cutthroat or steelhead, depending on the time of year. This fly was the first of my six Swift-Sure baitfish series which I tied commercially from 1966 through 1997. I have also tied variations of the patterns on tubes."

—Ted A. Schultz
Black Diamond, Washington

Waslick Sea Bait (Herring)

Originator: Mark Waslick
Tier: Brian Thielicke

Hook: Mustad 34007, size 1/0 and 2/0
Thread: Gudebrod BCS 93 monofilament
Underwing: Same as herring version
Topwing: Black over forest green bucktail with corresponding colors of Krystal Flash
Gills: Same as anchovy version
Head, Eyes and Finish: Same as Anchovy version
Tier's Note: "These patterns are variations on the original Sea Bait designed by Mark Waslick for tropical waters. Colors for the anchovy version are taken from the Abel Anchovy. The herring incorporates colors used by Bruce Ferguson for his herring flies.

—Brian Thielicke

"These bulky flies have worked extremely well in open-ocean conditions such as those encountered at the mouth of the Juan de Fuca Strait in Washington and at Langara Island on the north end of the Queen Charlotte Islands in British Columbia, Canada."

—Bruce Ferguson

Flies for Bucktailing

The fine sport of bucktailing first practiced in the 1930s was employed primarily for locating coho salmon since a lot of salt water could be covered with a trolled fly. The sport was refined and gained popularity slowly and steadily until the late 1940s. Then improved flies designed for bucktailing gave the sport a shot in the arm. Bucktailing has enjoyed yet another spate of resurgence during the past ten years or so, with more and more people fishing for salmon, and is now probably the number one method for taking coho and pink salmon on flies in marine waters.

Art's Special

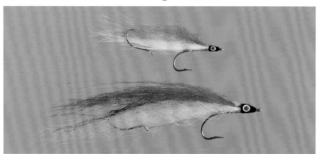

Originator and Tier: Art Limber

Hook: Primary, Mustad 3407, 2/0. Trailer, Mustad 925535, size 1
Thread: Black, 3/0
Body: Medium silver Mylar
Wing: Polar bear, or substitute; olive over purple over white. Top each color with 3 to 4 strands of Krystal Hair
Eyes: Red pupils on yellow background
Finish: Epoxy
Tier's Note: "The Art's Special is my favorite bucktail, particularly when there are herring schools around. It rarely fails to produce. In small sizes, 3 to 4 inches long, it is great for coho. For winter and spring chinook, I tie it 6 to 7 inches long. Either fly, however will take both coho and chinook depending on the size of bait that is in the water. Both sizes of the pattern are shown for comparison."

—Art Limber
Qualicum Beach, British Columbia

Campbell River Special

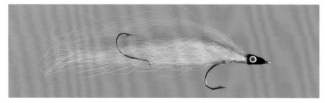

Originator and Tier: Art Limber

Hook: Primary, Mustad 3407, 3/0; trailer, Mustad 925535, 1/0

Body: Small silver Mylar tubing
Wing: Polar bear; blue over chartreuse over pink over white
    Flash and Topping: Pearl Krystal Flash, sparse
Eyes: Red pupils on a yellow background
Finish: Epoxy
Tier's Note: "The Campbell River Special has been an outstanding fly for winter and spring chinook for years. In smaller sizes it is good for coho."

—Art Limber

Coho Fly

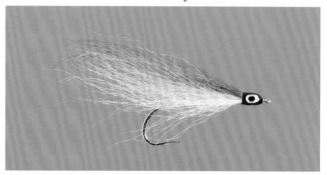

Originator: Unknown
Tier: Preston Singletary

Hook: Daiichi X472, 2/0
Rib: Oval silver tinsel to match hook size, five turns
Body: Flat silver tinsel
Optional Body: Silver Mylar piping slipped over hook shank, tied off and unraveled at the hook bend
Pattern Variations: All are dressed with equal bunches of polar bear, bucktail, yak hair, or synthetic material. Wing color combinations are: #1 blue, red, white. #2 blue, green, white. #3 green, yellow, white (shown above). #4 green, red, white. #5 yellow, red, yellow. #6 olive, red, white. #7 blue, olive, white. #8 olive, yellow, white. #9 blue, green, yellow, white. #10 peacock herl, green, white. #11 green, white. #12 blue, white. #13 orange, white. #14 blue, green. #15 red, white. #16 brown, white. #17 brown, orange, white. #18 yellow, red, white.
Head: Build up with black thread
Eyes: Witchcraft stick-on eyes covered with Softex or Hard Head
Tier's Note: "Roy Patrick noted that the Coho Fly was originated in about 1938 and was first tied in British Columbia. The original version was dressed with feather wings, streamer style, eventually making its way to Puget Sound. Patrick credited the redesign into a bucktail to anglers Jerry Hallum and Charles King who sometimes tied it with a tandem hook rig for trolling. Eighteen bucktail variations of the Coho Fly were recorded by Patrick in his self-published, milestone book, Pacific Northwest Fly Patterns."

—Preston Singletary

Coronation (Original version)

Originator: Roy Patrick
Tier: Preston Singletary

Hook: Daiichi X472 or equivalent, size 2/0
Thread: Black 6/0. 3/0 for larger dressings
Body: Flat silver tinsel
Rib: Silver rope, 5 turns. Tinsel and rib may be omitted if a stainless or nickel-plated hook is used
Wing: Bucktail: Medium blue over bright red over white
Eye: Black center on white background (stick-on eyes may be substituted for painted eyes)
Tier's Note: "The genesis of the Coronation is a bit sketchy. While Roy Patrick never took credit for the pattern there is considerable evidence that he was its originator. It may also have been a combination of ideas mulled together by Patrick, Letcher Lambuth, Bill Lohrer, Zell Parkhurst and other Seattle-area salt water tiers of the day. The original long-shank, bronzed Limerick-bend hooks used, which are no longer available, were at one time manufactured by Alcock, Mustad, Partridge and Sealy."
—*Preston Singletary*

Coronation (Canadian Bucktailing Version)

Originator: Roy A. Patrick
Tier: Art Limber

Hook: Primary, Mustad 34007, 2/0. Trailer, Mustad 925535, size 1
Thread: 3/0 black
Body: Silver Mylar, medium
Wing: Royal blue over red over white. Polar bear or bucktail
Flash: Add a few strands to match each color of wing hair
Eyes: Red pupils on yellow background
Tier's Note: "The Coronation, a pattern originated by Roy Patrick of Seattle, Washington, has been around for decades. This

is my bucktailing version of the original. It is always one of my top producers when coho are present. Tie it in lengths from 3 to 7 inches to match the size of baitfish."
—*Art Limber*

Grey Ghost

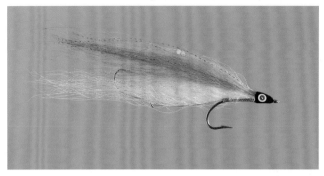

Originator and Tier: Art Limber

Hook: Primary, Mustad 3407, 3/0. Trailer, Mustad 925535, size 1/0
Body: Medium silver Mylar
Wing: Polar Bear, light gray over white
Topping: Three or four strands of rainbow Krystal Flash
Eyes: Red pupils on a yellow background
Finish: Epoxy
Tier's Note: "The Grey Ghost is my basic go-to herring bucktail. It works great dressed long and full for mature winter and spring chinooks. In smaller sizes it is a good coho fly."
—*Art Limber*

Gray Pink

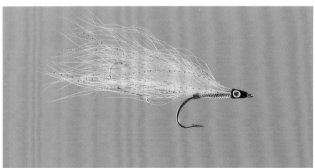

Originator and Tier: Art Limber

Hook: Primary, Mustad 3407, 2/0. Trailer, Mustad 925535, size 1
Thread: Black, 3/0
Body: Medium silver Mylar
Wing: Polar bear, light gray over pink over white
Topping: 3 or four strands of rainbow Krystal Flash
Eyes: Red pupils on a yellow background
Finish: Epoxy
Tier's Note: "This fly is excellent for fishing around schools of needlefish or crab spawn."
—*Art Limber*

Lambuth Herring

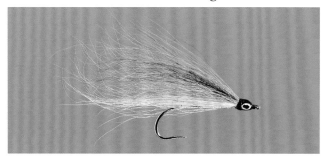

Originator: Letcher Lambuth
Tier: Preston Singletary

Hook: Daiichi X472, size 2/0
Body: Medium silver tinsel
Wing: Equal bunches of bucktail, polar bear, yak hair, or synthetic
Underwing: Pale green. Median line; gunmetal gray
Overwing: Dark green topped with a small bunch of dark blue
Head: Build up with black thread
Eyes: Spirit River stick-on eyes covered with Softex or Hard Head

Tier's Note: "This Letcher Lambuth original was a coho killer when he designed it more than sixty years ago and it shows no signs of slowing down. Whether the Lambuth Herring is used in the original saltwater form; updated to a Clouser-style fly; or tied to match small, immature baitfish for casting from the beaches, it continues to be a great pattern even in the face of all the new dressings that have come down the pike during the last few years."

—Preston Singletary

Mrs. Nelson

Originator and Tier: Bill Nelson

Hook: Tandem rig; 4/0-3/0 Mustad 34007. Front hook cut off at bend after pattern is complete. 2/0-1/0 Mustad 92553S trailer
Thread: Clear monofilament
Body and Wing: FisHair, 24-denier. Purple over pink over white
Flash: Pearl Flashabou over white FisHair; pink Flashabou over pink FisHair; purple Flashabou over purple FisHair; all sparse
Head: Built up over Flashabou butts with clear monofilament

Eyes: Witchcraft stick-on eyes covered with epoxy or Softex
Tier's Note: "Mrs. Nelson represents a herring in almost all stages. Have it tied and ready in several sizes to match available baitfish."

—Bill Nelson

Nelson Anchovy

Originator and Tier: Bill Nelson

Hook: Mustad 34007. Use hook for tying only. Trailer hook is Mustad 92553S, 1/0-2/0
Thread: Clear monofilament
Body: FisHair; white, purple, fluorescent pink and green
Flash: Flashabou; pearl, pink, bright blue and green
Eyes: Stick-on eyes
Finish: Any high build-up finish

Tier's Note: "Early in the year it is best to fish the Anchovy Fly slow and deep on the edges of the bait school. Anchovy schools seem to move very slowly…then suddenly disappear."

—Bill Nelson

Nelson Baitfish

Originator and Tier: Bill Nelson

Hook: Mustad 2/0-4/0 34007 for tying only. Hook cut off after pattern is complete. Mustad 9522SS 4/0-2/0 trailer
Thread: Clear monofilament or heavy flat waxed nylon
Body: White chenille on long hook. No body if tied as a trailing hook fly
Wing: Polar bear or white FisHair, tapered well back of Flashabou topping
Throat: Red hackle, clipped short
Eyes: Yellow stick-on eyes
Finish: Any high build-up finish

Tier's Note: "I generally fish this fly in areas where we find good fish in groups. When a salmon is being played we keep a fly rod set-up in the rack with this fly on the leader. Then we cast the fly behind the fish being played, careful not to get too close. The result is almost always a sure double-header as some fighting salmon expel their stomach contents when being played and the other fish follow to grab the regurgitated baitfish."

—Bill Nelson

Nelson Crab Spawn

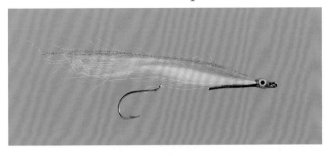

Originator and Tier: Bill Nelson

Hook: Mustad 34007, 2/0-4/0. Use shank to tie on only.
Trailing hook is Mustad 92553S, 1/0-2/0

Thread: White heavy-duty flat nylon, or clear, medium
monofilament

Wing: FisHair (24 denier), fluorescent orange over white

Topping: Orange and pearl Krystal Flash

Head: Clear monofilament

Eyes: Yellow with black pupils, covered with Softex, or any
high build-up cement

Tier's Note: "*I fish this fly in back eddies, very slowly. The color
is more attractive than the shape of the fly. It is most effective
when fished along crab spawn bundles.*"

—Bill Nelson
Eugene, Oregon

Nelson Dark Needlefish

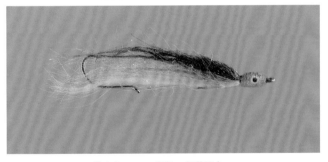

Originator and Tier: Bill Nelson

Hook: Mustad 34007, 2/0-4/0 for tying only. Trailer hook is
Mustad 922553SS, 1/0 or 2/0

Thread: Clear monofilament or heavy flat waxed nylon

Body: White hobby fur or Arctic fox tail, pearl Flashabou,
pink hobby fur, pink Flashabou, green hobby fur

Topping: Rainbow Lite-Brite

Eyes: Yellow or red stick-on eyes

Finish: Any high build-up finish

Tier's Note: "*This fly is extremely effective when needlefish
(sand lance) are working. Use a fly a bit smaller than the actual
bait. Most bait is camouflaged in some manner while the fly is
obtrusive. Again, fish this fly a bit slower than you would fish
the herring fly (Mrs. Nelson). Usually eight feet of water or a bit
deeper is about right.*"

—Bill Nelson

Nelson Needlefish (or Candlefish)

Originator and Tier: Bill Nelson

Hook: Mustad 34007, size 6-2. Can also be tied on a trailer
rig

Thread: Clear monofilament or heavy flat waxed nylon

Body: Rainbow Lite Brite topping over pink hobby fur, over
fluorescent green hobby fur over white hobby fur or
Arctic Fox with pearl Flashabou

Eyes: Red stick-on eyes

Finish: Any high build-up finish

Tier's Note: "*Early and late in the day the median line reflects
the pink more than the fluorescent green. As the azimuth
changes to midday the green is more prominent. This pattern
is deadly when needlefish are present. Fish it slower than you
would a herring fly.*"

—Bill Nelson

Nelson Shrimp Spawn

Originator and Tier: Bill Nelson

Hook: Mustad 34007, 2/0-4/0, shank only for tying. Trailing hook Mustad 92553S, 1/0 or 2/0

Thread: White flat waxed nylon or clear medium monofilament

Body: FisHair; 24 denier, fluorescent pink over fluorescent
chartreuse over white

Flash: Flashabou; white, chartreuse and pink

Eyes: Stick-on eyes, optional

Finish: Any tough, high-build finish like Joli-Glaze, epoxy or
Hard-As-Nails

Tier's Note: "*This is a deadly pattern during shrimp hatches.
Obviously the color is the most important factor. Fish the edges of shrimp spawn-filled back eddies. Sometimes the salmon
seem to herd the shrimp spawn into tight groups two to three
feet wide. That is when the bite can really turn on.*"

—Bill Nelson

Purple Gray

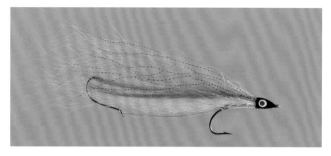

Originator and Tier: Art Limber

Hook: Primary, Mustad 3407, 3/0. Trailer, Mustad 925535, size 1/0

Body: Medium silver Mylar piping

Wing: Polar Bear: Purple over gray over white

Flash: Pearl Krystal Flash

Eyes: Red pupils on yellow background

Finish: Epoxy

Tier's Note: "This is one of my four favorites; the others being the Gray Ghost, Pink Gray and Campbell River Special."

—Art Limber

Tofino Special

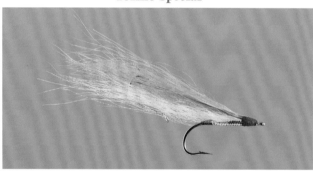

Originator and Tier: Art Limber

Hook: Primary, Mustad 3407, or 34007 in size 2/0. Trailer, Mustad 925535, size 1

Thread: Fluorescent red floss

Body: Medium silver Mylar

Wing: Polar bear, pink over orange over white

Flash: A few strands of pearl Krystal Flash along the sides

Tier's Note: "Orange is a terrific color in Clayoquot Sound at Tofino and most other areas on the west side of Vancouver Island. It works from the early season until the middle of September. You always want to have plenty of orange coho flies when you fish Tofino."

—Art Limber

Squid

Squid are important feed for Pacific salmon. Although squid have not received the attention from fly tiers that baitfish, shrimp, krill and attractors have enjoyed, they should not be overlooked as an important item on the salmon's diet. Co-author Les Johnson is convinced in fact that a good squid pattern may be as effective for taking mature, feeding chinook salmon as any fly and more effective than most. This may, in his opinion be in part due to the pattern, the Ever Glow, or the primary color, white. Legendary bucktailer Art Limber also favors white and goes to an all-white polar bear streamer when chinook salmon are on squid.

Calamarko

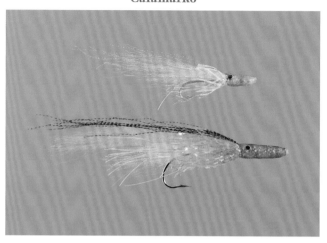

Originator and Tier: Mark Mandell

Tube: 1/16 to 3/16" tube in lengths from 3/8 to 1" overall for overall fly lengths of two to five inches. Soft plastic hook accommodator

Weight: Four to eight turns of lead wire on hard tube, against soft tubing. Use two layers for fishing heavy currents

Thread: White monocord

Short Tentacles: Polar bear white or pink FisHair

Long Tentacles: White or pink Everglow

Body: White or pink Everglow piping, picked out over tentacles. Pearl or red Krystal Flash down the sides

Eyes: Large Spirit River stick-on eyes, yellow or red

Topping: Pink, purple or lavender Krystal Flash, extending out over tentacles

Tier's Note: "Cast and trolled this tube squid pattern has taken chinook, coho, chum and pink salmon. I believe that its success in deep salt water (down to 90 feet) is primarily a testament to the phosphorescent head and skirt which glows lime green in low light from the Everglow. The fly, super-sparsely tied, also works well from the beaches in lengths down to two inches. I like to noseweight the heads a bit, even on the smallest, shallow-water versions because it balances out the hook at the aft end and makes the fly swim more realistically. For the pink version of the Calamarko simply replace all white materials with the same in pink."

—Mark Mandell
Port Townsend, Washington

Ocean Squid

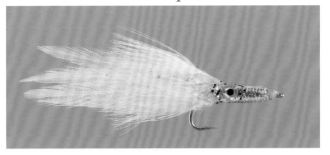

Originator and Tier: Bob Triggs and Richard Burge

Hook: Mustad 34011, size 2/0-1

Thread: Danville's flat waxed nylon, white

Tentacles: White marabou at hook bend. Four white hackles, coved in, on either side of the marabou

Underbody: Large fuchsia, pearl white or chartreuse cactus chenille or ESTAZ Glissen Glo wound tightly

Overbody: Pearl Mylar piping

Eye: Hareline stick-on eyes, .05mm., silver/black or gold/black

Finish: Epoxy over head and eyes, two coats

Tier's Note: "The Ocean Squid at times will out-fish the Clouser Minnow that is commonly used in Puget Sound and off shore for returning adult salmon. I use it shallow and deep for coho and pinks with good results. In bright daylight I combine the Ocean Squid with a fast-sinking, 350- to 450-grain integrated heads on 8- or 10-weight rods using 10- to 30-second countdowns. I like it in pink, green, white and orange Cactus Chenille under pearl piping although it works well at times tied with orange or green piping. I strip the fly reasonably fast in 8- to 12-inch pulls, letting it pause occasionally when it gets near the boat. Then I allow it to dive one more time. This is when I get about half of my strikes.*

—Richard Burge
Quilcene, Washington

Pink Squid

Originators: Mark Vinsel and Jay Fair
Tier: Mark Vinsel

Hook: Tiemco TMC 911S, 2/0 or equivalent long-shank salt-water hook

Thread: Danville Mono Cord, pink or white

Tentacles: Six to eight long, pink-dyed grizzly saddle hackles 3 to 4 inches long. Top with tuft of pink marabou

Body: White or pink Sparkle Chenille

Hackle: Pink grizzly schlappen or saddle hackle, tied in at the tip and palmered forward.

Eyes: Aluminum or plastic eyes, depending on the amount of weight needed, just forward of the hook bend

Finish: Any fast-drying finish

Tier's Note: "This squid is an adaptation of the sparkle leeches created by guide, Jay Fair of Eagle Lake, California. For decades, Jay has custom-dyed schlappen and marabou and sold gold sparkle chenille for his highly effective leech patterns. This was long before these materials were commonly available to fly tiers. By adding a few trailing tentacles of whole schlappen or hackle feathers, and adding eyes just ahead of the bend of the hook, the general form of Jay's leeches make for a realistic and effective squid pattern that has proven its worth both casting and trolling in open water for pink, coho and king salmon.*

—Mark Vinsel
Juneau, Alaska

Pacific Squid

Originator and Tier: Chris West

Hook: Tiemco 800S, size 1/0-6

Thread: Pink UNI-Thread, size 6/0

Hook: EZ-Body, pearl or natural, small to extra small

Skirt: Polar Fibre, pink Gliss N' Glow, MOP pink

Tentacles: Dry-fly hackle tips, white and grizzly on each side

Eyes: Spirit River stick-on eyes. Size 2.5-2.0

Finish: Devcon 2-Ton Epoxy

Weigh West Squid

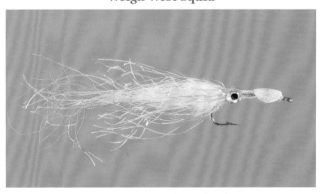

Originator and Tier: Shawn Bennett

Hook: Mustad 34011, 1/0-3/0

Thread: UNI fine clear monofilament

Head: Sequin, attached with waterproof glue

Body: White polar bear or substitute
Tail: Same as body
Overbody: Sleeved with pearl Mylar tubing that is frayed out
Eyes: Mylar stick-on eyes, large

Tier's Note: "Spending years around the cleaning tables of a charter operation has given me the opportunity to view salmon stomach contents on a daily basis. Seeing chinook and coho jammed full of needlefish, shrimp and euphausiids are clues to what I need in my box when I venture out.

Another item that occasionally shows up on the menu are squid. When a squid hatch goes off within inshore waters, salmon that are available to fly-fishermen will gorge themselves with squid, particularly chinook. I have seen chinook salmon hanging from the weigh scales so full that undigested squid are dropping out of their vents.

Squid patterns are easy to tie and some fishermen neglect to have this tasty morsel represented in their fly boxes. My Weigh West Squid is tied on a heavy hook and has a sequin added to the nose to mimic the rudder fins of a live squid. It can be tied in basic pearl white or a combination of colors. Just check out the Hootchies at your local salmon gear shop to see the possibilities. I always douse my squid with pearlescent powder while the epoxy is still wet to add sheen to the finished fly."

—Shawn Bennett

Saltwater Attractors

Cam Sigler Mid-Range Popper

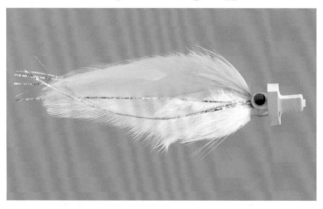

Originator and Tier: Cam Sigler

Tube: Small HMH tubing with soft tubing hook accommodator
Hook: Gamakatsu SC-15, or SC-15H, size to match size of fly
Body: Any combination of hair and feathers to create imitative or attractor dressing
Eyes: Doll eyes to match overall size of popper
Head: Cam Sigler popper heads, small or medium to match overall size of fly

Tier's Note: "This small version of my Offshore Popper has been very effective for resident coho starting in late spring and for large returning northern coho from late summer through fall."

—Cam Sigler
Vashon Island, Washington

Blanton's Jig Hook Rabbit's Foot

Originator: Dan Blanton
Tier: Steve Rohrbach

Hook: Eagle Claw EC 413, size 1 and 2
Thread: White Danville Flymaster Plus
Optics: 3/16" Spirit River Real Eyes Plus. Nickel/red or nickel/yellow
Flashtail: 10-15 strands pearl Flashabou, original limp
Tail: White rabbit strip
Underwing: Chartreuse Slinky Flash
Topping: Light blue Krystal Flash, 15-25 strands
Head: White tying thread

Blanton's Jig Hook Flashtail Clouser

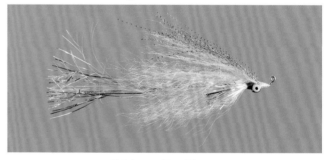

Originator: Dan Blanton
Tier: Steve Rohrbach

Hook: Eagle Claw EC 413, size 2 to 3/0
Thread: White Danville Flymaster Plus, white and red
Optics: Spirit River Real Eyes Plus, 7/32". Nickel/red or nickel/yellow
Flashtail: 50/50 mix of silver and pearl Flashabou, original limp. 75 strands
Tail: Bucktail white Slinky Flash
Side Flash: 50/50 mix of silver and pearl Flashabou, original limp. 25 strands
Belly: Bucktail white Slinky Flash
Under-wing: Chartreuse Slinky Flash
Mid-wing: Chartreuse bucktail
Over-wing: Chartreuse bucktail
Topping: 40 to 50 strands of light blue Krystal Flash
Head: White tying thread

Blanton's Jig Hook Flashtail Whistler

Originator: Dan Blanton
Tier: Steve Rohrbach

Hook: Eagle Claw EC 413, size 2 through 4/0
Thread: White Danville Fly Master Plus, chartreuse and red
Optics: Spirit River Real Eyes Plus, size 7/32". Nickel/red or nickel/yellow
Flashtail: 50/50 mix of silver and pearl Flashabou, original limp, 75 strands.
Side Flash: 15 to 20 strands, multi-color Krystal Flash
Tail: Bucktail white Slinky Flash
Belly-wing: Bucktail white Slinky Flash
Underwing: Bucktail white Slinky Flash
Middle-wing: Chartreuse Slinky Flash
Overwing: Chartreuse bucktail
Topping: Light blue Krystal Flash, 50 strands
Collar: Medium red Ultra Chenille, tied in with red thread
Hackle Collar: White medium webby hackle
Facing Hackle: Chartreuse medium webby hackle
Head: Chartreuse tying thread
Tier's Note: "These unique patterns, dressed on a jig hook, were Dan Blanton's choices when author Les Johnson requested flies for this book. I tied them for Les per the instructions on Blanton's web site. This hook also conjures up ideas for tying other patterns on the EC413. Dan refers to this threesome of attractors as his 'any ocean, any species flies'."

—Steve Rohrbach
Seattle, Washington

Clouser Minnow (chartreuse)

Originator: Bob Clouser
Tier: Barry Stokes

Hook: Mustad 3407, size 1/0-2

Thread: Fine clear monofilament, 3/0 Danville chartreuse, 3/0 Danville red
Body: White FisHair secured with clear monofilament and topped with red thread to suggest gills
Lateral Line: Chartreuse Mirage Flashabou
Topwing: Chartreuse FisHair and Glow Krystal Flash, mixed
Eyes: Dumbbell painted yellow with orange pupils. Epoxy over eyes, optional
Tier's Note: "This is my adaptation of Shawn Bennett's Clayoquot Clouser. It was developed by Shawn to target coho in the Tofino/Clayoquot Sound area. This version of the Clouser has proven to be a good searching pattern and for feeding pink salmon as well. This pattern also works for me tied with bead-chain eyes and fished off the beaches."

—Barry Stokes

Clouser Minnow (Pink)

Originator: Bob Clouser
Tier: Christopher Bentsen

Hook: Mustad 3407, size 8
Thread: Clear monofilament or Danville fluorescent pink
Tail: Pink kip tail, thin bucktail or FisHair
Body: Pink thread
Wing: Pink kip tail or thin bucktail topped with 6 strands of pink Krystal Flash
Eyes: Small chrome dumbbells, 1/64 or 1/32.

Tier's Note: "This is a standard Clouser Minnow. Its single distinction is that it is tied on a small hook using all pink wing material, a very effective color for Pacific salmon. It was shown to me by Mike Santangelo of Seattle when we were fishing in South Puget Sound one winter.
The Pink Clouser, which is an impressionistic imitation of a euphausiid, or shrimp, is fished on a floating line with a long leader and a slow stripping action. The fly should stop and dip during the retrieve. It is on the dip when the salmon usually hit it. In addition to silvers the Pink Clouser has been very effective on pink salmon in Washington and British Columbia. Don't use eyes larger than you need to give the pattern action."

—Christopher Bentsen
Sammamish, Washington

Ferguson Green and Silver

Originator and Tier: Bruce Ferguson

Hook: Mustad 34011, size 4, Tandem. Trailer, Daiichi 256, size 6

Thread: Black monocord, 3/0 waxed

Tail: Short tuft of polar bear or calf tail on a single hook version. A few strands of silver Krystal Flash on tandem hook version

Body: Rear half, silver Diamond Braid; front half, four turns of chartreuse chenille

Wing: White polar bear or bucktail, 1 1/2 to 2 inches, topped with several strands of pearl Krystal Flash.

Tier's Note: "This attractor pattern was originated in the 1970s for resident coho salmon feeding on zooplankton in Puget Sound. Over the years its use has expanded to include fall "waiting period" coho, chum and sea-run cutthroat year around. The Green and Silver has also taken mature fall chinook in southern Oregon rivers. It is always prominent in my fly box."

—Bruce M. Ferguson

Handlebar Fly #1

Originator: Thor Froslev (per Bob Hurst)
Tier: Bob Hurst

Hook: Size 6 and 8 Mustad 34007 or Gamakatsu SL11-3H

Thread: Clear monofilament

Body: Fluorescent pink Edgebright over flat silver tinsel or Diamond Braid

Throat: One strip of Pearlite on each side

Wing: Blue Crystal Hair topped with white polar bear, sparse

Eyes: Black painted and covered with epoxy

Tier's Note: "The unique feature of the Handlebar is the silver tinsel under fluorescent plastic which makes the plastic almost electric, so to speak. This material was first incorporated into a

steelhead fly by Thor Froslev, called Thor's Hammer. In the late 1970s I combined the body design with a polar bear wing for use beach fishing for pink and coho salmon. Results were outstanding. Modified numerous times since, the current pattern retains this important basic body style. The name "Handlebar Fly" came from the use of fluorescent plastic strips popular in a bygone era as decoration for bicycle handlebars. This material is now available as Edgebrite."

—Bob Hurst
Parksville, British Columbia, Canada

Handlebar Fly #2

Originator: Bob Hurst
Tier: Bill Nelson

Hook: Mustad 34007, size 2

Thread: Fine clear monofilament

Tail: Hot red FisHair, sparse

Body: Hot red strand from Hootchie skirt, or Edgebrite

Hackle: Pheasant rump feather

Eyes: Bead chain at bend of hook, silver or brass

Head: Clear monofilament over orange or fluorescent red thread

Finish: Epoxy or high-finish head cement

Tier's Note "I fished the original Handlebar with Bob Hurst and it is very successful. The modifications to the fly that I now use were made because it is handy for me to obtain the other materials and because I am fishing a different area. I found that some of the modifications seem to work better on other species. There aren't many sockeye south of Canada's border but we do have chum, pink and coho salmon; all of which like this version of the Handlebar Fly."

—Bill Nelson

Handlebar Fly #3, Simplified

Originator: Bob Hurst
Tier: Bruce M. Ferguson

Hook: Mustad 34007, size 2

Thread: Fine clear monofilament

Tail: Hot reddish-pink FisHair
Body: Silver Diamond Braid overlaid with fluorescent pink Edgebrite
Head: Fine, clear monofilament
Tier's Note: "In 1991 Bill Nelson introduced this fly to me in its simplified form. Every year for a decade this trimmed-down version of the Handlebar was the number one producer for me, fishing the offshore rips of N.E. Vancouver Island's Queen Charlotte Strait out of Telegraph Cove. It works at all depths from sub-surface to 70 feet down. The catch was a combination of pinks and coho with the occasional sockeye, all taken when they were feeding on euphausiids."

—*Bruce M. Ferguson*

Handlebar Fly #4

Originator: Unknown
Tier: Les Johnson

Hook: Gamakatsu SL13-3H size 8-4, or equivalent
Thread: Danville clear monofilament
Tail: Krystal Flash to match body, sparse
Body: Edgebrite over silver Mylar tinsel. Pink, red, hot orange, orange or green are all used
Eyes: Mini bead chain, black, silver, blue, chartreuse or red
Head: Thread to match Edgebrite
Tier's Note: "I found this version of the Handlebar at a small fishing tackle shop in Port Hardy on northern Vancouver Island a few years ago. As I recall it was tied locally, particularly for pinks staging in the surf. It turned out to be a very good fly not only for mature returning pinks but coho as well along the beaches near Port Hardy. I have also used it with success in all the Edgebrite colors at one time or another along the beaches of Puget Sound."

—*Les Johnson*

Handlebar Fly (pink) #5

Originator: Thor Frøslev (per Bob Hurst)
Tier: Barry Stokes

Hook: Mustad 34007 or Partridge CS 11, size 4-8
Tail: Pink polar bear and pink Krystal Flash, mixed; sparse
Body: Pink Laser Wrap over flat silver tinsel

Head: Epoxy over fluorescent red paint
Tier's Note: "This pattern was first shown to me by Bruce Ferguson and was originally tied with a piece of a pink streamer from a child's bicycle handlebar, now almost impossible to find. Fortunately Bob Wagoner brought out Edge Brite, now called Lazer Wrap which is now the standard body wrap for all Handlebar patterns. The pink Handlebar is my second most effective fly for fishing pink salmon from the beaches; right behind the Glow Worm."

—*Barry Stokes*

Johnson Beach Fly

Originator and Tier: Les Johnson

Hook: Gamakatsu SC13-3H, size 4 through 8
Thread: Danville flame orange, 6/0
Tail: Hot orange calf tail, sparse, fairly long, or orange hackle fibers.
Body: Danville Depth Ray fluorescent orange wool, or Spirit River Pseudo Seal dubbing
Rib: Flat gold Mylar tinsel, size 12 or 14, for wool body version only. For the dubbed body spin dubbing sparsely over a gold Mylar tinsel covered shank. Brush out to form a veil over the tinsel so it will show through when wet
Hackle: Brown, four turns (original), or hot orange hen hackle, three turns, on dubbed version
Wing: White polar bear, calf tail or bulky synthetic material length of body and tail, over a few strands of orange Krystal Flash. Top with a few strands of pearl Krystal Flash. The dubbed version is tied with a shorter wing and tail
Head: Softex
Tier's Note: "A nice perk when developing one's own pattern is that the originator can modify it without becoming one of those people who 'improves' other people's flies. I've enjoyed a nice relationship with my Beach Fly, keeping it essentially the same but trying different materials from time to time. The original design is something of a hodgepodge roughly taken from the Brad's Brat, Admiral, Thor and Polar Shrimp all of which preceded it by decades and any of which could raise the question as to its need. I've used the original Beach Fly along beaches and sometimes near to estuaries with good success for more than thirty years. The later dubbed version with the shortened wing is very good when there is crab or shrimp spawn in the water."

—*Les Johnson*

Knudsen Spider

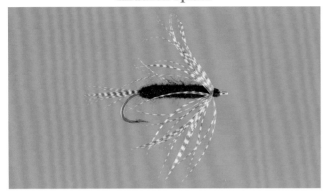

Originator: Al Knudsen
Tier: Bob Young

Hook: Mustad 34011, size 6
Thread: Danville, 3/0 black
Tail: Barred mallard flank fibers
Body: Black medium chenille
Wing: Mallard flank spun around hook shank as a hackle
Tier's Note: "This fly is a knock-off of one developed in the 1930s by noted fly tier of the period, Al Knudsen of Arlington, Washington. Originally called the 'Wet Spider' and tied mostly in bright colors, it became a classic sea-run cutthroat pattern. The version I tie is simplified considerably. While fishing from the beaches of Puget Sound, I tend to leave a few flies behind, decorating driftwood logs; hence my simplified dressing which makes replacement easy for me. Whenever I approach a beach, the black Knudsen Spider is the first fly I tie on. While various colors such as yellow, orange or red are tempting, I usually stick with black on a floating line, unless it gets windy when I switch to an intermediate sinking line to get my fly just under the choppy surface. My experience has shown that this is a reliable pattern for juvenile, early season resident coho as well as both feeding and mature 'waiting period' fish in the fall. And not abandoning its roots, anytime the black Knudsen Spider is being stripped through the Pacific Northwest salt, it is likely to coax up a nice sea-run cutthroat."

—Bob Young
Seattle, Washington

Medicine

Originator: Hugh Falkus
Tier: Art Lingren

Hook: Size 2-6, low-water salmon
Thread: Red, 6/0

Tail: None
Body: Paint hook shank silver, cover with silver Scribbles, or wrap with silver tinsel (Falkus covered the hook shanks of the first Medicine patterns with silver paint)
Hackle: Silver doctor blue
Wing: Bronze mallard, folded or bunched
Tier's Note: "I came across the Medicine when I purchased Hugh Falkus' Sea Trout Fishing in the mid-1980s. Falkus at that time was one of Great Britain's leading authors on Atlantic salmon and sea trout fishing. I liked its slim design and tied a few for my fly box to use on cutthroats. Digging around in my box, I noticed the Medicine when I was fishing on the Queen Charlotte Islands for pink salmon with my son, Charles. I handed him one to try. Charles was around twelve years old at the time. He managed to hook and land a pile of pinks that day on the Medicine. Afterward, I heard him tell his friend about how he caught more fish than his dad. Since that time the Medicine has produced fairly consistently for pinks and the odd coho and chum in saltwater."

—Art Lingren
Vancouver, British Columbia

My Favorite

Originator and Tier: Vernon J. Young

Hook: Size 4 or larger Mustad C71S SS Circle Streamer
Thread: Black
Body: Dubbing: Salmon Fly Orange or Burnt Orange
Wing: Olive over white arctic fox topped with 4 strands of Crystal Hair
Tier's Note: "Most fly-fishermen were using zooplankton patterns when I began fly-fishing for coho and cutthroat in southern Puget Sound. When the zooplankton was thick the coho would begin flock feeding and ignore my offerings. By presenting a baitfish pattern, they could occasionally be persuaded to strike. When they were on baitfish, they seem to prefer this pattern to the real thing.

I first tied it on a J hook, but now that I am using a circle hook, it works better. The circle hook can only grasp a convex surface and the only convex surface around a fish's mouth is its lips. Material in the bend of the hook can kick it away from the lip.

I am sold on circle hooks as a conservation tool for catch-and-release fishing. I have yet to gut-hook a fish with a circle hook as sometimes would happen using a J hook. It's also nice that I do not have to intentionally set the hook on the strike. In fact, it is recommended that you don't! Just take up slack and begin playing the fish. If you attempt to set the hook before the fish has a chance to turn, you will not hook it."

—Vernon Young
Gig Harbor, Washington

Pink and Gold

Originator and Tier: Ted Pearson

Hook: Mustad 92608 stainless, 4XL, size 6

Thread: White or pink 6/0. Switch to black to tie in the wing and form a head

Body: Short pink craft fur, dubbed and wrapped to form slightly thick body; brushed out to make it fuzzy

Wing: Long, light gold craft fur, small clump. Retain base fur but pick out longest hairs

Eyes: None

Head: Black thread

Tier's Note: "In about 1990 I acquired a box of mixed craft furs at a garage sale. I was impressed with the translucency of the material and decided to develop a fly patterns from it. The material proved to sink quickly; a plus when fishing from the beaches. The pink and gold combination worked well from the start for both resident coho and cutthroat. It is still the first fly I tie on when I start fishing our local salt water.

I had a great day in Vaughn Bay a few winters back when a school of blackmouth were hitting the Pink and Gold on nearly every cast. I also tie this fly with a white craft fur wing and find it to be an excellent change-up for the pink version. Lately I've been tying it on a smaller size 8 Mustad 3407 and find that it works when I am getting refusals on the longer shank dressing."

—Ted Pearson

Pink Eve

Originator: Barry Thornton
Tier: Clifford Barker

Hook: Mustad 34011, size 2-6

Thread: Bright pink

Body: Silver oval tinsel or Diamond Braid

Wing: Short, sparse pink hackle fibers

Head: Pink or red bead; or bright pink thread built up

Finish: Any high-gloss finish

Tier's Note: "This pattern originated by Barry Thornton of British Columbia has become a standby for taking both coho and pink salmon throughout the BC salt. Canadian fly-fishers use it regularly around kelp beds, the rips off Quadra Island and along the beaches of Vancouver Island."

—Clifford Barker
Bellevue, Washington

Pooch Persuader

Originator and Tier: Jay Taylor

Hook: Tiemco 9394, size 6

Thread: Black UNI-Thread, 8/0

Tail: Thin silicone chartreuse skirt holographic tinsel (rubber legs)

Body: Danville depth ray fluorescent nylon wool, chartreuse

Hackle: Chartreuse neck hackle, stripped on one side

Butt: Danville depth ray fluorescent nylon wool, hot orange

Finish: Any fast-drying finish

Tier's Note: "I developed the Pooch Persuader to fish for chum (dog) salmon in Hood Canal along the beach in front of the Hoodsport Salmon Hatchery. After having limited success using a chartreuse Woolly Bugger, I set forth to come up with a similar pattern that employed a sparser silhouette that would appeal to these hard-fighting fish. I fish the Pooch Persuader on an intermediate sinking-tip line using a slow finger-twitch retrieve, or when the tide is running, simply allow it to swing with the current.

The pattern has proven effective at the estuaries of Johns Creek, Potlatch and Chico Creek. It is also effective in hot orange with a chartreuse accent. The smaller hook size and shape of the 9394 seems to help avoid snagging chums when they are schooled up. I get many missed strikes between hook-ups, which is pretty common when fishing chums with small, non-snagging flies. It seems that by the time the strike is transmitted up the fly line, the salmon is gone."

—Jay Taylor
Seattle, Washington

(Original) Teeny Nymph

Originator and Tier: Jim Teeny

Hook: Custom Eagle Claw
Thread: Black
Body: Pheasant-tail feather section tied in at hook bend, twisted and wrapped forward
Legs: Tips of body feather pulled down as beard and tied off
Tier's Note: "The original Teeny Nymph has been a salmon-catching workhorse for me in rivers from California to Alaska for more than 30 years, and still is. Les Johnson told me though that he has been carrying the Teeny Nymph in sizes 6 through 10 with him during his saltwater fishing ventures for several years as a generic krill imitation in orange, pink, red and ginger to take bright, feeding pink salmon that are sipping amphipods, copepods or euphausiids from the surface. Les has also found the original Teeny Nymph to be an effective fly for big northern coho along the beaches of Vancouver Island and resident juvenile coho in Washington's Puget Sound during the winter. He recommends a floating or intermediate sinking line, depending on surface conditions and long leader for a gentle presentation to these often spooky fish."

—Jim Teeny
Gresham, Oregon

TUMS

Originator and Tier: Mike Croft

Thread: Gudebrod clear monofilament
Hook: Primary Mustad 34007, size 4. Trailer size 2 Octopus
Wing: Three strands of soft braided Mylar unraveled with Icelandic goat over the top
Gills: Red floss
Eyes: Mylar stick-on
Head: Epoxy
Tier's Note: "I was fishing with Charles Spring, whom I had been teaching to tie flies. We were fishing with Zonkers that we'd tied. Charles hadn't mastered the whip finish and the Mylar body of his Zonker soon began to unravel. With the unraveling Mylar flashing in all directions he suddenly was catching two or three coho salmon to my one.

If you are looking for a fly with as much flash as a spinner, this is your pattern. I've used it far and wide, almost always with excellent results. TUMS is a contraction for Triple Unbraided Mylar Streamer."

—Mike Croft

The Waiting Period

As the various runs of Pacific salmon near their natal streams, there comes a period when they must adapt themselves biologically to fresh water. They pause in their migration during this period and often flush in and out of the estuaries with the tide but never move far from the scent of 'home'. Low autumn flows will also cause salmon to hold outside of the estuaries to await a freshet before moving into the rivers. On short, coastal rivers salmon will begin to display the first flush of spawning colors at this time. On longer rivers where salmon travel considerable distances before spawning they will remain silvery bright for days or even weeks during their spawning run. The days or weeks that salmon begin staging near the estuaries prior to migration upstream has become known as the waiting period. The name was not used to the best of our knowledge prior to the publication of the original Fly Fishing for Pacific Salmon. However, the name has stuck and has become a common term among saltwater salmon fly-fishers.

Although waiting-period salmon are often concentrated and will reveal their presence by jumping and rolling, their feeding urge has become just a memory. Whereas, days earlier they could be taken readily on a bucktail as they slashed among the baitfish, these same salmon will distain such offerings. The waiting period is the time to find concentrations of salmon but hooking them consistently is something else again!

Through experience, anglers have found that large, often bulky, weighted attractor flies, long associated with freshwater fishing are not consistently effective for waiting-period salmon. The most productive flies for the waiting period are usually sparsely dressed on small, stout hooks, with some patterns sporting long, wispy wings.

Flies for the Waiting Period

Allard Orange

Originator: Al Allard
Tier: Bruce Ferguson

Hook: Size 2-6 Mustad 34007, Gamakatsu SL11-3H, or equivalent
Thread: Black monocord, 3/0
Tail: Sparse bunch of soft grizzly hackle fibers
Body: Burnt orange, or true orange chenille. Alternate body, medium yellow chenille
Rib: Flat silver tinsel
Hackle: Soft grizzly, two turns
Wing: Very sparse polar bear, yak hair or bucktail at least two inches long, topped with several strands of orange Crystal Hair
Head: Black thread
Tier's Note: "Al Allard was one of the most accomplished small boat and beach fly-fishers in southern Puget Sound and mentor to many of us. He introduced me to this fly in the 1970s. After perhaps a decade of use I put it aside for newer patterns. In the early 1990s I rediscovered it in the bottom of my fly box when other flies failed me. It has once again become a very dependable pattern along the beaches for returning mature fall coho—and sea-runs year around. Key to its success is the long, sparse white wing. The Allard orange or yellow is best fished with a clear intermediate line using an erratic 6-inch retrieve punctuated with a snap of the wrist."

—*Bruce Ferguson*

Chief Fat Dog

Originator: Unknown
Tier: Les Johnson

Hook: Gamakatsu SL11-3H, size 2-8, or equivalent
Thread: Black and orange Danville, 3/0
Body: Silver Mylar piping over wool underbody
Tail: Picked-out ends of braided Mylar piping body
Wing: Purple bucktail
Throat: Hot orange bucktail, extending to hook barb
Tier's Note: "The unassuming Chief Fat Dog was a sleeper offered by the folks at Bristol Bay Lodge in Alaska as a coho fly when the first edition of this book was being written. However, I first used the Chief Fat Dog to catch steelhead from the Salmon Creek estuary in California in the mid-1980s. As a coho fly it has served me well from the Snoqualmie River in Washington to the Thorne River in Alaska. A longtime California pal and rare book dealer Gene Fassi likes the fly so well that he simply refers to it affectionately as 'The Chief'. We were first told that Chief Fat Dog was a freshwater pattern. However, it has proven to work equally well for waiting period salmon. Pat Trotter noted that it would be interesting to find out the origin of its name."

—*Les Johnson*

Crazy Ben

Originator: Bob Nauheim and Charley Smith
Tier: Steve Damm

Hook: Mustad 34007, size 6
Thread: Danville black, 6/0
Tail: Red and pink Krystal Flash

Body: Danville silver Mylar tinsel, size 12

Wing: Cerise or hot pink marabou

Eyes: Lead eyes, small, 1/40 ounce

Tier's Note: "The Crazy Ben, named after my nephew, Ben Magnano, is an offshoot of the Crazy Charlie originated by Bob Nauheim and Charley Smith. After fishing salmon in the saltwater of the Pacific Northwest for twenty years I had been searching for a 'waiting period' fly for chum salmon. Finally, after realizing that the estuaries where we found chums were flat and shallow, similar to bonefish flats I decided to try a variation of the Crazy Charlie which is one of my favorite bonefish patterns. I first fished the Crazy Ben on a 10- to 12-foot leader, retrieving it with slow, 6-inch strips, letting the fly create its own action. It turned out to be very effective for chum salmon on beach flats throughout Puget Sound. Later, I found it to be a winner on pink and coho salmon, not only in Washington but in British Columbia and Alaska as well. Other wing colors that work well are chartreuse and yellow."

—Steve Damm
Seattle, Washington

Crazy Plankton

Originator and Tier: Leland Miyawaki

Hook: Mustad 3407 or 34007, size 10 or 8

Thread: Pink floss

Eyes: Smallest bead-chain or chrome lead eyes

Tail: 4-5 strands of Pink Krystal Flash

Body: Clear small V-rib over pink floss underwrap

Beard: 4-5 strands of pink Krystal Flash

Tier's Note: "Tie the Crazy Plankton short and sparse. Vary the weight of the eyes to increase or decrease the sink rate. I fish it on a floating line with a long leader; or a shorter leader if I'm using and intermediate sinking line. I cast to working salmon, allowing the Crazy Plankton to drift with the tidal current, keeping just enough tension to maintain contact with the fly without letting it swing. It is often very effective for immature coho during the December through February season in South Puget Sound."

—Leland Miyawaki

Croft's Spider

Originator and Tier: Mike Croft

Hook: Mustad 3399 or 3366, size 10-2

Thread: Gudebrod clear monofilament

Body: Gold Mylar laid in over a bead of Super Glue

Hackle: One large palmered golden pheasant crest and three wraps of pumpkin orange saddle hackle

Head: Gold bead to match size of hook

Tier's Note: "You can increase your waiting-period coho hookups by using high-carbon hooks as opposed to stainless-steel hooks. I hate to lose my flies to rust but the bronze hooks are much more effective. This fly is the great granddaughter of the Comet. Over the years it has gone through various changes, seemingly to become sparser and finer with each new generation. I made the Spider with cutthroat in mind but it has worked out to be an equally good, if not better pattern for coho salmon."

—Mike Croft

Disco Sand Lance

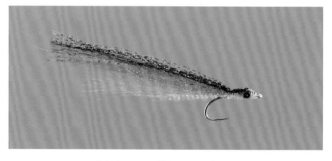

Originator and Tier: Les Johnson

Hook: Size 2-6 Gamakatsu S11 3H

Thread: Clear monofilament

Wing: Super Hair; black over olive over pink over white

Topping: Grizzly/black Krystal Flash

Side Flash: Pink Krystal Flash, sparse

Eyes: Small to medium Spirit River black bead chain, depending on hook size

Head: Build up with thread

Head: Build up with head cement or Softex

Tier's Note: "This flashy little generalized sand lance imitation has proven to be excellent at times over waiting period salmon near the creek mouths entering Puget Sound and Hood Canal."

The Disco Sand Lance has also hooked some large coho salmon in the fall when they are returning to parent rivers along Puget Sound beaches. The bead-chain eyes are not heavy enough to turn the fly upside down but do provide the right amount of weight to make the Disco Sand Lance dip up and down on retrieve and dive for the bottom when I pause the retrieve—just like a live frightened sand lance."

—*Les Johnson*

Flashabou Comet

Originator: Unknown
Tier: Les Johnson

Hook: Gamakatsu SL11-3H, size 6 and 8

Thread: Clear monofilament for body and tail. Danville flat waxed nylon to match to match hackle

Tail: Chum salmon; Bright green Flashabou, a dozen strands, one and one-half times longer than hook shank. Pink salmon; Pearl and solid pink Flashabou, mixed. Coho salmon; silver Flashabou

Body: Remaining Flashabou wrapped forward tightly. Criss-cross monofilament thread to the hook bend and back to the eye for durability

Hackle: Chum; Kelly green. Pink; fluorescent shell pink. Coho; hot red

Eyes: Spirit River nickel barbells, x-small

Head: Danville fluorescent green, shell pink or red flat waxed nylon to match hackle

Finish: Softex or other finish

Tier's Note: "This is my variation of the classic Comet made famous in Northern California rivers in the 1940s. It has been effective on waiting-period pink and coho salmon along the beaches of Puget Sound and in the tidal reaches of Puget Sound rivers. It is however exceedingly deadly on staging chum. I tied the Flashabou Comet small and sparse when I was searching for a fly that would hook these fish in low or clear water conditions when larger patterns sometimes snagged them or were refused. The Green Flashabou Comet was launched several years ago when Bruce Ferguson and I used it to light up some moody Hood Canal chums; every one fair-hooked. It has become my go-to fly for chums when they reach the estuaries. The tiny nickel barbell or bead chain eyes provide just enough weight to make the

fly dance enticingly on retrieve without rolling it over. For pink salmon the pink version is usually best. The silver body and red hackle is most effective for coho."

—*Les Johnson*

Glo Worm

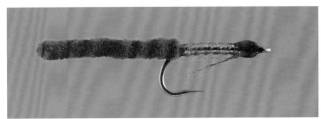

Originator and Tier: Barry Stokes

Hook: Mustad 3407, size 4-8

Thread: Danville 6/0, fluorescent pink

Tail: Twisted hot pink chenille

Beard: Pink Fluoro Fibre

Head: Epoxy over built-up thread head

Tier's Note: "This pattern is the result of an experiment combining two of my favorite flies for fishing pink salmon from the beach: The Pink Handlebar and the Pink Worm. The process of twisting the chenille was developed by Bernie Marchildon from an original procedure by Dave Lornie. I combined the best features of my two favorite pink salmon flies and came up with this: the Glow Worm. It is now my go-to fly for pink salmon anywhere I find them."

—*Barry Stokes*

Hubert Humpy

Originator and Tier: Preston Singletary

Thread: Fine clear monofilament

Hook: Mustad 34007, size 4-8

Body: Pearl Diamond Braid

Gills: Several turns of red floss (optional)

Wing: Pink rabbit strip

Eyes: Medium silver bead chain

Tier's Note: "Although I originally tied the Hubert Humpy for pink salmon in fresh water, it has proven to be an exceptional waiting-period fly for coho in salt water as well. I have also tied and fished it with olive, orange or white rabbit strips. Olive, in particular, makes an excellent small candlefish imitation."

—*Preston Singletary*

Monty's Zuma

Originator: Ian Montgomery
Tier: Steve Sunich

Hook: TMC 9394, size 6-1

Thread: Red or hot pink, size 6/0

Tail: Extension of body material frayed with red tag

Body: Pearl Mylar tubing over hook shank

Wing: Overwing, pink bucktail; Underwing, white bucktail; lateral line, blue Fluoro Fibre

Head: Red thread coated with epoxy

Tier's Note: "I first used this pattern, an Ian Montgomery creation, in preparation for a trip to Tofino, British Columbia. Shawn Bennett at Weigh West suggested it for silvers. After a successful trip casting for silvers in Clayoquot Sound, BC I have used Monty's Zuma in smaller sizes for casting from the beaches of Puget Sound It is a wonderful casting fly as it never tangles and is not too bulky or heavy for casting with a 6- or 7-weight rod. I have not tried it in different colors but the pink version has caught some very respectable silvers—and sea-run cutthroat in Puget Sound. The blue lateral line contrasts very well with the pink and white material. I have mostly fished it near the surface using a floating line during cloudy days, or early in the morning. It has brought some nice returning ocean-run silvers to the surface."

—Steve Sunich

Pink Streak

Originator and Tier: Tim Tullis

Hook: Mustad 34011, size 6

Thread: UNI Mono, fine

Body: Silver holographic Mylar

Wing: Pink over white Everglow Flashabou

Head: Epoxied medium Mylar cord

Eyes: 1/8" silver Witchcraft holographic stick-on eyes

Tier's Note: "The Pink Streak was developed for pink salmon beach fishing on the waters around north and east Vancouver Island. It is very productive when fished with an intermediate line using a quick snap retrieve. It also works well to get things going when there are fish around but the bite is off."

—Tim Tullis

Secret Weapon

Originator and Tier: Peers Pendlebury

Hook: 8-12 Mustad 9671, Gamakatsu SS 15, or equivalent

Thread: 6/0 pink

Body: Flat silver tinsel

Wing: Four strands each pearl Krystal Flash, pearl Flashabou. A few strands each of white, pink, yellow, orange and olive hair (calf or polar bear), mixed. Bunch and tie on as wing

Head: Pink thread

Tier's Note: "I developed the Secret Weapon to hook coho salmon that are being fussy on those late fall days when they have been around for a while waiting for rain to swell the creeks. Cast on a 6-pound-test leader you will get a lot of action and consistently hook coho on the Secret Weapon. You are however only likely to land one out of every five you hook, due to the small hook. It is especially valuable in flat, calm conditions when larger flies and heavy leaders only spook the fish. I have fished the Secret Weapon 'when necessary' for the past two seasons and have enjoyed excellent results."

—Peers Pendlebury
Qualicum Beach, British Columbia

Silver Slammer (Cerise)

Originator and Tier: Mike Telford

Hook: Daiichi Alec Jackson Spey, or Mustad 34007, size 1/0

Thread: UNI-Thread, white for body, black for head

Tail: Cerise kid goat hair

Tag: Lagartun medium oval tinsel, silver

Body: Pink Flashabou over-wrapped with Stalcup's standard midge tubing filled with mineral oil

Hackle: Cerise kid goat hair woven George Grant style

Finish: Sally Hansen's Hard-As-Nails or similar durable finish

Tier's Note: "This is essentially a classic comet pattern given a bit of a facelift with new materials and an old hackling method. I've enjoyed great success on coho salmon with the Slammer while fishing estuaries of Sheep Bay, Simpson Bay and Sheep River in Prince William Sound, Alaska."

—*Mike Telford*

Silver Slammer (Purple)

Originator and Tier: Mike Telford

Hook: Daiichi Alec Jackson Spey, or Mustad 34007, 1/0

Thread: UNI-Thread, white for body, black for head

Tail: Purple kid goat hair

Tag: Lagartun medium oval tinsel, silver

Body: Grape Flashabou over-wrapped with Stalcup's standard midge tubing filled with mineral oil

Hackle: Purple kid goat hair woven George Grant style

Finish: Sally Hansen's Hard-As-Nails or similar durable finish

Tier's Note: "The Purple Slammer is the companion pattern to my Pink Slammer. I use them interchangeably for coho salmon. If one doesn't bring grabs for some reason, the other usually will."

—*Mike Telford*

SS Minnow

Originator and Tier: Steve Sunich

Hook: TMC 9394, 200R, or 5263, size 10-6

Thread: Red, 6/0

Tail: (Tag), silver tinsel counter-wrapped with red wire. Epoxy over the entire body for durability

Wing: White blood quill marabou, one white saddle hackle on each side

Topping: 8-10 strands of extra-limp silver Flashabou

Head: Finish with red thread and cover with head cement

Tier's Note: "This pattern was originated at the tying bench while playing with some marabou and Flashabou. The idea was that it would be a thin attractor to represent a variety of baitfish found in fresh and salt water that is the prey of coho salmon and sea-run cutthroat. It can be tied in a range of sizes. I have used saltwater versions of the SS Minnow down to size 10, especially early in the season. The larger version should be in the size-6 range with an overall length of about 3 inches. The saddles in the wings provide a bit of rigidity and mass while the marabou and Flashabou provide very good swimming characteristics. I've used the SS Minnow weighted and unweighted. Epoxy on the body provide both durability and a bit of shine."

—*Steve Sunich*
Issaquah, Washington

ST Clouser Minnow

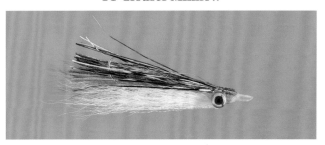

Originator: Bob Clouser (Modification by Roger Stephens)
Tier: Roger Stephens

Hook: Gamakatsu SC 15, size 4

Thread: Clear monofilament

Sequin: 10mm pearl, found in fabric or craft shops

Tube: HMH 3/32" OD cut at a 45-degree angle on the side when fly is finished. Soft plastic accommodator added to hold hook in position

Body: Pearl Krystal Flash over white bucktail

Top: 4 strands of peacock herl over #6923 Flashabou over white bucktail

Eyes: Spirit River Eye Balz, 3/16"

Finish: Zap-a-Gap or other durable finish

Tier's Note: "The up-and-down jigging action of a traditional Clouser Minnow helps to make it a very effective pattern. The erratic side-to-side action is created by the sequins angled at 45 degrees created by the cut at the front of the tube. I use two of the 10mm sequins for durability. I find that a fast retrieve of 4- to 6-inch strips with a snap at the end like shaking down a thermometer is most effective. Long, steady strips of 12 to 18 inches are a good change-up retrieve. This has proven to be an excellent pattern for coho salmon on Puget Sound. "To give the S.T. Clouser Minnow even more side-to-side movement cut off the last 1/3 of the tube and add a small clear or pearl bead between the two sections. Attach the hook sleeve to the end of the 1/3 section."

—*Roger Stephens*

Tryityou'lllikeit

Originator and Tier: Peter Caverhill

Hook: Size 6 Mustad 34011, Gamakatsu SL11-3H or equivalent. (Any 2X-3X long-shank hook will do)

Thread: 6/0 UNI-Thread, yellow

Tail: Small clump of yellow hackle fibers

Body: Medium green UNI-yarn, slim and tapered toward up to eyes

Hackle: None

Wing: Yellow hackle fibers tied in behind eyes, tips forward. Pull hackle forward, tie and pull back and finish tying off behind eye. Wing should be short, 3/4 body length

Eyes: Translucent green plastic bead chain

Tier's Note: "For several years I resisted using this fly. It sat in my salmon fly box and stared up at me with those ridiculous transparent eyes every time I would open the lid. I'd tied a couple of the flies some years ago because I had discovered the plastic bead chain and wanted to see how it would look on a quickly tied fly. Then, one fall in a freshwater situation that seemed impossible, with lock-jawed coho cavorting all around, I said to myself, 'What the hell?' Wow! It worked. And it has been working ever since. It seems to do best in the freshwater and estuary realm, where coho are staging (sometimes called the waiting period) to make their upstream dash when the conditions of tide and flow tickle their instincts.

Perhaps the best thing about this pattern, and what I seek more and more as life speeds along, is dumb simplicity in the tying department. This is truly the '3-minute fly'—perfect for those night-before-the-trip tying sessions. Probably the hardest part of this fly is finding the translucent green plastic eyes (and who knows how critical they actually are?). Part of the ease and speed of tying this fly is that the plastic eyes come affixed on a chain of beads. All a lazy tier has to do is snip off a pair and whip it to the hook shank. These bead eyes add little, if any, weight to the fly. If anything they may be slightly buoyant which isn't an issue, when using slow-sinking fly lines, preferably the clear or camo ones.

Since this pattern has come out of the closet, several friends have reported good salmon success with it. Its name Tryityou'lllikeit at first glance seems like a foreign language, but in truth it states a simple fact in English."

—*Pete Caverhill*
Port Moody, British Columbia

Tsapee Clouser

Originator and Tier: Don McDermid

Hook: Mustad 34007, size 4 to 10

Thread: Danville pre-waxed 6/0 chartreuse

Eyes: Chartreuse-colored brass, 3/16"

Wing: 3/8 chartreuse, over 1/4 pink, over 3/8 white polar bear or substitute

Topping: Four strands of pearlescent Krystal Flash. The completed wing should be very sparse

Tier's Note: "This fly proved to be very fishy at Tsapee Narrows in September 2005, as well as in the vicinity of Marina Island near Campbell River. It does require further use however before I can declare it a 'killer'".

—*Don McDermid*
Campbell River, British Columbia

Flies for the Freshwater Migration

Fly patterns used during the freshwater migration period of Pacific salmon reflect the influence of the modern renaissance that occurred on the Eel and Smith rivers of northern California and the Chetco and Rogue in southern Oregon. Accordingly, we opened the freshwater fly section by stating that success on salmon in the rivers depended on getting your flies deep. That is still essentially true if you are fishing for chinook salmon, which seek out the deepest runs and pools when they enter fresh water.

When the Alaska fishery opened up and anglers became aware of the sporting qualities of the other species of Pacific salmon, they also found that the different species could be targeted to a degree by where in the water column and in what stretches of a river they fished their flies. Chum salmon they discovered prefer a small, sparse fly stripped not too far under the surface, especially in the lower reaches and tide pools of a river. Coho strikes often occur very near the surface and on the surface. Sockeye salmon have a penchant for small flies drifted through the mid-level of their holding water. These are generalities. Nothing about the strike zones for various salmon species should be considered hard and fast. It is simply the observation of anglers based upon their experience over the years. The complete freshwater salmon fly-fisher always has an arsenal of flies in order to put a fly in front of a salmon's nose regardless of the species, or where it is holding in the water column. They range from small and sparse to large and heavily dressed from black to bright red; depending on water height and clarity—and the species of salmon that is being sought.

In recent years some beautifully dressed patterns reminiscent of classic steelhead or Atlantic salmon Spey flies have been developed for Pacific salmon in fresh water. This is likely a trend that will increase as dedicated steelhead fly-fishers spend more time fishing over coho and chinook salmon.

Freshwater Attractors

Beadhead Electric Leech

Originator: Unknown
Tier: Cecilia "Pudge" Kleinkauf

Hook: Size 6-2, Mustad 9674
Thread: UNI-Thread, 6/0 to match the colors in the fly
Tail: Fluffy marabou with several strands of rainbow or solid color Flashabou along each side
Body: Medium chenille (purple, black, white, etc.) with rainbow or solid color Flashabou down sides. Weighted hook shank is optional
Hackle: Webby saddle hackle feather palmered down the fly body
Eyes: Bead to match size of fly (Optional). For swift water a conehead is sometimes used in place of a bead
Finish: Any fast-drying finish
Tier's Note: "This is just a decorated Woolly Bugger with a bead head that is effective in various body and Flashabou combinations for all salmon. Some people omit the lead wire underbody and just rely on the weight of the bead or conehead to sink the fly."

—Cecilia "Pudge" Kleinkauf
Anchorage, Alaska

Dumbbell Marabou

Originator: Unknown
Tier: John Thompson

Hook: Tiemco 7999, size 2, or equivalent
Thread: Danville 6/0 chartreuse
Tail: Light green marabou
Body Flash: Silver Flashabou tied as collar, length of marabou
Hackle: Light green marabou plume, spun around hook shank
Eyes: Silver dumbbells, size determined by water depth and speed
Tier's Note: "This fly has been successful in southeast Alaska rivers for several years when it was given to me by a friend when I had gone fishless after nearly an hour of flogging the water with the usual popsicle and flash flies. Using the Beadhead Marabou I hooked up eleven bright coho salmon with just the one fly, or what was left of it.

Design of this fly has apparently undergone many slight modifications as it passed from one angler to the next. Although the originator is unknown, I like him."

—John Thompson
Seattle, Washington

Big Magenta

Originator: Bill Lee
Tier: Paul Carnes

Hook: Partridge Bartleet Supreme CS12/2, Mustad 36890 or Tiemco MMC, size 2/0-4
Thread: Red
Tail: Magenta dyed polar bear
Body: Fluorescent magenta SLF dubbing

Rib: Silver tinsel

Wing: A few strands of pink Krystal Flash topped with white polar bear over magenta-dyed polar bear

Hackle: Magenta-dyed guinea hen tied as throat

Head: Any fast build-up finish

Tier's Note: "I found this fly on the web, called Bill's Big Red as described by Phil Rowley. The original called for a wool body and fox fur wing. I substituted SLF for the body and a polar bear wing for a bit more visibility, movement and durability. The Big Magenta has been one of my best patterns for coho in the Bella Coola River in September and October which is oftentimes milky from glacial runoff."

—Paul Carnes
Williams Lake, British Columbia

Big Pink

Originator: Bill Lee
Tier: Paul Carnes

Hook: Same as Big Magenta

Thread: Red

Body: Fluorescent pink SLF dubbing

Rib: Silver tinsel

Wing: A few strands of pink Krystal Flash topped with white polar bear over pink dyed polar bear hair

Hackle: Pink-dyed magenta guinea hen tied as a throat

Head: Any fast build-up finish

Tier's Note: "A reliable variation of the Big Magenta."

—Paul Carnes

Big Red

Originator: Bill Lee
Tier: Bill Carnes

Hook: Same as Big Magenta and Big Pink

Thread: Red

Body: Fluorescent red SLF dubbing

Rib: Silver tinsel

Wing: A few strands of pink Krystal Flash topped with white polar bear over red dyed polar bear

Hackle: Red-dyed guinea hen tied as throat

Head: Any fast-build up finish

Tier's Note: "This is the original dressing of which the Big Magenta and Big Pink are color modifications. Outstanding for coho fresh in from salt water."

—Paul Carnes

Bjorn's Super Prawn (Black)

Originator and Tier: Bjorn Beech

Hook: TMC 7999, 2/0-1/0; Tiemco 777SP, 1/0-2; Gamakatsu Spinner-bait 3/0 for large kings (Read your regulations, as this hook has a 5/8" gap)

Thread: Danville 210 denier, color to match fly

Tail: Black bucktail and Flashabou

Shellback: Scud Back (to part and hold marabou)

Body: Black chenille

Hackle: Marabou Spey blood quill, spun; one kingfisher blue spun at mid-shank and one black at the head

Wing: American black-laced hen neck (at least three)

Eyes: Barbells (optional)

Tier's Note: "I first tied this fly in the mid-1980s for anglers chasing spring chinook salmon in Alaska and needed a large profile fly. As time passed, and with some minor alterations in size and color, this fly has also tallied an impressive numbers of coho, chum and pink salmon, steelhead, Arctic char, Dolly Varden and coastal cutthroat. Fishing for salmonids, the fly has produced through entire river systems but is seems to shine from a few miles above tidewater down to the estuary. I fish it on the swing, dredge it through deep holes or strip it along school edges in the salt chuck."

—Bjorn Beech
Lacey, Washington

Bjorn's Super Prawn (Purple)

Hook: TMC 7999, 2/0-1/0; Tiemco 777SP, 1/0-2; Gamakatsu
 Spinner-bait 3/0 for large kings (Read your regulations,
 as this hook has a 5/8" gap)
Thread: Danville to match color of fly
Tail: Purple marabou and bucktail
Shellback: Scud Back (to part and hold marabou)
Body: Purple chenille
Hackle: Purple Marabou Spey blood quill, spun; one at mid
 shank and one at the head
Wing: American black-laced hen (at least three)
Eyes: Barbells (optional)
Tier's Note: *"This variation of Super Prawn that has been ef-
fective as a change-up. Also, try it in red, orange, chartreuse, or
pink; all colors that produce well at times."*

—*Bjorn Beech*

Bunny-Winged Salmon Leech

Originator: John Gilbert
Tier: Cecilia "Pudge" Kleinkauf
Hook: Size 4-2, Mustad 36890
Thread: UNI-Thread, 6/0, color to match the fly
Eyes: Beach chain, lead dumbbell or Spirit River Eye-Balz, de-
 pending on how heavy you want the fly to be
Tail: One-inch-long strip of straight-cut bunny fur. Do not cut
 as remaining bunny will be brought forward as a wing
Body: Orange, fluorescent green, white or purple polar che-
 nille to match the bunny strip. Pull remaining bunny
 strip forward and tie off behind the eyes
Collar: Webby hackle feather in color to match the bunny and
 polar chenille, wrapped in from the butt, collar style, just
 behind the eyes
Finish: Any fast-drying finish
Tier's Note: *"I first saw the Bunny-Winged Salmon Leech in
Cy's Sporting Goods in Kodiak, Alaska where John Gilbert had*

*just tied it up for his customers to try. Cohos love this fly! I tie
it in both weighted and un-weighted versions to use in different
water conditions. Coho salmon take it as it sinks, on the swing,
or when the two-hand strip makes them chase it. It is also effective for chums."*

—*Cecilia "Pudge" Kleinkauf*

Clouser Mickey

Originator: Bob Clouser
Tier: Clifford Barker
Hook: Mustad 34011, size 2-6
Body: None
Wing: Blue over yellow over red over yellow polar bear or syn-
 thetic
Throat: Red synthetic material
Eyes: Gold bead chain
Tier's Note: *"This is a Mickey Finn dressed Clouser style. It
works well in freshwater pools for active pink and coho salmon."*

—*Clifford Barker*

Coho Muddler

Originator and Tier: Jerry Daschofsky
Hook: Size 2/0 DaiRiki 930, Tiemco 811S, Daiichi 2456 or
 Mustad 34007
Thread: Danville flat waxed nylon, fluorescent neon red
Body: Braided and tapered. Top: silver Diamond Braid.
 Bottom: UNI-Yarn, light pink
Wing: 15-20 strands of silver Flashabou, beyond hook bend
Head/Hackle: Pink deer belly hair spun and tapered to eye of
 hook. Leave top and bottom hair long and flared as wing
 and hackle
Tier's Note: *"I was looking for a good attractor pattern for catch-
ing silver salmon in the tidal flux areas of the Chehalis River
in southwest Washington. I always liked the Don Gapin Muddler Minnow for trout, so modified it several years ago to try it*

on silvers. I used a heavy, saltwater hook for weight, durability and to get a good sink rate in the tidal water. I've modified the Coho Muddler over the years, the most recent upgrade being the braided body. Depending on how deep and fast the slot is where I'm fishing I use lines ranging from a floater to a very fast-sink tip. After allowing the fly to sink to the desired depth I make three fast strips, pause and then three more fast strips. I keep up this retrieve until the fly is nearly at the rod tip, having experienced coho salmon attacking it right up to the surface. The Coho Muddler has also taken chinook salmon. For a change-up I tie the fly with a chartreuse, or bright green head. The Coho Muddler is a terrific fly for salmon fresh in from the salt."

—Jerry Daschofsky
Tacoma, Washington

Comet, (gold)

Originator: Unknown
Tier: Gene Fassi

Hook: Partridge CS2, Gamakatsu T10-6H, or equivalent, size 1/0-8
Tail: Orange calf tail, one and a half times body length
Body: Gold Sparkle Braid or Diamond Braid (or flat silver tinsel)
Hackle: Orange and yellow saddle hackle, mixed
Eyes (optional): Bead chain to match size of fly. Gold bead chain for Gold Comet, silver bead chain for Silver Comet
Finish: Any quick-drying head cement
Tier's Note: "The Comet's origin goes back to about 1949 for use on Russian River steelhead. It is thought that Grant King was involved in its development and is credited with the similar Boss and Flaming Boss patterns. The bead-chain eyes are optional but the Comet is rarely seen without them. A few years later, the Comet soon gained favor on the Eel and Smith rivers for fall chinook salmon as it would sink quickly into the deep, holding pools in the lower reaches of these rivers. In addition to the Gold Comet, there is a Silver Comet, Black Comet, Howard Norton Special and the two Boss variations. Early on, Comets were often tied on hooks down to size 6 and 8, even for mature chinook salmon upwards of 40 pounds due to the very clear water of the rivers of Northern California.*

—Gene Fassi
San Rafael, California

Comet, (silver)

Originator: Unknown
Tier: Larry Kovi

Tier's Note: "The Silver Comet is identical to the Gold Comet with the exception of using silver tinsel or Diamond Braid as a body and nickel bead-chain eyes. Although they are very similar, some California salmon anglers favor one over the other."

—Larry Novi
Novato, California

Egg Head

Originator and Tier: Mike Foster

Hook: Size 2/0-8 Mustad 36890, TMC 7898, Gamakatsu T10-6H
Thread: Danville flat waxed nylon to match fly
Tag: Medium oval gold tinsel
Tail: Black Russian squirrel, calf tail or equivalent, fairly long
Body: Danville light fluorescent orange wool
Rib: Medium oval gold tinsel
Hackle: Fire orange fluorescent, four turns
Head: Fluorescent medium orange chenille. Fluorescent green chenille for the Green Head
Eyes: Gold bead chain to match size of fly
Tier's Note: "I first tied the Egg Head in the late 1970s. It came about as a semi-joke to incorporate all the colors and shapes that worked in the South Fork of the Eel River into one fly. I had immediate success with it and have use it extensively ever since. I wrote an article about the Egg Head in February, 1981 that was published in Fly Tyer magazine. Since that time many variations and color versions have emerged, some by me and some by others. The Green Head, a variation tied by my neighbor Rex

Collingsworth is very good, although I still enjoy my best results with the original."

—Mike Foster
Miranda, California

Egg Sucking Leech, Purple

Originator: Unknown
Tier: Cecilia "Pudge" Kleinkauf

Hook: Mustad 36890, size 6-2

Thread: UNI-Thread, 6/0, color to match other materials

Tail: Marabou plume fluff with several strands of rainbow Krystal Flash

Body: Medium purple chenille or cactus chenille tied three-quarters down the hook shank

Hackle: Webby saddle hackle palmered

Head: Medium salmon pink chenille tied egg-style just behind the hook eye

Eyes: (Barbells, optional) if used, wrap chenille around them

Tier's Note: "The Egg Sucking Leech is known as the "All Alaska Fly" because in different sizes and colors, it catches virtually every species in Alaska at one time or another. With salmon, hits can be very hard or very subtle. Fish will take as the fly sinks, on the swing, or when being stripped. Vary material colors as you wish."

—Cecelia "Pudge" Kleinkauf

Everglow Fly

Originator: John Foley
Tier: Cecilia "Pudge" Kleinkauf

Hook: Size 4-2/0, Mustad 34007

Thread: UNI-Thread, 6/0, or flat waxed nylon in color to match Everglow piping

Underbody: Build up with wool yarn or lead wire from behind eye to bend of hook

Tail: Everglow piping with center removed, secured behind hook eye and extending beyond hook shank about 1 inch where it is secured at hook bend

Wing: A few strands of Everglow Flashabou, body length

Collar: Webby hackle feather in color to match Everglow, wrapped collar style over the wing

Eyes: Bead-chain, lead dumbbell, or Spirit River Real Eyes to match size of fly

Tiers' Note: "This is an old stand-by for both chinook and coho salmon in Alaska. Originally designed for chinook in its larger sizes, its success on coho and chum salmon quickly became apparent. Primarily fished on the bottom, salmon nevertheless take as the fly drops on a dead drift, and on the strip. Depending upon water level and clarity, vary your tactics until you find what works. The Everglow Fly is very effective in glacial water."

—Cecelia "Pudge" Kleinkauf

Fish Candy

Originator: Unknown
Tier: Cecilia "Pudge" Kleinkauf

Hook: Size 6-4, Mustad 7970, or Gamakatsu Octopus (red), 4-6

Thread: UNI-Thread, 5/0 in color to match the fly

Tail: Optional, clump of Flashabou or Krystal Flash as used in the tail adds interest and movement in the water

Weight: Lead wire, optional

Body: Hot pink, fluorescent green, orange or white, medium-large Cactus wrapped one turn in front of the other so that spikes in Cactus Chenille will stand up

Wing: Optional. A wing of Flashabou, Krystal Flash or marabou adds movement to the fly

Eyes: Optional. Bead-chain, lead dumbbell, or Spirit River Real Eyes can be added for faster sinking. Beads and cones are also added for attraction and sinking weight

Tiers' Note: "When Cactus Chenille came on the market, salmon anglers quickly learned of its appeal to all Pacific salmon. The Fish Candy combines ease of tying with incredible effectiveness for sockeye salmon, in spite of their reputation for a lack of chasing instinct and being 'uncatchable'. The Fish Candy does not really need the tail, eyes or wing. Just the Cactus Chenille wrapped around the hook is all it really takes. I *tie the fly in different colors and sizes to meet various water conditions—and for different species. Smaller sizes area best for pinks and sockeye while larger sizes tempt chum, coho and chinook salmon."*

—Cecilia "Pudge" Kleinkauf

Fraser River Sockeye Fly

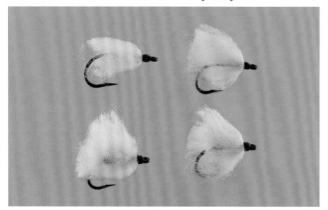

Originator and Tier: Cliff Olson

Hook: Tiemco 811S, or equivalent, size 6-8

Thread: Red

Body and Wing: Steelhead wool, chartreuse or green, split

Underwing: Hot red wool

Tier's Notes: "This simple fly in four basic configurations will usually coax up Fraser River sockeye salmon for me. It is easy to tie and when the sockeye are in, they will take it readily and hit it hard. The red Underwing gives it a bit more of a krill appearance, which sometimes is effective. I swing the fly downstream using either an intermediate sinking line or a fast-sinking tip, depending on the flow and depth of the area I'm fishing."

—Cliff Olson
New Westminster, British Columbia

General Practitioner

Originator: Col. Esmond Drury
Tier: Ronn Lucas, Sr.

Hook: Partridge Bartleet or Gamakatsu T10-6H, size 2/0-6

Thread: Black

Tail: 10 bucktail hairs dyed bright orange

Eyes: Golden pheasant tippet; trimmed

Body: Pink and orange seal or substitute; mixed

Back: Two golden pheasant rump feathers; under feather with concave side up, the top one with concave side down

Finish: Red lacquer

Tier's Note: "The General Practitioner, a beautiful shrimp-imitating pattern, has been around for a good many years and was originally tied as an Atlantic salmon fly. It has, however proven to be effective for Pacific salmon in coastal rivers. The light-colored version uses yellow-gold dyed golden pheasant feathers and 'Hold On Iridescent Dubbing' to represent sand shrimp for use in lower river pools and tidal areas."

—Ronn Lucas, Sr.
Milwaukie, Oregon

General Practitioner (Black)

Originator: Col. Esmond Drury, variation by Art Lingren
Tier: Arthur Lingren

Hook: Size 1/0-10, Partridge low-water salmon, TMC 7999, Gamakatsu T10-6H, or equivalent, size 10 to 6/0

Thread: Black 6/0

Tail: Black squirrel, with or without a few strands of black, pearl, or red Krystal Flash

Body: Black mohair

Rib: Oval silver tinsel

Hackle: Black, palmered

Wing: Two black-dyed golden pheasant breast feathers tied in to lay flat over the body

Tier's Note: "The first GP Black variation came from my tying vise in January 1984 and was an instant producer for both winter and summer-run steelhead. I designed the GP Black, based on Col. Esmond Drury's original orange General Practitioner for use on winter-run steelhead. It quickly became a staple in my steelhead box. My standard is dressed on a number 2 hook, but I have dressed it on hooks up to 5/0 for larger fish and down to size 10 for trout. Since its inception, I have altered the original fly's dressing somewhat and have regular, marabou and low-water versions. Over the seasons I have found it to be* an effective fly for most species of game fish that swim in the waters I fish.

One of the things I noticed early on was this fly's attraction to other salmonids and it was not uncommon for me to pick up chinooks on the Dean River with the GP Black. My largest chinook salmon, taken in the summer of 2003 was just over 42 inches long and would have tipped the scales at more than 40 pounds. Besides chinooks, I have caught pinks and chums on the GP Black. However it is as a coho fly that the GP Black shines. I have taken coho up to 20 pounds from fifteen rivers and three freshwater lakes on the GP Black."

—Art Lingren
Vancouver, British Columbia

Glo Bug

Originator: Unknown
Tier: Les Johnson

Hook: Gamakatsu C14S, size 6-12

Milt: (optional) A few strands of pearl Krystal Flash

Body: Several short strands of fat Glo Bug yarn (standard or tinsel) in pink, orange, or pink, plus a small amount of alternate color for an eye. The bundle is tied to top of hook and trimmed round

Finish: A dab of head cement on thread wraps

Tier's Note: "This original version of the Glo Bug has been primarily used as a trout fly, fished behind spawning salmon and steelhead. It is however, effective for salmon that have moved into the middle reaches of a river where they are still in good shape but beginning to show a hint of spawning color. It is popular to fish the Glo Bug under a strike indicator but I prefer to swing it deep on a sink tip line and a short leader using a 2X stout hook or a split shot about a foot above the fly. Coho, chum, pink and occasionally chinook salmon will all grab a Glo Bug at times. Myriad variations of the original Glo Bug have been created using all the new synthetic materials available and all of them seem to work, so be creative."

—Les Johnson

Horner's Brown Shrimp (or Silver Shrimp)

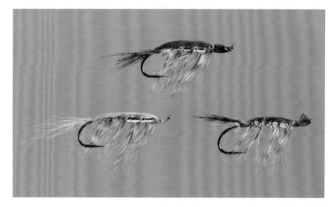

Originator: Jack Horner
Tier: Les Johnson

Hook: Gamakatsu T10 6H, size 1/0-8

Thread: Brown or gray, 3/0 waxed nylon

Weight: Several turns of lead wire slightly forward of center on the hook shank

Body: Silver tinsel over tapered floss underbody

Legs: Grizzly hackle palmered and trimmed on sides and top

Tail and Back: Brown or gray-dyed bucktail tied in at the hook bend; brought forward and tied off at head. Cover the back with Softex for durability. Gray bucktail is used for the Silver version

Head: Tied off as a trim tapered head or with an Elk Hair Caddis style burr cut (both styles shown).

Eyes: Painted, or small Witchcraft stick-on eyes, optional

Tier's Note: "Horner's Brown Shrimp, also tied as the Silver Shrimp was developed, according to Trey Combs' classic steelhead book, Steelhead Fly-fishing and Flies, by San Franciscan Jack Horner in September 1938. Sleek, trim and unassuming, it was one of the early successful shrimp imitations for fishing salmon and steelhead in the estuaries and gin-clear tide pools of Northern California coastal rivers.

I began using the three Horner Shrimp variations shown here when I lived in the San Rafael, California in the mid 1980s. I enjoyed success with it and continued using it when I returned to Washington. The rather unassuming Horner's Shrimp has gotten lost amongst all of the glitz, glitter and glow of some contemporary salmon flies but the subdued brown and gray versions remain very effective. For extremely low, clear water and dour salmon, the gray Horner's Shrimp may be slightly more effective than the brown. That however is an opinion that I don't hold with unflagging confidence, as they have both worked so well. There have been many variations of the Horner Shrimp over the years and I'm sure that they've all been effective. For me the brown, silver and burr-cut have been my favorites.

To shake up the most uncooperative salmon Horner liked the burr-cut version of his shrimp as it had more action and left a bubble trail when retrieved."

—Les Johnson

Iliamna Floozie

Originator: Ted Gerken
Tier: Robert Triggs

Hook: Daiichi 246, size 4-1/0
Thread: Danville hot pink flat waxed nylon
Tail: Bubble Gum pink Marabou
Body: Large hot pink Cactus Chenille overwrapped with Estaz Metallique
Hackle: Large schlappen, hot pink
Eyes: Bead chain, nickel or stainless to suit size of fly and weight needed
Tier's Note: "This is my adaptation of the Pink Floozie, a silver salmon fly tied by the late Ted Gerken of Iliaska Lodge on Lake Iliamna, Alaska. On my first trip out to Big River in Katmai Park, Ted told me, 'All you need is a box full of Pink Floozies.' He was right. I added Krystal Flash, larger eyes and the Estaz Metallique overwrap for a little more glitter and larger eyes for a deeper presentation. This fly has since taken silvers in fresh and salt water in Alaska and Washington. It is also good for pink salmon, coastal cutthroat and char. I fish it with a floating line and long leader. Short, brisk strips elicit strikes."

—Bob Triggs
Port Townsend, Washington

Kate's Prawn

Originator and Tier: Vernon Jeremica

Hook: Size 4 to t5/0
Tail: Super Spey pink peacock eye

Tag: Four turns of medium silver tinsel
Butt: Peach Tri Global dubbing and cut-out of six sections of golden pheasant tippet cutouts
Body: Red Super Wrap divided in three parts with dyed red golden pheasant
Hackle: Pink Super Spey hackle
Wing: Green phase of black Amherst body feather overlaid with dyed red golden pheasant
Finish: Any high-gloss finish
Tier's Note: "I named this pattern after Kate Davidson, one of the originators of Super Spey Hackle. My largest fish landed on Kate's Prawn was a 65-pound king salmon. I normally fish this pattern on a swing. In rivers with a bit of color I go to the larger 3/0 to 5/0 hooks. Body variations are; red/pink, black/purple, black/blue and black/chartreuse. The black/ blue Kate's Prawn has been a good pattern when fishing over bright fish."

—Vern Jeremica

Kingfisher

Originator and Tier: Paul Carnes

Hook: Partridge Bartleet-Supreme CS10/2, Mustad 36890 or Tiemco 7999, size 2/0-4
Thread: Black Danville 6/0
Tail: Kingfisher blue polar bear
Body: Kingfisher blue SLF dubbing
Rib: Silver tinsel
Wing: A few strands of blue Krystal Flash topped with white polar bear hair over kingfisher blue polar bear
Hackle: Blue-dyed guinea hen tied as a throat
Head: Any fast build-up finish
Tier's Note: "I developed the Kingfisher as part of the Big Red series for use in low, clear water on bright, sunny days. Its success on coho salmon during these conditions has earned it a permanent spot in my coho fly box."

—Paul Carnes

Lemon Fly

Originator: Jerry Lemon
Tier: Cecilia "Pudge" Kleinkauf

Hook: Size 6-4, Mustad 7970, or 92567R
Tail: None
Body: None
Hackle: None
Wing: Several strands of multi-color or solid-color Flashabou extending about 1/2 inch beyond the end of the hook
Head: Small clump of Glo Bug yarn, hot orange or chartreuse, to match or contrast with the wing and allowed to fuzz out
Finish: Any fast-drying finish

Tier's Note: "Jerry Lemon, an original member of the Alaska Fly Fishers, designed this fly as a 'quick tie' for sockeye salmon fishing, but we also use it for chum and coho salmon. Its original name is lost in history. Now we just call it the Lemon Fly after Jerry, who ascended to fish heaven a few years back."

—Cecilia "Pudge" Kleinkauf

Mike's Marabou (Rotor Special)

Originator and Tier: Mike Foster

Hook: TMC 7999, Gamakatsu T10-6H, or equivalent
Thread: Danville fluorescent orange, 3/0
Body: Shoulder; orange tinsel chenille. Rear half: orange Edgebright
Wing: Orange and yellow marabou plumes spun together.
Collar: Orange dyed guinea
Head: Orange thread

Tier's Note: "I first tied this take-off on a Popsicle about ten years ago and called it Mike's Marabou. I intended it for steelhead but it proved to be very good for salmon in northern California rivers as well. I have named several flies after family members. This one, the Rotor Special is named for my son Todd, who has the nickname of Rotor."

—Mike Foster

Moose's Ugly

Originator: Lloyd "Moose" Murray
Tier: Gavin Grapes, MD

Tube: Kennebec small clear plastic tube, or a section of Q-Tip stem
Thread: Bright green or chartreuse, 3/0
Hook: Gamakatsu Octopus 4/0-7/0 or SC-15 2/0-4/0
Wing: Strip of chartreuse rabbit strip
Flash: Pearl Krystal Flash
Hackle: Chartreuse marabou fronted by Kingfisher blue marabou. Both are spun around the tube as hackle
Finish: Head cement

Tier's Note: "This fly was originated to imitate anchovies for use on chinook salmon in the lower Dean River in the late 1980s. The first patterns were not very good looking, hence the nickname, 'Ugly'. It evolved into a much more elegant fly when tied in the round like George Cook's Alaskabou series. Moose's Ugly has proven to work not only on the Dean but the Kitimat as well.

For a good change-up, tie Moose's Ugly with a black rabbit strip."

—Gavin Grapes MD
Quesnel, British Columbia

Orange Sparkle Shrimp

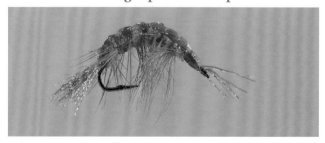

Originator: Unknown
Tier: Mike Foster

Hook: Size 2 to 12, TMC 207B, Mustad 37160, or equivalent

Thread: Danville flat waxed nylon, flame orange
Tail: Orange calf tail and fire orange Krystal Flash, mixed
Body: Fluorescent orange chenille, or Spirit River Pseudo Seal to match hook size
Hackle: Orange, palmered
Shellback: Mixed orange bucktail and fluorescent orange Krystal Flash tied down over the back
Tier's Note: "Randy Stetzer credited me for the Orange Sparkle Shrimp in his book, Flies: The Best One Thousand. I'm sure however that I saw flies like it as a youngster on the Russian River. The Krystal Flash is a fairly recent revision I made to the original pattern for a bit more attraction."

—Mike Foster

Polar Shrimp

Originator: Clarence Shoff
Tier: Les Johnson

Hook: Size 2-8 Gamakatsu T10-6H
Thread: 6/0 Danville, black or fluorescent orange
Tail: Hot red hackle fibers
Body: Hot orange fluorescent chenille, fairly full
Hackle: Hot orange saddle
Wing: White bucktail, polar bear, calf tail, or yak hair length of body and tail
Flash: A few strands of pearl Krystal Flash mixed with wing material
Head: Black thread (original), or hot orange
Tier's Note: "The Polar Shrimp was designed about 1936 by Clarence Shoff, another of the Washington pioneer fly-fishing innovators and founder of Shoff's Sporting Goods, a fine fishing and hunting emporium in Kent, Washington. This easy-to-tie pattern was intended for winter steelhead and was an instant success on the Green River that flowed through the Kent Valley, not far from Shoff's establishment. The Polar Shrimp soon gained popularity as a coho and chinook salmon fly in northern California and eventually enjoyed a great following among Alaskan fly-fishers. The Polar shrimp is particularly effective when worked through the depths of a salmon pool where chinook and coho salmon are stacked up and crowded."

—Les Johnson

Red Hot

Originator: Hank Pennington
Tier: Cecilia "Pudge" Kleinkauf

Hook: Size 6-1/0, Gamakatsu Octopus, red
Thread: UNI-Thread, 6/0 red
Tail: None
Body: None
Hackle: None
Wing: A clump of bright red Flashabou extending just past the bend of the hook.
Finish: Any fast-drying finish
Tier's Note: "You just can't get a simpler fly than the Red Hot; just a hook and Flashabou. However, it does take salmon. Sockeye salmon particularly find this fly irresistible, taking it just as the line straightens out. Coho also take it in the larger sizes as do chum salmon. For a change-up, you can also tie the Red Hot with bright, Kelly green Flashabou on the green Gamakatsu Octopus hook."

—Cecilia "Pudge" Kleinkauf

Salmon Creek Special

Originator: Irwin Thompson
Tier: Gene Fassi

Hook: Partridge CS2, size 2-8
Thread: Sue Burgess, black 6/0
Tail: Black squirrel tail
Body: Fluorescent fire orange floss
Rib: Silver Mylar tinsel. After winding on the tinsel cover the entire body with several coats of Sally Hansen's Hard-as-Nails
Hackle: Yellow saddle, four turns

Wing: Alaska Roe Glo Bug yarn, topped with white marabou tip

Finish: Sally Hansen's Hard-as-Nails

Tier's Note: "*The late Irwin Thompson was a well-known fly tier in the San Francisco Bay Area. This was one of his most popular patterns for salmon in the streams north of San Francisco, including its namesake, Salmon Creek where Les Johnson and I enjoyed great fishing for several years when he lived in San Rafael. Thompson's flies were famous for their fish-catching characteristics and extreme durability. He was reputed to cast a line farther with a 7 1/2-foot 5-weight rod than most people could with a 9-foot 8-weight.*"

—*Gene Fassi*

Sand Shrimp

Originator and Tier: Jerry Daschofsky

Hook: Size 2/0 DaiRiki 930, Tiemco 811S, Daiichi 2546 or Mustad 34007

Thread: Danville flat waxed nylon, fluorescent white

Tail: 10-15 strands, pearl Krystal Flash

Body: Four sections of Ice Dub pearl dubbing

Ribbing: Pearl oval medium tinsel

Hackle: White saddle hackle tied in four separate sections, tied down

Shellback: Prismatic pliable pearl sheet back, pointed at head, rounded at tail

Eyes: Black bead-chain eyes tied on underside of hook

Tier's Note: "*My inspiration for this fly was the General Practitioner. However, I wanted something a bit simpler to tie, since some of the places I fish this pattern would have a chance to hang it up. Also, I wanted certain colors and matching the shell casings with gold pheasant feathers was nearly impossible. I usually tie the Sand Shrimp in pearl, pink or peach. The sand shrimp it is one of the better baits used on the river systems that I fish; in areas of brackish, tidal flux where salmon are in transition from the salt. I always fish my Sand Shrimp on a fast, sometimes very fast, sinking tip line as the kings I'm looking for are often holding nearly 60 feet deep. I let the line go straight to the bottom, then slowly strip the fly back to the surface. I have coaxed some very aggressive strikes with this fly. Although I target chinook salmon with the Sand Shrimp I've also caught fresh-run silver and chum salmon—and steelhead with it as well.*"

—*Jerry Daschofsky*

Sockeye Orange

Originator: Unknown
Tier: Cecelia "Pudge" Kleinkauf

Hook: Size 2-8 Mustad 36890 or 7970

Thread: UNI-Thread in color to match the fly

Tail: None

Body: Flat silver tinsel or Diamond Braid wrapped down the hook shank

Wing: Black squirrel, or calf tail tied under, or on top of the collar

Collar: Webby orange hackle feather wrapped in from the butt, just behind the eyes.

Eyes: (Optional) Bead chain, or Spirit River Eye-Balz to match size of fly

Tier's Note: "*Tied sparsely the Sockeye Orange is one of old-time Alaskans' favorite flies for sockeye and coho salmon. Fish usually take the Sockeye Orange as it is sinking. Or, it can be stripped slowly to get the salmon's attention, or very fast to trigger a coho's chase instinct. For variety, substitute green, purple, etc., for orange.*"

—*Cecelia "Pudge" Kleinkauf*

Spun Marabou Streamer (or Dressed Hook)

Originator: Unknown
Tier: Les Johnson

Hook: Size 1/0 to 4, Gamakatsu T10-6H

Thread: 6/0 Danville

Body: Flat silver or gold Mylar tinsel

Flash: A few strands of silver, gold, or pearl Flashabou, your choice, extending slightly beyond marabou

Wing: Marabou plume tied in by the tip and spun forward around the hook. Most colors are used, including plumes tip-dyed in contrasting colors

Hackle: Dyed hen saddle to match or contrast marabou, optional

Head: High-gloss cement

Tier's Note: "The Spun Marabou was shown to me by veteran angler, fly tier and fishing companion, Dan Lemaich of Camano Island, Washington about 1987. He called the spun marabou a 'dressed hook' and first employed it several years earlier, primarily for Skagit River and Sauk River steelhead. He noted however that he took a lot of coho salmon with it every fall as well. This proved to be true for me when I landed several big, fresh-run coho while fishing a hot red Spun Marabou the first time I fished the Thorne River on Prince of Wales Island, Alaska. Unlike so many heavily dressed marabou patterns, the Spun Marabou, as Dan dresses it is sparse and simple to tie, calling for a single marabou plume. This gives it a lot of swimming action in the current—and it rarely requires added weight to sink quickly into deep runs. Almost any color combination of marabou, hackle, Flashabou and thread will work at times. To make the spun marabou, or 'dressed hook' longer, simply add a marabou tube."

—Les Johnson

Spun Marabou Tube

Originator: Dan Lemaich
Tier: Les Johnson

Tube: Small (fresh water) Kennebec clear plastic tube, 1-1/2 inches long

Body: None

Wing: Marabou plume tied in by tip and spun around tube

Hackle: Dyed hen hackle, optional

Flash: A few strands of Flashabou trailing just beyond marabou

Head: Head is built up with chenille or crystal chenille of any color to match or contrast marabou, optional

Finish: Any high-build-up finish

Tier's Note: "This tube marabou, another innovation I was shown by Dan Lemaich can be used as is, in front of a bare hook, or slid onto the leader ahead of the spun marabou fly that Dan

calls a 'dressed hook' to present a longer silhouette in the water. When fishing his two-handed rod Dan doesn't hesitate to string up to three tubes ahead of a spun marabou fly, mixing and matching colors, when the water is murky in order to present a highly visible offering."

—Les Johnson

Squimp

Originator: Jack Cook
Tier: Chris Ringlee

Hook: Gamakatsu T10 6H, size 2/0, green. Targus 7999, size 2/0

Thread: Gudebrod, white 3/0

Tail: Two chartreuse dyed grizzly saddle hackle feathers

Flash: Silver Flashabou

Body: White Cactus Chenille, large

Hackle: Chartreuse marabou

Eyes: 30-pound-test mono, black beads

Tier's Note: "The Squimp is a variation of a Waddington Squid tied by Jack Cook. The fly is simple and effective. I fished the Squimp on the Alagnak River when I was a guide during the summer of 2005. I fish this fly deep on a sinking line at the high tide turn when the river has stopped flowing in. That is when the kings enter the river. A slow, erratic retrieve allows the Squimp to have good movement. I also use a smaller version tied on a size 1 hook for coho salmon. Red, blue, pink and white are also good colors."

—Chris Ringlee
Gig Harbor, Washington

Starlight Leech

Originator: Joe Howell
Tier: Cecilia "Pudge" Kleinkauf

Hook: Size 4-1/0, Mustad 36890

Thread: UNI-Thread, 6/0, color to match the body

Eyes: Dumbbell lead eyes or Spirit River Eye-Balz with fuchsia or chartreuse chenille wrapped around them, place on hook before tying the rest of the fly

Tail: One-inch length of straight-cut bunny fur strip

Body: Cactus chenille the same or contrasting color as bunny strip tail. Weight hook shank with lead wire

Collar: Webby hackle feather wrapped in from the butt, collar style to match the tail or body color

Finish: Any fast-drying finish

Tier's Note: "The Starlight Leech, originated by Joe Howell of Roseburg, Oregon is tied in many sizes and color combinations. It is particularly effective for chinook and coho salmon, but chum salmon will also take it. Because of its weight the fly-fisher can often avoid the use of split shot. Black is the most common color for the tail and the body."

—Cecilia "Pudge" Kleinkauf

Teeny Egg-Sucking Leech

Originator and Tier: Jim Teeny

Hook: Size 2-12 Teeny Custom by Eagle Claw

Thread: Hot orange

Tail: Pheasant-tail fibers, long

Body: Pheasant-tail feathers, tied in at butts, twisted and wrapped forward

Underwing: Feather tips tied off and pulled under as a beard

Head: Built up with hot orange thread

Tier's Note: "I designed the Teeny Egg Sucking Leech as an alternative to some of the bulkier patterns used for Pacific salmon. It has proven to be especially effective in low, clear water when cast to wary fish. Being trim this pattern is easy to cast, sinks quickly, and is taken without hesitation most of the time."

—Jim Teeny
Gresham, Oregon

Teeny Sparkle Leech

Originator and Tier: Jim Teeny

Hook: Teeny Custom by Eagle Claw

Tail: Pheasant hackle fibers, long

Body: Rear half; silver tinsel

Shoulder: Pheasant-tail fibers tied in by butts, twisted and wrapped forward

Underwing: Feather tips pulled down and tied off

Head: Black thread

Tier's Note: "The Sparkle Leech has been very effective on king salmon in both the spring and fall. Chum and pink salmon also like the Sparkle Leech in smaller sizes. The extra sparkle I worked into the Sparkle Leech adds a bit of needed attraction in some of the murky, glacier-fed rivers I fish in Alaska."

—Jim Teeny

Teeny Sparkle Nymph

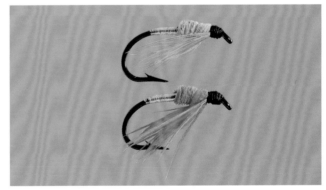

Originator and Tier: Jim Teeny

Hook: Teeny Custom by Eagle Claw

Body: Rear half; silver tinsel

Shoulder: Pheasant-tail fibers tied in by the butts, twisted and wrapped forward

Underwing: Points of hackle fibers pulled down and tied off

Head: Black thread

Tier's Note: "The Sparkle Nymph has proven to be a very good pattern for sockeye salmon in the lower tide pools of rivers. I cast out, mend and swing it past the edge of school then start my retrieve keeping the rod tip low. The first few pulls will generally do the trick."

—Jim Teeny

Tillamook Tube Eel

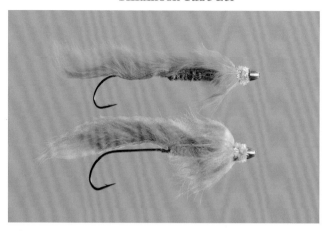

Originator and Tier: Glenn Young

Tube: 3/16-inch OD Kennebec River tubing

Hook: Gamakatsu B10S, size 1/0 or 2/0, depending on tail length, tied as trailer

Thread: Gudebrod pink or blue, 3/0

Body: Variegated blue/purple or pink chenille

Tail: Blue or pink rabbit strip

Hackle: Palmered rabbit strip

Wing: Rabbit strip tied in at head and extended beyond the end of tube

Weight: Kennebec River tube conehead. Lead eyes can also be used

Head: Pink sparkle chenille (egg color)

Tier's Note: "*As a guide in the Tillamook region of Oregon from 1989 through 1997 I relied on a few variations of this same pattern for all species of salmon in the rivers. My friend, an innovative tier, Guy Fullhart, also helped in the evolution of this fly during his many years of guiding in Alaska and Russia. After reading Tube Flies by Mark Mandell and Les Johnson, I immediately saw the benefits of tying the pattern on a tube. The tube allows me to tie a longer body and longer tail without risking short strikes and eliminates the leverage issues of long shank hooks. Once the salmon enter the rivers I have found that it is important to get their attention and a big fly like this one does just that. While guiding during the salmon season I found that I only needed two colors, blue for clear water and pink for off-colored water. All five species of Pacific salmon have taken this fly. It has also proven effective for estuary chum salmon in Hood Canal in Washington. My best chinook on the Tillamook Tube Eel was a 54-pounder that smacked a blue one. If I'm into large salmon I don't hesitate to use a Tube Eel up to 7 inches long. A fly that large will either trigger a chinook's territorial instincts—or cause it to abandon the pool.*"

—Glenn Young
Puyallup, Washington

Right: Here is a peek into the fly box of saltwater fly-fisher, Steve Rohrbach of Seattle, Washington. Like most other saltwater fly-casters, Steve believes in having a big box crammed with every good fly pattern he has ever seen—new or old.

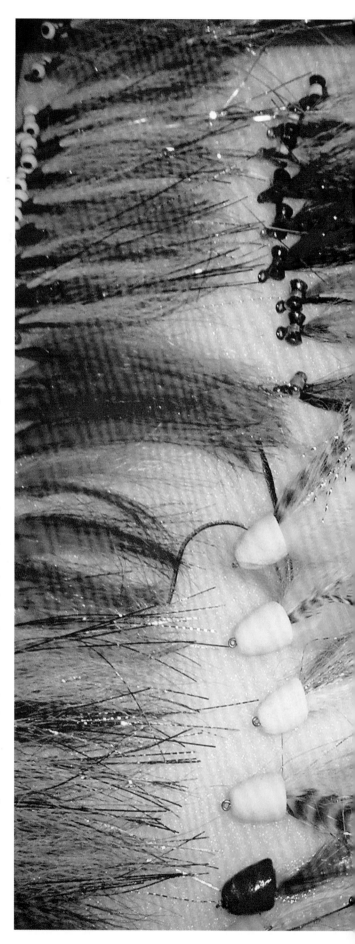

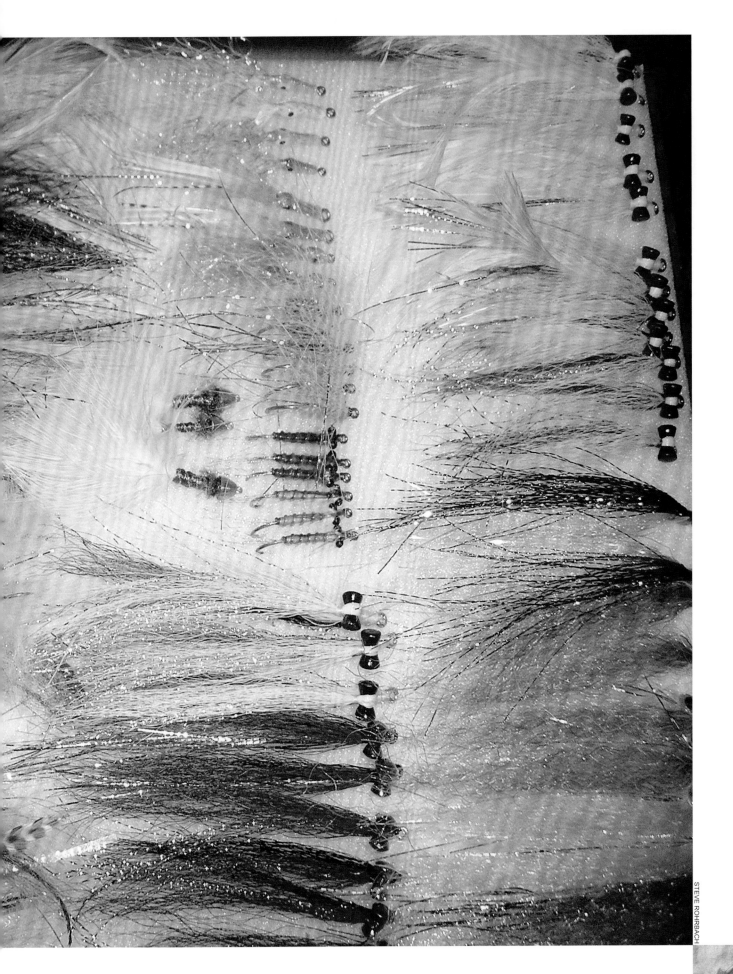

CHAPTER ELEVEN

Tackle

By Les Johnson

In my opinion, the mystique and prestige surrounding fly tackle is unparalleled by any other type of fishing gear. This includes the glitzy assortment of big-game rods and reels that are found in the racks of sleek Bertram and Baja sport-fishing cruisers.

Fly rods for salmon require enough flexibility to cast gently to spooky coho or pink salmon in shallow estuarine water with long leaders. They must also be strong enough to handle the gyrations of a frenetic hooked chinook salmon. Well-constructed reels with strong drag systems are the order of the day. Fishing from a boat, along the beach, or waist-deep in the swift flows of western rivers, our fly tackle has to combine strength and lightweight for throwing big flies, sometimes at long range. Bear in mind, our goal is to cast to and we hope, play a salmon now and then without losing the use of a rotator cuff.

In the early 1980s, when the first edition of *Fly Fishing for Pacific Salmon* was being compiled, we had already jumped light years ahead of the cane and fiberglass rods, spring and pawl reels and silk lines upon which the sport of salmon

Chris Bentsen used an intermediate line that carried his fly just below the surface to catch this small coho salmon taken while fishing from the beach on northern Vancouver Island.

Shooting-head and knot-tying maestro, Bill Nash was able to reach way out from the beach to connect with this nice coho. It hit a size 10, brown bucktail Clouser tied up by Chris Bentsen and shortly thereafter was destined to become an evening meal entrée.

fly-fishing was founded. Technological advances had given us fly rods that would cast a shooting head into the teeth of a gale, disk drags on reels capable of stopping a runaway motor home and lines that would sink quickly in a fast-running river current or saltwater tide rip.

Today we have even more tackle choices available for use in every category of Pacific salmon fly-fishing, and as good as our equipment was in the 1980s, it is even better today. Designers incorporating new generations of graphite have

Tom Worsfold caught this nice coho while wading along Rupert Inlet on the west coast of Vancouver Island. Good waders are a must for much of the beach fishing that is becoming increasingly popular.

CAROL FERRERA

continued to tempt us with faster, lighter, stronger, easier casting rods. We have a great many more reels to choose from than ever before. For shallow water and spooky fish, we even have clear and camouflage lines that are practically invisible.

When establishing tackle requirements there are a few factors that hold true whether we fish in fresh or salt water, for chum, coho, chinook, pink or sockeye salmon. Salmon-fishing tackle is subjected to some very severe treatment from the environment, the salmon, or the hand of the owner, so durability is a concern. Day-long casting with heavy shooting heads or sinking lines can tweak the sturdiest shoulder or elbow, so light weight in a rod and reel obviously has to be a consideration—but not the point of sacrificing structural integrity. Generally speaking, the quality of a fly-fishing product goes up in direct correlation with the price tag and quality should never be a place for cutting corners in our salmon-fishing equipment. There is, however an acceptable range of quality and cost that a new salmon-fisher can work within and still be assured of buying gear that will stand up to the task. The thing to do when tooling up for Pacific salmon angling is to *buy the very best tackle you can afford.* This will guarantee that your rod, reel and line will last for several seasons with reasonable care. For example, I own a No. 2, anti-reverse Fin-Nor reel that has been fished hard for going on forty years and only recently received its first minor repair; which will probably keep it going for forty more years. This is the quality I look for in all of the reels I purchase. Similarly, I have several rods that are more than ten years old and lines that are still in excellent shape after seven or eight hard seasons. So, *do not* second mortgage the condo, or raid the kids' college funds, but *do* plan for your tackle purchases so that you can own the best gear that you can afford.

When it comes to rod design, Don Green, one of the founders of Sage Rod Company, has few peers in the industry. Don was kind enough to provide some insight on selecting a fly rod:

Purchasing a Fly Rod

"When considering how to select a new fly rod for saltwater angling let me give you a few thoughts to consider. Many times wind will be a factor and a rod that will deliver a high line speed for pinpoint accuracy as well as cutting into the wind will be an advantage. This means the rod should be one of a faster, progressive action. Long-distance casting is also very important; therefore I would recommend a graphite rod of 9 to 10 feet in length. The light weight of graphite makes it easier to deliver longer casts as well as reduce fatigue.

Also to consider is the rod's ability to lift a long line. For example; a cast is made and needs to be redirected quickly. The ability to pick up the long line with a single back cast and forward delivery requires a rod that is not too soft in the butt. Because wind is always a potential factor, the need for long casts and pinpoint accuracy, plus the weight of the fly, I recommend a 7- or 8-weight rod. When you are working through heavy currents, casting large bucktails, or handling large salmon, a 9- or 10-weight is called for.

River fishing for salmon, either from a boat or wading, has a different requirement than fishing for salmon in salt water. You have the river current to deal with and most often the need to get the fly down deep. Therefore, fast-sinking lines will be used. The fish can run in size from 15 to 50 pounds, or more. With the need for a sinking line, wet fly and potentially large fish, a 9- or 10-weight rod should be considered. When making long casts with a sinking line, the need to pick up at the end of the drift can best be accomplished with a rod of 9 to 10 feet. The action should not be overly stiff in the butt to allow the rod to flex into the butt section for better utilization of the full rod to lift the line out of the water.

Because the rod is going to be used hard, sometimes in a saltwater environment, the need to consider the quality and workmanship is important. The rod should have an anodized aluminum, double-nut locking reel seat. A large stripper guide of high quality is needed to feely allow the line to clear when shooting extra line for distance. Guide wraps should be well finished and the wraps completely sealed. A small fighting butt is a great asset when fighting large fish. I like an uplocking reel seat to help keep the reel away from my body when fighting these large fish. Also, with the reel closer to my casting hand, the rod is in better balance and less fatiguing. A reverse half wells cork handle is desirable as it puts a place for my thumb to be directly behind the rod for maximum power when casting or fighting a fish.

When making a final fly-rod selection, choose from well-established companies that specialize in fly-rod design and manufacture."

—Don Green
Sage Rod Company
Bainbridge Island, Washington

Preston Singletary, associate editor of Flyfishing & Tying Journal *magazine caught this nice coho salmon while testing tackle in the Italio River in Alaska.*

CHARLES VULLIET

Fly Rods

There are very few tools of the fishing trade that have been intellectualized as much as the fly rod. Every rod designer has his own ideas as to what makes the perfect rod and threads posted on Internet fly-fishing bulletin boards ramble on at great length scrutinizing the most minute aspects of a rod's action, how it will function with various lines and if another manufacturer offers one just as good at a more attractive price. Fact of the matter is most graphite fly rods on the market today have better intrinsic casting properties than the majority of us will ever bring out when casting them. So, if you are planning to purchase your first rod to use for Pacific salmon fishing, you are certain to find something ranging from very serviceable to exceptionally good in the range of $140- $700. Remember, you can always start with something very serviceable and work your way up into the rarified air of the very high-end rods as your take-home pay increases.

Through the years I have used rods from St. Croix, Fenwick, Lamiglas, Sage, Scott, Orvis and Temple Fork Outfitters. Other rods that I have tried but not used extensively are made by G.Loomis, Powell, Cabela's and Cortland.

My friend, fishing partner and co-author, Bruce Ferguson has been a Sage man since I first met him many years ago. Bruce has an arsenal primarily of Sage RPLx and RPLxI rods. During the past several years I have primarily employed Lamiglas rods and more recently Temple Fork Outfitters. This is not to say that the other fly rods that we've used are not excellent because they are indeed very good and have established dedicated followings among Pacific salmon fly-fishers.

Rod Action

For all practical purposes, any one-handed rod offered as a steelhead/salmon rod will have a fast action compared to anything we owned in the old cane and fiberglass days. Some will be advertised as moderately fast, fast or very fast. For the fishing you will be doing, a rod rated as moderately-fast to fast, will be a good choice.

A two-handed rod will almost always have a slow to moderate action. This is the nature of the beast for a rod that has to sort of build up a head of steam before sending all of that line out over the water. Since two-handed rods fill the bill primarily for fishing rivers, any of them 13 to 15 feet in length for a 9- to 11-weight line will do the job very well.

Rod Length

The highest percentage of the single-handed graphite rods used for salmon fishing are 9-footers. The rest are comprised of rods of 9 1/2 to 10 feet in length.

Anglers who fish rivers more than beaches and estuaries often go for the 9 1/2- to 10-foot rod as the additional length will mend line more easily. In addition, a 10-foot, fast-action 8-weight in the hands of a good, strong caster will send a weight-forward line or shooting head to astonishing distances that are not as easily reached with a 9-footer. The angler who fishes primarily along beaches and estuaries uses

Jimmy LeMert, owner of Patrick's Fly Shop in Seattle, uses a stripping basket while fishing for coho in Puget Sound. Many anglers make stripping baskets from Rubbermaid dishpans at very little expense.

BOB YOUNG

Author Johnson having it out with a large, stubborn Skagit River chum salmon. He was using a two-handed 10-weight rod. It was put to the test but up to the challenge. A lot of fly-fishers use two-handed rods to swing flies for salmon in the rivers. When landing a salmon with a two-hander you sometimes need a lot of beach to back up on.

a 9-foot rod since a longer rod can actually become a disadvantage in working a played-out salmon close enough to net.

Rod Line Weight

Rods used for year around Pacific salmon fishing run the gamut of weights. Fly-fishers pursue immature salmon in the salt that are little more than a foot long. They also go after mature chinook salmon that can weigh upwards of 50 pounds. Thus the line weights for salmon rods can range from a 5-weight at the light end of the range on up to 10-, 11- or 12-weights when going after large chinook salmon. The average salmon fly-fisher generally gets by with a 5-weight and an 8-weight, a tandem that will cover most of the situations one might face when fishing for coho, chum or pink salmon. Anglers do land the occasional huge chinook salmon with an 8-weight outfit, but it is an exhausting ordeal that almost always kills the fish, and often breaks the rod.

The angler who fishes exclusively from the beaches often opts for a 5- or 6-weight, which will handle coho salmon from a pound to larger resident salmon upwards of 6 pounds. A reel with a good drag and capacity of 125 yards of backing is suggested for this rod. Some anglers will stretch the use of their 5- and 6-weights with mature northern coho or chum salmon but it is not recommended by the authors.

If a person wants to purchase a single rod for all of his or her beach fishing for immature coho salmon to big adult chum and coho returning from the north Pacific, a fast-action 7-weight is a good choice. The 7-weight will do the job along the beaches and estuaries but is often overmatched on big

rivers where salmon have the advantage of a heavy current to supplement their bid for freedom.

On the other hand, the angler who fishes primarily in rivers and only occasionally fishes the salt will be better served with an 8-weight. It will be a bit on the heavy side for beaches and estuaries but have more strength for handling big chum and coho salmon in rivers. In addition to its line-mending capabilities, an 8-weight will pick up a long length of line from the surface so that the fly can be quickly redirected to a salmon that has shown itself by swirling or jumping.

Two piece, four piece, or what?

Other than one three-section rod, a 9 1/2-foot 7-weight, all of my salmon-fishing rods are four-piece models. I prefer four-piece rods for ease of transporting during my travels. Furthermore, I can find no good reason not to own four-piece rods. They cast just as well as two-piece rods and if they weigh more, the additional weight is nearly undetectable.

As for the technology of a four-piece rod, remember that nearly all of our early cane rods were of three- and four-piece construction. In the late 1960s, the J. Kennedy Fisher Rod Company was producing four-piece rods of fiberglass (one of which I still own). In the mid-1970s Fisher brought out four-piece graphite rods of up to 10 feet in length. The technology is long-standing and has been improved over the years. Today we can expect good actions from rods that have four to seven sections. Any slight differences in the actions of multi-piece rods are probably undetectable to the average angler.

The All-Around Two-Rod Salmon Tandem

The fly-fisher who wants to cover 95 percent of the salmon fishing—in fresh and salt water—as simply as possible will get most of it done with a 6-weight/8-weight brace of fast-action, four-piece rods. These rods have to be designed for use in salt water with corrosion-proof fittings throughout. An all-around tandem meeting these criteria will handle all salmon from 2 to 15 pounds very nicely. The occasional chinook up to 20 pounds, or so can also be handled on the 8-weight. For monster chinook salmon that tip the scales at 30 to more than 50 pounds, which makes up the other 5 percent, a 10- to 12-weight rod would be a better choice.

I have fished extensively with two sets of rods that are designed for estuary and saltwater use, but can also be used nicely in fresh water. They are action-matched 6- and 8-weights. One set is the Jim Teeny *Signature Series* from Temple Fork Outfitters, which have anodized aluminum reel seats, short fighting butts and corrosion-resistant hardware. The other is a brace of Temple Fork Outfitter TiCr rods with fast actions for saltwater use, designed by Lefty Kreh. With a set of rods like these, the Pacific salmon fly-angler can fish confidently from California to Alaska in fresh water or salt.

Purchasing a Fly Reel

A fly reel for salmon fishing is a purchase worthy of serious consideration. Dave Lock, a fly-fishing expert and long-time fishing tackle manufacturing representative, offers his personal observations for purchasing a salmon fly reel:

"A fly reel for Pacific salmon fishing should satisfy realistic needs for line capacity and backing—and be the proper weight to balance the rod to be fished. Depending on the need for durability and lightness, adequate reels are available at prices ranging from garage sale, to thousands of dollars. Allowing for the principle of "buyer beware", reels costing more will usually offer more features and reliability.

Quality freshwater reels with click-and-pawl drags and exposed palming rims can give years of service with good care and maintenance. I have been out-fished for sea-runs and small salmon on more than one occasion by fellows whose aging equipment did not hamper their experience. I have also seen trips end abruptly when a lightweight or poorly maintained reel failed beyond repair and the hours and dollars invested were wasted.

In the last fifteen years or so, numerous new highly corrosion-resistant reels have come onto the market, responding to the demands of the saltwater aficionados in the sport. Most are beautifully designed, creatively engineered and manufactured on computer controlled equipment to exacting tolerances. They run smoothly, usually on sealed ball bearings and employ reliable adjustable drags.

As you travel farther from home, your need for a reputable, dependable reel increases because your ability to find parts and repair is usually diminished. Look for reels that can be serviced easily in the field, by yourself or a guide—and be sure to take along any manufacturer's suggested replacement parts and lubricant.

If your quarry is of larger size and capable of long, hard runs, your need for a quality drag system becomes the heart of your fly reel. It should be of proven design and easily adjustable. The drag adjustment knob should be accessible and easily gripped and smoothly progressive for controlled changes to drag resistance. The foundation for a drag is the structure supporting the revolving spool. If the reel foot, frame, spindle or bearings cannot resist the force generated by the fish, eventually the reel will fail. When you are fly-fishing for fish at the 200-pound threshold, the design requirements are different than at the 10- to 30-pound mark. You will do a lot more casting for Pacific salmon than for tuna, Dorado or sailfish, so the weight of the reel is important from the standpoint of fatigue.

Do you need 50 or 250 yards of backing? Will you need to turn a fish quickly on heavy tippet or let them run long on a light leader? Pink salmon from the beach are quite different

Fishing tackle representative, Dave Lock has fished salmon on the fly for years in his home waters around Vancouver Island.

sport than king salmon in a river or coho along the outside of a kelp bed. When your fishing will encompass several species and situations you will need to average the demands, or purchase additional tackle.

The newest generation of reels use large-arbor spools with the best of them light enough to balance the newest lightweight rods. When a salmon is way out at the end of your backing, the advantage can be 12X that of the conventional arbor; and when it is in close, making that last desperate run, the larger diameter spool reel releases line smoothly, with fewer revolutions.

Anti-reverse reels are also worthy of consideration. The part that is anti-reverse is the spool handle. The advantage is that when a fish is running out line, you do not need to be concerned about injuring your hand or fingers on a rapidly revolving spool handle. Experienced anglers will argue that they lose some control when fighting a fish. However, an angler who does not have the benefit of frequent fishing and many hours on the water will land more fish with an anti-reverse reel. Look for a reel with a simple anti-reverse mechanism so that you do not increase the opportunity for problems or failure.

How do your choose from so many quality reels? Ask questions from the shops that sell them so that you know their features, characteristics and price range. A good fly-fishing shop will dispense good advice. They want satisfied customers to return. If you need more help, ask people who have fished the reels you are interested in seeing if their experience matches the claims for performance and serviceability. Do your homework and when possible, try before you buy. A good fly reel should be a lifetime investment and never be the cause of you losing a lifetime salmon."

—Dave Lock
Saanichton, British Columbia, Canada

These Islander reels 4-inch (left) and 4.5-inch diameter, are considered big-game reels best suited to fishing sailfish or dorado. Johnson also uses them for salmon in the salt and to hold Spey lines for use in fresh water as well. They have seen front line use for more than ten years without a whimper.

Fly Reels

We presently have a mind-boggling selection of high-quality, high-priced fly reels available. To this end it is prudent to consider reels only from reliable manufacturers, preferably those who have been making reels for a long time. The manufacturing companies whose reels you check out should offer a complete repair service based within reasonable shipping distance of your home.

It is important to always purchase a reel that has adequate capacity for the fly line and backing. To this end it is always better to purchase a reel that is a bit oversized than one that you have to jam full to have enough capacity. An overly full reel often binds up if you don't rewind line exactly evenly

Two reliable old reels belonging to author Johnson, both anti-reverse models. The Fin Nor (bottom) is forty years old. The top reel is a twenty-five-year-old Fenwick World Class. Both have been discontinued but are still going strong. The message here is to buy the best reels that you can afford and they will likely be passed on to your kids.

when fighting a salmon. I know that even after fifty years, I still get excited enough when playing a salmon that I need the comfort of a bit of extra space on my reel spool.

When selecting a reel for salmon fishing, I use the following rule of thumb for line capacity. It has worked for me without a hitch for years:

Reel	Line	Backing
6 weight	Weight forward	125-150 yards, 20 pound
7 weight	Weight forward	150-175 yards, 20 pound
8 weight	Weight forward	175-225 yards, 20 pound
10 weight	Weight forward	200-250 yards, 30 pound
12 weight	Weight forward	250-300 yards, 30 pound

Note: If your present reel has too little capacity for the manufacturer's backing recommendations you can go to Gel Spun backing which will increase the capacity of any reel by 15-20 percent, or purchase a larger reel.

Brian O'Keefe had someone else taking his picture for a change when he landed this nice chinook salmon from an Alaska river. He was checking out a two-handed rod when the chinook grabbed the fly.

Reels that have served me well over the years include: Fenwick, Fin Nor, Islander, Scientific Anglers and Temple Fort Outfitters. For a bit less outlay of your hard-earned cash, but still very serviceable and up to the task of tangling with Pacific salmon, take a look at the saltwater models offered by Cabela's, Cortland, Okuma or Tioga. There are, of course many more reels on the market in a range of prices that are up to the task of handling Pacific salmon. Be patient, shop long and hard, and take good care of the reel you finally decide to purchase.

Fly Lines

There is a large selection of fly lines available to the contemporary salmon fly-fisher that are offered in a wide range of prices, from relatively inexpensive to pricey. They all work;

LES JOHNSON

When fishing beaches of shallow inlets the right fly line is critical to success. These anglers used floating lines designed for distance to put their flies over coho swimming in less than five feet of water.

some better than others. We have fly lines tapered to turn over heavy bucktails. We have fly lines that float like corks, even when gunked up from extensive use in salt water. We have lines that will sink fast and deep to reach salmon in almost any situation that can be negotiated with a cast fly. In between we have fly lines that will allow us to work a fly through every level of the water column. One of the latest developments are superb fly lines that are clear, or clear camouflage, a feature that has proven to be a distinct advantage when fishing spooky salt water salmon that are feeding along the surface, or holding in the shallow margins of large western rivers.

There has also been an upsurge in the use of long, two-handed Spey rods for salmon in coastal rivers. This is a spin-off by fly-fishers who employ two-handed rods for steelhead fishing and have extended their method to salmon fishing. There are several salmon/steelhead line options for long-rod anglers.

We have not listed line colors since they are subject to change. Colors can be introduced—or discontinued—in any line category; by any manufacturer, at any time. Floating lines range from somber tans and grays to bright yellows, greens and reds. Most sinking lines are offered in various shades of blue, green and gray to black. Remember, line function is more important than line color in most angling situations.

Make your fly line purchases prudently—and don't begin arbitrarily hacking them up to design a custom line on the recommendation of a fishing buddy, streamside guru, or a thread on an internet bulletin board unless you are sure the formula is valid. Even a fly shop with the most liberal return policy is not likely to take back a line that has been cut into several useless pieces. Fly lines are expensive and as a complete salmon fly-fisher you are going to need several.

Fly lines recommended in this chapter include only those that the authors have either tested, or used extensively. All have application in angling for Pacific salmon with some being more useful specifically for salmon than others. Although the information presented was current at the time this book went to press, new lines are being introduced on a regular basis. Professionals at better west coast fly-fishing shops keep up on fly line development and stock the lines you'll need to get started. Some fly shops have test lines available from major manufacturers for you to *try before you buy.*

Well known fly-fishing writer and shooting-head expert Dan Blanton with a nice coho taken in the salt off Baranoff Island in Alaska. Dan was using one of his jig-hook patterns.

DAN BLANTON

The Floating Fly Line

Floating fly line development—primarily in weight-forward fly lines—has been rolling along at a brisk rate during the past several years, in large measure to meet the needs of the fly-fisher who finds diverse conditions near home or at remote fishing destinations. Although Pacific salmon fly-fishing is considered to be primarily the domain of the sinking fly line, the floater is equally important particularly when working from the beaches, casting to near-surface salmon in the salt, or retrieving flies over active salmon in a freshwater pool.

Most floating lines that fall into the category of *saltwater taper*, or something similar, have a powerful front taper, a standard length belly and long running line section. They are designed for easy casting with bulky flies and quick pick-up for redirecting a cast in order to cover a distant salmon with a minimum of false casting. There are some very good lines on the market for this work such as the Orvis Salmon/Steelhead Taper, Rio Steelhead & Atlantic Salmon Line and Scientific Anglers Steelhead Taper.

Bruce Richards, product development engineer for 3M Scientific Anglers, trying out a new fly line at his Midland, Michigan "office". Bruce generously helped the authors edit the fly line section of the tackle chapter for accuracy.

Even on sunny days, saltwater fishing areas can get chilly. Marsha McDermid (left) and Linda Caverhill needed both polarized sunglasses and warm clothing during this successful trip to Tofino, British Columbia.

The Orvis Salmon/Steelhead Line, Scientific Anglers Steelhead Taper and Rio Steelhead & Atlantic Salmon Line are designed with powerful front tapers to delay turnover of the fly, which is best for long casts. These lines have long rear belly tapers for easy pickup and redirection. The finishes are designed for cold, northern rivers and salt water.

Floating fly lines in weights from 6 through 10 are commonly employed by the Pacific salmon angler. Six-weights are excellent for immature resident coho salmon that are fished extensively throughout Washington and British Columbia marine waters and for pink salmon upon returning to natal rivers. Seven- through 10-weight lines are used by anglers who fish heavier single-handed rods in fresh or salt water. Eleven- and 12-weight lines, at one time used only for southern saltwater species like tarpon, sailfish or dorado, are becoming more commonly seen in use on rivers like the Hoh, Skeena, Alagnak or Kenai where chinook salmon of more than fifty pounds are often encountered.

Multi-Tip Floating Fly Line

A floating line with multiple-tips has become popular across the country during the past few years. Actually, this innovative line is one of the many offshoots of West Coast fly-fishers' ingenuity at creating lines that will cover many situations. Multiple-tip lines, called Change-A-Tip, Quad Tip, Multi-Tip, or something similar depending on the manufacturer, are simply weight forward floating lines with four changeable tips; floating, intermediate sinking, fast sinking and very-fast sinking. Spare tips are carried in a small wallet that is provided with the line. Changing tips is quick and easy to meet different water conditions by means of the loop-to-loop connecting system.

For the angler who wants to get the maximum options from a single fly line, multiple-tip lines are worthy of consideration and are available from 6-weight through 12-weight.

Tackle boxes made of plastic like this Plano model 3500 with adjustable dividers, are perfect for saltwater use. Plastic does not corrode or rust.

There is also a full complement of multi-tip lines available for two-handed rods.

The Sinking Fly Line

Since its introduction by Scientific Anglers more than fifty years ago, the sinking fly line has continued to be improved and dominates the arsenal of the successful Pacific salmon fly-fisher because it is available in a wide variety of types and sinking rates. It is doubtful that any Pacific salmon angler does not own at least one sinking fly line and the more serious among us own several.

We have fly lines that sink very slowly, for working a fly just under the surface and very fast sinking fly lines that plumb the depths of the swiftest current. And, we have sinking fly lines that allow us to search through the water column at every depth in between. Of primary importance, every type of sinking fly line is offered to match every Pacific salmon fly rod from 6-weight through 12-weight.

Within the gamut of sinking lines, there are full sinking lines and floating lines with sinking tips of various lengths. Shooting heads, backed with a variety of shooting lines, remain justifiably popular although they are receiving competition from integrated shooting head lines. All are manufactured in a wide range of sinking rates, usually listed in *inches per second*.

Scientific Anglers fly line sinking rates are established by dropping a short length of each fly line weight and type through the water column in a tank that has electric eyes to accurately start and stop a timer that measures the sink rate. Other companies probably use a similar system.

While the method for establishing sinking rates (how fast a line sinks) of lines is pretty well standardized, there is no industry standard for labeling these sinking rates for comparison, so that the buyer must carefully read all information available to compare them and it isn't easy. One manufacturer may rate its sinking lines 1 through 5 while another will use a 1 through 6, or 1 through 8 designations. In practical fishing applications, the speed at which a certain line will sink varies considerably according to line weight, water depth, current speed and water salinity if fishing in the salt.

In most cases, fly shops specializing in saltwater salmon fishing will have people on staff that can help you get started on the right track. Most fly-fishers eventually build up a battery of sinking lines or shooting heads to meet the various conditions that must be dealt with to successfully fish for Pacific salmon from the surface film to the depths of a river or saltwater bay.

Fly Line Sinking Rates

The following is an average compilation of sinking rates for most fly lines. The sinking rate can even vary within a designation depending on the weight of the line. For instance; a type IV, 7-weight sinking line will sink slightly slower than a type IV 8-weight. A shooting taper will sink at the same rate as a weight forward but it might fish a little deeper because the shooting line does not tend to plane the line up as much as a weight-forward running line will. This is admittedly nit-picking but such things are factors when checking out sinking rates of lines.

Sinking Fly Line Designations	Sink Rate
Standard Sinking and Sinking Tip Lines	
Type I/Intermediate	1.25 - 1.75
Type II	2.00 - 3.00
Type III	3.25 - 4.00
Type IV	3.75 - 5.00
Type V	5.25 - 6.00
Type VI	6.25 - 7.00
Integrated Shooting Heads	
Cortland *Quick Descent*	4.00 - 9.00
Orvis *Depth Charge*	4.5 - 7.5
Rio Striper 26 DC	6.5 - 9.0
Scientific Anglers *Express Wet Tip*	4.00 - 8.00
Teeny Nymph Company *T/TS*	4.00 - 10.00

Note: The accuracy of these inches-per-second sink rates are as stated by the manufacturers and have not been verified by the authors.

Integrated Shooting-Head Lines

When Jim Teeny introduced us to his revolutionary Teeny Nymph fly line in August, 1983 we never dreamed that it would become one of the most widely used lines and type of line employed for fishing Pacific salmon in fresh and salt water. Utilizing a very fast sinking head section with a small diameter floating running line the Teeny Nymph line was actually a one-piece, integrated shooting head first available in weights of 200 through 400 grains. The Teeny lines with a smooth junction between the head and running line became tremendously popular with salmon and steelhead fly-fishers and have since been followed by similar lines from Cortland, Orvis, Rio and Scientific Anglers. Nearly every major fly-line manufacturer now offers a line of this type in a wide range of weights and sinking front sections from 10 to 32 feet long. The astute salmon angler keeps close tabs on integrated shooting head lines as it is probably the category where the most intensive design work is taking place at this time.

Manufacturers offer their lines from 150 through 700 grains or more. To build in a bit of exclusivity they have tweaked line weights so that each manufacturer offers a slightly different selection. Also, these lines are available with either a floating or intermediate sinking running line section. For fresh water fishing a floating running line is generally desired for its mending qualities, although running lines of .025 to .035 inches have limited mending capabilities. For saltwater fishing an intermediate sinking running line pulls straighter allowing the head to sink deeper.

Presently, specialty sinking lines from all major manufacturers are available in 150, 175, 200, 225, 250, 275, 295, 300, 325, 350, 375, 400, 425, 450, 475, 500, 525, 550, 575, 600, 625, 650 and 750 grains. With each manufacturer offering at least five of the line weights shown, it will take a bit of studying to find just the right one for your rod. This already long list of integrated shooting head line weights is destined to keep growing and changing so the weights listed here will probably be somewhat dated by the time this book is published. The list will, however remain useful as a general reference of line weights.

When testing integrated shooting-head lines you will learn that each one will work with two to three different rod weights. They cast very smoothly once you have learned to *launch* them (see Lob Shot in the saltwater techniques chapter) with a minimum of false casting and a nice, firm stroke. For instance, I can cast specialty sinking lines from 275 through 350 grains with my 8-weight rods.

Once you have mastered the casting technique you will quickly learn to count on these lines for a variety of salmon fishing situations. You can rest assured that additional line weights and types of specialty sinking lines will be coming your way in the future.

Clear and Camouflage Fly Lines

A relatively new addition to the already burgeoning variety of fly lines available to the Pacific salmon angler are the clear, or clear camouflage fly lines in floating, sinking or sinking-tip models in a full range of weights. Early models had some coiling problems. However, once this wrinkle was worked out by manufacturers clear and camouflage fly lines

Don McDermid combines a long-billed cap and polarized glasses for spotting bait or leaping salmon to minimize glare.

MARSH MCDERMID

quickly became a big hit with fly-anglers up and down the Pacific Coast.

Clear/Camouflage Floating Lines

Clear or clear camo floating lines can be a boon to the angler who is working over skittish salmon such as pinks or cohos feeding in the surface film on Euphausiids or small, immature herring. This is a time when presentation of the fly to a salmon becomes every bit as critical as setting out a tiny Blue-Winged Olive over a demanding brown trout. There are floating lines available that are completely clear and others that have a 9- to 15-foot clear tip. Either type works very well for this situation.

Clear/Camouflage Intermediate Sinking Lines

This is a line that casts easily and is virtually tangle-free when using a stripping basket or having a good spot to strip it onto your boat deck. With its very slow sink rate, the clear intermediate line slips just under the surface where it nearly disappears and can be fished without being pushed around by wave action that may range from a gentle chop to foot-high waves. It is considered to be a must-have line by most fly-fishers who fish Washington's Puget Sound and the marine waters of British Columbia. Clear camo lines are available in line weights from 6 through 10 to cover every situation that will confront a Pacific salmon fly-fisher who is working near the surface.

Clear/Camo Integrated Shooting Heads

The first clear camo integrated head introduced by Cortland combines the clear camo running line with a dark head section. Scientific Anglers has a similar line called Streamer Express that has a translucent running line. These are the only two lines of this type that we've tried to date. Both have excellent casting properties and minimal tangling problems.

Shooting Heads

With the off-the-shelf cornucopia of front-loaded, shooting head-style lines available from Cortland, Orvis, Rio, Scientific Anglers and Teeny, one would be hard pressed to believe that experienced salmon fly-fishers need more options. However, even in light of the almost endless array of lines commercially manufactured the venerable shooting taper, commonly called a shooting head, a 30-foot fly line dreamed up in the 1950s by innovative west coast fly-fishers, is still widely used and highly regarded.

Shooting heads began as home-made lines constructed by weighing (using a powder scale which weighs in grains), cutting and splicing lengths of level or double taper floating and sinking fly lines together to create short, compact fly lines, 30 to 40 feet long. These *heads* were employed for use in specific angling situations found most often on the Pacific Coast. Shooting heads could be cast a hundred feet or more

by capable casters and quickly became so popular that they dominated the sport of salmon and steelhead fly-fishing from the 1950s through the 1980s.

Not only has custom-built shooting head construction maintained a solid position in west coast fly line development; this intriguing regional fly line building process continues to attract new devotees every season. Around 1993, custom shooting head construction enjoyed a second surge from anglers who began devising custom heads, some with detachable sinking tips, to glean the best casting properties from their two-handed salmon rods. As a result, we now see expert casters using 14- and 15-foot, 10/11-weight rods routinely casting more than a hundred feet of line to reach far holding water in rivers like the Chetco, Skagit and Skeena.

Fly Line and Shooting Head Standards		
Line Weights		
No. (line or head)	**Weight** (1)	**Range** (2)
1	60	54-66
2	80	74-86
3	100	94-106
4	120	114-126
5	140	134-146
6	160	152-168
7	185	177-193
8	210	202-218
9	240	230-250
10	280	270-290
11	330	318-342
12	380	368-392
(1) In grains (437.5 grains equal one ounce) based on the first 30 feet of line exclusive of any taper or tip.		
(2) Manufacturing tolerances		

Shooting Lines

Shooting lines, small-diameter, level-floating, intermediate-sinking, or fast-sinking fly lines are used behind both custom and factory shooting heads. There is a variety of floating shooting lines available in .024 through .042 diameters for use with the lightest to the heaviest salmon shooting-head systems. These are excellent for distance casting but due to a rather light surface coating over a small core—and being accelerated through the rod guides time after time at very high speed—shooting lines are prone to wearing out more rapidly than the larger-diameter running section of a standard fly line.

Amnesia, a low-memory monofilament distributed by Sunset Line and Twine Company in Petaluma, California, is another popular shooting line that has been in use for many years. You can find Amnesia in most full-service West Coast fly shops in 20- through 40-pound test.

Pontoon boats are also useful when fishing the salt in an area of light current. Bob Young is playing out a Vancouver Island coho while knot master Bill Nash of San Jose, California offers assistance.

A Shooting-Head System

I almost always use full lines in either floating or sinking configurations when fishing from a boat where I have the luxury of having two or three rods strung up. When I'm fishing beaches for chum, coho or pink salmon though, my preference for shooting heads is unflagging. When it comes to making long-range casts time after time, and being able to carry four or five lines (heads) in a jacket pocket, a shooting head system is still pretty hard to beat.

For salmon fishing my shooting head system in line weights 6.8 and 10 include: floating, intermediate, type 1, type 3 and type 6 (or type 7, depending on the manufacturer) sinking heads. I also have a couple of heads made of Cortland LC-13, Rio T-14 and Scientific Anglers Deep Water Express on hand as well, just in case I really have to get a fly down deep.

All of my shooting heads and shooting lines are set up with loops for easy changing. In every fishing situation, I use a shooting head two sizes larger than the line rating marked on the rod. Most anglers always use a shooting head that is two, or sometimes three, sizes heavier than the rod rating. The reason for this is that a heavier shooting head will load most rods more easily, thus requiring less back casting and quicker delivery of the fly.

Another plus for a shooting-head system is that in the event of a reel breakdown or loss of a line (mine or a friend's), an easy-to-carry, shooting-head system can save the day and takes up very little space in my duffle. Even in view of all the technological advances in line design since the 1950s, I still consider a selection of shooting heads to be one of the very best systems ever conceived for versatile day-to-day salmon fishing.

Shooting-head kits are presently being offered by Rio and Orvis and are already weighted for the rod listed on the box. Scientific Anglers has a list in its Mastery catalog recommending that shooting heads two sizes heavier than the rod weight be used for most efficient casting. I expect another surge in shooting head popularity with the systems being simplified.

Some conventional shooting-head devotees blow them off as "chuck and duck" heads (not to be confused with Jim Teeny's Chuck and Duck fly lines) but there is a cadre of fly-casters centered in the San Jose/Monterey area of central California who have become experts at building and casting heads made of very dense and heavy lines and consider them to be integral to their shooting-head systems. Furthermore, they contend that these heads are not only useful but are as easy to cast as any other shooting head once a person gets to know how they work.

A fine gentleman whom some friends and I had the pleasure of salmon fishing with on Vancouver Island is Bill Nash of San Jose, California. Bill, a retired college professor, is incurably curious about everything from the true strength of knots to the exact dimensions, weights and balance-to-the-rod requirements of these extra-high-density lines. He has in fact become such a respected authority in this pursuit that he has published an excellent book on the subject, *Flycasting Systems*. So, I asked Bill for a rundown on the popular lines, LC-13, T-14 and Deep Water Express, which he uses for most everything, from trout to big game species, when the situation requires them:

LC-13, T-14 and Deep Water Express

High-Density Sinking Lines, Lc-13, T-14 and Deep Water Express

Extra-High-Density Lines LC-13 and T-14

When there is a need to go deep, to compensate for swift flows, or keep a fly down when fast-stripping rates are required, the extra high density of lead-core or tungsten loaded lines will help get the job done.

LC-13 is a plastic coated lead-core line, marketed by Cortland. T-14 is a powdered tungsten loaded plastic line with a monofilament core, marketed by RIO. Both LC-13 and T-14 are offered in 30' coils or on bulk spools and should be cut to a desired weight/length, for use as shooting heads. After cutting to size, braided loops should be installed on each end for attachment to a running line and a leader,

Bill Nash of San Jose, California selects a fly to tempt a northern coho salmon on Vancouver Island.

Relative Characteristics

Diameters: LC-13 & T-14 are both nominally 0.040".
Break Strength: LC-13 = 24lbs, T-14 = 35lbs.
Density: LC-13 = 2.05 oz/in³· T-14 = 2.12 oz/in³.
Sink Rates: LC-13 = 9"/sec., T-14 = 9.7"/sec.
Weight Variations: LC-13 ± 1 grain/ft, T-14 ± 0.6 grain/ft.

As you can see, based upon measurements, I find that the line weight per foot varies considerably from one spool or coil to another, often-in excess of "Manufacturing Tolerances".

As an aid in making adjustments I advise the use of an economical line weight scale, so that once the desired line load is determined for a rod it can be easily matched when getting/ making a new line (measure the weight of 30' to get grains/ft and cut accordingly).

Rod Selection for LC-13 and T-14

Shooting heads much longer than 30', or shorter than 26' become a bit awkward to cast, so, except for specialty situations, head length should be confined to that range.

To get the best performance from a rod, when most all of the line weight is concentrated within 26' to 30', the weight of these heads should approximate the weight of about 50' of a double-taper line that matches the rod number, this is because rod design requires that a rod must be able to cast at least 50' of a double-taper line (that is why we advise up-lining by at least two when selecting a standard 30' shooting head).

LC-13

At 13.2 grains-per-foot, the LC-13 weight range (26' to 30') would be 343 grains to 396 grains, which suggests that it be used with 8wt through 10wt rods (26' for 8wt, 28' for 9wt and 30' for 10wt on up).

T-14

At 14 grains-per-foot, the weight range of T-14 would be 364 grains to 425 grains, suggesting that it be used with 9wt or 10wt rods (27' for 9-weight and 30' for 10-weight on up).

This isn't to say that these rods can't be used with greater loads than suggested above but the ease of casting diminishes as higher loads are used and may give rise to the expression "chuck and duck" lines.

The belief that using lead core requires a chuck-and-duck casting approach probably arises from a tendency to try to use 7-, 8- and 9-weight rods with 30' of LC-13 or T-14 type lines. If the proper length (weight) is chosen for the rod to be used these heads will cast as easily as any other shooting head properly matched to a rod.

Where Do Braided-Core Shooting Heads, Like Scientific Anglers' Deepwater Express, Fit Into This Discussion?
Deep Water Express

Scientific Anglers' Deep Water Express (DWE) is an example of braided-core 30' shooting heads and RIO'S T-14 is an example of a mono-core line. Most of the various line manufacturers produce both types but for comparison, because of my experiences and tests, DWE and T-14 will be used as examples for comparison.

These lines/heads are weighted by coating the cores with a plastic that has been loaded with tungsten powder. Assuming that both were coated with the same plastic mix, such that the weight per unit length were the same, it would be found that the line densities would be un-equal because the braided-core diameter would be greater than that of the mono-core due to the air space between the fibers of the braid (There are other factors but that is the way it works out for the materials being used). As the coatings become thicker (making the cores less significant) the densities would approach being the same.

LC-13 is structurally different in that it may be considered a tri-axial line where the core is a lead wire inserted into a braided sleeve (sleeve provides the line strength) and then covered with a protective plastic coating. It will have some of the attributes of a braided-core line but is more like a mono-core line in characteristics and performance. Since its loading and casting characteristics are closely the same as T-14 only a comparison of T-14 and DWE will need to be made to establish the DWE position.

Comparisons

Scientific Anglers' DWE is offered as 30' heads with tapered ends and is available in line weights of 400, 550, 700, and 850 grains. DWE may need to be cut to a desired weight/length to match the rod to be used or to make a suitable sinking tip for other lines and SA has included a weight distribution chart in the package to assist in determining how and where to cut.

Rio T-14 is a linear line available in 30' coils or on bulk spools; it weighs about 14gn/ft and is cut to get the desired weight/length for proper rod loading.

Diameters:

DWE (400gn) 0.049", (550gn) 0.053", (700gn) 0.056", (850gn) 0.081"

*(Note: Diameters are for the mid-section. DWE has tapered ends)

T-14 (420gn for 30') 0.040"

*(Note: T-14 has a smaller diameter because of a monofilament core)

Density:

DWE (400gn) = 1.52 oz/in³, (550gn) =1.88 oz/in³, (700gn) = 2.10 oz/in³, (850gn) = 2.15 oz/in³
T-14 (420gn) = 2.12 oz/in³

*(Note: The DWE density increases, as expected, as the thickness/weight of the plastic coating is increased and weighs about 700gn (28gn/ft mid section) before the density of T-14 is reached)

Sink Rates:

DWE (400gn) = 7.0"/sec., (550gn) = 8.5"/sec. (700gn) = 9.0"/sec., (850gn) = 9.5"/sec. T-14 (420gn) = 9.7"/sec.

*(Note: When the densities are about equal so are the sink rates).

Break Strength:

DWE 28 lbs, T-14 = 35 lbs

Why and When Should One of These Lines/Heads Be Chosen?

It is obvious, from the data above, that if the sink rates are to be approximately matched a DWE shooting head must have a weight of 700gn to 850gn, to match the rate of a T-14, 30' shooting head weighing about half as much (420gn).

Excluding heads cut to less than 25' (short heads may have special applications but introduce casting complications) DWE type heads will be too heavy for anything under a 12-weight rod, making it a candidate for dredging up big-game fish. However, when used for big-game and/or deep presentations, it will have the advantage of being much heavier which will help prevent the line from being buoyed up by currents and stripping action, keeping the fly in the strike zone longer.

Also, the thicker coatings of DWE type lines provide good protection from abrasions and a braided core will accept minor cuts/nicks without seriously weakening the line.

A fast sink rate combined with the lower weight of T-14 type lines makes it possible to have fast-sinking shooting heads, in the 25' to 30' range, that can be cast using much lighter action, 8-weight to 10-weight, rods and provide excellent performance when chasing stripers, salmon, bluefish, dorado and the like (this applies to LC-13 as well).

T-14 type shooting heads also work well on the bigger rods but due to a thinner coating and monofilament core, they don't hold up as well to abrasion, nicks and/or cuts as the DWE types (Think of the effect of a nick in a monofilament leader). When used in a big-game environment, occasional line failure is not uncommon.

Knot and shooting-head maestro Bill Nash found an intermediate shooting head just the ticket to put his fly at eye level with this nice coho salmon.

LES JOHNSON

Conclusions

DWE type lines are long-lasting heads best suited to be used with big rods for big-game applications and/or deep-water presentations where the extra weight helps put and keep a fly in the strike zone.

T-14 type lines make deep presentations possible while using the mid-range rods and are best used while seeking fish in environments that are not likely to nick or cut into the line.

LC-13, like T-14, can be used on mid-range rods, is more durable than T-14, because of the braided sleeve construction but not as durable as DWE.

Except for the very deep presentations possible with DWE type 700gn and up heads, LC-13 is the most versatile and cost effective of these lines.

—Bill Nash
San Jose, California

Rigging Fly Lines and Shooting Lines

When I began fly-fishing in the 1950s, we put loops onto the ends of fly lines and shooting heads by whip finishing the first inch or so of the fly line back on itself and coating it with varnish or Pliobond. Today many of us still make our own loops, only we use either Cortland or Gudebrod braiding running line in 30- through 50-pound test. The loops are used for joining backing to fly line, running lines to shooting heads and for building a variety of sink-tips for either a full line or shooting-head system. These loops are strong, sleek and rarely, if ever, hang up in the guides. I have some on old saltwater lines that have been wearing the same loops for the past ten years.

There is considerable information available on building your own loops. Two of the best sources are:

•www.DanBlanton.com, Click on Tackle and Techniques and then navigate to Getting Looped.

•*Flycasting Systems* by Bill Nash. This little self-published volume discusses knots, loops, splices and everything else you need to know about assembling a fly-line system—from the master. Contact Bill via billsknots@aol.com

During the past few years fly-line manufacturers have been integrating welded loops into the front end of fly line. The first ones were pretty clunky and clattered through the guides noisily, often hanging up. These factory loops have been improved dramatically of late and are now small, smooth and strong. With continued improvement being a certainty in my opinion, factory loops will eventually lessen the need for all of us old loop-building alchemists to continue our work but will never completely do away with it.

There is no substitute for incorporating a loop system into your salmon tackle. It makes any needed changes in a fly line quick and easy. For keeping things simple you can have a reel holding a running line as the basis for building any type of line you will need to meet any situation you may face during a day of fly-fishing for salmon by simply looping on the appropriate head or tip from your line wallet.

Auxiliary Fly Line Sinking Tips/Leaders

West Coast fly-fishers have not only made their own shooting heads for years but have also crafted short lengths of sinking line and lead core that they keep stashed away in a vest pocket. These auxiliary tips, usually from 1 to 10 feet in length can be added to the end of a shooting head or the sinking tip of a fly line so that a bit deeper probe of the fly can be achieved.

By saving old sinking lines and purchasing several feet of Cortland LC-13, Cortland 444 Type 6 Sinking Trolling Line, or Rio T-14 from your local fly shop you can easily make up a versatile set of auxiliary sinking tips by serving a loop onto each end. A set of these tips in 3 through 10 feet take up very little space. Some day, in the right situation, one of these tips might be just the ticket when you have to deliver your fly just a wee bit deeper to reach that salmon of the trip—or a lifetime.

If you don't wish to make your own tips there are tailor-made poly leaders available from Cortland, Orvis and others in lengths from 6 to 10 feet in at least four sinking rates. It is worth the small cost to have a couple on hand at all times. One caveat regarding some of these sinking leaders is that they have stiff or bulky loops that do not like to clear the tip top of rods easily or sometimes hang up in a guide. This can be rectified by snipping off the loop and adding one of your own, at least until manufacturers have their loop problems rectified.

Leader and Tippet

There is nothing unique about leaders for salmon fishing. Leaders from 12 feet to 4 feet and tippet weights from 6- to 16-pound test will do the job for any salmon that the Pacific salmon angler will ever confront. The following leader weights and lengths provide a good baseline.

Author Johnson's essentials; a stripping basket, fly box and the right rod for the job at hand.

Leader Strength	Length	Species	Flies
6-8 pound test	12'	Resident coho	Zooplankton
10-12 pound test	12'	Larger coho and mature pink salmon	Zooplankton Sm. Baitfish
12-16-pound test	9'	Mature northern coho, chinook and chum salmon	Baitfish
12-pound test	6-71/2'	Coho, chum, chinook in rivers	Attractors
16-pound test	4-6'	Large chinook, chum and coho salmon in rivers	Attractors

Tippet material should be carried in the same breaking strength as the main leader. A spool of lighter material is also needed. For instance the angler using a leader of 12-pound test should have spools of 12- and 10-pound test on hand. This way a leader that has been shortened from several changes of the fly can be re-lengthened with either the same breaking strength or lightened for clear conditions and spooky fish.

Excellent leader and tippet material is available from Climax, Orvis, Rio and Scientific Anglers. It is best to decide which brand you like and stick with it. I prefer to purchase leader and tippet material from the same manufacturer for uniformity of strength and finish.

Fluorocarbon Leader

Fluorocarbon leader is advertised as being less visible to fish and highly abrasion resistant. Many salmon anglers like to add a short length of fluorocarbon to the end of their leader for both reasons. Fluorocarbon leader does not float, thus is best used for work either just under the surface or deep into the water column.

Fluorocarbon leaders are also offered in full-length tapered leaders from Climax and Rio. Under the toughest clear water conditions some veteran salmon fly-fishers are convinced that a 9-foot leader made completely of fluorocarbon can make a difference in coaxing strikes from wary salmon that are turning away from their flies.

These two Plano bags hold all of Johnson's salmon fishing gear. The large bag on the bottom carries five large boxes of flies, leaders, spare hooks, and all miscellaneous gear for a day's fishing, or a destination trip. The smaller bag holds either four large Scientific Anglers or model 3500 Plano boxes for a day's fishing.

Bruce Ferguson's grandson Josh Carnahan used a 7-weight outfit to take his very first salmon—a feeding sockeye no less! A 6- or 7-weight is usually a good outfit for a youngster.

The Stripping Basket

Another innovation of West Coast anglers, the stripping basket, was first built in Washington and later manufactured locally by various small companies. During the past few years most stripping baskets have been devised from Rubbermaid dishpans, which can be found anywhere. However it is constructed, the stripping basket has become a standard item among fly-casters on both coasts.

A stripping basket is strapped around the waist so that retrieved line can be dropped into it rather than falling into the water when wading or onto the deck of a boat where it can get stepped on. This simple but unique innovation is actually a portable casting platform that allows the angler routinely longer casts and considerably less frustration over the fly line becoming tangled in flotsam, or sinking around one's boots which makes it very difficult to shoot.

There are many stripping baskets on the market at this time, some better than others, many of which sport more bells and whistles than are actually needed. The best stripping basket available according to many veteran fly casters is the one offered by Orvis. The Orvis basket has nine cones in the bottom to keep line shifting to a minimum, and notches to hold the rod while tying a fly or leader tippet. It fits comfortably against one's stomach.

Anyone who needs to fire long casts time after time in order to reach distant salmon lies should make stripping basket standard equipment.

Carrying One's Trappings

The salmon angler generally needs a vest, shoulder bag or boat bag for carrying the flies, leaders, tippet material, hones, nippers and all the trappings. An angler who fishes both on foot and from a boat many need all three.

A vest or shoulder bag need not be overly busy with an excessive number of pockets and tricky doodads for securing pliers or sunglasses because not many items are needed when fishing for Pacific salmon. One box of flies will handle most fresh water fishing needs and more than two boxes approaches gilding the lily. Anglers who prefer a compact shoulder bag usually have found a way to get by with less tackle than the person who wears a vest.

A boat bag is a different story altogether. A good boat bag should be waterproof if it's being used in an open craft as it will be subjected to heavy rain and get bounced around in the bottom of a boat or raft. In addition to flies and other paraphernalia, a boat bag carries spare reels, fly boxes and expensive cameras. For this reason the angler is well served to find a bag that is genuinely waterproof—and very few are. Even some of the most highly priced boat bags from very toney manufacturers leak to beat hell in a hard rain or when doused with sea water. You can be cheered to know that there are bags available from Offshore Angler and Cabela's catalog houses that will stand

Anglers who prefer to travel light often carry just a compact shirt-pocket box jammed with small "waiting period" flies while fishing the beaches of Washington and British Columbia.

A small skiff gives the angler more mobility when chasing salmon in the salt. Cam Sigler (left) and Bruce Ferguson used Bruce's aluminum skiff to chase fast-moving salmon in south Puget Sound.

up to a relentless pounding from rain or the sea and never leak a drop. These are the bags to consider because no matter how nifty a boat bag may look or the trendy brand name it carries, it isn't worth its weight or the space that it takes up, if it leaks.

The final part of an angler's duffle is a good soft-sided gear bag, the better ones for our purposes usually designated "expedition" or something similar. This is the bag that must engulf all the clothing and related angling equipment one needs when fishing near home for the weekend or at some distant hotspot. Shop carefully for your duffle bag because there are some marginal offerings out there that are very pricey and others that are very well designed and economically priced. The bag I own, for instance, will swallow up to six four-piece rods in a hard-sided bottom compartment, tubes and all, plus my clothing, rain gear and other essentials in the main compartment.

Clothing

The Pacific salmon angler who fishes year around will need clothing that ranges from lightweight shirts and shorts to heavy fleece undergarments, woolen mittens, stocking caps along with good insulated bootfoot waders and a rain parka.

Staying cool or warm or dry is as critical to fly-fishing Pacific salmon successfully as a good rod and reel.

Clothing for salmon fishing is straightforward and can be purchased either from the many outdoor catalog houses, local outdoor stores, or from a good army-navy surplus. For spring, summer and early autumn fishing khaki trousers and shirts, or any of the specialty fishing apparel available does the job. For late autumn through winter and early spring, polypropylene underwear, fleece tops (with zipper-closing pockets to secure one's car keys, money and fishing license), wool shirts and sweaters, socks, gloves, caps and the like, don't have to be either fancy or expensive. If you don't have a local store that handles outdoor clothing it can be purchased easily and delivered quickly from Cabela's, Ex Officio, Land's End, Orvis, L.L. Bean or Feather-Craft. All of these companies offer their products by catalog or on the Internet.

Waders

Most waders used today are made of tough, breathable material. They incorporate a membrane of Gore Tex or are treated with a breathable coating. Neoprene waders are still favored by many West Coast fly-fishers who continue on through the winter steelhead season as they are perceived to be warmer

The two most popular size outfits for mature Pacific salmon are 7 and 8 weights. Shown here is a Temple Fork Outfitters 8-weight Jim Teeny rod and #375 reel (top). Lower outfit is a Temple Fork 7-weight rod and #340 reel.

than breathables. If the angler layers fleece properly under breathable waders they are, in my experience, every bit as warm as neoprene and far more comfortable due to the fact that they breath, allowing perspiration to pass through into the atmosphere. Neoprene waders conversely hold moisture and must be turned inside out or placed on dryers overnight after a day of fishing, particularly if a person is fishing for several days straight. Breathable waders hung up at day's end will be dry as a bone the next morning.

Breathable waders have gotten a reputation of leaking easily and this may be the case with some of the lower end models but more often it is a matter of proper fit. Neoprene waders have a certain amount of built-in stretch. Some breathable have built-in stretch but not to the extent of neoprene waders. For this reason one should not purchase breathable waders to fit like a nice pair of chinos. Breathable waders should have ample room for high-stepping over logs or boulders without unduly stressing the seams in the crotch-area and big enough through the chest and seat to accommodate a heavy layering of fleece or wood. Waders may not look as snappy with baggy knees but they will be far less prone to give out around the crotch seams. I owned a pair of breathable waders that served me for eight seasons of hard use before springing a leak.

Waders are available in either stocking-foot (worn with a separate wading shoe) or boot-foot models. Stocking-foot waders which have a neoprene foot are comfortable, offer ankle support, and are warm enough for most fishing. They are also excellent for float tubing since regular wading shoes can be exchanged for lightweight booties for wearing with fins. Boot-foot waders are offered with thick insulation and are warm during the coldest weather.

Boot-foot waders and wading shoes are offered with either lug soles which work well for most gravelly saltwater beaches or felt soles which are preferred for river fishing and slippery

tidal areas. For very slippery river rocks which occur late in the season, cleats in addition to felt soles are recommended.

It is a good idea to always wear a wading belt with one's waders. Some new models of waders have built-in wading belts; a nice feature. A wading belt is the only item I know that will keep out most of the water you can take in when going over the top of your waders, or getting dunked. More recently, some wader manufacturers are providing back-support belts with their waders. These belts really do provide extra support for the back during a day of casting.

Excellent waders in a range of sizes to fit everyone (although some extremely tall or heavy folks will require

Shooting-head systems are included in author Johnson's fishing duffle for front line and back-up use from spring through fall. Above, a 6-weight Islander 3.4 LX and below an 8-weight system on a Scientific Anglers LA 890 reel and TFO Jim Teeny rod.

custom-made waders, offered at extra cost) are available from Cabela's, Dan Bailey, Hodgman, Orvis and Simms.

Rain Parkas

A good rain parka made for fishing should be constructed of sturdy, breathable material with a generous hood and visor that helps to shield eyeglasses from rain. A parka should have enough large pockets to handle fly boxes, leaders and all other items required for a day of salmon fishing in the rain. Serviceable breathable parkas range in price from about $120 to $400. As with most equipment you get what you pay for. Going below the low end listed here is not a good idea as you are almost certain to wind up with a garment that is liable

straight to the bottom. The angler simply has to come to terms as to what tools and accessories he or she really needs to make it through a day of fishing. When this is achieved, the weight of the gear we carry is usually reduced by half.

I carry a pair of stainless-steel pliers for removing hooks from a salmon's jaw, pinching down hook barbs, or cutting heavy leader material. I also carry a small belt knife for bleeding any salmon I am taking home for the barbeque. On a neck lanyard I keep a nipper, a tiny knot-tightening bar and hook hone. I always have two or three leaders and appropriate spools of tippet handy and carry a small wallet that holds spare shooting heads or sink-tips. Add a couple of boxes of flies and I am pretty well set for a day on a river or the beach.

Two-handed rods have been gaining popularity for several seasons. Author Johnson uses this 13' 6" 8-weight TFO rod with a Scientific Anglers Skagit line for fishing large rivers.

to quickly develop leaks. This does not mean that you should opt for the top of the line parka if your budget will not handle the strain. Do, however, purchase the best rain parka you can afford. Excellent parkas in an acceptable range of prices are available from Cabela's, Hodgman, Orvis, Pacific Fly Group, Simms and Drift Creek.

Pliers, Doodads and Gizmos

There is no end of items to stuff into unfilled vest pockets or pin onto one's vest. We all go through a period of insecurity that we attempt to ward off by jamming our vest or shoulder bag to critical mass with nippers, forceps, leader organizers and other gadgetry of fly-fishing. With all that added weight, a dunking would surely drag the most vigorous among us

When fishing from a boat where I have the luxury of my boat bag I carry all the equipment already listed plus a great deal more including a spare reel or two, fly lines and a line winder, a camera, and a 6-ounce flask filled with good bourbon. My boat bag also carries five large Plano 3700 boxes filled with flies.

When building up one's tackle and related equipment for fishing Pacific salmon it is wise to add it slowly and carefully. Diving recklessly into a salmon-equipment buying spree will usually ensure that a lot of hard-earned bucks will be wasted. It is better to take your time, examine gear carefully and add it slowly. Don't worry; you will eventually have your vest, boat bag and duffle just as full as those of us who have been fly-fishing Pacific salmon for fifty years.

CHAPTER TWELVE

Pacific Salmon Fly-Fishing Ethics

By Les Johnson and Bruce Ferguson

> *Ethic: A set of moral principles; a theory or system of moral values. The principles of conduct governing an individual or group. A guiding philosophy.*

Fly-fishing for Pacific salmon has grown in popularity at a rate that the authors could not have dreamed of when the first edition of this book was published more than twenty years ago. This growth is comprised of nearly two generations of anglers, who began fly-fishing for Pacific salmon, in some measure at least, through interest engendered from the information we provided. We were hoping for a positive response but it has in fact been completely overwhelming. Salmon fishers carrying fly-rods roam the rivers and estuaries from mid-summer through late fall; saltwater fly-fishers hike the beaches, or run small boats along the shorelines of Puget Sound, the Strait of Juan de Fuca, Vancouver Island, the BC mainland and southeast Alaska. Lodges that once catered only to gear fishermen looking for big chinook salmon are now putting out the welcome mat for fly-fishers. Many more resorts have been built since 1985 with some of them offering boats designed specifically for fly-fishing, operated by skilled fly-fishing guides. The bottom line is that a sport that just two decades ago offered mile after mile of uncrowded beaches and vast expanses of open water has become a robust activity as a result of its escalating popularity.

Since fly-fishing for Pacific salmon is not likely to lose favor with anglers, provided the runs of fish are maintained and we hope, increased, the importance of angling ethics comes squarely into focus. The ethics we practice are critical to Pacific salmon fly-fishing if the pleasures of the sport are to be maintained for the enjoyment of all who participate.

The simple fact is that increasing numbers of us are now fishing in places that were enjoyed by relatively few anglers not all that many years ago. Boaters must sometimes wait for a turn to anchor up on a good river pool, or are lining up in the salt for a chance to work a productive rip line. As Pacific salmon fly-fishing continues to grow, we will have to learn to fish a bit closer together, value the other angler's space a bit more by respecting private property and public property—and to always give other boaters room to fish.

A treatise on ethics could provide a complete list of do's and don'ts that would cover everything, chapter and verse, from absolute rules of the road when boating; to a strict policy for wading through a good drift so that everyone has an opportunity to fish the entire run; to giving a beach-bound angler room enough for a decent backcast. As adults we should be able to simply apply our personal ethics to fishing as we do to other facets of our lives and rest assured that everything would work out just fine.

There is a problem with this application of ethics in actual practice though. For one thing the practices and courtesies that apply to more traditional methods of salmon fishing; mooching and trolling, or even casting Buzz Bombs don't necessarily apply to fly-fishing.

Bob Young revives a coho salmon so that it can continue its journey up river to its natal spawning gravel. Care of our salmon from birth to spawning, including catch-and-release regulations, will be vital to the future of the fishery.

For instance, a surface disturbance caused by a boater racing into a good spot at full throttle, or loud footfalls on the deck of an aluminum skiff may not bother a salmon sixty feet down, but it will almost certainly spook salmon that are feeding on, or near the surface along the shoreline. Frightened salmon may be put down anywhere from several minutes—to the remainder of the day. Conversely, it is amazing how many boats can work over a school of salmon provided they maintain comfortable fishing space and operate quietly.

If a fly-caster is working a stretch of beach, additional fly-fishers will not usually cause a problem as they realize the distance needed to efficiently work a fly along a current seam or to cast diagonally in either direction. A couple of anglers that come in not understanding the dynamics of fly-fishing and begin tossing large wobblers or Buzz Bombs may not realize the amount of room the fly-fisher needs and effectively crowd him/out without meaning to. In this regard we have to count on the powers of observation and ethical behavior of the gear fishermen for all to enjoy the beach.

And in the best of situations we need to practice ethical fishing, even when we chant the mantra of "catch-and-release" as a panacea against the population decline of salmon stocks. The practice of catch-and-release fishing has certainly helped us keep fishing, but pounding on schools, or complete runs, of salmon just to rack up obscene numbers is darkened by an underlying element of harvest. There is no denying that we lose a small percentage of the salmon released even with the most careful release procedures. Never forget that catch-and-release fishing is, and will always be, a blood sport.

What is critical for the future good health of the sport is that ethically, we to embrace the fishing in all of its many wonderful aspects. It is so much more than just catching fish.

CHAPTER THIRTEEN

Future Prospects for Pacific Salmon Fly-Fishing

By Les Johnson and Bruce Ferguson

Salmon have been swimming the rivers of the Pacific Coast drainage, in the footprint of the ancient rain forests, for more than ten centuries. For nearly nine of these ten centuries, they flourished, regardless of floods, droughts, wildfires, changing ocean conditions or seismic events. Throughout this period salmon provided a vital source of food for wildlife and were harvested by the native people who lived along the rivers.

We would all like to continue to enjoy evenings with salmon broiling on the barbeque after a day of fishing.

The dynamics of salmon harvest changed about the mid-point of the nineteenth century, when settlers began descending upon the Pacific Coast from California to Alaska in burgeoning numbers hoping to acquire land, mine for gold, cut timber and build communities. They soon joined Native Americans in harvesting Pacific salmon which were incredibly abundant; at their zenith along the Pacific Coast. The tonnage of salmon harvested for subsistence and commercial sale from the Sacramento River in California to the Fraser in British Columbia was soon escalating at a phenomenal rate. At the same time, other natural resources, essential to the well-being of the salmon were also being harvested or harnessed.

The great stands of timber along Pacific Coast watersheds began falling under the loggers' saws in the mid to late 1800s. Regrettably, logging practices of the day often left a wasteland of denuded and severely degraded hillsides which resulted in water runoff that in some cases silted entire river systems, burying miles of spawning gravel.

As the population continued to grow, settlements expanded; some into large cities. Rivers were impounded behind huge hydroelectric dams built to provide inexpensive electricity for industry and growing communities. Many of these dams blocked major rivers without allowing passage for salmon, shutting off invaluable upriver spawning grounds forever. When farming was implemented on the once-barren desert along the inland prairies of the Columbia and Sacramento rivers, water was diverted for irrigation in enormous volume and the land suddenly bloomed with alfalfa, barley, wheat and market produce.

All of the human growth and industrial development that occurred, beginning in the middle of the Nineteenth Century along the West Coast has steadily eroded the salmons' environment and populations. From approximately 1850, until today, a period of about 155 years, Pacific salmon have been either harvested, or forfeited to other avenues of economic progress in such extraordinary numbers that hundreds of individual stocks have been in sharp decline for several decades. In fact, many salmon runs that were amazingly robust and prolific for nearly 900 years, taking everything that nature could throw at them have, in the relatively short span of 158 years, been depleted so severely that they are presently listed as threatened, endangered or extinct. So, now that we've outlined a rather grim history, what might the future hold for our incomparable Pacific salmon?

Well, first of all we have to be encouraged that despite all that we've put the Pacific salmon through from harvest to habitat degradation, the species remains at least guardedly

DOUG SCHAAD

Cleaning up small streams is critical to the future health of our salmon runs today, and will be more so in the future. Griffin Creek, a tributary of the Snoqualmie River in Washington, was cleaned up as a cooperative project of the Washington Fly Fishing Club and the Washington Department of Fish and Wildlife. Its once depleted population of coho salmon and coastal cutthroat are now recovering.

healthy in some areas of the Pacific coast. Things could be worse.

The importance of healthy habitat and easy passage to spawning water has become more and more evident throughout the range of our Pacific salmon. Timber companies are doing a better job of minimizing impact on the salmon's habitat during harvest operations. Community "adopt a stream" programs have been very successful where they have been put into practice, and redesigned road culverts have reopened miles of once pristine spawning habitat; seemingly small incremental measures for improving stretches of small streams that are paying off in big dividends. This is particularly good for coho salmon which are small-stream spawners.

Giving over river-bank property or draining wetlands to build apartment and condominium tracts or strip malls for immediate gain will almost always become a long-term loss for a community, a county or state; and for the salmon. Such riverbank or near-river construction has to be protected by tough, no-nonsense regulations. This includes far more hard-nosed environmental impact statements, and economic studies that state the true value of a healthy salmon run against an apartment complex or golf course. While some land developers continually lobby against any additional protection for the environment, others have signed on, albeit grudgingly, to work within the constraints of environmental protection laws.

LES JOHNSON

Passing along knowledge is an important part of the future of fly-fishing. Bill Nelson, shown here at a fly-tying seminar, has taught people how to tie his noted bucktailing flies for years at FFF expositions.

Our salmon runs will have to be maintained and improved if small towns like Tofino on the west side of Vancouver Island, shown here, are to continue to enjoy a robust economy. From Northern California to Alaska people who live in similar coastal communities have traditionally depended on salmon for a large measure of their annual income through a balanced commercial and sport fishery.

LES JOHNSON

Fly-fishers at Lincoln Park in Seattle discuss the fishing while they await the tide change. From the left: Dave Potts, Charley Norton, Bob Young and Jimmy Chang (sitting). Fishing from the beaches of Washington and British Columbia has been ongoing since the 1930s and should be factored into the regulations, particularly regarding access.

It is true that much of the Pacific salmon's habitat has been lost forever behind Coulee Dam, Dworshak Dam and Shasta Dam; examples of monolithic structures that block hundreds of miles of important salmon spawning habitat. Most of these old, existing dams are too imbedded within our economy to ever be removed. However, it is important to note that some dams have been removed and others are scheduled

Prudent hatchery supplementation of wild-salmon runs will be important to the future of our fishery. For example, the Rowdy Creek Hatchery in Smith River, California carefully high grades the Smith River's famous chinook salmon for hatchery production.

for removal. For example, Elwha Dam completed in 1913 on the lower Elwha River in Washington is scheduled for removal to begin in 2008 (as this is written). The Congress still has Glines Dam, also on the Elwha which was completed in 1927, on the bubble for environmental impact studies before it will be taken out. If both of these dams which have blocked the river for ninety years—and were built without fish passageways—are removed, nearly 70 miles of a vast historic and unspoiled watershed will once again be open to receive all five species of Pacific salmon plus steelhead and sea-run cutthroat trout. So, while we may never see much of the salmons' precious lost spawning water restored we can fight to maintain all of the remaining flood plain habitat and watersheds where they are born and where they return to spawn. And we can assemble shoulder-to-shoulder with those who are standing up for the removal of the dams on the lower Snake River and on other historic salmon streams throughout the west; dams that are legitimate candidates to be taken out to reopen vital salmon habitat.

State, Provincial and National fishery departments in the U.S. and Canada, in control of commercial and sport salmon harvest bear watching by sportsmen and conservation groups. Harvest administrators have a long history dating back to early England, the Atlantic Coast of the United States and most recently the Pacific Coast for managing salmon stocks into a perilous downward spiral.

This ongoing *managed* loss of salmon stocks is being monitored and challenged on an ever increasing basis. Organizations like Save Our Salmon, American Rivers, the Nature Conservancy, Federation of Fly Fishers, Trout Unlimited, Cal Trout, the Sierra Club and a legion of independent sportsmen's guilds are spearheading the conservation drive to protect our salmon and restore stocks wherever possible rather than merely slow the decline. For a solid conservation and restoration effort to continue moving forward though, all of these groups need dedicated financial support and increased membership from citizens who care about the future of our natural resources, whether they are salmon anglers or not. Last but not least, native tribes along the Pacific Coast also must share in the responsibility for rebuilding salmon stocks. They also have a dismal track record for conserving salmon stocks.

Hatchery reform is another hot-button issue, as this is written, that has been taken on by teams of scientists, biologists and engineers to improve the abysmal returns of hatchery stocks based on the huge numbers of juvenile salmon that are released every year. The scientific community is working to increase the number of salmon that actually return from the numbers released. This results-oriented approach to hatchery programs all along the Pacific Coast should help to supplement dwindling wild stocks rather than try to be a replacement for salmon runs that have been seriously

Here we have three generations of salmon fly-fishers. From left: Ferguson's grandson, Bruce Ferguson, and Dave Carnahan, his son-in-law, after a day of fishing for pink salmon on Vancouver Island. Passing along the tradition of fly-fishing for Pacific salmon will be a large part of seeing the sport move forward to future generations.

Rick Grange, founding owner of West Coast Fishing Club on Langara Island in the Queen Charlotte archipelago, presents anglers a full-size fiberglass wall mount of any chinook salmon over 40 pounds that they release to conserve the largest trophy fish. This is the first such conservation move by a lodge owner that the writers have witnessed.

weakened by over harvest and habitat degradation. Supplementing wild salmon with hatchery fish can allow anglers to continue sport fishing and even keep a few salmon while releasing wild fish to spawn wherever stocks are weak.

Lodges and fishing camps throughout Washington, British Columbia and Alaska are welcoming increasing numbers of fly rod toting guests each season for both fresh and saltwater fishing. Although the primary theme of these establishments has been to promote big chinook salmon, called springs in Canada and kings in Alaska, they do not make nearly as strong a case for chum, coho, pink and sockeye salmon. This is a marketing approach that would benefit from revision because chum, coho, pink and sockeye salmon are key species for the fly rod angler to pursue. Chinook salmon, although they are taken in both fresh and salt water on the fly, tend to be the big-game fish of the Pacific salmon family rather than a regularly targeted species like the chum, coho, pink and sockeye. Let the fly-fishers know that these welterweights and middleweights of the Pacific salmon species are absolutely incredible fighters when hooked, especially those actively feeding in salt water, and they will come, fly rods in hand. This will add to the voices already declaring that these light, fast sluggers are great fly-rod fish.

As we grow long in the tooth, it is our wish to pass on the responsibility of enlightening others to the importance of Pacific salmon history, fishing and conservation. If you should elect to take a stand to ensure the future of Pacific salmon populations, we urge you to do so with a sense of stewardship. Ours has been a long, exciting, at times arduous, and ultimately rewarding journey; one that has taken us from our home waters to some of the most remote reaches of the Pacific salmon's range. It was accomplished only with your support. We thank you.
—Les Johnson and
Bruce Ferguson

So, while we certainly haven't done the Pacific salmon many favors over the decades, there is evidence that a concerted effort to protect them on all fronts can indeed make their future brighter. It will be a slow, tedious process fraught with victories and setbacks that really will have no end. It will be ongoing and require an army of vigilant, devoted citizens to maintain the momentum. We cannot count on our state and federal agencies to do the job right. Their sorely outdated management methods do not warrant our confidence. The future of the Pacific salmon is in our hands and it is a responsibility that we need to embrace.

If we all have the courage and commitment to take up our shields in defense of the Pacific salmon we just might be able to hand over the care of healthy populations of these great fish to our grandchildren and great-grandchildren and all who follow.

APPENDIX I
Taxonomic List of Baitfish Species

COMPILED BY BRUCE FERGUSON

Scientific Classification	Common Name
Phylum Chordata	
Sub Phylum Vertebrata	
Class Osteichthyes	
Order Clupeiformes	
Family Clupeidae	
Genus *Clupea*	
Species *harengus pallasi*	Pacific herring
Genus *Sardinops*	
Species *sagax*	Pacific sardine
Family Engraulidae	
Genus *Engraulis*	
Species *mordax*	Northern anchovy
Order Salmoniformes	
Family Osmeridae	
Genus *Thaleichthys*	
Species *pacificus*	Eulachon
Genus *Allosmerus*	
Species *elongatus*	Whitebait smelt
Genus *Hypomesus*	
Species *pretiosus*	Surf smelt
Genus *Mallotus*	
Species *villosus*	Capelin
Order Perciformes	
Family Ammodytidae	
Genus *Ammodytes*	
Species *hexapterus*	Pacific sand lance

APPENDIX II
Taxonomic list of invertebrates identified from zooplankton samples and stomach contents
COMPILED BY BRUCE FERGUSON

Scientific Classification	Common Name
Phylum Cnidaria	Coelenterates
Class Hydrozoa	
Genus *Velella*	"Purple sailor"
Class Scyphozoa	
Class Anthozoa	
Phylum Ctenophora	
Phylum Nematoda	Round worms
Phylum Mollusca	
Class Gastropoda	
Order Mesogastropoda	Snails
Genus *Littorina*	
Order Thecosomata	Sea butterflies
Class Bivalria	Clams, oysters
Class Cephalopoda	
Subclass Coleoidea	
Genus *Loligo*	Squids
Genus *Octopus*	Octopus
Phylum Annelida	Segmented worms
Class Polychaeta	
Subclass Errentia	
Family Syllidae	
Genus *Autolytus*	
Family Nereidae	
Genus *Platyneris*	
Subclass Sedentaria	
Family Spionidae	
Family Opheliidae	
Phylum Arthropoda	
Class Arachnida	Spiders, mites
Order Araneae	Spiders
Class Crustacea	
Subclass Branchiopoda	
Order Cladocera	Water fleas
Genus *Podon*	
Subclass Ostracoda	Mussel or seed shrimp
Order Myodocoda	
Subclass Copepoda	Copepods
Order Calanoida	Calanoids
Genus *Calanus*	
Genus *Evcalanus*	
Genus *Paracalanus*	
Genus *Aetidius*	
Genus *Metridia*	
Genus *Epilabidocera*	
Genus *Acartia*	
Genus *Candacia*	
Order Harpacticoida	Harpacticoids
Order Cyclopoida	
Genus *Oncaea*	
Genus *Corycaeus*	
Order Monstrilloida	
Order Caligoida	
Subclass Cirripedia	Barnacles
Suborder Balanomorpha	Sessile barnacles
Genus *Balanus*	
Subclass Malcostraca	
Order Mysidacea	
Family Mysidae	Oppossum shrimp
Genus *Boreomysis*	
Order Cumacea	
Genus *Cumella*	

Scientific Classification			Common Name
Order Tanaidacea			
Order Isopoda			
Suborder Epicaridea			
Suborder Flabellifera			
Order Amphipoda			
Suborder Hyperiidea			
		Genus *Parathemisto*	
		Genus *Hyperia*	
Suborder Gammaridea			Sand fleas, scuds
		Genus *Calliopius*	
		Genus Corophium	
		Genus *Anisogammarus*	
		Genus *Paraphoxus*	
		Genus *Accedomoerra*	
Suborder Caprellidea			
		Genus *Caprella*	
Order Euphausiacea			Krill
		Family Euphausiidae	
		Genus *Euphausia*	
		Genus *Thysanoessa*	
Order Decapoda			
Suborder Natantia			Shrimps, crabs
Section Penaeidea			Shrimps
Section Pleocyemata-Caridea			
		Family Hippolytidae	
		Genus *Heptacarpus*	
		Family Pandalidae	
		Genus *Pandulus*	
		Genus *Pandalopsis*	
		Family Crangonidae	
		Genus *Crangon*	Sand shrimps
Section Macura			
		Family Callianassidae	
		Genus *Callianassia*	
		Genus *Upogebia*	
Section Anomura			Crabs
		Family Poecellanidae	
		Family Paguridae	Hermit crabs
		Genus *Pagurus*	
Section Brachyura			True crabs
Infrasubsection Brachyrhyncha			
		Family Cancridae	Cancer crab
		Genus *Cancer*	
		Family Pinnotheridae	Pea crabs
Infrasubsection Oxyrhyncha			Decorator crabs
		Family Majidae	
Class Insecta			Insects
Order Ephemeroptera			Mayflies
Order Isoptera			Termites
Order Plecoptera			Stoneflies
Order Psocoptera			Lice
Order Homoptera			Aphids
		Family Psyllidae	
Order Neuroptera			Alderflies
Order Diptera			True flies
		Family Chironomidae	Midges
Order Hymenoptera			Ants, bees, wasps
Phylum Chaetognatha			
		Genus *Sagitta*	
Phylum Chordata			
Class Larvacea			
		Genus *Oikopleura*	

APPENDIX III

COMPILED BY BRUCE FERGUSON

Salmon Feed by Species[1]
In order of importance 1-5 (5 is most important) for Marine Adults.

Chinook (Oncorhynchus tshawytscha)

Scientific Name (Taxa)	Common Name	Importance
Decapoda	Crab megalops	3
Euphausiacea	Euphausiids	4
Mollusca	---	1
Cephalopoda	Squid	2
Pisces	Fish	5

*Most important food—herring and sand lance, euphausiids, crab zoea and megalops, squid, pelagic amphipods.
NOTE: No feeding observed in estuaries on spawning return.

Coho (Oncorhynchus kisutch)

Scientific Name (Taxa)	Common Name	Importance
Decapoda	Crab megalops	3
Hyperiidae	Amphipods	2
Euphausiacea	Euphausiids	4
Cephalopoda	Squid	1
Pisces	Fish	5

* Most important food—pelagic (hyperiid) amphipods, herring, sand lance, anchovy, sardine. Also, euphausiids and squid.
NOTE: No feeding observed in estuaries on spawning return.

Pink (Oncorhynchus gorbuscha)

Scientific Name (Taxa)	Common Name	Importance
Hyperiidea	Amphipods	5
Euphausiacea	Euphausiids	3
Cephalopoda	Squid	2
Limacina sp.	Sea Butterfly	1
Pisces	Fish	4

*Most important food—hyperiid amphipods, fish, euphausiids, squid and sea butterflies.

---

[1] Excerpts from *Physiological Ecology of Pacific Salmon*, edited by C. Groot, L. Margolis & W.C. Clarke, 1995.

Chum (Oncorhynchus keta)

Scientific Name (Taxa)	Common Name	Importance
Calanoida	Copepods	1
Hyperiidea	Amphipods	5
Euphausiacea	Euphausiids	2
Limacina sp.	Sea Butterfly	3
Pisces	Fish	4

*Most important food—ocean adults: Hyperiid amphipods and fish are most frequently consumed. Pteropods, euphausiids and calanoids are consumed to a lesser degree.

NOTE: Hyperiid amphipods preferred even when other plankton available—highly visible pigmented eye and relatively large size (eye).

Sockeye (Oncorhynchus nerka)
Marine Adults

Scientific Name (Taxa)	Common Name	Importance
Calanoida	Copepods	1
Hyperiida	Amphipods	4
Euphausiacea	Euphausiids	5
Cephalopoda	Squid	2
Pisces	Fish	3

Returning Adults
(Final Spawning Migration)

Scientific Name (Taxa)	Common Name	Importance
Crustacea	---	3
Decapoda	Crab megalops	2
Hyperiida	Amphipods	4
Euphausiacea	Euphausiids	5
Mollusca	Squid	4
Pisces	Fish	1

*Most important food—ocean adults: Euphausiids (*pacifica* and *thysanoessa* sp.) hyperiid amphipods (*parathemisto* sp.) fish, squid and calanoid copepods.

NOTE: Gillnet analysis of sockeye approaching river mouths—24% of stomachs contained food. Crab larvae dominated in Alaska.

British Columbia Run Timing
Regional Information

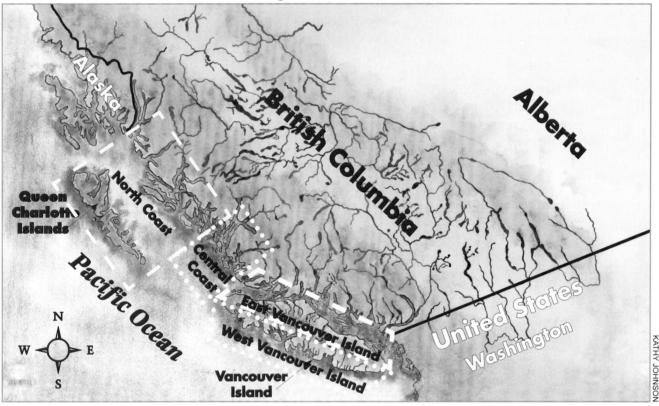

KATHY JOHNSON

Marine Salmon Maturity Definitions
(Applies to all species)

1. **Immature feeders:** Fish not developing any sign of sexual maturity. Either not spawning that year or early in their final year.
2. **Mature feeders:** Mature fish in their final year, but still actively feeding. Sexual organs developing, and have signs of digestion in progress.
3. **Mature non-feeders:** Obviously maturing fish, usually found along beaches, estuaries and river mouths with little or no food in digestive tract. Stomach starting to atrophy.

Run-Timing Charts

Information contained in the run-timing charts provide a general idea of when each salmon species—in various stages of feeding activity—are accessible to fly-fishers. It must be remembered however that there can be signifcant yearly fluctuations in both run timing and run sizes. A serious long-term effort is currently underway in British Columbia to protect and re-build weak salmon stocks. For this reason there can be large areas either closed or open to catch-and-release fishing only. This is particularly true for chinook and coho salmon. It is therefore vital to check regulations as part of your trip planning.

More than twenty interviews were conducted with British Columbia Fisheries and Oceans staff members to develop the run-timing data shown here. We are especially indebted to Terry Gjernes for his extraordinary help in assembling this information before retiring. Terry was Recreational Fisheries Coordinator for the South Coast Pacific Region of Fisheries and Oceans, Canada.

Chinook

Week	Mar 1	2	3	4	Apr 1	2	3	4	May 1	2	3	4	Jun 1	2	3	4	Jul 1	2	3	4	Aug 1	2	3	4	Sep 1	2	3	4	Oct 1	2	3	4
Immature feeders																																
Mature feeders													X	X	X	X	X	X	X	X	X	X	X	X	X							
Mature non-feeders																																

Coho

Week	Mar 1	2	3	4	Apr 1	2	3	4	May 1	2	3	4	Jun 1	2	3	4	Jul 1	2	3	4	Aug 1	2	3	4	Sep 1	2	3	4	Oct 1	2	3	4
Immature feeders									X	X	X	X	X																			
Mature feeders													X	X	X	X	X	X	X	X	X	X	O	O								
Mature non-feeders																		X	X		X	X	X	X	X	X	X					

Pink

Week	Mar 1	2	3	4	Apr 1	2	3	4	May 1	2	3	4	Jun 1	2	3	4	Jul 1	2	3	4	Aug 1	2	3	4	Sep 1	2	3	4	Oct 1	2	3	4
Immature feeders																																
Mature feeders														X	X	X	X	X							O	O						
Mature non-feeders																	X	X	X		X	X										

Chum

Week	Mar 1	2	3	4	Apr 1	2	3	4	May 1	2	3	4	Jun 1	2	3	4	Jul 1	2	3	4	Aug 1	2	3	4	Sep 1	2	3	4	Oct 1	2	3	4
Immature feeders																																
Mature feeders																	O		X	X	X											
Mature non-feeders																					X	X	X	X	X							

Sockeye

Week	Mar 1	2	3	4	Apr 1	2	3	4	May 1	2	3	4	Jun 1	2	3	4	Jul 1	2	3	4	Aug 1	2	3	4	Sep 1	2	3	4	Oct 1	2	3	4
Immature feeders																																
Mature feeders																																
Mature non-feeders																	X	X	X	X	X	X	X									

North Coast

Chinook
Immature feeders – Always present but not in any concentration.

Mature feeders – Always present. Best opportunity when feed is shallow.

Mature non-feeders – Real variation. Most river systems don't have Chinook holding at river mouths, because the rivers are large.

Coho
Immature feeders – Limited knowledge.

Chum
Mature non-feeders – Depends on river system.

Sockeye
Mature feeders – Very rare.

Mature non-feeders – Some early runs. Depends on river system.

Key	
X	Fisheries and Oceans, Canada
O	Authors added experience

Chinook	March				April				May				June				July				August				Sept				Oct			
Week	1	2	3	4	1	2	3	4	1	2	3	4	1	2	3	4	1	2	3	4	1	2	3	4	1	2	3	4	1	2	3	4
Immature feeders																																
Mature feeders													X	X	X	X	X	X	X	X	X	X	X	X								
Mature non-feeders																																

Coho	March				April				May				June				July				August				Sept				Oct			
Week	1	2	3	4	1	2	3	4	1	2	3	4	1	2	3	4	1	2	3	4	1	2	3	4	1	2	3	4	1	2	3	4
Immature feeders									X	X	X	X	X	X																		
Mature feeders															X	X	X	X	X	X	X	X										
Mature non-feeders																			X	X	X	X	X	X	X							

Pink	March				April				May				June				July				August				Sept				Oct			
Week	1	2	3	4	1	2	3	4	1	2	3	4	1	2	3	4	1	2	3	4	1	2	3	4	1	2	3	4	1	2	3	4
Immature feeders																																
Mature feeders													X	X	X		X	X	X	X												
Mature non-feeders																	X	X	X	X		X	X	X								

Chum	March				April				May				June				July				August				Sept				Oct			
Week	1	2	3	4	1	2	3	4	1	2	3	4	1	2	3	4	1	2	3	4	1	2	3	4	1	2	3	4	1	2	3	4
Immature feeders																																
Mature feeders																																
Mature non-feeders																																

Sockeye	March				April				May				June				July				August				Sept				Oct			
Week	1	2	3	4	1	2	3	4	1	2	3	4	1	2	3	4	1	2	3	4	1	2	3	4	1	2	3	4	1	2	3	4
Immature feeders																																
Mature feeders																																
Mature non-feeders																	X	X	X		X	X	X	X								

Central Coast

Chinook
Immature feeders – Always present but not in any concentration.

Mature feeders – Always present. Best opportunity is when feed is shallow.

Mature non-feeders – Difficult. Real variation. Most river systems don't have Chinook holding at river mouths, because the rivers are large.

Coho
Immature feeders – very much depends on local knowledge.

Pink
Mature feeders – Dates uncertain.

Sockeye
Mature non-feeders – Limited to a few spots.

Chinook

	March 1	2	3	4	April 1	2	3	4	May 1	2	3	4	June 1	2	3	4	July 1	2	3	4	Aug 1	2	3	4	Sept 1	2	3	4	Oct 1	2	3	4
Immature feeders																																
Mature feeders											X	X	X	X	X	X	X	X	X	X	X	X	X									
Mature non-feeders																																

Coho

	March 1	2	3	4	April 1	2	3	4	May 1	2	3	4	June 1	2	3	4	July 1	2	3	4	Aug 1	2	3	4	Sept 1	2	3	4	Oct 1	2	3	4
Immature feeders									X	X	X	X	X																			
Mature feeders													X	X	X	X	X	X	X	X	X	X	X									
Mature non-feeders																					X	X	X	X	X	X	X	X	X			

Pink

	March 1	2	3	4	April 1	2	3	4	May 1	2	3	4	June 1	2	3	4	July 1	2	3	4	Aug 1	2	3	4	Sept 1	2	3	4	Oct 1	2	3	4
Immature feeders																																
Mature feeders																																
Mature non-feeders																					X	X	X									

Chum

	March 1	2	3	4	April 1	2	3	4	May 1	2	3	4	June 1	2	3	4	July 1	2	3	4	Aug 1	2	3	4	Sept 1	2	3	4	Oct 1	2	3	4
Immature feeders																																
Mature feeders																																
Mature non-feeders																									X	X	X	X	X	X	X	

Sockeye

	March 1	2	3	4	April 1	2	3	4	May 1	2	3	4	June 1	2	3	4	July 1	2	3	4	Aug 1	2	3	4	Sept 1	2	3	4	Oct 1	2	3	4
Immature feeders																																
Mature feeders																																
Mature non-feeders									X	X	X	X	X	X	X	X	O	O	O													

West Coast Vancouver Island

Chinook
Immature feeders – Immature fish around at all times. (Fly-fishing opportunities depend on feed distribution).

Mature feeders – Depend on feed distribution.

Mature non-feeders – Difficult. Real variation. Most river systems don't have Chinook holding at river mouths, because the rivers are large.

Coho
Immature feeders – Limited knowledge.

Pink
Mature non-feeders – Very limited. (Quatsino Sound).

Chum
Mature non-feeders – Not well known.

Sockeye
Mature non-feeders – Very limited. Some possibility in May and June at Gold River Estuary also in Alberni Inlet.

Key
X	Fisheries and Oceans, Canada
O	Authors added experience

British Columbia: East Coast Vancouver Island
Straight of Georgia, E. Coast of Vancouver Island and Mainland from Sheringham Point to Cape Scott

Chinook

	March				April				May				June				July				August				Sept				Oct			
Week	1	2	3	4	1	2	3	4	1	2	3	4	1	2	3	4	1	2	3	4	1	2	3	4	1	2	3	4	1	2	3	4
Immature feeders																																
Mature feeders											X	X	X	X	X	X	X	X	X	X	X	X	X									
Mature non-feeders																																

Coho

	March				April				May				June				July				August				Sept				Oct			
Week	1	2	3	4	1	2	3	4	1	2	3	4	1	2	3	4	1	2	3	4	1	2	3	4	1	2	3	4	1	2	3	4
Immature feeders		X	X	X	X	X	X	X	X	X	X																					
Mature feeders														X	X	X	X	X	X	X	X	X	X	X	X							
Mature non-feeders																						X	X	X	X	X	X	X	X	X	X	

Pink

	March				April				May				June				July				August				Sept				Oct			
Week	1	2	3	4	1	2	3	4	1	2	3	4	1	2	3	4	1	2	3	4	1	2	3	4	1	2	3	4	1	2	3	4
Immature feeders																																
Mature feeders																			X	X	O	O	O									
Mature non-feeders																					X	X	X		X	X	X					

Chum

	March				April				May				June				July				August				Sept				Oct			
Week	1	2	3	4	1	2	3	4	1	2	3	4	1	2	3	4	1	2	3	4	1	2	3	4	1	2	3	4	1	2	3	4
Immature feeders																																
Mature feeders																																
Mature non-feeders																									X	X	X	X	X	X	X	

Sockeye

	March				April				May				June				July				August				Sept				Oct			
Week	1	2	3	4	1	2	3	4	1	2	3	4	1	2	3	4	1	2	3	4	1	2	3	4	1	2	3	4	1	2	3	4
Immature feeders																																
Mature feeders																						O	O	O								
Mature non-feeders																	X	X	X	X	X	X	X	X								

East Coast Vancouver Island

Chinook
Immature feeders – Fish around at all times (Fly-fishing opportunities depend on feed distribution).
Mature feeders – Depend on feed distribution.
Mature non-feeders – Very difficult. Most river systems don't have Chinook holding at river mouths, because rivers are so large.

Coho
Immature feeders – This fishery starts in March around Victoria.

Pink
Mature feeders – Can be very productive from Port Hardy to Johnstone Strait, including Telegraph Cove area.

Chum
Mature non-feeders – Very much depends on local knowledge.

Sockeye
Mature feeders and non-feeders – Mainly from Port Hardy to Johnstone Strait, including Telegraph Cove area.

Bibliography

COMPILED BY BRUCE FERGUSON

Alaska Flyfishers, 1983. *Fly Patterns of Alaska*. Frank Amato Publications, Portland, OR.

Association of Professional Biologists of British Columbia-North Pacific International Chapter of The American Fisheries Society, 1993. *Proceedings of the 1992 Coho Workshop, May 26-28th, Nanaimo, B.C., Canada*.

Bell, Gordon, Ph.D., 1996. *Pacific Salmon From Egg to Exit*. Hancock House Publishers, Ltd., Surrey, B.C., Canada.

Caolo, Alan, 1995. *Fly Fisherman's Guide to Atlantic Baitfish and Other Food Sources*. Frank Amato Publications, Inc., Portland, OR.

Carleton, Frank E., Chairman, 1985. Proceedings of the Tenth Annual Marine Recreational Fisheries Symposium, April 26-27th, 1985, Seattle, Washington. *Recreational Uses, Production and Management of Anadromous Pacific Salmonids*. Published for the International Game Fish Association, The National Coalition for Marine Conservation, and The Sport Fishing Institute by National Coalition for Marine Conservation, Savannah, Georgia.

Crawford, Jim, 1995. *Salmon to a Fly: Fly Fishing for Pacific Salmon in the Open Ocean*. Frank Amato Publications, Portland, OR.

Ferguson, Bruce, Johnson, Les, and Trotter, Pat, 1985. *Fly Fishing for Pacific Salmon*. Frank Amato Publications, Inc., Portland, OR.

Groot, C., and Margolis L., Edited by, 1991. *Pacific Salmon Life Histories*. Published in cooperation with the government of Canada, Department of Fisheries and Oceans. UBC Press, Vancouver, B.C., Canada.

Groot, C., Margolis, L., and Clarke, W. C., edited by, 1995. *Physiological Ecology of Pacific Salmon*. Published in cooperation with the government of Canada, Department of Fisheries and Oceans, UBC Press, Vancouver, B.C. Canada

Hamner, William H., May 1984. "Krill: Untapped Bounty From the Sea" P. 626, *National Geographic*, Vol. 165, No. 5.

Hart, J.L., 1973. *Pacific Fishes of Canada*. Bulletin 180, Fisheries Research Board. Information Canada, Ottawa, Canada.

Inland Empire Fly Fishing Club, Randy Shaber, Editor-In-Chief, 1998. *Flies of the Northwest*. Frank Amato Publications, Portland, OR.

Kosloff, Eugene N., 1973. *Seashore Life of Puget Sound, The Strait of Georgia and the San Juan Archipelago*, University of Washington Press, Seattle, WA.

Lingren, Arthur J., 1993. *Fly Patterns of Roderick Haig-Brown*. Frank Amato Publications, Portland, OR.

Martin, Dr. Anthony R., 1990. *The Illustrated Encyclopedia of Whales and Dolphins*. Portland House, New York, NY.

Pacific Salmon Commission, 2003. *Report of the Fraser River Panel on 2000 Fraser River Sockeye Salmon Fishing Season*, Vancouver, B.C., Canada.

Pearcy, William G., 1992. *Ocean Ecology of North Pacific Salmonids*. Washington Sea Grant Program, University of Washington Press, Seattle, WA.

Raymond, Steve, 1996. *The Estuary Flyfisher*. Frank Amato Publications, Portland, OR.

Roberts, George V., Jr., 1994. *A Fly-Fisher's Guide to Saltwater Naturals and Their Imitation*. Ragged Mountain Press, Camden, ME.

Route, Anthony J., 1989. *Flyfishing Alaska*. Johnson Publishing Co., Boulder, CO.

Route, Anthony J., 1991. *Flies for Alaska*. Johnson Publishing Co., Boulder, CO.

Schmitt, Waldo L., 1965. *Crustaceans*. Ann Arbor: University of Michigan Press.

Smith, D.L., 1977. *A Guide to Marine Coastal Plankton and Marine Invertebrate Larvae*. Dubuque: Kendall/Hunt Publishing Company.

Strickland, Richard M., 1983. *The Fertile Fjord*. Seattle: University of Washington Press.

Thorton, Barry M., 1995. *Saltwater Fly Fishing for Pacific Salmon*. Hancock House Publishers, Ltd., Surrey, B.C., Canada.

Uoya, Toshinori, Deputy Director, *North Pacific Anadromous Fish Commission, Statistical Yearbook 1999. Salmon Catch Data by Species*. Vancouver, B.C., Canada.

Index